VARGAS AND BRAZIL

STUDIES OF THE AMERICAS

Edited by
James Dunkerley
Institute for the Studies of the Americas
University of London
School of Advanced Study

Titles in this series are multidisciplinary studies of aspects of the societies of the hemisphere, particularly in the areas of politics, economics, history, anthropology, sociology, and environment. The series covers a comparative perspective across the Americas, including Canada and the Caribbean as well as the United States and Latin America.

Titles in this series published by Palgrave Macmillan:

Cuba's Military 1990–2005: Revolutionary Soldiers during Counter-Revolutionary Times
By Hal C. Klepak

The Judicialization of Politics in Latin America
Edited by Rachel Sieder, Line Schjolden, and Alan Angell

Latin America: A New Interpretation
By Laurence Whitehead

Appropriation as Practice: Art and Identity in Argentina
By Arnd Schneider

America and Enlightenment Constitutionalism
Edited by Gary McDowell and Johnathan O'Neill

Vargas and Brazil: New Perspectives
Edited by Jens R. Hentschke

Caribbean Land and Development Revisited
By Jean Besson and Janet Momsen

Vargas and Brazil

New Perspectives

Edited by
Jens R. Hentschke

VARGAS AND BRAZIL

Cover Photo:

Brazilians lighting candles to pay their respects on the death of President Getúlio Vargas, August 1954.

Arquivo Nacional do Brasil, Correio da Manhã—PH/FOT/18089

First published in 2006 by
PALGRAVE MACMILLAN™
175 Fifth Avenue, New York, N.Y. 10010 and
Houndmills, Basingstoke, Hampshire, England RG21 6XS
Companies and representatives throughout the world.

PALGRAVE MACMILLAN is the global academic imprint of the Palgrave Macmillan division of St. Martin's Press, LLC and of Palgrave Macmillan Ltd. Macmillan® is a registered trademark in the United States, United Kingdom and other countries. Palgrave is a registered trademark in the European Union and other countries.

ISBN-13: 978–1–4039–7391–7
ISBN-10: 1–4039–7391–1

A catalogue record for this book is available from the British Library.

Library of Congress Cataloging-in-publication data is available from the Library of Congress.

Design by Newgen Imaging Systems (P) Ltd., Chennai, India.

First edition: December 2006

10 9 8 7 6 5 4 3 2 1

Printed in the United States of America.

Contents

List of Tables

List of Contributors

Gunter Axt has a doctorate in Social History from the University of São Paulo and is currently working on his *pós-doutorado*. Until 2006, he was a researcher at the Memorial do Ministério Público in Rio Grande do Sul, and he now presides over the Instituto Hominus de Desenvolvimento Sócio-Cultural. Axt is the author of *De homem só a guardião da cidadania: história associativa e institucional do MPRS* (Procuradoria-Geral de Justiça do Rio Grande do Sul/Memorial, 2003) and of 21 other books.

John J. Crocitti is Associate Professor of History at San Diego Mesa College, San Diego, CA. In 1999, he coedited *The Brazil Reader* (Duke Univ. Press) with Robert M. Levine. His current projects include a twentieth-century social history of a secondary Brazilian city and a history of popular culture among Brazilian railroad workers.

Jerry Dávila is Associate Professor of History at the University of North Carolina at Charlotte. He is the author of *Diploma of Whiteness: Race and Social Policy in Brazil, 1917–1945* (Duke University Press, 2003) and has research interests in the relationship between racial thought and public policy and in the formation of historical memory. He has been Fulbright Distinguished Chair in American Studies at the Pontifícia Universidade Católica in Rio de Janeiro (2005) and visiting Fulbright scholar at the Universidade de São Paulo (2000).

Oliver Dinius is Croft Assistant Professor of History and International Studies at the University of Mississippi. He received his Ph.D in Latin American history from Harvard University in 2004. His research focuses on the history of labor, industry, and economic development in Brazil, where he did extensive field work for his dissertation on the history of the country's foremost state enterprise, the Companhia Siderúrgica Nacional.

Jens R. Hentschke obtained his *Habilitation* (*Livre-Docência*) at Heidelberg University and is Professor of Latin American History and Politics at Newcastle University, U.K. He is the author of *Estado Novo* (Verlag für Entwicklungspolitik Saarbrücken, 1996), *Populismus* (CeLA Münster, 1998), *Positivism gaúcho-Style* (Verlag für Wissenschaft und Forschung, 2004), and numerous articles and chapters on nineteenth and twentieth century Brazil. Currently, he is completing a research monograph on Vargas's educational reforms and their implementation in the states of Rio de Janeiro and Rio Grande do Sul.

Frank D. McCann is Professor of History at the University of New Hampshire. His publications include: *The Brazilian-American Alliance, 1937–45* (Princeton Univ. Press, 1973); *A Nação Armada: Ensaios sobre a História do Exército Brasileiro* (Ed. Guararapes, 1982); and *Soldiers of the Pátria: A History of the Brazilian Army 1889–1937* (Stanford Univ. Press, 2004). In 1986, the Brazilian government gave him the rank of "Comendador" in the Order of Rio Branco.

Thomas D. Rogers is Assistant Professor of Africana Studies at the University of North Carolina at Charlotte. He completed his Ph.D in Latin American History at Duke University in 2005, writing a dissertation that combines elements of environmental and labor history to offer a new interpretation of the historic 1963 and 1979 strikes in the sugar region of Pernambuco. A Fulbright Fellowship funded a year of archival research and extensive oral history interviewing in Pernambuco. Tom Rogers also studies labor and politics in the Caribbean and has published an article on the early career of Jamaican labor leader Alexander Bustamante.

Lisa Shaw is Reader in Brazilian Studies at the University of Liverpool, U.K. She is the author of *The Social History of the Brazilian Samba* (Ashgate, 1999), and coauthor of *Popular Cinema in Brazil* (Manchester UP, 2004) and *Brazilian National Cinema* (Routledge, 2006). In the autumn term of the 1999–2000 academic year, she was Visiting Lecturer in Brazilian Civilization and Popular Culture at the University of California, Los Angeles.

Daryle Williams, Associate Professor at the University of Maryland, College Park, is author of *Culture Wars in Brazil: The First Vargas Regime, 1930–1945* (Duke University Press, 2001), 2001 winner of the American Historical Association's John Edwin Fagg prize. He has also authored several articles and book chapters on twentieth-century Brazilian cultural history. Recent research has examined the cultural politics of World Heritage in Argentina, Brazil, and Paraguay;

humanities computing; and blackness in nineteenth-century Brazilian fine arts. Daryle Williams is Associate Editor of the *Hispanic American Historical Review.*

James P. Woodard (Ph.D., A.M., Brown University, B.A. University of North Carolina) has written widely on twentieth-century Brazilian history, including articles published in the *Hispanic American Historical Review*, the *Journal of Latin American Studies*, the *Luso-Brazilian Review, Estudios Interdisciplinarios de América Latina y el Caribe*, and the University of São Paulo's *Revista de História*. After being a postdoctoral fellow at Emory University's Center for Humanistic Inquiry, he joined the Department of History at Montclair State University in September 2006.

List of Acronyms and Abbreviations

AGC	Arquivo Gustavo Capanema (Gustavo Capanema Archive)
AGV	Arquivo Getúlio Vargas (Getúlio Vargas Archive)
ANL	Aliança Nacional Libertadora (National Liberation Alliance)
AOA	Arquivo Oswaldo Aranha (Oswaldo Aranha Archive)
CLT	Consolidação das Leis do Trabalho (Consolidation of Labor Laws)
CPDOC	Centro de Pesquisa e Documentação de História Contemporânea do Brasil (Center for Research and Documentation of the Contemporary History of Brazil)
CSN	Companhia Siderúrgica Nacional (National Steel Company)
DASP	Departamento Administrativo do Serviço Público (Administrative Department of the Public Service)
DHBB	*Dicionário Histórico-Biográfico Brasileiro. Pós 1930* (Historical-Biographical Dictionary of Post-1930 Brazil)
DIP	Departamento de Imprensa e Propaganda (Department of Press and Propaganda)
FGV	Fundação Getúlio Vargas (Getúlio Vargas Foundation)
IPM	Inquérito Policial Militar (Military Police Inquiry)
NARA	(United States) National Archives and Records Administration
PCB	Partido Comunista Brasileiro (Brazilian Communist Party)
PD	Partido Democrático (Democratic Party)
PDT	Partido Democrático Trabalhista (Democratic Labor Party)
PRP	Partido Republicano Paulista (Paulista Republican Party)

PRR   Partido Republicano Rio-Grandense (Republican Party
            of Rio Grande do Sul)
PSD   Partido Social Democrático (Social-Democratic Party)
PTB   Partido Trabalhista Brasileiro (Brazilian Labor Party)
UDN   União Democrática Nacional (National Democratic
            Union)

Chapter 1

The Vargas Era Institutional and Development Model Revisited: Themes, Debates, and Lacunas. An Introduction

Jens R. Hentschke

In October 2005, Brazilians commemorated the seventy-fifth anniversary of Getúlio Vargas's Revolution of 1930. This jubilee followed 14 months after the fiftieth anniversary of Vargas's suicide in August 1954 and 17 months after the fortieth anniversary of the 1964 military coup that, as the generals and many analysts during the following decade claimed, but more recent studies questioned, marked a major rupture with the previous polity. These three events should have prompted scholars to look afresh at the era and legacy of Brazil's most important, but also most controversial, statesman of the twentieth century. Yet, as that country's leading news magazine *Veja* soberly noted, critical scholarly studies are missing.[1] As a result, the initiative has been left to staunch *getulistas* in politics, media, and academia that continue to remind us that Vargas was the modernizer of the economy, unifier of the nation, organizer of the state, and father of the poor.[2]

This book unites historians, political scientists, and Cultural Studies specialists from Brazil, the United States, and Europe who, rather than attempting a synthesis of the Vargas era,[3] focus on key problems and offer a revisionist approach. All these scholars have already published, or will publish in the near future, major monographs based on extensive research. This includes work with the Vargas diaries, recently opened police archives and local depositories, previously unused statistical sources and newspapers, newsreels and films, and interviews with protagonists of Vargas's regimes. The authors apply different methodologies and some focus on so-far unexplored areas. This empirical approach allows us to challenge some long-standing myths and obsolete interpretations.

It is no accident that independent scholars felt little compelled by the anniversaries to reconsider Vargas's personal role in the reshaping of Brazil's state and society after 1930. For too long even they had been guided by the promises of Vargas and his protégés, the centralist and interventionist institutions they created, and the nationalist and social legislation they promulgated, instead of asking how these institutions worked in practice and to what extent and in what form the new policies were implemented throughout the vast and regionally divided country with a socially, racially, and ethnically stratified society. Treatment of these questions over the past 20 years, whether from a Marxist, functionalist, or structuralist perspective, has increasingly considered Vargas himself to be a secondary figure who, as José Nilo Tavares expressed, was "made by history, adjusted himself to history, and changed with it."[4] Since John Dulles's *Vargas of Brazil*, published in 1967,[5] no authoritative biography of the dictator-turned-populist has been written.

Following his "presidency" of Rio Grande do Sul (1928–30), Getúlio Vargas governed Brazil from 1930 to 1945, initially as provisional ruler (1930–34), then as indirectly elected president (1934–37), and finally as dictator (1937–45). However, his sustenance in power for 15 years and his comeback as democratically elected leader in 1951 do not per se imply he had a coherent political-ideological project, as the notion of a "Vargas era" suggests. If he did, was he capable of adjusting it to changing circumstances (which would demonstrate strength, rather than weakness, of political leadership)? Contributors to this volume reexamine major caesuras of the Vargas years and search for the variables that caused the characteristic continuity in change. Therefore, it is sensible to place chapters in roughly chronological order.

Read together, they allow us to distinguish five major themes: the 1930 Revolution; regional politics; Vargas's role as the arbitrator of the political system; social policies and the control of labor relations; and the deconstruction of the representations and symbolisms of this period. This introductory chapter places the findings of these analyzes within the international debate and highlights the way they challenge the prevalent views about Vargas and his era.

The 1930 Revolution—Catalyst for a "Depression Dictatorship"?

It may at first be surprising that no chapter in this volume focuses on the 1930 Revolution, though all contributors refer to it, in particular Jerry

Dávila. From the perspective of the Vargas era institutional and development model, what was the historical place of this event in Brazilian history and why does it seem to be overshadowed by the rupture of 1937?

Rosemary Thorp's edited volume *Latin America in the 1930s: The Role of the Periphery in World Crisis*, published in 1984, shed new light on the effects of the Great Depression on Latin America and prompted Charles Kindleberger to revise some of his classical theses. For Thorp, it was only with the world recessions of the mid-1970s and early 1980s that import-substituting industrialization (ISI) had exhausted itself.[6] Her argument challenged periodizations according to which the military dictatorships of the 1960s and early 1970s, with Brazil's 1964 regime being their prototype, had replaced this modernization strategy by a new model, coined "associated-dependent development."[7] Thorp's book revived interest in the origins of ISI that can be traced back to at least World War I. Brazil shows that notwithstanding the continuing predominance of the agrarian-export sector until long after 1930, industrialization was possible and the state became more active during the 1920s. The managers of the 1929–33 crisis could rely on previously established industries and an acceptance of (at least casual) state intervention.

The discussion initiated by Thorp's team found its continuation among German and Swiss academics during the following decade. Heidelberg became the center of both economics[8] and political science debates. A group of scholars, led by Dieter Nohlen, reinvestigated the institutional changes of the 1930s and 1940s and their link to the economic policies the world recession had instigated. In the 1960s, Charles Anderson had identified typical "depression regimes" or "depression dictatorships" in Central America, but Swiss historian Hans-Werner Tobler has warned against such a generalization.[9] Nohlen's research group extended this debate to other Latin American countries, the United States, and Canada. In case studies and comparative analyses, presented at an international symposium, these scholars asked to what extent the Great Depression represented an independent or an intervening variable in the transformation of the region's political systems.[10] During the ensuing years, some participants produced revisionist articles and monographs on the topic. My own *Estado Novo* resulted from these debates.[11] Like most scholars in the group, I have argued that, while the Great Depression paved the way for the installation of the authoritarian-corporatist Estado Novo, the dictatorship would not be explainable without taking into account the socioeconomic and political-institutional changes of the previous decade at both national and regional levels.

After World War I, urban industrial centers in the dynamic southeast experienced an unprecedented social mobilization. Labor and a new, wage-dependent middle class articulated their demands for more political participation. Yet, initially the oligarchic regime, dominated by the states of São Paulo and Minas Gerais, proved unable to absorb and institutionally channel these new tendencies. Instead, it responded with force and "de-institutionalization" thereby contributing to the 1922 political crisis. In that year, the Reação Republicana (Republican Reaction), an intraoligarchic conflict for the most advantageous cooptation of secondary oligarchies, among them Rio Grande do Sul's elites, demonstrated the fragility of the Old Republic's clientelistic system of interstate compromise. An insurrection of lower-rank military (*tenentes*) from Rio de Janeiro's Fort Copacabana revitalized the tradition of the "young officers" who, during the last years of the Empire, had defended their rights, as citizen-soldiers, to criticize the government. The Partido Comunista Brasileiro, founded in 1922, was Brazil's first supraregional party, at least in outlook. The crisis triggered generational conflicts as well as dissidences within the ruling Partido Republicano Paulista, leading to the foundation of the still little-researched Partido Democrático in 1926,[12] the formation of a broader *tenentismo* movement, and a previously unknown labor militancy.

However, by 1928 most of these movements had ebbed away. A competent foreign observer realized early that the PD increasingly lost programmatic definition.[13] *Tenentismo* began to disintegrate. Some of its activists contented themselves with the liberal-constitutionalist demand for "representation and justice." Luís Carlos Prestes converted to Marxism[14] and advocated a social ("agrarian and anti-imperialist") revolution. His comrade-in-arms, Juárez Távora, did not believe in the revolutionary potential of the lower classes[15]; he and other national-revolutionary *tenentes* wanted to overcome the country's backwardness and dependency by installing a strong, interventionist state that promoted industrialization and national integration. Yet, the PCB's and Prestes's voluntaristic understanding of Brazil's political conflicts led to the self-destruction of the party, a weakening of working-class front groups, and a further disintegration of *tenentismo*.

As with the other major ruptures in Brazil's history, the *Independência* (1817–22/24) and the transition from a slaveholders' monarchy to abolition and republic (1888–89/94), the regime change did not coincide with the climax of social mobilization but followed it with a delay of some years. The fact that the tactics of cooptation of dissident elites failed this time resulted from the Great Depression. The external crisis did not cause, but accelerated, the decomposition of the Old Republic. It revitalized the opposition movement, precipitated further dissidences from the hegemonic oligarchic bloc, and forced the new regime to go much further in its state-building pretensions than it had ever intended, though Vargas would never mobilize the urban middle class and workers or politicize rural protests such as Caldeirão (1926–38). Therefore, the 1930 "Revolution" itself appeared to be little more than the typical mixture of conspiratorial movement, military coup, and reforms, so well known from the other caesuras in Brazilian history. Only in the long run did Vargas's takeover of power prove to be a revolution, that is, the catalyst for more profound and lasting changes in Brazil's political system and, on that basis, a new development model. These changes did not become clearly noticeable prior to the installation of the Estado Novo. Yet, it has only been since the *abertura* of the late 1970s that historians have been able to explore this regime[16] and come to this conclusion.

Regionalism versus Centralism in the Vargas Era: São Paulo and Rio Grande do Sul

My argumentation against a "depression regime" can also be supported from another perspective: regionalism. Given the extreme dual federalism of the Old Republic, it is no wonder that historians have devoted much attention to regionalist studies. Pioneering in this field was an American project in the 1970s that focused on the most important units of the Brazilian federation and analyzed their interaction with an increasingly integrated nation-state.[17] The 1930 Revolution accelerated this process. Vargas's Provisional Government witnessed a civil war, followed by a vehement debate, between regional oligarchies and *tenentes*, on the reasons for the failure of the Old Republic and how the state was to be reconstructed. In the volume *Regionalismo e centralização política: partidos e constituinte nos anos 30* [Regionalism and Political Centralization: Parties and Constituent Assembly in the 1930s], Ângela Maria de Castro Gomes concludes that, "for either side, the binomial centralization *versus* federalism represented the touch-stone from which all other questions developed" (emphasis in the original).[18] However, further research was needed to identify alternative political and societal models proposed in the 1920s and explore their long-term impact. Moreover,

Barbara Weinstein points to the "fact that regionally-based political studies virtually never go beyond 1937," thereby reinforcing "the notion that Vargas effectively centralized Brazilian politics."[19] This book questions the alleged eradication of regional identities by Vargas's regime and reexamines his political socialization in Rio Grande do Sul.

Brazil's economic powerhouse, São Paulo, has remained a special focus of interest. One might speculate how differently from Vargas *paulistas*, had they not been removed from power, would have responded to the world recession. The demands for a federalization of coffee valorization, the 1926 constitutional reform (in which Getúlio Vargas took an active part), and the creation, at least nominally, of a number of advisory councils, such as the Conselho Nacional do Trabalho (National Labor Council) and Conselho de Defesa Nacional (National Defense Council), are clear expressions of an ongoing recentralization as early as the mid-1920s. Also, as Jerry Dávila reminds us in his chapter concluding this volume, Edgar de Decca and Weinstein have revisited the alleged conservatism of pre-1930 *paulista* industrialists. For Weinstein, it was precisely the redefinition of their role, or at least the reshaping of their image, as "industrial owner managers" that recommended them for a prominent position in the formulation of public policies and control over social welfare programs during the Estado Novo.[20] The point at issue in the con-flicts of the early 1930s was not so much self-sustainable economic development and social reform but political and cultural hegemony. Politically, *paulistas'* main target was the *tenentes* who fiercely opposed reconstitutionalization because in a country whose rural population had remained personally dependent on the landowning class and by far outnumbered the urban electorate, a call to the ballot would inevitably lead to a manipulation of the vote and a return of state particularists (not just *paulistas*) to the national assembly. Weinstein, influenced by the "linguistic turn," also emphasizes the *paulistas'* successful construction of a hegemonic discourse that repre-sented their state "as the vanguard of progress and civilization, while the rest of the nation served as the 'other,' in a cultural relationship reminiscent of that between colonizer and colonized." In the 1932 revolt, the northeastern-born soldiers amongst government troops could be portrayed as backward, nonwhite barbarians who threatened São Paulo's, and thereby the country's, future. The uprising may have been the last regional revolt in Brazil but for Weinstein these repre-sentations survived the Vargas era and the "Paulistas' insistence on a hierarchy (rather than a diversity) of regional identities . . . formed the greatest impediment to a more progressive and democratic national culture in the early 1930s."[21]

Rather surprisingly, the crucial relationship between Vargas and *paulistas* after 1930 has remained clouded in myth. In his contribution to this volume, JAMES P. WOODARD directs our attention to Vargas's journals that reveal that indeed São Paulo, and not the extreme Left and Right, as so many historians believe, was his "greatest political concern during the 1930s." In São Paulo's 1932 uprising, Woodard maintains, Vargas aimed at "flushing out" his *paulista* opponents, and after the Intentona Comunista in 1935 he had his eyes firmly on state governor Armando de Salles Oliveira who was about to challenge his presidency in the abortive elections of 1937–38. For Woodard, Salles did not, as is so often claimed, head a reactionary movement; on the contrary, his program was reformist. Despite Vargas's interventions, Woodard warns us of denying him the sensitivity for persisting regional loyalties. Indeed, Vargas actively manipulated *paulista* identity and regionalist symbolism from 1929. Even during his dictatorship, also dubbed the "National State," he was not unattuned to São Paulo's peculiarities and traditions. Senior politicians of the former PRP regained influence. Yet, São Paulo's conservative and racist upper classes increasingly hated Vargas, and the more they did so the more he appealed to the region's common people. This, according to Woodard, may explain why Vargas was able to reinvent himself as a populist and return to power in 1951.

An incorporation of the Estado Novo into an analysis of regionalism is equally significant in the case of Rio Grande do Sul. Not only were its elites "who had been traditionally oriented towards domestic markets, [. . .] the least dependent on the international economic system and therefore the least discredited by its collapse,"[22] but Rio Grande also represented the only authoritarian polity between 1894 and 1930. It is remarkable that historians and political scientists who have researched the Estado Novo's eclectic political-ideological project[23] and identified, among others, Alberto Tôrres, Oliveira Viana, Jackson de Figueiredo, Azevedo do Amaral, Benito Mussolini, Francisco de Oliveira Salazar, Józef Piłsudski, and William F. Willoughby as its fathers have often overlooked another spiritual mentor: Julio de Castilhos, the first republican governor of Rio Grande do Sul and arbitrary interpreter of Auguste Comte. This omission may be explainable by the fact that Brazilian history has usually been written and rewritten from the perspective of the southeast and its archives.[24] For historians who have closely studied the normative ideas that guided *gaúchos*, there can be little doubt about the region's significant influence on state and nation-building in Vargas's Brazil and beyond,[25] though a detailed analysis of this long-term impact is still missing.[26] Castilhos despised the liberal constitutionalism of other regional oligarchies that seemed to expose the state to destructive forces. Following the so-called Federalist Revolution (1893–95), the last war at Brazil's open frontier, he installed a developmental and educational dictatorship. The young Vargas, born in the border town of São Borja in 1883, breathed the spirit of this regime and would, at both state and national level, preserve some of its characteristics: a centralization of political power in the state's chief executive; the latter's engineering of elections and constitutional law; a tutelary state (to borrow Ricardo Vélez Rodríguez's term); a special responsibility of the public administration for primary and vocational education; and a close cooperation with the Roman Catholic Church in the moralization of society. However, having witnessed the eroding hegemony of the ruling Partido Republicano Rio-Grandense under Castilhos's successor, Antônio Augusto Borges de Medeiros, Vargas and his protégés, among them the mastermind of the 1930 Revolution, Oswaldo Aranha, and the later generals Pedro Aurélio de Góes Monteiro and Eurico Gaspar Dutra, understood that the state had to play a more active role in transforming the economy and state-society relations. Vargas, influenced by Oliveira Viana, increasingly thought in national terms.[27]

GUNTER AXT whose chapter follows this introduction represents a more recent, revisionist school of historians in Rio Grande do Sul that questions the alleged exceptionalism of the southern state during most of the Old Republic. It distinguishes between the ruling PRR's positivist political discourse and the reality of (rather fragile) clientelistic relations of power and stresses the programmatic discontinuities in the history of the hegemonic party.[28] Axt shows that Getúlio Vargas's rise to the state "presidency" resulted from his ability to form new alliances between center and regions at both national and state level, but not in the way historiography has usually described them. As leader of the *gaúcho* caucus in congress and President Washington Luís's finance minister, Vargas restored Rio Grande's position in the Union after *gaúchos'* help for the Reação Republicana. Porto Alegre's renewed strategic alliance with São Paulo included lending support to the liberal agrarian policy of the dominant *paulistas* at national level. Yet, when in charge of state politics, Vargas also had to address Rio Grande's own divisions. In contrast to those who see the Litoral in the driving seat and its allies shift from the Campanha to the Serra, Axt argues that Vargas abandoned Castilhos's and Borges's political alliance with the commercial and financial interests in Porto Alegre, Pelotas, and Rio Grande city, restored the prominence of cattle farmers at the Argentinean and Uruguayan borders, and incorporated the previously neglected sectors, industrial capital and labor, in *all* regions, including in the zones of foreign colonization. Not only did Vargas overcome Rio Grande do Sul's isolationism; he also defended a more interventionist state.

In the analysis of this new state, Axt comes close to a thesis Bolívar Lamounier developed, first in his collaboration with the Heidelberg School. According to Lamounier, the Vargas era institutional model could be compared to a tripod resting on the corporatist representation of (professional) interests; cooperative (Lamounier actually speaks of "consociational"), but fragmentary, structures of political representation "in the strict sense," that is, in the federal, electoral, and parliamentary spheres; and a plebiscitary presidency.[29] Indeed, the origins of this model can be traced back to Vargas's Rio Grande do Sul. As Céli Regina Pinto shows, *gaúcho* discourses had always been nonoligarchic, or protopopulist, though never antioligarchic.[30] With the state's legislative chamber in recess for ten months of the year and its functions reduced to those of a finance chamber, Rio Grande's "president" concentrated all power in his own hands but the 1891 state constitution forced him to publish draft decrees for public discussion. Vargas, less autocratic than Castilhos and less wooden than Borges, would find the search for quasi-plebiscitary approval relatively easy. Furthermore, he did not wait for smallholders, workers, and industrial capital to organize independently but created a system of cartels and cooperatives under the auspices of the modernizing state.[31] Finally, a new deal with the liberal opposition guaranteed more honest elections, did not prevent their elected candidates from taking up their seats in parliament or municipal councils, and allowed them to retain control over some municipalities. Moreover, as Axt emphasizes, the opposition even gained access to public credits. The success of this polity generated the image of a president who stood above political parties and daily politics; the chief-of-state seemed to represent an impartial arbitrator and the supreme administrator of the public good. This image helps to explain why Vargas, until the very end of his political career, "presided over regimes but survived their collapse,"[32] though we have to return to the question of his actual arbitrary powers later on.

The 1930 presidential elections gave *gaúchos* the opportunity to present themselves as an alternative generation of leaders. Indeed, for the next 50 years *gaúchos* would provide six presidents and numerous other civilian and military key figures and imprint their renewed political philosophy on Brazilian institutions and policies. However, those who had hoped the 1930 Revolution would follow the examples of the *Independência* and the installation of the republic and simply replace one regional oligarchy by another felt bitter disappointment when Vargas, in 1931, claimed to represent all Brazilians.[33] This attitude, prompted not least by the need to tackle the problems arising from the Great Depression, divided the *gaúchos* in Vargas's government. While Aranha, Góes, and Dutra remained in leading civilian and military posts, others returned to Rio Grande and reunited with *borgistas*. Some would support São Paulo's elites in their quest for a quick restoration of the constitutional regime. The political divisions that Brazil's reconstitutionalization exposed strengthened *gaúchos'* deep distrust, rooted in *castilhismo* as much as in the influences of European totalitarianism, in the capability of a liberal democracy to provide political stability. In 1934, Góes seemed to have contemplated about proclaiming Castilhos's authoritarian 1891 constitution at national level, though Vargas did not follow this proposal.[34] He knew he had to bargain with the other contenders for power. Nonetheless, with the 1932 Electoral Law and 1934 charter, the Vargas era institutional tripod, described by Lamounier, began to take shape at national level. The regime opted for corporatism, rather than trade union pluralism, and allowed for a more cooperative federalism, a peaceful, but engineered, competition of political parties, and elements of proportional representation in order to protect (elite/state) minorities against (arbitrary) rule by overwhelming majorities. Though corporatism would change its form and the following authoritarian regimes, behind a more or less legalist façade, tried to concentrate power in the center, forbid or reduce party competition, and abolish or restrict the legislative, both institutional solutions have survived until the present day. Toward the end of the Estado Novo, when Vargas embraced populism, thereby adjusting clientelism to an emerging mass society, the Vargas era institutional model received its third leg at national level: plebiscitary presidentialism.[35]

Notwithstanding the centralist provisions in the 1937 constitution, Vargas's dictatorship missed the opportunity to redivide the national territory for economic (reallocation of resources), social (regional adjustment of public services), and political reasons (weakening of the oligarchies' power). The size and number of inhabitants of states and municipalities differed in the extreme. All attempts to establish rational criteria for the formation of municipalities and to reduce their number in São Paulo, Piauí, and Bahia failed.[36] The territorial integrity of states was never seriously questioned. As a consequence, the polarization between powerful states and municipalities, which offered excellent conditions for investment, and small administrative units with precarious economic foundations would aggravate. Vargas's unprecedented visits to states in the interior and the construction of cities in the centralwest had symbolic value but an incorporation of the hinterland into the nation would have required building streets and rail tracks, promoting land reform and the formation of well-equipped agricultural cooperatives, and providing schools and health services. Little was achieved (and even tried) on this front.[37] Political clientelism survived the Estado Novo (as it would later survive the military dictatorship[38]) and it would quickly undermine the parties founded after 1945[39] (and 1966, respectively[40]).

The official memory of Vargas and his era differs from region to region and has more to do with challenged identities and the place in national politics a particular state's elites played after the 1930 Revolution than with the actual socioeconomic progress that state made, as we discuss. São Paulo's upper classes felt demoted; the state parliament and a main avenue still today carry the name "July 9," the day when the 1932 uprising started, while there is no public building, and not a single street, named after Getúlio Vargas.[41] In contrast, the government of the capital city Rio de Janeiro would eventually, as Daryle Williams shows in his chapter, remember Vargas, their honorary citizen, as the creator of a new urban landscape for their city and architect of a new Brazil and erect a memorial to him in 2004. Interestingly, it stands on the same place where the states' flags, and with them liberal constitutionalism, went up in flames in 1937. It was a *carioca*, Oscar Niemeyer, whom Rio Grande do Sul's Legislative Chamber charged with designing the only other major memorial (and new burial-place) for the *gaúcho* president: on the Praça XV de Novembro of his provincial home town of São Borja. In Porto Alegre, Vargas, the "president of all Brazilians," could never escape from the long shadow of Castilhos.

Was Vargas the Arbitrator of the Political System?

This book challenges the notion, widespread in historiography, that Vargas acted as an arbitrator in national politics during a crisis of hegemony. While this was certainly the image he and his propaganda apparatus projected, it was rarely matched by reality. While Vargas was a clever manipulator and had the missionary zeal, so typical for *castilhistas*, to use government not merely as a source of private enrichment but as a chance to transform the country, a reading of his diaries shows, in day-to-day politics he often felt overwhelmed by circumstances. Only more recently have we learned that he contemplated suicide at all critical conjunctures of his political career: in 1930, 1932, and 1945.[42] The role of an arbitrator would have required more political-institutional autonomy than he ever enjoyed. Despite Vargas's indefatigable efforts in administrative reform, paternalism survived, many reforms remained mere *"reformas de organograma,"* and interinstitutional conflicts were commonplace. The state lacked sufficient infrastructural power to implement public policies throughout Brazil.[43]

All attempts to place the regime on a firm political basis failed. The Aliança Liberal (Liberal Alliance), which backed Vargas in the 1930 Revolution, was no more than a loose coalition of state parties without a coherent ideological basis, united by little more than their wish to end the rule of the PRP. Its rapid decay and the reintegration of dissident elites into regional fronts were predictable. Only the national-revolutionary *tenentes* could guarantee Vargas's survival in power during the critical years of the Provisional Government. He shared with them an interest in breaking the monopoly of power that the states' republican parties had held during the Old Republic but left the socioeconomic and political foundations of oligarchic rule intact. The (engineered) reconstitutionalization that Vargas conceded to *paulistas*, in spite of their defeat in 1932 and the *tenentes'* resistance to such a step, followed a shrewd calculation: the registration of political parties would, he hoped, contribute to a further division of the regional oligarchies and allow for the mobilization of his supporters in the states. Similarly, the introduction of a corporatist element in the 1933–34 constituent assembly was to strengthen the government. While Vargas was right with regard to the atomization of Brazil's party system[44] and his indirect election to the presidency on the basis of the new political organizations and "class representation," he eventually lost his military ally. The *tenentes*, with their regional basis in the northeast, were forced to reorganize and created their own political block, the União Cívica Nacional (National Civic Union). It supported Vargas. However, Aranha's attempt to extend it to a lasting national movement that would include the organizations of other *situacionistas*, first and foremost Rio Grande do Sul's new Partido Republicano Liberal (PRL; Liberal Republican Party) failed. Moreover, the *tenentes* began to be absorbed by the states' political machines.

The short history of two national organizations with a broad membership, the Far Right Ação Integralista Brasileira and Far Left popular front Aliança Nacional Libertadora, founded in 1932 and 1934 respectively, shows that mass mobilization would have been possible. Both the AIB's model of an "integral state" that was to revitalize the values of the agrarian and patrimonial society and to strengthen Roman Catholic religion as a way of "brazilianizing" Brazil and the ANL's goal of a revolutionary popular government based on (class) "solidarity" reveal the search for social integration in a society characterized by a lack of institutionalized participation.[45] Yet, the regime's inability to overcome its elitism left large parts of the lower and middle classes to extremist forces.

All too often Vargas has been incorrectly portrayed as the clever manipulator who knew about the preparations of the *Intentona Comunista*, a series of Communist-inspired barrack revolutions in November 1935, but did not intervene because the revolt would offer him the pretext for imposing a state of war, playing off the Left and the Right, and preparing his 1937 coup d'etat. In a letter to Aranha, then ambassador in Washington, Vargas himself called this coup a "revolution from above"[46] since it had cut the Gordion knot and gave him *carte blanche* to implement his program of national reconstruction. Such an interpretation can make us overlook that he needed the military to crush first the *Intentona Comunista* and then, in 1938, an *integralista* revolt, not to speak of holding in check *paulistas* and *gaúchos*. Axt's claim that the state executive in Rio Grande do Sul's pre-1930 *republiqueta* lacked the power to establish a one-party regime, also applies to the Estado Novo. However, in contrast to the former (and the military dictatorship after 1966), the volatile situation after 1935 did not even allow for the installation of a controlled two-party system. The banning of all political parties during the Estado Novo increased Vargas's dependence on the right-wing army command. At one point the generals thought of overthrowing him and provisionally establishing a *junta* under their control. Such plans failed due to a lack of both unity within the armed forces and an alternative to Vargas.[47] But what really restrained the army from such a step?

In his contribution to this volume, FRANK D. MCCANN reconstructs the events and maneuverings that produced the 1937 coup. He considers the presidential campaign to be just the "backdrop for the main drama" that unfolded after the failed *Intentona*: the formation of an alliance between Vargas and the army generals, especially Minister of War Dutra and Chief of the General Staff Góes Monteiro. The latter were increasingly worried about the army's difficulties in mobilizing and training sufficient soldiers, the poor state of its weaponry and equipment, and Brazil's lack of a steel industry. The events in Spain, China, and Abyssinia seemed to be the prelude for a much greater battle, and Argentina and Chile had begun rearmament. Domestically the fear of Soviet-influenced uprisings, military mutinies, or armed revolt by regional bosses was strong. A dictatorial regime seemed to be inevitable in order to save Brazil from catastrophe and to start making it a prosperous nation. Yet, as McCann demonstrates, *neither* Vargas *nor* Góes had absolute power, even after tighter control over the officer corps was established, renegade *gaúcho* governor Flores da Cunha had been disarmed and forced out of the country, and *integralistas* had lined up with Vargas. This, McCann argues, was the background for a pledge, or *compromisso*: Vargas "would equip and arm the armed forces so that they could carry out their assigned duty, in return they would provide the muscle for a regime of force and national development." It was on the basis of this *compromisso*, McCann continues, that the army would become the moderator of the political system over the next five decades. This argument undermines the long-accepted view that the military had gained this position after the overthrow of the monarchy in 1889.

Only recently have researchers focused on the institutional implications of the events of 1934–35. It was at this political conjuncture, and not only after the foundation of the Escola Superior de Guerra (Superior War School) in 1949, as historiography usually claims, that the positivist slogans of "progress" and "order" were increasingly replaced by the new terms of "economic development" and "national security," respectively, and the architecture of a national security state began to take shape.[48] Yet, OLIVER DINIUS's chapter in this book shows that Vargas proved unable to control another institution that was to act preemptively in securing his power: the political police. By applying a long-term perspective, stretching from the installation of Vargas's dictatorship to the 1964 coup, Dinius discovers a growing autonomy of this force during and after Vargas's second administration. For the political police, the president's "populist pact" with labor jeopardized political stability. Marginalized and in quiet opposition, it pursued its own agenda and gathered intelligence on labor militants. After 1964, this intelligence would facilitate the repression of the Left. Since Dinius's chapter focuses on labor control, it is to be discussed in detail in the next section.

Vargas Era Social Policies and Industrial Labor Control

Vargas has been given credit for the extension of state interventionism to the social sphere. The claim that the Old Republic had only considered the "social question" to be "a case for the police" ignores the fact that Castilhos's 1891 state constitution was pioneering in at least nominally defending the rights of workers and that Borges introduced Brazil's first workers' compensation scheme, increased salaries in government enterprises, and encouraged private capital to follow suit.[49] This background, though insufficient of itself, is important for understanding Vargas's promise, before his 1930 Revolution, of a "valorization of man," the foundation of two new Ministries for Education and Public Health and for Labor, Industry, and Commerce days after his victory, and the demand in his 1934 national charter that private ownership should carry with it social responsibility. He understood his legislation as a preventative measure aimed at incorporating a politically active, but still divided, labor movement into the polity. Interestingly, *paulista* entrepreneurs pursued a different strategy from Vargas's government. Both were interested in controlling labor but the former favored workers' incorporation into the enterprise while the latter preferred a state-corporatist solution.[50] Early historiography stressed that Vargas decreed this legislation against the resistance of many entrepreneurs but shunned open conflict with them when it came to the implementation of his reforms.[51]

Research over the past 20 years, less consumed by Vargas's paternalistic role, has revealed the hollowness of high-sounding promises in government programs. The Estado Novo's self-styled social democracy excluded destructive elements that refused to integrate into the labor market and subversive groups that opposed the tutelary state.[52] The edifice of a national security state included the social ministries. Leading educators, like chief statistician Mário Augusto Teixeira de Freitas, cooperated with the army and the notorious Tribunal de Segurança Nacional (National Security Tribunal), and the Ministry of Labor, Industry and Commerce became the coordinator of repressive policies against activists.[53] Vargas's regime did not only separate political from social participation; it also hierarchicized the beneficiaries of social reforms, focusing on skilled and organized workers in strategic industrial enterprises, ignoring rural laborers, and further marginalizing black Brazilians through a technocratic and eugenicist approach to educational reform.[54] While labor regulation and educational policy have attracted much attention by scholars, we still know relatively little about health care, housing, and nutrition during Vargas's regimes, especially the Estado Novo. In his chapter, JOHN J. CROCITTI fills this gap. He is interested in how common people fared during the dictatorship, and nutrition offers, in his opinion, an especially suitable area to test the actual impact of state

interventionism. Vargas's government committed itself to improving
the material well-being of the nation and made nutrition a prominent
part of social reforms. It had various reasons for such a commitment.
A hungry population could become prone to extremists. It would be
ill-suited for the planned industrialization or the recruitment of
soldiers during the war. Nutritional programs could help controlling
and coopting the working class, improving the race, and generating
development. Crocitti paints a dire picture of urban workers' living and working conditions in Vargas's Brazil. Moreover, he shows
that, by partly blaming workers' miseducation and traditions for the
selection of an unhealthy diet, nutritionists missed addressing the
main reason for Brazil's food problem: the inadequacy of workers' real
wages. Using data from the *Anuário Estatístico*, Crocitti calculates the
cost of a sample basket, as suggested by these nutritionists, and the
income distribution of workers nationally and in six major urban areas
during the Estado Novo and the late 1940s. The comparison of food
prices and wages demonstrates that the living conditions improved for
a substantial part of the population, especially Vargas's major target
groups: unionized workers in big enterprises and commercial and
bureaucratic sectors. Nowhere was this progress more tangible than in
the Federal District, São Paulo, and Porto Alegre. However, the
majority of Brazilians remained undernourished, as figures for Belo
Horizonte and especially northeastern Salvador da Bahia and Recife
illustrate.

Recent research has also asked to what extent the Estado Novo's
authoritarian corporatism succeeded in making workers passive clients
of the state. Historians have given revisionist, but controversial,
answers. John D. French, relying on his research on metropolitan São
Paulo's industrial belt, insists that labor activists at local level successfully used the channels of controlled participation the regime offered
them and actually gained concessions. The "invention of *trabalhismo*"
(to use Gomes's expression[55]), that is the emerging alliance between
government and labor, further strengthened unions' bargaining
power.[56] In contrast, Joel Wolfe argues this may be true but few
working people joined unions, especially outside the federal capital
with its long tradition of labor activism. These *sindicatos* were perceived as tightly controlled government agencies that were unable to
guarantee the improvement of living conditions they promised. As
soon as workers were allowed to do so, they would negotiate directly
with their employers.[57]

With regard to the postwar period, traditional historiography has
stressed that Vargas, when faced with demands for democratization,

was clever in placing the corporatist system upon new foundations, rather than dismantling it. At the end of his nonparty dictatorship, he founded, "from above," two political parties, the Partido Social Democrático and the Partido Trabalhista Brasileiro. While the former represented the interests of most state *interventorias* and some industrial entrepreneurs, the urban middle class, and government employees who had profited from Vargas's economic policy and administrative reform, the PTB was the party of those who had bene- fited from *trabalhismo*, especially the trade union bureaucracy. In the 1945 poll, with a greatly enlarged electorate, both parties and other pro-Vargas groups supported the former dictator, and eventually his handpicked successor, General Dutra, in order to preserve economic nationalism, state interventionism, and *trabalhismo* (i.e., their public jobs, concessions, privileges, and social rights) against the economi- cally liberal and socially conservative União Democrática Nacional. Such an assessment ignores, as French demonstrates, that Vargas endorsed Dutra's candidacy only under pressure, that both the PSD and the UDN competed for the support of the traditional local elites, and that it was precisely the issues of mass mobilization and labor rights that separated PSD and PTB, especially in the first years after the war. Within the trade unions, the Left (including the PCB) and Centre gained ground and rejected both the UDN's proposal of union pluralism and state tutelage. Instead, they defended union rights within the existing structures, redefined their relation to the state, and isolated the careerist right-wing bureaucracy that had remained influential within the PTB and even cooperated with the political police.[58] Following this interpretation, it is the divisive actions of these leaders that have to be blamed for the difficulties the PTB initially had in mobilizing workers, and not the party's links with the Estado Novo's unpopular trade unions.[59]

The alliance between a more combative PTB and large numbers of PSD dissidents only emerged at the end of the 1940s and remained rather fragile. Vargas's comeback in the 1950 presidential elections had more to do with the inflationary effects of Dutra's deficit- financed public investment, an increasingly repressive response to labor activism, and Vargas's ability to unite his union supporters and the PTB than with the political consolidation of his parties. Equally, it was the dynamics of Vargas's last administration and the symbolic cap- ital they could gain from his death, which allowed these parties to form the government, with one short interruption, until 1964.[60]

Lamounier addresses the root problem of trade union corporatism: it indexed, and thereby multiplied, demands. Weaker enterprises in a given sector had to implement what had been negotiated in stronger ones, and the achievements in one sector would serve as a point of reference for the others.[61] Toward the end of his 1951–54 administration, Vargas was haunted by the ghosts he had conjured up: while, due to an increasing balance-of-payment problem arising from a dramatic drop in world coffee prices, the government faced difficulties in maintaining welfare policies for organized workers in the cities, tensions began to increase in rural areas in which a more politicized peasantry demanded its own "1930." Moreover, Vargas now also faced dilemmas in the two other subsystems of the institutional tripod, as described by Lamounier: his government lacked the stable political majority and legitimacy it needed to implement or adjust its program to a more crisis-ridden economy. By having concentrated power in a highly personalized executive, not only the survival of the incumbent administration, but the stability of the whole political system, depended on an unpredictable and diffuse popular support.[62]

This leads us back to DINIUS's chapter. Latin America's biggest steel plant in Volta Redonda, state of Rio de Janeiro, symbolized, more than any other project, Brazil's ambition to become what modernization theorists would later call a take-off country. True, it remained a "modernization island." However, as Dinius stresses, Vargas's goals of "fostering rapid industrialization, expanding labor rights, and maintaining order in an increasingly complex industrial society [intersected there]." This makes the Companhia Siderúrgica Nacional the perfect case for exploring the coherence of Vargas's legacy. During the Estado Novo his three goals were considered to be interdependent. Continuous production implied social peace. Therefore, the plant's workforce was among the first to benefit from Vargas's social legislation and to receive the right to unionize. In 1944, a local metalworkers' union was founded and recognized. However, Dinius shows that Volta Redonda, the foundation stone of a state-run basic and defense industry, also became a prime target of the ever-expanding police apparatus. "The political police in particular shaped the relations between CSN management and the workers as it became a tool for the State to forestall labor organization under Communist leadership." In reality, we learn, the PCB's influence was exaggerated, and police repression against labor activists reached its climax after the prohibition of the party in 1947. This was when the mill started full production, and managers and the Dutra government would not allow any disruption. However, Vargas's return to the presidency strengthened union power, restored labor rights, and restricted the role of the political police who had increasing difficulties in distinguishing between new, radicalizing PTB union leaders and their PCB supporters. If forced to choose, claims Dinius, this police force would now defend its concept of social "order" against the advocates of socioeconomic "progress" (*desenvolvimentismo* and *trabalhismo*), once complimentary goals.

Deconstructing Vargas Era Representations

In a recent issue of *LASA-Forum*, Timothy J. Power refers to Antônio Carlos Jobim's *bon mot* "Brazil is not for beginners." While he disagrees in part, pointing to the fact that the students he takes there immediately fall in love with the country, he admits: "after landfall on Brazilian shores, it takes a while before things truly come into focus."[63] Indeed, a first encounter with the official construction of Vargas's image can be disturbing for a foreign undergraduate, as Dávila describes in vivid terms in his chapter. The three generations of Brazilianists who have contributed to this volume have, some over many years, tried to come to grips with Vargas's multifaceted personality and the ways in which his memory has been cultivated and twisted. Given the dictator-turned-populist's continuing frictions with regional elites, his lack of political-institutional autonomy, and the limited impact of his social reforms, how could the myth of him standing above regions, institutions, and classes emerge in the first place and why has it survived until now? In consonance with more recent trends in historiography, several authors in this book explore and deconstruct the representations, images, and symbols of Vargas and his era. Collectively, they show how much Vargas himself and his protégés were concerned with molding not only institutions but also people's minds. They knew that the adoption and adjustment of an alternative political model at national level depended decisively on gaining cultural hegemony. The search for modernity and a new national identity, the meaning of *brasilidade* (often painted in regional colors), had gathered momentum in the early 1920s[64] and was strongly manipulated during the Estado Novo. *Gaúchos* were experienced in masking political and social ruptures, such as 1928 or 1937, with a subtle personality cult, a pseudo-scientific political discourse, and symbolic gestures that reconciled past and future, order and progress (*conservar melhorando*, "to preserve by improving," as Castilhos had put it).

DARYLE WILLIAMS points to the fact that Vargas and his "revolutionary" coalition did not have to militarily conquer the federal capital; yet, when arriving in Rio de Janeiro, they immediately took symbolic control of the old regime's built environment. The subsequent remake of civic time and civic space was to provide the new rulers with their own historical legitimacy and to instill in the capital city's population a sense of civic belonging and sociability. Consecutive interventions into the civic calendar and the gradual transformation and occupation of Rio's public spaces reflected, as Williams demonstrates, both the changing priorities of Vargas's 1930–45 administrations and his overarching goal of reconstructing the Brazilian nation. Rio de Janeiro was to become a model of urban planning emblematic of the moral improvement of its citizenry. Vargas could draw on the 1927 Agache Plan that had emphasized functionality, sanitation, and modernist splendor. Though his regime was never able to fully implement Agache's project, Williams argues that, by 1945, the Estado Novo had, at least in the downtown area, "urbanized a functional cityscape that doubled as a spectacular 'theatre of power.'" Nonetheless, Vargas and his protégés could never completely regulate civic culture and behavior, even at the height of the Estado Novo. The state-led modernization, with its centralist, antiliberal, and technocratic attributes, remained contested until the very end of the dictatorship.

Vargas and his propaganda apparatus always aimed at reshaping both "high" and popular culture. JERRY DÁVILA analyzes textbook writing and orpheonic singing during and immediately after the Estado Novo. High school history books addressed the offspring of the elites and aspiring elites who could afford to buy such luxury items. These textbooks, produced without government interference, depicted the 1930 Revolution as a major rupture and Vargas as the political genius who realized its objectives and integrated society. Manuals reflected the changes in Brazil's international alignments and polity transformations but it was always Vargas who acted as the far-sighted steersman of the nation's progress. Heitor Villa Lobo's cocurricular nationalist music program, implemented especially in the federal capital, was not restricted to elite schools; on the contrary, mass musical manifestations aimed at transforming what Williams calls the capital city's "civicscape" and at using the cohesive power of the chorus to forge "a strong, corporate race unified under the leadership of the chief of the nation." Dávila shows that Vargas's image as nation-builder and protector of the popular classes still figures prominently in today's texts and even samba performances, but Vargas's praise is no longer sung uncritically.

LISA SHAW explores Vargas's screen image in both the newsreels and the popular musical comedies, or *chanchadas*, from the early 1930s to the end of the populist era. Her analysis is pioneering in that she places these media in the context of a shared viewing experience. When Vargas took power in 1930, he lost little time in exploiting the new medium of cinema to educate the nation. Newsreels and feature-length documentaries, screened not only in public theaters but also in schools, cultural centers, sporting associations, and big enterprises, were to instill into the viewers values such as patriotism, respect for the established social order, pride in the country's and its leader's achievements, (reproductive) hygiene, work discipline, and optimism in Brazil's industrial progress. It should be added that these were all values that had already figured prominently in Rio Grande before 1930. What may be surprising is Shaw's conclusion that the themes and didactic language of the newsreels did not change fundamentally from Vargas's first regime to his "populist" government. It is a different matter with the *chanchadas*. At the height of the Estado Novo, the state had taken firm control of the production and distribution of films. Yet, there remained one niche, low budget comedies that, it seems, were largely neglected by the regime's censors or allowed to act as a little-threatening valve through which the (semi-)illiterate masses could relieve the tensions of everyday life. However, it was during the 1950s when the production of *chanchadas* particularly prospered, primarily because of the high costs (and lesser popularity) of (subtitled) imported films. Carnivalesque *chanchadas* ridiculed (in a subtle way during the Estado Novo, more aggressively in the 1950s) the official pomp, societal norms, and bureaucracy of the Vargas years, but also the leader's iconic status.

A whole generation of Brazilians was exposed to these representations and images (which linked Vargas increasingly with the military), from primary school to the work place, professional associations to recreational activities, radio broadcasts to cinema, and mass rallies to Carnival processions. Yet, we can also conclude from this research that contemporaries saw through, and even debunked, the official myths. Had Vargas simply been overthrown in the fateful summer of 1954, it is questionable whether they would have survived. Nobody knew this better than Vargas whose speech at Castilhos's funeral had compared Rio Grande's patriarch to a saint who had made his state the helmsman of the nation. When Vargas's power waned, he would not just resign but shape the legacy of his death. For THOMAS D. ROGERS, this was the main function of his suicide note. "The letter and Vargas's death clearly drew meaning from one another and this fact is crucial to understanding the document as an intervention. The *Carta Testamento* was the exclamation point following the suicide and the suicide sealed the letter with blood." Though we have a reasonable knowledge of the events that culminated in Vargas's death, both the authorship and the meanings of this short, but enormously powerful, text have remained disputed. Rogers's careful reconstruction of the context in which it was written and exegesis of not only the *Carta Testamento*, but also the documents closely related to it, shed new light on the crucial events of August 1954 and explain the longevity of Vargas's last words. Vargas used an almost biblical language, declaring himself chosen by destiny and now willing to make the ultimate sacrifice for "the people"; yet, he was also full of his own importance and aware that this letter would be a weapon to defeat his opponents. Vargas's PTB and the three populist successors who followed him as president would exploit the symbolic capital of his last gesture, adopt his language, and (badly) imitate his political maneuvers. As Rogers points out, those who had worked with Vargas, like Tancredo Neves and Lionel Brizola (who symbolically died in the year of the fiftieth anniversary of his Master's suicide[65]), would not stop reminding Brazilians of Vargas's sacrifice and link the struggle for democracy after 1964 with his person and era.

Conclusion

What failed as a consequence of the world recessions of the mid-1970s and early 1980s was not only the military regime but the technocratic strategy Vargas had embraced to implement ISI. This strategy enabled Brazil's transformation into a take-off country but it also neglected agriculture in favor of industry and perpetuated regional, social, and ethnic distortions. It fostered modernization but failed to produce what is now called development that includes, apart from full national sovereignty and economic growth: the generation of productive and sufficiently paid work/employment; a reasonable level of social equality and justice in the distribution of land, income and access to public goods, especially education; and the participation in political decision making.[66] Ultimately Vargas failed because of his inability to abandon the course of a conservative modernization. If there was one pattern characterizing all of Vargas's regimes, it was his failure to implement profound social reforms, first and foremost an agrarian reform, to extend citizenship universally, and to develop civil society. A *castilhista* would always consider social problems to be of a technical nature. He would rely on *técnicos* in the expanding, but little amalgamated, bureaucratic apparatus who, allegedly apolitical, in reality preferred a (semi-)authoritarian regime and constituted the pool the 1964 military regime could draw from. Or he would bypass fragile representative institutions and directly mobilize the masses through carefully orchestrated campaigns of a plebiscitary character. However, neither one nor the other could guarantee Vargas's survival and, what is more, make the state sufficiently effective and the nation sufficiently coherent to allow for the gradual consolidation of democracy after 1945.[67] What survived were the hopes of a decent life for all that the dictator-turned-populist had raised.

Contributors to this volume have not only tried to decipher some of the enigmas surrounding Vargas and his Brazil; some have also raised new questions. Axt shows how little we have understood the complex relationship between regions before 1930, especially the "strategic alliance" between Rio Grande do Sul and São Paulo. In the assessment of "1932," many students of Brazil still follow the *getulista* interpretation and refer to São Paulo's counter-revolution.[68] Though being one of the key events in twentieth century Brazilian history and vital for an understanding of the Vargas era, an authoritative scholarly study of São Paulo's revolt has not yet been written and one *paulista* historian told me years ago that probably only a foreigner could fill this lacuna. Such a study would have to explore the cycles of action and reaction of Republicans and Democrats who issued different manifestos and only united after the crisis had begun.[69] Woodard points to the superficiality with which São Paulo's main parties after 1930 have been treated so far. The same applies to Rio Grande's political organizations: PRR, PRL, and Partido Republicano Castilhista (Castilhista Republican Party). McCann raises another question: why did, in 1937, as in 1889 and 1922, the military establishment, resort to lies (the Cohen Plan) in order to justify its intervention? Did Vargas know that the Communist plot was fake? Contemporaries and *getulistas* emphasized that Vargas's second government differed significantly from his first 15 years in office.[70] Yet, historiography has paid less attention to this period,[71] and Vargas's journals stop in 1942. Dinius reminds us that the social and institutional conflicts of these years indeed hold the key to understanding Vargas's legacy as all but monolithic and static.

As the editor of this volume, I would like to thank all contributors for their meticulous work and reliable collaboration. All of us would like to thank the anonymous readers for their advice. We are grateful to Professor James Dunkerley and editor Gabriella Georgiades for the inclusion of our book into the ISA-Palgrave series "Studies of the Americas." Thanks go to assistant editor Joanna Mericle, production manager Erin Ivy, and Maran Elancheran and his team at

Newgen Imaging Systems in Thiruvanmiyur, India, who guided us competently through the production process. Last but not the least we owe a word of gratitude to copyeditors Newton Samraj and Sumathi Ellappan and indexer Lisa Rivero for their excellent work.

Notes

I wish to thank Michael Derham for the proof-reading of this text.

1. "O enigma Getúlio Vargas: No cinqüentenário da morte do presidente, faltaram obras sérias para decifrar a personagem e o seu legado," *Veja*, August 25, 2004.
2. The Partido Democrático Trabalhista dedicated part of its official webpage to "Getúlio." These texts are prime examples of an uncritical reflection on Vargas's legacy. See http://www.pdt.org.br/personali-dades/getulio.asp, accessed November 15, 2005.
3. See Robert M. Levine's *Father of the Poor? Vargas and his Era* (Cambridge: Cambridge Univ. Press, 1998) and Maria Celina d'Araújo's *A era Vargas* (São Paulo: Ed. Moderna, 2004).
4. José Nilo Tavares, "Getúlio Vargas e o Estado Novo," in *O feixe e o prisma: uma revisão do Estado Novo*, ed. José Luiz Werneck da Silva, 2 vols. (Rio de Janeiro: Jorge Zahar Ed., 1991), 1:80.
5. John W. F. Dulles, *Vargas of Brazil: A Political Biography* (Austin: Univ. of Texas Press, 1967).
6. Rosemary Thorp, "Introduction," in *Latin America in the 1930s: The Role of the Periphery in World Crisis*, ed. Rosemary Thorp (London: Macmillan/Oxford: St Antony's College, 1984), 13–14. For Kindleberger's afterword, see 315–329.
7. Fernando Henrique Cardoso, "Associated-Dependent Development and Democratic Theory," in *Democratizing Brazil: Problems of Transition and Consolidation*, ed. Alfred Stepan (New York: Oxford Univ. Press, 1989), 299–326.
8. Dietmar Rothermund further researched the Great Depression's effects on the underdeveloped world in *The Global Impact of the Great Depression, 1929–1939* (London/New York: Routledge, 1996).
9. Charles Anderson, *Politics and Economic Change in Latin America: The Governing of Restless Nations* (Princeton: Van Nostrand 1967), 215; Hans-Werner Tobler, " 'Depressionsdiktaturen' in Zentralamerika? Einige Bemerkungen zu einem historischen Begriff," in *Staatliche und parastaatliche Gewalt in Lateinamerika*, ed. Hans-Werner Tobler and Peter Waldmann (Frankfurt am Main: Vervuert, 1991), 217–226.
10. Results were published in Dieter Nohlen et al., Section 7 "Die langfristigen Auswirkungen der Weltwirtschaftskrise auf die heutigen politischen Systeme," in *Nord und Süd in Amerika: Gegensätze, Gemeinsamkeiten,*

europäischer Hintergrund, ed. Wolfgang Reinhard and Peter Waldmann, 2 vols. (Freiburg i. Br.: Rombach, 1992), 2:785–958.

11. Jens R Hentschke, *Estado Novo: Genesis und Konsolidierung der brasilianischen Diktatur von 1937. Eine Fallstudie zu den sozioökonomischen und politischen Transformationen in Lateinamerika im Umfeld der Großen Depression* (Saarbrücken: Verlag für Entwicklungspolitik, 1996). The conclusions of the section are based on the findings of this book.

12. For a recent revisionist analysis, see James P. Woodard, "History, Sociology and the Political Conflicts of the 1920s in São Paulo, Brazil," *Journal of Latin American Studies* 37, no. 2 (2005): 333–349.

13. See the statement of long-serving Austrian envoy Anton Retschek in Report 11. 10. 1926, Liasse Brasilien 2, 2/3, Karton 514, Neues Politisches Archiv, Österreichisches Staatsarchiv/Archiv der Republik.

14. William Waack, to my knowledge the first Brazilian to visit the recently opened Comintern archives, explores Moscow's role in this process. William Waack, *Camaradas: nos arquivos de Moscou. A história secreta da revolução brasileira de 1935* (São Paulo: Companhia de Letras, 1993), 26–47.

15. See Prestes's 1930 May Manifesto and Juárez Távora's answer in Hélio Silva, *O ciclo de Vargas*, vol. 3, *1930—a revolução traída*, 2nd ed. (Rio de Janeiro: Ed. Civilização Brasileira, 1966), 417–426.

16. See Edgard Carone's introduction to his *A Terceira República (1937–1945)*, 2nd ed. (São Paulo: Difel, 1982).

17. Joseph Love's *Rio Grande do Sul and Brazilian Regionalism, 1882–1930* (Stanford: Stanford Univ. Press, 1971) and *São Paulo in the Brazilian Federation, 1889–1937* (Stanford: Stanford Univ. Press, 1980); John D. Wirth, *Minas Gerais in the Brazilian Federation, 1889–1937* (Stanford: Stanford Univ. Press, 1977); Robert M. Levine, *Pernambuco in the Brazilian Federation, 1889–1937* (Stanford: Stanford Univ. Press 1978); Eul-Soo Pang, *Bahia in the First Brazilian Republic* (Gainesville: Univ. Presses of Florida, 1979).

18. Ângela Maria de Castro Gomes, "Introdução," in *Regionalismo e centralização política: partidos e constituinte nos anos 30*, coord. Ângela Maria de Castro Gomes (Rio de Janeiro: Ed. Nova Fronteira, 1980), 29.

19. Barbara Weinstein, "Racializing Regional Difference: São Paulo versus Brazil, 1932," in *Race and Nation in Modern Latin America*, ed. Nancy P. Appelbaum, Anne S. Macpherson, and Karin Alejandra Rosemblatt (Chapel Hill and London: Univ. of North Carolina Press, 2003), 237–262; the quote is from note 1.

20. Barbara Weinstein, *For Social Peace in Brazil: Industrialists and the Remaking of the Working Class in São Paulo, 1920–1964* (Chapel Hill: Univ. of North Carolina Press, 1996).

21. Weinstein, "Racializing Regional Difference." The quotes are from 239 and 255, respectively.

22. Joseph Love, "Regionalism and Federalism in Brazil, 1889–1937," in *Politics, Society, and Democracy in Latin America: Essays in Honor of*

Juan J. Linz, ed. Scott Mainwaring and Arturo Valenzuela (Boulder/Oxford: Westview Press, 1998), 224.

23. See, for example, the essays in Lúcia Lippi Oliveira, Mônica Pimenta Velloso and Ângela Maria Castro Gomes, eds., *Estado Novo: ideologia e poder* (Rio de Janeiro: Jorge Zahar Ed., 1982).

24. Had the private archives of Vargas and most of his protégés been placed in the National Archive, they would have become part of Brazil's national heritage more generally. The creation, in 1973, of a relatively well-funded single research institution, the Centro de Pesquisa e Documentação de História Contemporânea do Brasil within the Fundação Getúlio Vargas in Rio de Janeiro, to "administer" the public memory of Vargas's era guaranteed that this legacy has remained a subject of political debate until the present day.

25. The most significant analyses are Ricardo Vélez Rodríguez, *Castilhismo: uma filosofia da República* (Porto Alegre: Escola Superior de Teologia São Lourenço de Brindes/Caxias do Sul: Ed. da UCS, 1980); Antônio Paim Filho, *História das idéias filosóficas no Brasil*, 3rd rev. ed. (São Paulo: Convívio/Brasília: INL, Fundação Pró-Memória, 1984), 101–102, 112–117; Décio Freitas, *O homem que inventou a ditadura no Brasil* (Porto Alegre: Ed. Sulina, 1998); *Julio de Castilhos e o paradoxo republicano*, ed. Gunter Axt, Ricardo Vaz Seelig, Sirlei Teresinha Gedoz, Omar Luiz de Barros Filho, and Sylvia Bojunga Meneghetti, Coleção Sujeito & Perspectivas 1 (Porto Alegre: Ed. Nova Prova, 2005).

26. Closest comes Carlos E. Cortés's *Gaúcho Politics in Brazil: The Politics of Rio Grande do Sul, 1930–1964* (Albuquerque: Univ. of New Mexico Press, 1974), though it does not focus on the *gaúchos'* normative ideas. See also my interpretative essay *Positivism gaúcho-Style: Júlio de Castilhos's Dictatorship and its Impact on State and Nation-Building in Vargas's Brazil* (Berlin: Verlag für Wissenschaft und Forschung, 2004).

27. Ricardo Vélez Rodríguez, "Castilhismo: uma filosofia da República— atualidade da doutrina de Julio de Castilhos, no centenário da sua morte," *Julio de Castilhos*, 43.

28. See Gunter Axt's "O governo Getúlio Vargas no Rio Grande do Sul (1928–1930) e o setor financeiro regional," *Estudos Históricos* no. 29 (2002): 119–140, and Luciano Aronne de Abreu's *Getúlio Vargas: a construção de um mito* (Porto Alegre: EDIPUCRS, 1997).

29. For the original, see Bolívar Lamounier, "Das institutionelle Modell der dreißiger Jahre und die gegenwärtige brasilianische Krise," in Nord und Süd in Amerika, 2:918–932; a Portuguese version appeared as "Do modelo institucional dos anos 30 ao fim da era Vargas," in As instituições brasileiras da era Vargas, ed. Maria Celina d'Araújo (Rio de Janeiro: Ed. da UERJ/ Ed. da FGV, 1999), 35–53. Lamounier does not define the term "consociational" as the concession of guarantees and special rights to ethnic, religious, and linguistic minorities.

Rather he refers to the creation of legal mechanisms (such as the equal representation of states after 1932–34 and extremely favorable conditions for the formation of new parties and their access to the media after 1945) that facilitate the fragmentation of the political system at different levels, thereby generating multilateral blockades to the exercise of power. Despite their origins in an oligarchic and (semi-)authoritarian Brazil, these legal mechanisms are, according to Lamounier, modern formulas for integration. I have difficulties in following this argumentation. They may have broken the power of the *café-com-leite* cartel and strengthened Vargas's and populist leaders' middle class bases in the cities but they also and primarily protected the interests of regional oligarchies and deliberately dispersed the opposition. The term "consociational" is definitely misleading.

30. Celi Regina J. Pinto, *Positivismo. Um projeto político alternativo (RS: 1889–1930)* (Porto Alegre: L & PM Ed., 1986), 105.

31. Joan L. Bak, "Cartels, Cooperatives and Corporativism. Getúlio Vargas in Rio Grande do Sul on the Eve of Brazil's 1930 Revolution," *Hispanic American Historical Review* 63, no. 2 (1983): 255–275.

32. James Dunkerley, *Political Suicide in Latin America and other Essays* (London/New York: Verso, 1992), 27.

33. Cortés, *Gaúcho Politics in Brazil*, 34.

34. General M. Rabello to General P. A. de Góes Monteiro, AGV, GV 34.03.18 cor, folhas 0870/1–2, FGV/CPDOC; Getúlio Vargas, *Diário*, 2 vols. (Rio de Janeiro: Ed. da FGV/São Paulo: Ed. Siciliano, 1995), 1:279.

35. Lamounier, "Do modelo institucional," esp. 44, 46–51.

36. T. Lynn Smith, *Brazil. People and Institutions*, 2nd rev. ed. (Baton Rouge: Louisiana State Univ., 1954), 630–631, 644–646.

37. For Teixeira de Freitas's project of "colony-schools," see ibid., 566–569, 630–631. Few agricultural colonies were created. Even prosperous states struggled to construct, inspect, and staff rural schools. The failure of the *ruralismo* policy of Vargas's son-in-law and governor of Rio de Janeiro state during both the Estado Novo and Vargas's second government, Ernani do Amaral Peixoto, is telling.

38. Frances Hagopian, *Traditional Politics and Regime Change in Brazil* (Cambridge/New York: Cambridge Univ. Press, 1996).

39. Klaus Lindenberg, "Politische Parteien in Lateinamerika: Ein kritischer Essay," in *Lateinamerika. Kontinent in der Krise*, ed. Wolf Grabendorff (Hamburg: Hoffmann und Campe, 1973), 152.

40. Gláucio A. D. Soares, "El sistema político brasileño: nuevos partidos y viejas divisiones," *Revista Mexicana de Sociología* 44, no. 4 (1982), 929–959.

41. I am grateful to Antônio Carlos Alves dos Santos for the verification of this information.

42. "Escritos de Vargas: I. Cartas-testamento," in *As instituições brasileiras da era Vargas*, 155–161.

28   JENS R. HENTSCHKE

43. Beatriz M. de Souza Wahrlich, *Reforma administrativa na era de Vargas* (Rio de Janeiro: Ed. da FGV, 1983), esp. 851–853 (quote on 852; read: existed on paper only); Sônia Draibe, *Rumos e metamorfoses. Estado e industrialização no Brasil: 1930/1960* (Rio de Janeiro: Paz e Terra, 1985), 79–80, 131–134; Michael Mann, "The Autonomous Power of the State: Its Origins, Mechanisms and Results," in *States in History*, ed. John A. Hall (London: Basic Blackwell, 1986), 109–136.
44. For a list of all parties, see Bolívar Lamounier and Judith Muszynski, *O processo eleitoral brasileiro da Velha a Nova Republica* (São Paulo: IDESP, 1989).
45. For an estimate of the AIB and ANL membership, see Robert M. Levine, *The Vargas Regime. The Critical Years, 1934–1938* (New York: Columbia Univ. Press, 1970), 79, 84–85, 95.
46. G. Vargas to O. Aranha, Rio de Janeiro 7. 12. 1937, AOA, OA 37.11.08/2 cp, folhas 0198–0199, FGV/CPDOC.
47. See a "very confidential" report by British Navy Attaché Mack on a conversation with Admiral Vasconcellos, commander of the Navy School: Captain P. Mack to H. Gurney, enclosure to H. Gurney to Viscount Halifax, Rio de Janeiro 18. 6. 1938, Foreign Office 371/21422, A 5307/29/6, Public Record Office London.
48. Hentschke, *Estado Novo*, 451–461.
49. Sandra McGee Deutsch, *Las Derechas: The Extreme Right in Argentina, Brazil, and Chile, 1890–1939* (Stanford: Stanford Univ. Press, 1999), 45.
50. John D. French, *The Brazilian Workers' ABC: Class Conflict and Alliances in Modern São Paulo* (Chapel Hill: Univ. of North Carolina Press, 1992), 78.
51. Peter Flynn, *Brazil: A Political Analysis* (London: Ernest Benn/Boulder: Westview Press, 1978), 102.
52. Ângela Maria de Castro Gomes, "A construção do homem novo. O trabalhador brasileiro," in *Estado Novo: ideologia e poder*, 151–166; on political persecution, see Walter R. Sharp, "Brazil 1940—Whither the 'New State'?," *The Inter-American Quarterly* 2, no. 4 (1940): 12.
53. Joel Wolfe, "The Faustian Bargain Not Made: Getúlio Vargas and Brazil's Industrial Workers, 1930–1945," in "Getúlio Vargas and His Legacy," ed. Joel Wolfe, special issue, *Luso Brazilian Review* 31, no. 2 (1994): 81–82.
54. Regarding the weaving of elite assumptions about race into educational policy, see Jerry Dávila, *"Diploma of Whiteness:" Race and Social Policy in Brazil, 1917–1945* (Durham/London: Duke Univ. Press, 2003).
55. Ângela de Castro Gomes, *A invenção do trabalhismo* (São Paulo: Vértice-Ed. dos Tribunais; Rio de Janeiro: IUPERJ, 1988).
56. French, *The Brazilian Workers' ABC*, 82–92.
57. Wolfe, "Faustian Bargain," 82–86.
58. French, *The Brazilian Workers' ABC*, 104–106, 112–118, 146–151, 174–175.

59. Wolfe, "Faustian Bargain," 86–88.
60. Ângela de Castro Gomes, "Trabalhismo e democracia: o PTB sem Vargas," in "Getúlio Vargas and His Legacy," ed. Joel Wolfe, special issue, *Luso Brazilian Review* 31, no. 2 (1994): 119.
61. Lamounier, "Do modelo institucional," 45.
62. Ibid, 47, 50–51.
63. Timothy J. Power, "Why BRASA?," *LASA Forum* 36, no. 2 (Summer 2005): 8.
64. See Helena Carvalho de Lorenzo and Wilma Peres da Costa, eds., *A década de 1920 e as origens do Brasil moderno* (São Paulo: Fundação Ed. UNESP, 1997).
65. Mario Sabino, "As mortes de Brizola. Caudilhismo, populismo, nacionalismo: as idéias e os conceitos em que acreditava o político foram sepultados antes dele," *Veja*, June 30, 2004.
66. Dieter Nohlen and Franz Nuscheler, "Was heißt Entwicklung?," Handbuch der Dritten Welt, ed. Dieter Nohlen and Franz Nuscheler, 3rd rev. ed., 5 vols. (Bonn: Dietz, 1992), 1: 55–75.
67. See Michael Mann, "The Crisis of the Latin American Nation-State," (paper, University of the Andes, Bogotá, April 10–13, 2002), http://www.sscnet.ucla.edu/soc/faculty/mann/publications.htm; Shaoguang Wang, "State Effectiveness and Democracy: Asia Cases," esp. 1–17, http://www.cuhk.edu.hk/gpa/wang_files/State&Dem-Asia.doc (both accessed January 15, 2006).
68. Aranha equated the victory of government forces with the fall of Brazil's Bastille. O. Aranha to Flores da Cunha, Rio de Janeiro 29. 10. 1932, AOA, OA 32.10.29 cp, folhas 974–979, FGV/CPDOC.
69. See last page of Carlos Henrique Davidoff's entry on the "Revolução de 1932," in *DHBB*, ed. Alzira Alves de Abreu, Israel Beloch, Fernando Lattman-Weltman, and Sérgio Tadeu de Niemeyer Lamarão, 2nd ed., 5 vols. (Rio de Janeiro: Ed. da FGV, 2001), 5:5006–5013.
70. See later President-Elect Tancredo Neves, quoted in Valentina da Rocha Lima, *Getúlio: uma história oral*, 2nd ed. (Rio de Janeiro: Ed. Record 1986), 195.
71. Two analyses that focus on Vargas's second government date back to the 1980s. See Maria Celina Soares d'Araújo, *O segundo governo Vargas, 1951–1954*, 2nd ed. (São Paulo: Ed. Ática, 1992) and S. Besserman Vianna's *A política econômica no segundo governo Vargas* (Rio de Janeiro: BNDE, 1987).

Chapter 2

The Origins of an "Enigma": Getúlio Vargas, Rio Grande do Sul's Decaying *coronelismo*, and the Genesis of the Interventionist State before the 1930 Revolution

Gunter Axt

How did Getúlio Vargas appear on the political scene in the state of Rio Grande do Sul, Brazil? What was the political orientation of his government between 1928 and 1930, and to what extent did Getúlio's experience of his home state's political environment at the beginning of the twentieth century influence his later political trajectory? By answering these questions, I aim to contribute to a better understanding of the roots of the historical phenomenon "Getúlio Vargas."

This analysis is based on my doctoral thesis and further study of Rio Grande do Sul's political system during the First Republic.[1] In my original research, I used the annals of the state's Assembly of Representatives and Brazil's National Congress, between 1891 and 1929, official reports of government agencies and ministries, presidential addresses, documents from private companies, articles from newspapers and magazines of the period, and especially correspondence exchanged between state President Antônio Augusto Borges de Medeiros and local or national leaders. Due to the extensive nature of Borges's archive, they received little systematic attention from researchers. However, the institutional, thematic, and extremely contingent approaches that prevailed, and continue to prevail, in historiography impede attempts at viewing the political process in Rio Grande do Sul as a whole, and in particular the relationship between the government and society. The purpose of this chapter is to take a long-term perspective and explore the political transformations in the state's major regions.

My study of Getúlio Vargas's role in Rio Grande focuses on three interrelated issues: the *gaúcho* governments' public policies, especially those concerned with ports, inland navigation and railroads, tax and the state budget; the continuities and discontinuities in the official and opposition discourses regarding these policies, and the strategies of those that sought to defend and combat Rio Grande do Sul's republican regime; and, finally, the power structure in the *gaúcho* state, especially the relationship between central and local authorities.

In my study, I rely on three theoretical paradigms: the theory of *coronelismo* (Brazil's variant of political clientelism),[2] primarily developed by such Brazilian authors as Victor Nunes Leal, Maria Isaura de Queiroz, Maria de Lourdes Janotti, and José Murilo de Carvalho[3]; Gramscian theory from which I have used the concepts of "hegemony" and "factions within the dominant class"[4]; and recent neo-Marxist critiques of the state-society relationship, especially the concepts of the "relative autonomy" of the state, the private appropriation of public space,[5] and "infrastructural power."[6]

Rio Grande do Sul's Political System Reconsidered

Generally, the historiography of the First Republic (1889–1930) in Rio Grande do Sul tends to identify a line of political and ideological continuity between Julio de Castilhos, the so-called patriarch of the *gaúcho* republic, Borges de Medeiros, and Getúlio Vargas. Those students of Rio Grande who emphasize the impact of the "Generation of 1907" (graduates from Porto Alegre's Law School in that year), which included Getúlio, typify this position.[7] By contrast, I stress the programmatic discontinuities in the history of the Partido Republicano Rio-Grandense and ask to what extent Getúlio's membership of this party influenced his political career.[8] On a theoretical level, while remaining in disagreement with the greater part of current historiography, I recognize the existence, in Rio Grande do Sul, of the same system of *coronelismo* that characterized the First Republic in Brazil as a whole, though with specific features. Like Loiva Félix,[9] I am unconvinced of the explicative potential of the *coronel burocrata* concept (*bureaucrat-colonel*), used by Joseph Love and Sérgio da Costa Franco,[10] among others. However, unlike Félix, I not only seek to analyze the *coronelismo* system beyond case studies; I also attempt to point out the discontinuities in the power relations of the period, identifying, moreover, the specificity of the *gaúcho* model independently of the geographic determinants that attempt to associate different regions of the state to different partisan colors. The characteristics of the so-called *coronelismo* model that can be said to be specific to the *gaúcho* context are the rigid authoritarianism, the emphatically persecutory attitude of the hegemonic party toward the opposition, the "administrative continuity" (which does not assume political linearity), and the great value given to political discourse as a strategy to justify the institutionalization of an authoritarian regime (in contrast to the more liberal scenario of the national institutions). In fact, the *coronelismo* system in Rio Grande do Sul was built upon the bloody fields of a cruel civil war, the Federalist Revolution.

Another specific feature of the *gaúcho* variant of *coronelismo* is the existence of a considerable number of small rural properties, the result of the immigration process, constituting the so-called colonial districts. Within the power structure, their existence implied the weaving of more communitarian, transverse loyalties, leading to political instability within the conventional model of traffic of influence and power between local *coronéis* and regional central power, and thus decharacterizing to some degree the classical blur between public and private space, characteristic of Brazil's political tradition.

However, despite having a powerful regional army, the Military Brigade, harnessing the Judiciary and draining the legislative power of its attributes and responsibilities, the state executive was not "*infrastructurally*" strong enough to implement a full dictatorship. They lacked the bureaucratic instruments and the modern administrative organs capable of suffocating inconvenient outbursts from local powers and to control civil society. Elections could not be expunged from the political process and the ruling elite could not do without the *coronéis* and the local electoral canvassers to organize the PRR. Though bloodied and reduced, the opposition continued to exist, preventing the establishment of a one-party regime. At those times when the state government was out of step with the government of the Union, the opposition could gain new life. Despite the widespread use of electoral fraud, even at the level of the vote-counting commissions in the legislative, the opposition could still create instability. The threat of instability increased whenever the president of the state and/or chief of the PRR appointed their own candidate as *intendente temporário* (temporary mayor), instead of respecting the will of the local membership of the party, thereby undermining and causing disaffection in the ranks at local level. This sometimes led to disputes between factions of the PRR in the municipalities, in which alliances could even be made with factions of the opposition. This was quite a common phenomenon after the death of Julio de Castilhos in 1903.[11]

Castilhos's authoritarian 1891 constitution and dictatorial style of government faced strong resistance. Dissident Republicans and leaders of the old monarchical parties, both the Conservatives and Liberals, united to overthrow Castilhos in the revolution of November 12, 1891. In March 1892, in Bagé, ex-Liberals and ex-Conservatives founded the *Partido Federalista Brasileiro* (Brazilian Federalist Party), splitting away from republican dissidents whose politics differed little from those of Castilhos. With the return of Castilhos to political command of the state through the revolution on June 17, 1892, the Federalist opposition suffered relentless persecution, precipitating migration "en masse" to the Republic of Uruguay. In February 1893, the bloody Federalist Revolution broke out and continued until August 1895. In general terms, the revolutionaries of 1893 advocated a civilian parliamentary republic with honest elections and more power for the Union, the municipalities, and the legislative assemblies.[12]

Minority elite groups in the municipalities who owed their political dominance to the imposition of a regime of force joined Julio de Castilhos's authoritarian undertaking. From a socioeconomic perspective, cattle owners, traders, and financiers (based in the cities of Porto Alegre, Pelotas and Rio Grande) tended to support the political proposals of Castilhos, while in exchange demanding government commitments to establish their hegemony over commerce within the state. This would imply their capability to effectively capture the surplus capital from the mountain region colonized by Europeans and to neutralize the growth of commerce on the southern border that was more integrated with the River Plate region and the ports of Montevideo (Uruguay) and Buenos Aires (Argentina) than with the markets of Rio de Janeiro and São Paulo.[13]

The so-called middle classes and urban proletariat did not always adhere to the policies of Castilhos and his successors. On the contrary, when two prominent Republicans, João de Barros Cassal and Demétrio Ribeiro, dissented from Castilhos soon after the proclamation of the republic these sectors tended to follow them. The repression of the labor movement enforced by Castilhos's successor Borges during the general strike of 1919 led to a further rift between workers and the regime and determined the approximation of the former and middle class sectors to the elite opposition who rose in arms against Borges and his PRR in 1923. In an apparent contradiction, in the previous general strike of 1917 the PRR-controlled state and capital city governments had intervened in the market, to freeze prices and raise salaries, in favor of the urban working class. However, this was because Borges's "network of personal commitments"[14] was temporarily weakened and it was politically inconvenient to open new fronts of conflict in society. This situation was fully overcome in 1919. As to the famous positivist concept of "incorporation of the proletariat into society," which was in fact included in the state constitution of 1891, it was never followed by a systematic social policy of inclusion, but was employed in 1917 to justify government action in favor of the commercial sectors of the dominant class.[15]

Contrary to conventional understanding, the areas of European colonization did not constitute a pool of passive voters. There is growing evidence that the electoral results, generally in favor of the PRR, seem to have been levered by a permanent and delicate game of negotiations. Submission was definitely not the rule, as the areas of colonization were subject to insubordination, which produced instability amidst the PRR-dominated scene. For example, this was the case in the election campaign for the state succession in 1907, when many supporters of the *coronelismo* system tended to reject the tax policy of the Borges government, especially the *imposto territorial* (rural land tax).[16]

The relationship of the PRR and the republican governments with the industrial sector has been another source of controversy and confusion for historians. When viewed from a long-term perspective, the speeches made by PRR politicians at the Assembly of Representatives and the National Congress indicate that, while diversification of the economy and support for industrialization through tax incentives were defended within Rio Grande do Sul, at the national level *gaúcho* Republicans tended to concur with politicians from São Paulo, criticizing the so-called artificial stimulation of industry and defending the agricultural vocation of Brazil. Also, analysis of the tax incentives created in Rio Grande do Sul indicates they were intended to promote the industrial investments and interests of the urban-coastal financial and mercantile sectors. In fact, the industrialization that originated from the capital surplus created in the area of colonization counted on little government support, and at times faced hostility from government quarters. Moreover, the manufacturers from the colonial zone managed to organize their class association and become independent from Porto Alegre's Mercantile Association only in 1930.[17]

Finally, the majority of the members and supporters of the socially inexpressive, but symbolically and culturally relevant, positivist movement also supported Castilhos, especially after the dissidents João de Barros Cassal and Demétrio Ribeiro had been neutralized with the failure of the Federalist Revolution. However, the influence of the positivists within Rio Grande's government was limited, notably to the Secretariat of Public Works, and this influence tended to decline after the death of Castilhos in 1903, especially with the expropriation of the railroads and the port of Rio Grande, between 1919 and 1920.

Contrary to much of the current historiography, I do not believe that positivist ideas underlie the public policies conceived and implemented by the republican governments in Rio Grande do Sul during the First Republic. On the contrary, diachronic analysis of the official discourse on the economy clearly indicates contradictions between Castilhos and his successors, and conceptual and programmatic mutations of the former's ideas, even though political agents of Borges and Getúlio Vargas successively reiterated a new edition of Castilhos's legacy. Moreover, it is not possible to verify an automatic correlation between Comte's positivism and Castilhos's ideas, since there are significant discrepancies between these two ideologies.[18]

To conclude: on the one hand, the social alliance that supported the regimes of Castilhos and Borges in Rio Grande do Sul had a much more conservative profile than the one the greater part of the historiography has tended to recognize. On the other, the Federalist Revolution seems to have been a much more complex social phenomenon than a simple intraoligarchic war in which the *estancieiro* group (large landowners) from the border were opposed to the smallholders from the center and manufacturers from the coast, as was believed for some time.

There is no doubt that the sociopolitical situation, here briefly outlined, was in practice considerably conditioned by volatile personal loyalties that resulted from the nondistinction between political and private spheres, a typical feature of Brazil's political culture and policy of personal commitments. The agrarian faction of the ruling class seems to represent the clearest example of this diagnosis, as the *estancieiro* group from all regions of the state was to be found evenly distributed among the different groups involved in the struggle for power. In fact, according to Duncan Baretta, the Federalist Revolution was more violent in those *gaúcho* municipalities in which land ownership was most disputed within the ruling class and within the *estancieiro* group.[19]

In the following section, I examine the relationship between the Vargas family and the state government because it is exemplary of the volatile nature of such loyalties. I look at three critical conjunctures. First, there is the rise to leadership of the Vargas clan in 1907, which coincided with an apparently contradictory, but in reality very logical, policy by Borges. While the state president broke with the "network of personal commitments" associated with Castilhos, he affirmed, within the discursive sphere, his predecessor's positivist concept of power. Second, I explore the reasons that led to the rupture of the Vargas family with Borges in 1913. Though, as a consequence of this dispute, the Vargas' political power at local level was initially weakened, later there seems to have been a rearrangement of their relationship with Borges that allowed the young Getúlio to play at least a subordinate role within Borges's power structure. Finally, with the constitutional reform imposed by the Pedras Altas Treaty in December 1923, result of a revolutionary challenge to Borges's hegemony, the president's clientelistic network was undermined and therefore allowed Getúlio to pursue an increasingly independent political career and to eventually take over power in Porto Alegre in 1928. Administrative vigor, together with the power to overcome the partisan political differences in Rio Grande do Sul, were the touch-stones of Vargas's state government. It led to a rearrangement of the political alliance that supported the political group in power.

Political Clientelism, Subsequent Crises of Hegemony, and the Changing Fortunes of the Vargas Clan from 1890 to 1923

Getúlio's formation needs to be understood in the context of the patrimonial power relationships during the First Republic. He was the son of Colonel Manuel do Nascimento Vargas, of the National Guard, a landowner in São Borja, a town on the remote frontier of Rio Grande do Sul and Argentina whose economy relied essentially upon extensive cattle-farming. Between 1907 and 1911, Manuel Vargas was São Borja's Municipal Superintendent; later he was replaced by his son Viriato.[20]

The political rise of the Vargas family is related to the crisis of hegemony that shook the PRR after the death of Júlio de Castilhos in 1903. With the end of the Federalist Revolution, in August 1895, Castilhos's model of state was consolidated. Nevertheless, if fortified at the regional level, Castilhos came out of the 1893 revolution partially weakened at the national level. The army, which had given him considerable support during the conflict, now proved less willing to demonstrate its alignment, which was to cause him problems. In the same way, the strategic alliance with the politicians from São Paulo had begun to fade. The relationship with the government of Prudente de Moraes was uncomfortable because of his demand for the pacification of the state. Moreover, in 1897–98 Castilhos, discreetly harboring federal presidential ambitions, expressed open opposition to the candidacy of Prudente's successor, Campos Salles.[21]

In 1897, politically isolated in Rio Grande do Sul, Castilhos appointed Chief Judge Antônio Augusto Borges de Medeiros to the presidency of the state, though he maintained control of the leadership of the PRR. Borges's fidelity entitled him to reelection in 1902. After the PRR leader's premature death he attempted to embrace both the government and the command of the hegemonic party. His plan was repelled by other leaders. This impasse caused a division within the PRR and culminated in a tense campaign for the state presidency in 1907, when Borges found himself obliged to negate his own candidacy and recommend Carlos Barbosa Gonçalves in his place to face a prominent dissident, Fernando Abbott. To secure Barbosa Gonçalves's victory and to consolidate his position within the party, thereby paving his way back to the state presidency in 1913, Borges used the authoritarian juridical structure, based in the constitution of 1891, and intervened in many municipalities. Between 1903 and 1908, countless local leaders were substituted by factions of the PRR who were loyal to Borges's clientelistic network.[22]

Although the Vargas family had joined the PRR at its foundation, their political rise resulted from Borges's attempt at forming new alliances in order to confront the crisis of 1906–07. This is a crucial point, because it signals a rupture between the Vargas family and the factions originally loyal to Castilhos in São Borja. Colonel Manuel Vargas substituted the Mariense family in the control of both the administration of São Borja and the municipal leadership of the PRR. At the same time, Getúlio, prior to graduating from Law School in Porto Alegre, traveled through the areas of Italian and German colonization, in the company of his colleague João Neves da Fontoura, campaigning on behalf of the government. In Porto Alegre, João Neves led the formation of the Bloco Acadêmico (Academic Block), a student organization that also organized support for the government's candidate. Therefore, the campaign offered Getúlio an opportunity to affirm his loyalty to Borges and to begin his political career.[23]

Getúlio was rewarded with the position of Public Prosecutor of the Capital. A few months later the president of the PRR, Borges, requested his inclusion in the official candidate list. With peace reigning within the party, Getúlio was easily elected in March 1909.[24]

His reelection in 1913 was equally uncomplicated. However, Getúlio gave up the mandate soon afterward, in protest against Borges's intervention in the politics of Cachoeira do Sul. Colonel Isidoro Neves, João Neves's father, falsified the official electoral list by distributing ballots on which the name of an opponent had been omitted. As a disciplinary measure, Borges forced Isidoro Neves, the elected candidate, to resign and replaced him with his adversary. In solidarity with his colleague Getúlio also resigned.[25]

In retaliation against Getúlio Vargas's insubordination, Borges encouraged a dispute for local power in São Borja, between the Vargas family and a group led by Benjamin Torres and Rafael Escobar. In 1913, the administration of the appointed mayor, Viriato Vargas, was threatened by an inquiry set up to investigate accusations made by local dissidents and held under the command of the general prosecutor of justice, who was an appointee of the state president. When Benjamin Torres, a doctor in medicine, was murdered in March 1915, the political tension reached its peak. Viriato Vargas came under suspicion, as one of the thugs captured by the police accused him of having ordered the murder.[26] Denounced by the Prosecuting Counsel, Viriato went into hiding in Argentina.[27]

With the weakening of the Vargas family at the local level, the situation once again favored Borges, to whom the family began to owe its political and, moreover, economical survival.[28] The state president was interested in a rapprochement. While the lawsuit against Viriato proceeded, he allowed Colonel Manuel to stay in the leadership of the local PRR. Furthermore, Borges used his position as chief executive to have the case relocated in order to benefit the Vargas family. However, when the local political situation was favorable to the Vargas' again, the judiciary allowed the reinstatement of the lawsuit in São Borja, which was an unusual decision.[29] Viriato was finally cleared by the jury, as the local opposition to the Vargas family denounced.[30]

Meanwhile, Getúlio made a point of getting closer to Borges. An opportunity came with the hegemonic crisis that shook the PRR between 1915 and 1916. This crisis arose as a result of the indication, by Senator Pinheiro Machado, Rio Grande do Sul's powerful voice in the Brazilian Congress, of *gaúcho* Hermes da Fonseca as candidate for a senatorial vacancy in Rio de Janeiro. Rio Grande's overlooked contender, senator Ramiro Barcellos, who had hoped for reelection, rallied the dissidents and disaffected in several towns. Weakened, Borges, who had been acting with considerable autonomy from regional local powers since 1913, relied again on the support of his allies. Borges's political situation improved after the demise of Senator Pinheiro Machado, who was murdered in September 1915.[31] The Vargas family, under pressure due to the ongoing lawsuit, remained faithful to the government. In exchange, Getúlio was included in the list of candidates for the Assembly of Representatives, and he took up his duties in 1917.[32]

In the Assembly, Vargas was particularly effective in justifying the contraction of loans by the state government, particularly after 1920, as until then any form of public debt was criticized from the original *Castilhista* standpoint. In the same way, state intervention in the economy was now defended by Vargas in the Plenary as fundamental principle of the party.[33]

In view of his performance, Vargas's reelection to the Assembly in 1921 was easily assured. Faithful to the party line, Vargas went along with Borges in the so-called Reação Republicana (Republican Reaction), between the end of 1921 and the beginning of 1922, when the Republican Party machines in Rio Grande do Sul, Rio de Janeiro, Bahia, and Pernambuco tried to defeat the candidacy of Artur Bernardes to the presidency of the Republic. Bernardes had been proposed by Minas Gerais and São Paulo. As a result of his victory in the elections in March 1922, Borges became isolated. A dramatic financial and economical crisis at regional level was added to the unfavorable political situation at national level. This crisis was a direct consequence of the state government's interventionist policy and caused the third serious hegemonic crisis of Borges's regime.[34]

Trying to avoid incurring foreign debt, which could make the state more dependent on the Union, and at the same time attempting to take advantage of the assets accumulated in the regional financial institutions due to the retraction of imports during World War I, Borges used loans from local banks to finance the expropriation of the railroad and the port of Rio Grande city in 1919 and 1920. This operation caused a drastic reduction in the volume of money in circulation in the region. The situation further deteriorated with the resumption in the demand for imports in 1920, the inflation of the period, and the increased speculation with foreign currency. Furthermore, the lack of cash started to hamper production and led the banks to demand mortgage repayments from the farmers. This discouraging situation was aggravated by the dizzying increase in government-controlled public transport fares. In fact, in order to constrain the companies that provided the services, Borges had pressed for a policy of low fares. However, when he took up the direct administration of railroads, he had to face an enormous operational deficit and increased the fares.[35]

The opposition used its chance and, in 1922, presented its candidate for the state government. Francisco de Assis Brasil, a long-standing Republican who had fallen out with Julio de Castilhos at the end of 1890, also received support from sectors of the students' and workers' movements, which had been so vigorously repressed by Borges in 1919.

The state elections took place on November 25, 1922, amid rumors of an armed revolt against Borges and accusations of fraud from both sides. Getúlio Vargas was appointed president of the Constitution and Powers Committee of the Assembly of Representatives. Vote counting and acknowledgment of the elected candidates were carried out by legislative committees such as this, as there was no Electoral Justice System existent in Brazil at that time. According to the testimony of José Antônio Flores da Cunha,[36] having been assured of the impossibility of reelection to the state presidency, since he would not have met the constitutional demand of a three-quarter majority of the votes, the Committee was urged by Borges to perform electoral alchemy, rigging the result. On January 17, 1923, the Committee formalized Borges's victory by 106,360 votes, compared to the 32,216 obtained by Assis Brasil.[37]

Still in January, discontent with the result among supporters of Assis and the Federalist opposition sparked a chain of insurrection that led to the revolution in 1923. Faced with this violent crisis of hegemony, Borges was forced to seek the support of his old allies, many of whom among the up-state leaders and families who had fallen out with him between 1913 and 1920. While support for maintaining Borges in power was reaffirmed, the membership subtly indicated that the party would no longer submit itself to the leader's unilateral intervention.[38]

The civil war ended in December 1923 with the signing of the Treaty of Pedras Altas. Mediated by the Brazilian army and the president of the republic, the treaty guaranteed Borges's position in power until the end of his mandate, which had started the previous January, but it demanded a constitutional reform that, among other things, limited the intervention of the state executive in the municipalities and required that the vice president of the state also be elected and no longer nominated solely by the president. Therefore, although Borges was permitted to conclude his presidential mandate, the reform and the rearticulation of the Republican Party constrained the power of his network of personal commitments. In fact, the political influence that Borges had enjoyed began to wane as from 1923. In compensation, up-state Republican leaders were strengthened and, on the other hand, the opposition party grew, as was clearly demonstrated during the federal congressional elections in 1924, when the vote for the new Partido Libertador (Liberator Party) increased in several cities of the state.[39]

Getúlio Vargas's Rise to Power after 1923 and the Construction of a New Alliance

During the 1922 election campaign, Getúlio Vargas received the commission of lieutenant-colonel of Rio Grande's Military Brigade and took command of the Seventh Auxiliary Corps in São Borja, a troop composed of civilians recruited to face the rebel enemy. However, he did not see battle, because he went to Rio the Janeiro, where he took his seat in the Federal Chamber of Representatives and dedicated himself to the vital task of avoiding the federal intervention in Rio Grande do Sul that the insurgent Federalist leaders proposed. He took the opportunity to expand his contacts with representatives from other states, above all São Paulo with whom, with the exception of the period of the Reação Republicana, *gaúcho* republicanism had maintained a historical and strategic alliance since the antimonarchical struggles and Julio de Castilhos's dictatorship.[40]

Reelected federal representative in 1924, Vargas assumed the leadership of the *gaúcho* group in the Chamber, in recognition of the important services rendered to Borges's regime. In 1925, Vargas was appointed to a legislative committee, entrusted to evaluate the reform of the 1891 federal constitution.[41] These new roles smoothed the way for him to occupy a seat on the influential Committee of Finances of the Chamber, in May 1926. Being the most high-profile *gaúcho* representative in the Congress, in October, Vargas was invited to take up the Treasury Ministry by the recently elected President Washington Luís. Among the new president's aims were the reconciliation of the divided oligarchy, the implementation of a financial stabilization plan, and monetary reform, objectives that required him to form a coalition government. The assignment of the Treasury Ministry to Rio Grande do Sul conferred prestige on the southern state and strengthened the bonds between São Paulo and Rio Grande, particularly with regard to economic policy. Borges, however, was unhappy with the appointment, as shown in correspondence exchanged between the *gaúcho* leader and Getúlio Vargas. Borges, who retained the leadership of the PRR, with an eye on the state succession in 1927, had proposed representative Simões Lopes for the Ministry of Agriculture. Getúlio Vargas withheld the news of his invitation to take up the post from Borges, and so forced him to accept Getúlio's appointment to the Treasury Ministry as a fait accompli.[42]

Being the only *gaúcho* in a federal ministry, Getúlio became a natural candidate for the state succession in 1927. His candidacy, together with that of João Neves da Fontoura as vice president, was finally announced by Borges in August 1927 and approved by acclamation at the PRR convention in October of the same year. In fact, Getúlio Vargas's candidature won wide acceptance among those groups within the party that had been strengthened during the revolution in 1923. On the other hand, the opposition Partido Libertador looked favorably on the change in political command, because it was understood that the removal of Borges would open the way for an understanding.[43]

Vargas and João Neves took up the government of the state on January 25, 1928. Although they sought to follow the political directives given by Borges, they underlined their political autonomy from the outset. In fact, Borges did not succeed in forming the secretariat that he would have preferred, and Getúlio Vargas named the young Oswaldo Aranha as secretary of the Home and Justice Department, the state government's political office, as well as his brother-in-law, Florêncio de Abreu, as head of the Police Department.[44]

Right from the start, Vargas tried to give an impression of dynamism, retrieving old projects and proposing new ones, while confronting the serious financial crisis inherited from Borges's administration. He summoned an extraordinary meeting of the Assembly and asked for authorization to borrow 42 million dollars. This was the largest external loan ever contracted by Rio Grande do Sul, and it consolidated the preeminence of North American capitalism over foreign investments in the state. The situation was favorable because Brazil had recovered credibility due to Washington Luís's program of financial stabilization, which Vargas had implemented during his stay at the Treasury Ministry, and since capital was available on the international market, especially in the United States. The interest rates on the loan were 6 percent and the period of amortization was 40 years. These were much better conditions than those negotiated by Borges for previous loans. For the first time, state tax income would not constitute a guarantee of interest on a credit operation, which indicated that the state was in first-rate structural condition. In fact, with the expropriations of 1919 and 1920, the state had acquired assets that acted now as natural guarantees for external loans.[45]

The combined sums were used, fundamentally, to pay off the floating debt, to convert the internal and external debt, and to create a mortgage bank. Borges had left Getúlio Vargas with a distressing financial situation. While state budgets showed successive positive balances, in practice state debt with regional bank institutions was increasing alarmingly. This constituted bad, short-term debt, subject to very high interest rates. Moreover, the number of bonds, promissory notes, and public debt securities that saturated the market was so large that they depreciated. This debt resulting from the intrinsic costs of the expropriation of the port and the railroad was exacerbated by the government's extraordinary expenses with the military campaign during the Revolution of 1923. In 1927, the state was on the verge of insolvency.

Payments to suppliers were delayed and the administration was no longer able to guarantee the value of and the interest on the so-called *depósitos populares* (popular deposits), the personal savings deposited in private institutions. Savers had no liquidity and their investments were registered in bank savings books that depreciated in commercial transactions. The commercial sector, choked with these savings books and promissory notes and other securities, which in practice represented a parallel currency, experienced regional inflation and the cost of living soared. Finally, banking operations to satisfy the needs of the public debt created a shortage of resources to finance production, making credit particularly expensive. Therefore, the financial operation carried out by Vargas was aimed at consolidating a public debt that was suffocating the government and production, reestablishing the investment capacity of the private sector, and avoiding an imminent chain of bankruptcies.[46] This policy was complemented by the creation of the state mortgage bank, in June 1928, which met a longstanding demand of cattle farmers from Rio Grande do Sul for wider and cheaper credit. The credit was made available without any distinction based on party political allegiance, a practice that had been common during the regimes of both Borges and Castilhos. This new policy contributed to overcoming political discord. The extraordinary financial turnover involving the port of Rio Grande and the railroad company, now administered by the government, as well as the public service payroll, were concentrated in the new state bank. These changes reduced the deposits in the region's private banks, at the same time weakening those financial institutions and freeing the administration from an almost structural dependence upon them.[47]

Initially, the creation of the Banco do Estado do Rio Grande do Sul (BERGS; Bank of the State of Rio Grande do Sul) was supported by the regional banks, because it released them from the heavy debt of land mortgages, freeing them to negotiate rediscounting operations and short-term investments. However, the weight of the public budget in the state bank and the creation of commercial agencies indicated that the administration had entered the financial market as a competitor. When the 1929 New York Crash hit, check account holders tended to seek official agencies, which seemed to have more credibility. That was a terrible blow to regional private banks. In January 1930, the directors of the private banks were on the warpath against the BERGS. In April, the Banco Popular (Popular Bank) went bankrupt, causing the "*gaúcho* bank drama." In fact, regional bank institutions, in spite of their structure of multiple branches, preserved a model of local management. Besides, in pursuit of easy profit, they administered limited cash reserves and did business without always obtaining good guarantees. This situation, together with the creation of the BERGS, made them vulnerable to speculative attack. The following year, the powerful Banco Pelotense (Bank of Pelotas) went bankrupt. A few years before, during a hearing in São Borja, its management had discovered embezzlement, which led the local manager—Antônio Sarmanho, Getúlio Vargas's father-in-law—to commit suicide. Vargas, in fact, refused to aid the bank, intervening in the crisis only after bankruptcy had been declared.[48]

The closure of the Banco Pelotense marked the definitive end of the strategic alliance that had been the force behind the years of Borges's political reign, namely between the ruling elite and the *charqueadores* (entrepreneurs in the dried meat industry), the urban-littoral import merchants, and the bankers. In fact, the fiscal policy of Julio de Castilhos and Borges and the policy for the transport sector tended to benefit the combined interests of those factions of the dominant class, thereby consolidating the hegemony of the commercial centers of Porto Alegre, Pelotas, and Rio Grande in detriment to the frontier region and the area of Italian and German colonization. Politically a minority at the end of the Empire, these factions of the dominant class had supported Castilhos's authoritarian project precisely because they understood that a centralized, strongly presidentialist, and interventionist state would facilitate the implementation of their plan for mercantile hegemony in the whole state.

This strategic alliance supported Castilhos's regime in the policy to combat smuggling on the frontier, the effort to standardize municipal taxes, the introduction of a rural land tax, the convergence of the rail network in Porto Alegre and Rio Grande city, and, above all, the granting of tax incentives to banks and sectors of production that received direct investment from those class factions, such as rice farming, the electrical power generation, and distribution industries. Although the official discourse of the PRR indicated otherwise, this alliance was markedly conservative and harmed the interests of the frontier merchants, neglected the big cattle farmers', sought to economically dominate the area of Italian and German colonization—from which it obtained resources—and despised the incipient industrialization that grew in these areas, with the spread of the local commercial capital. The survival of the *charqueadores*, the import merchants from the coastal cities, and the regional bankers is, in great measure, due to the incentives received from the state government, which on several occasions hampered the diversification of the economy and economic progress. Two outstanding examples of this are: the delay in the installation of frozen meat packing plants in Rio Grande do Sul, programmed for 1903 but only carried out in 1917; and the boycott of the construction of a hydroelectric plant in the Jacuí valley, in 1919. The latter would have provided abundant cheap energy for industrialization. However, it would have made the public concessions in large urban centers unfeasible for the thermal energy generating companies.

Final Considerations

Ultimately, with the creation of the state bank, Getúlio Vargas deepened the interventionist policy initiated under Borges, but he broke with the strategic political alliance that had supported the authoritarian model adopted by Castilhos's regime. His policy of conciliation with the opposition organized in the Partido Libertador reinforced this break, paving the way for the creation of a Frente Única (Single Front) in 1929, the base of the famous Campanha Liberal (Liberal Campaign) and the Revolution of 1930.[49]

Three other measures complemented the renewal brought by Getúlio to the regional political scene. First, Vargas was particularly disposed to face the infrastructural problems of the state, seeking solutions for the deficient transportation and electrical power services. Second, a tax reform designed to face the fiscal deficit was based on increasing taxes on trade and services. Vargas, thereby, acknowledged the structural changes in the economy and the growing importance of industry. If this measure first brought the closure of small businesses in the up-state regions, it favored the concentration of industrial capital and highlighted its economic importance.

Finally, Vargas started to encourage cooperatives and associations. Borges had struggled vigorously against such tendencies, fearing the mobilization of opinion and of political pressure in civil society. In fact, industrialists had been trying unsuccessfully to organize themselves into an autonomous association since 1906, but were forced to stay under protection of the Associação Comercial de Porto Alegre (Porto Alegre Trade Association), dominated by the urban mercantile and financial elite. Another example: in 1921, Borges managed to frustrate the creation of a federation of municipal trade associations, which would have covered the whole territory of the state. From 1926 on, however, with Borges's influence in definitive decline, the formation of associations boomed in Rio Grande do Sul. After 1928, this process was supported and encouraged by Getúlio Vargas.[50]

Vargas, in fact, saw class associations as important instruments for economic and social development. He also recognized the failure of Castilhos's representative model that deprived the legislature of effective power while forging an oligarchic representation that was out of step with the alterations in the social structure. At the same time, Vargas did not show signs of valuing a typically liberal parliamentary government, far from it. He attempted, through the class associations, to establish a channel of direct communication with sections of society that were more economically dynamic, balancing the classic oligarchic representation of the Old Republic.[51]

This criticism of both the liberal representative model and the institutional authoritarianism of Castilhos, full of positivist oratory, never diminished the value that Vargas attributed to government institutions and to public political speech, aspects that represent the most palpable characteristics of Castilhos's and Comte's legacies and that pulsated in this enigmatic *gaúcho* politician. Vargas was deeply interested in, and concerned with, governmental reports, good administration, and the maintenance of a balanced budget.[52]

However, when compared to the authoritarian conservatism of the Borges period, the Vargas administration in Rio Grande do Sul, in spite of having been prematurely interrupted because of Getúlio's departure to lead the national Provisional Government after the Revolution of 1930, brought about an important political and administrative renovation. Taking Rio Grande do Sul out of its isolationism, Vargas managed to negotiate the huge external loan, with which he balanced the state finances and removed the main obstacle to economic growth. Indeed, the deficit had paralyzed the state since 1920. Vargas extended the interventionist tendency initiated under Borges, recognizing the need to strengthen the "infrastructural power" of the state as a strategy to control local powers and implement macroeconomic projects. But he used interventionism as a means to overcome political division, while Borges had used it to consolidate an authoritarian model. In fact, the expropriations of 1919 and 1920 were intended, above all: to remove the autonomous power of the large foreign company that had administered public services and whose interests diverged from those of the government; to permit the convergence of road communication toward Porto Alegre and Rio Grande; and to strengthen the executive power.

By using interventionism in order to implode the alliance of factions of the dominant class that until then had supported the Borges regime, Vargas paved the way for a new, broader pact of class factions that would support the government: while the influence of the commercial and financial sectors in the urban-littoral zone decreased, the prominence of cattle farmers' interests was rehabilitated and the nascent industrial bourgeoisie integrated into the political system. Finally, in promoting association as a solution, Vargas demonstrated his lack of faith in the oligarchic representative model and signaled the need for an alternative channel of communication between the government and the more economically dynamic sections of society. The success of these initiatives greatly influenced the prestige of Vargas's candidacy within the Liberal Alliance, in the elections in 1930, and helped to design a new concept of state for the nation.

Notes

I would like to thank Timothy Donovan for his translation of my Portuguese manuscript.

1. My doctoral thesis, supervised by Maria de Lourdes Janotti, was defended at the University of São Paulo in 2001. It has not yet been published in its entirety but is quoted in several of my articles and books that have been used for this chapter.

2. *Coronelismo* describes a system of political control in Brazil's states that rested on so-called *coronéis* ["colonels"], usually big landowners who controlled life in the municipalities. Historically, these local strongmen had held the position of a colonel in the National Guard (1831–1918); after the latter's abolition, they would still keep their rank or were at least referred to as "*coronel*."

3. José Murilo de Carvalho, *Pontos e bordados. Escritos de história e política* (Belo Horizonte: Ed. da UFMG, 1998); Victor Nunes Leal, *Coronelismo, enxada e voto. O município e o regime representativo no Brasil*, 4th ed. (São Paulo: Alfa-Ômega, 1978); Maria de Lourdes Mônaco Janotti, *O coronelismo: uma política de compromissos* (São Paulo: Ed. Brasiliense, 1981); Maria Isaura Pereira de Queiroz, "O coronelismo numa interpretação sociológica," in *História geral da civilização brasileira*, ed. Sérgio Buarque de Holanda, tome 3, *O Brasil republicano*, ed. Boris Fausto, vol. 1, *Estrutura de poder e economia (1889–1930)*, 5th ed. (Rio de Janeiro: Ed. Bertrand, 1989), 153–192.

4. Giuseppe Staccone, *Gramsci: 100 anos—revolução e política* (Petrópolis: Ed. Vozes, 1991).

5. Among others, see Martin Carnoy, *Estado e teoria política*, 4th ed. (São Paulo: Ed. Papyrus, 1994); Adam Przeworsky, *Estado e economia no capitalismo* (Rio de Janeiro: Ed. Relume Dumará, 1995); John F. Padgett, "Hierarchy and Ecological Control in Federal Budgetary Decision Making," *American Journal of Sociology* 87 (1981): 75–129; Theda Skocpol, "Political Response to Capitalist Crisis: Neo-Marxist Theories of the State and the Case of the New Deal," *Politics and*

Society 10 (1980): 155–201; Kenneth A. Shepsle, *The Private Use of the Public Interest*, Center for the Study of American Business 46 (St. Louis: Washington Univ. Press, 1979).

6. Michael Mann, "The Autonomous Power of the State: Its Origins, Mechanisms and Results," *Archives Européennes de Sociologie* 25 (1984): 185–213.

7. Joseph L. Love, *O regionalismo gaúcho e as origens da Revolução de 1930* (São Paulo: Ed. Perspectiva, 1975).

8. Gunter Axt, "Contribuições ao debate historiográfico concernente ao nexo entre estado e sociedade para o Rio Grande do Sul castilhista-borgista," *Métis: História & Cultura* 1, no. 1 (2002): 39–70.

9. Loiva O. Félix, *Coronelismo, borgismo e cooptação política* (Porto Alegre: Ed. Mercado Aberto, 1987).

10. Sérgio da Costa Franco, *Júlio de Castilhos e sua época* (Porto Alegre: Ed. UFRGS, 1988); Love, *O regionalismo gaúcho*.

11. See my own publications "Votar por quê? Ideologia autoritária, eleições e justiça no Rio Grande do Sul borgista," *Justiça & História* 1, no. 1–2 (2001): 175–216, and "Coronelismo indomável: especificidades do sistema coronelista no Rio Grande do Sul (1890–1930)," in *As múltiplas dimensões da política e da narrativa*, ed. Teresa Malatian, Marisa Saenz Leme, and Ivan Aparecido Manoel (Franca: Ed. UNESP/Ed. Olho D'água, 2003).

12. See my "Introdução" [passages "Antecedentes da Revolução Federalista" and "Os diários e a Revolução"] in Joca Tavares and Francisco da Silva Tavares, *Diários da Revolução de 1893*, 2 vols., org. by Gunter Axt, Coralio B. P. Cabeda, and Ricardo Seelig, Série Memória Política e Jurídica do Rio Grande do Sul 3 (Porto Alegre: Ed. Nova Prova, Memorial do Ministério Público—Procuradoria-Geral de Justiça do Estado do Rio Grande do Sul, 2004), 1:15–38, 47–66; and my article "A história contada pelo dragão," in: Rafael Cabeda and Rodolpho Costa, *Os crimes da ditadura*, org. by Coralio B. P. Cabeda, Ricardo Vaz Seelig and Gunter Axt, Série Memória Política e Jurídica do Rio Grande do Sul 1 (Porto Alegre: Memorial do Ministério Público—Procuradoria-Geral de Justiça do Estado do Rio Grande do Sul, 2002), 15–28. See also Francisco das Neves Alves and Luiz Henrique Torres, eds., *Pensar a Revolução Federalista* (Rio Grande: Ed. da FURG, 1993); Lurdes G. Ardenghi, *Caboclos, ervateiros e coronéis. Lutas e resistência no norte do Rio Grande do Sul* (Passo Fundo: Ed. UPF, 2003); Sílvio Rogério Duncan Baretta, "Political Violence and Regime Change: A Study of the 1893 Civil War in Southern Brazil" (PhD diss., Univ. of Pittsburgh, 1985); Sérgio da Costa Franco, "O sentido histórico da Revolução de 1893," in *Fundamentos da cultura rio-grandense: Quinta série* (Porto Alegre: Ed. UFRGS, 1962), 191–216; Ana Luiza Gobbi Setti Reckziegel, *A diplomacia marginal. Vinculações políticas entre o Rio Grande do Sul e o Uruguai (1893–1904)* (Passo Fundo: Ed. UPF, 1999).

13. See my dissertation "Gênese do estado burocrático-burguês no Rio Grande do Sul (1889–1929)" (PhD diss., Universidade de São Paulo, 2001) and my publications "A dimensão política e social do contrabando no Rio Grande do Sul," *História em Revista* no. 8 (2002): 69–110; "Constitucionalidade em debate: a polêmica Carta Estadual de 1891," *Justiça & História* 2, no. 3 (2002): 305–344. See also Baretta, "Political Violence and Regime Change;" Sandra J. Pesavento, *A República Velha gaúcha: charqueadas, frigoríficos, criadores* (Porto Alegre: Ed. Movimento/IEL, 1980); Jean Roche, *A colonização alemã e o Rio Grande do Sul*, 2 vols. (Porto Alegre: Ed. Globo, 1969); *O Estado do Rio Grande do Sul* (Barcelona: Monte Domeq e Cia, 1916).

14. My translation is based on the Portuguese expression "rede de compromissos." This is a key concept of Brazilian historical-social theory on the *coronelismo* system and therefore widely used in the literature. See, for example Janotti, *O coronelismo*.

15. See Joan L. Bak's "Classe, etnicidade e gênero no Brasil: a negociação de identidade dos trabalhadores na greve de 1906, em Porto Alegre," *Métis: História & Cultura* 2, no. 4 (2003): 181–225; and her "Cartels, Cooperatives, and Corporativism: Getúlio Vargas in Rio Grande do Sul on the Eve of Brazil's 1930 Revolution," *Hispanic American Historical Review* 63, no. 2 (1983): 255–275; see also my "A dimensão política e social do contrabando."

16. See, for example, the following sources, all part of the Borges de Medeiros Papers (hereafter BMP) in the Instituto Histórico e Geográfico do Rio Grande do Sul (hereafter IHGRS): Izidoro Neves da Fontoura to Antônio Augusto Borges de Medeiros, Cachoeira do Sul, August 22, 1904, no. 680; José Gonçalves Ferreira Costa to Antônio Augusto Borges de Medeiros, Caxias do Sul, April 22, 1905, no. 1.278; Tancredo A. Feijó, Antônio Giuriolo, André Fossati, Antônio Azambuja Kroeff, Martim Francisco Ayres, and Jacinto Targa to Antônio Augusto Borges de Medeiros, Caxias do Sul, December 18, 1906, no. 1.309. See also Henrique Blaskesi de Almeida, "Coronelismo, justiça e relações de poder em Caxias do Sul" (paper, presented in the Salão de Iniciação Científica, Memorial do Judiciário, Ministério Público do Rio Grande do Sul, Porto Alegre, October 2002); Elsa Avancini, *Coronelismo, cooptação e resistência—1200 votos contra o coronel—a eleição da banha em Ijuí, 1934* (Porto Alegre: Secretaria de Educação do Estado, 1993); Gunter Axt, "O Judiciário e a dinâmica do sistema coronelista de poder no Rio Grande do Sul," *Justiça & História* 4, no. 8 (2004): 55–118; René E. Gertz's publications "Aspectos da Revolução Federalista na zona de colonização alemã," in *Pensar a Revolução Federalista*, ed. Alves and Torres, 115–122, and *O aviador e o carroceiro: política, etnia e religião no Rio Grande do Sul dos anos 1920* (Porto Alegre: EDIPUCRS, 2002); Sérgio da Costa Franco, "O despertar político da região colonial

italiana," *Revista do Instituto Histórico e Geográfico do Rio Grande do Sul* no. 133 (1998): 11–14; Silvana Krause, "Economia, política e religião em Santa Cruz do Sul na República Velha" (master's thesis, Universidade Federal de Rio Grande do Sul, 1991).

17. Axt, "Gênese do estado burocrático-burguês"; N.a, *O Estado*; Sandra Jatahy Pesavento, *Os industriais da República* (Porto Alegre: IEL, 1991); Bak, "Cartels, Cooperatives, and Corporativism."

18. Gunter Axt, "Os guardiães da lei: aspectos da influência política e cultural dos positivistas religiosos sobre os governos republicanos no Rio Grande do Sul," *Métis: História & Cultura* 1, no. 2 (2002), 33–52; Nelson Boeira, "O Rio Grande de Augusto Comte," in *RS: Cultura e ideologia*, ed. J. H. Dacanal and S. Gonzaga (Porto Alegre: Mercado Aberto, 1980); Ricardo Vélez Rodriguez, *Castilhismo: uma filosofia da República* (Caxias do Sul: Ed. da UCS, 1980).

19. Baretta, "Political Violence and Regime Change." See also Janotti, *O coronelismo*; Leal, *Coronelismo, enxada e voto*; Queiroz, "O coronelismo numa interpretação sociológica;" and my "Coronelismo indomável."

20. Rubens Vidal Araújo, *Os Vargas* (Rio de Janeiro: Ed. Globo, 1985).

21. Axt, "Introdução."

22. See my own "Gênese do estado burocrático-burguês" and "Coronelismo indomável"; *A Federação* (Porto Alegre), August 27 and October 24, 1907, November 11 and 22, 1907, and October 26, 1908, Museu de Comunicação Social Hipólito José da Costa (hereafter MCS).

23. "Manifesto," *O Debate* (Porto Alegre), no. 1, June 2, 1907, and "Os excursionistas," *O Debate*, no. 132, November 6, 1907, IHGRS; *A Federação*, April 24 and 29, 1907, MCS; Carmen Aita and Gunter Axt, eds., *Perfil parlamentar de João Neves da Fontoura: discursos (1921–1928)*, Série Perfis Parlamentares 1 (Porto Alegre: ALERS/Corag, 1997); Carmen Aita and Gunter Axt, eds., *Perfil parlamentar de Getúlio Vargas: discursos 1903–1929*, Série Perfis Parlamentares 2 (Porto Alegre: ALERS/Corag, 1997); João Neves da Fontoura, *Memórias: Borges de Medeiros e seu tempo*, 2 vols. (Porto Alegre: Ed. do Globo, 1969), 70–71, 78–80.

24. *Correio do Povo* (Porto Alegre), February 7, 1908, MCS; Processo no. 2.238, Réu: Praxedes e José da Silva, 1908, Maço 101, and Processo no. 2.255, Réu: José Maria de Carvalho, 1908, Maço 102, both in Arquivo Público do Estado do Rio Grande do Sul (hereafter APERS); Aita and Axt, eds., *Perfil parlamentar de Getúlio Vargas*, 31–32; Álvaro Walmrath Bischoff and Cíntia Vieira Souto, "Getúlio Vargas e o Ministério Público," *Revista do Ministério Público*, no. 53 (2004): 15–47.

25. See the following records in BMP, IHGRS: Horácio Borges to Antônio Augusto Borges de Medeiros, Cachoeira do Sul, August 21, 1913, no. 864; Arlindo Leal to Antônio Augusto Borges de Medeiros, Cachoeira do Sul, August 23, 1913, no. 868; Isidoro Neves da

Fontoura to Antônio Augusto Borges de Medeiros, Cachoeira do Sul, November 11, 1914, no. 688; see also Carmen Aita, Wladimir Passos Araújo and Gunter Axt, eds., *Parlamentares gaúchos das Cortes de Lisboa aos nossos dias (1821–1996)*, 2nd ed. (Porto Alegre: ALERS/ Corag, 1996), 85; Aita and Axt, eds., *Perfil parlamentar de João Neves da Fontoura*, 20; Aita and Axt, eds., *Perfil parlamentar de Getúlio Vargas*, 32–33.

26. Processo Crime no. 2802, Réus: Viriato D. Vargas e João Gago, 1915, Comarca de São Borja, Maço 107, folha 4, APERS.
27. Aita and Axt, eds., *Perfil parlamentar de Getúlio Vargas*, 32–34.
28. In Rio Grande do Sul's clientelistic political system, the State controlled important political, judicial, and economic means in order to discipline *coronéis*. See Baretta, "Political Violence and Regime Change"; Coralio Bragança Pardo Cabeda, "José Antônio Martins, pioneiro esquecido do desenvolvimento da Campanha rio-grandense," *Revista do Instituto Histórico e Geográfico do Rio Grande do Sul* no. 130 (1994): 53–61; Coralio Bragança Pardo Cabeda, "Desafiando Castilhos e Borges de Medeiros: o caso Bernardino Mota" (paper, IHGRS, Porto Alegre, November 30, 2000).
29. Processo Crime, Viriato D. Vargas e João Gago, no. 2803, maço 107, Comarca de São Borja, 1922, folhas 2, 10, 55–56, 58, APERS.
30. Aita and Axt, eds., *Perfil parlamentar de Getúlio Vargas*, 34.
31. Axt, "Coronelismo indomável," 285–286.
32. Aita and Axt, eds., *Perfil parlamentar de Getúlio Vargas*, 35; Axt, "Constitucionalidade em debate," 327–332.
33. Axt, "Gênese do estado burocrático-burguês."
34. Ibid.; Miguel Frederico do Espírito Santo, *A abertura da Barra do Rio Grande* (Porto Alegre: BRDE/Palloti, 1982).
35. Gunter Axt, "O governo Getúlio Vargas no Rio Grande do Sul (1928–1930) e o setor financeiro regional," *Estudos Históricos*, no. 29 (2002): 119–140; Alcibíades Oliveira, *Um drama bancário: esplendor e queda do Banco Pelotense* (Porto Alegre: Livraria do Globo, 1936).
36. José Antônio Flores da Cunha, *A Campanha de 1923* (Rio de Janeiro: Ed. Zélio Valverde, 1943).
37. *Anais da Assembléia dos Representantes*, 1922 e 1923 (Porto Alegre: Oficinas Gráficas d'A Federação 1923 and 1924), Arquivo da Assembléia Legislativa do Estado do Rio Grande do Sul (hereafter AALERS).
38. Axt, "Coronelismo indomável," 287; *Congresso do Partido Republicano Rio-grandense* (Porto Alegre: Oficinas Gráficas d'A Federação, 1923).
39. Axt, "Coronelismo indomável," 286–287; Franco, "O despertar político," 11–14.
40. Aita and Axt, eds., *Perfil parlamentar de Getúlio Vargas*, 36–37.
41. Aita and Axt, eds., *Perfil parlamentar de Getúlio Vargas*, 37, 413–492; Edgar Carone's *A República Velha*, vol. 1, *Instituições e classes sociais*, 4th ed. (São Paulo: Difel, 1978); and vol. 2, *Evolução*

política, 4th ed. (São Paulo: Difel, 1983); Lenine Nequete, *O Poder Judiciário no Brasil a partir da independência*, 2 vols. (Porto Alegre: Ed. Sulina, 1973).

42. Aita and Axt, eds., *Perfil parlamentar de Getúlio Vargas*, 38–39, 495–500.
43. Ibid., 42.
44. Ibid., 43–45.
45. See Parecer da Comissão de Orçamento, sess. November 14, 1927; sessions of June 1928, *Anais da Assembléia dos Representantes* (Porto Alegre, Oficinas Gráficas d'A Federação, 1928 and 1929), AALERS; Gunter Axt, "Política portuária e de navegação e a formação do Estado no Rio Grande do Sul (1900–1930)," in *Breve inventário de temas do Sul*, ed. Luiz Roberto Pecoits Targa (Porto Alegre: UFRGS/FEE; Lajeado: UNIVATES, 1998), 147–194; Axt, "O governo Getúlio Vargas," 123–124.
46. See Adolfo Peña in the sess. of December 4, 1935, *Anais da Assembléia Legislativa* (Porto Alegre, Oficinas Gráficas d'A Federação, 1936), AALERS; Oliveira, *Um drama bancário*, 55–57.
47. Anonymous, *General Paim Filho: homem dum só parecer, um só rosto, uma só fé . . . Rebatendo infâmias* (Erechim: Tipografia Modelo, 1930), 29–30; Pesavento, *Os industriais da República*; Eugênio Lagemann, *O Banco Pelotense e o sistema financeiro regional* (Porto Alegre: Ed. Mercado Aberto, 1985); Oliveira, *Um drama bancário*, 110–120; Axt, "O governo Getúlio Vargas," 124–129.
48. Lagemann, *O Banco Pelotense*; Marli Mertz, "A burguesia industrial gaúcha e suas tentativas de organização," *Ensaios* 12, no. 2 (1991): 422–444; Sandra J. Pesavento, "Republicanos, industriais e o protecionismo alfandegário," in *Rio Grande do Sul: 150 anos de finanças públicas*, ed. Eugênio Lagemann (Porto Alegre: FEE, 1985), 57–86; Oliveira, *Um drama bancário*, 111–115; Axt, "O governo Getúlio Vargas," 124–129; *O Estado*.
49. Vavy Pacheco Borges, *Getúlio Vargas e a oligarquia paulista* (São Paulo, Ed. Brasiliense, 1984), 131–184.
50. Axt, "Gênese do estado burocrático-burguês."
51. Ibid.; Bak, "Cartels, Cooperatives, and Corporativism."
52. Jens R. Hentschke, *Positivism gaúcho-Style: Júlio de Castilhos's Dictatorship and its Impact on State- and Nation-Building in Vargas's Brazil* (Berlin: Verlag für Wissenschaft und Forschung, 2004).

Chapter 3

Civicscape and Memoryscape: The First Vargas Regime and Rio de Janeiro

Daryle Williams

In 1927, Antonio Prado Junior, the mayor of Rio de Janeiro, contracted French urbanist Alfred Agache (1875–1959) to design a master plan for the Brazilian capital city. A sweeping physical and aesthetic reform of Rio seemed within the reach of municipal authorities and their federal protectors. By the time Prado Junior received the plan's final version, in October 1930, the enthusiasm for large-scale reform in a city that had a population of 1.1 million plus had diminished significantly. The global economic seizure that began the previous October had wreaked havoc on public and private finances, while an armed insurrection, emerging out of a breakdown in civilian power-sharing arrangements, was bearing down on the capital. On paper, the so-called *Plano Agache*[1] held the potential to elevate Prado Junior to the peerage of Francisco Pereira Passos, the prefect credited with the urban and sanitation reforms of Rio's *belle époque*.[2] For Agache and his team, the plan would be a major accomplishment for the cause of the Société Française D'Urbanistes and its particular style of applied sociology. However, the upheavals of 1929–30—which included continued bad economic news, the arrest of the president and Prado Junior, and the arrival of a reformist civilian-military coalition rallying behind *gaúcho* statesman Getúlio Vargas (1883–1954)—rendered unviable any full-scale implementation of Agache's plan. By 1934, Rio's municipal authorities had formally scrapped the plan. Agache, in the meantime, had come to treat his plan as an exercise in the *theories* of urbanism, rather than as an actual blueprint for specific interventions into a specific city.[3]

A victim of the overthrow of the First Republic (1889–1930) and the onset of the Vargas era, the *Plano Agache* nevertheless points to the keen awareness among urban planners and public officials of the interwar years concerning the intimate connection between the built environment and the regulated socialization of an urban citizenry. The coalition that brought down the First Republic and tabled the Frenchman's plan still took inspiration in its predecessors' understandings of the central state as engineer and regulator of urban space. Inspired by a vision of moralization through urban planning, the Vargas regime treated urban reform as a tool in civic improvement. The reform of the capital's public spaces, alongside the careful management of civic time, guided Rio and its residents toward habits of civic sociability consistent with the political goals of urbanists and the urban goals of politicians. The construction and regulated occupation of civic space, in turn, afforded the residents of Rio opportunities to make, and remake, the *civicscape* of the Vargas era.[4] This chapter concentrates on the physical development of the capital city during the first Vargas regime and its attendant civic meanings.

City Planning and "Theaters of Power"

A close study of the *Plano Agache* proper is beyond the scope of this chapter, but it is important to underscore that Agache and his team were animated by the belief that any plan to renew Rio had to address the city's irregular urbanization, spectacular but uneven topography, and inadequate infrastructure. Drawing upon extensive statistical and observational evidence, Agache made the case that Rio required strong measures to correct shortcomings in functionality, hygiene, and grandeur.[5] Agache recognized that the success of past reforms had been mixed, due to the significant engineering challenges presented by the natural environment as well as residents' episodic resistance.[6] Agache's solution, then, was to envision a set of strategic interventions into Rio's natural and manmade environments capable of separating and rationalizing the functionality of urban space. The plan entailed the elimination of irregular and unhealthy districts and the surgical removal of *foci* of resistance.[7]

At the radiant point of the newly orderly capital would be the grand Porta do Brasil (Gateway to Brazil), a semicircular plaza fronting Guanabara Bay. Located approximately where the Aeroporto Santos Dumont now stands, the Gateway was to be built atop landfill created by the razing of the Morro do Santo Antônio. Monumental in scale and surrounded by grand government palaces styled in art-deco lines, the plaza was the epicenter of a rationalized city plan of well-organized streets and pleasing public spaces dominated by functional and artistic monuments to good public administration and good city living.

Many of the principles informing the Agache plan had already been part of city planning in Rio since the turn of the century. Notions of zoning, *favela* eradication, improved sanitation and transportation, and general urban beautification could be found in several small and grand plans for the capital, some dating back to the late colonial period. Even the focal point of the Agache Plan—the Porta do Brasil—had precedents in older public squares that unified significant public architecture, distinguished public monuments, and afforded easy access to economic centers. The bayfront Praça XV de Novembro, originally known as the Largo do Paço, is a prime example of a precursor to the Porta do Brasil.

Where the Agache Plan was to make its mark was in its totalizing scope, marrying the technical requirements of *citywide* construction and zoning to a vision of *citywide* moral improvement. The Porta do Brasil was quite special in this regard: an open "stage" surrounded by government palaces. On the gateway, key government functions would be performed in a tightly regulated urban space built specifically for the purpose of public administration and public sociability. On a day-to-day basis, some residents of the Federal District might stroll from the plaza to the Ponto do Calabouço, visiting a pantheon of national heroes, or the formal gardens at the Praça Paris. Others might head into the adjacent commercial-financial district, to grease the wheels of consumer capitalism. On special occasions, the Porta was to serve as the welcome parlor for national and international guests. The illustrations that accompanied the *Agache Plan* depicted the Porta as a site of large military processions and grand civic rallies.[8] When seen as part of a larger city plan—a plan that encompassed the oceanfront residential neighborhood of the South Zone, a secondary hub of government buildings on the Esplanada do Castelo, industrial and port installations, and transportation links to São Paulo and beyond—the Porta do Brasil was the spatial condensation of a project for structural and social modernization through urbanism.

The young Vargas regime, attracted to the idea of modernization, had neither the political might nor the economic resources to put the *Agache Plan* into action *in toto*. The regime instead adapted key aspects of the plan's underlying principles, including the rationalization of zoning, the concentration of public buildings, and the improvement of traffic circulation, especially between the downtown and the burgeoning suburbs. Most germane to our purposes here, the marriage of monumental public architecture and a vibrant, state-regulated civic culture became an important dimension to public power for the Vargas regime. That is, the interface of architectural monumentalism and grand civic pageantry envisioned for the Porta do Brasil took root in Rio de Janeiro even though the Porta was never actually built. Moreover, the patterns of sociability and urban citizenship implied by Agache's plan took shape as the residents of Rio occupied the spaces built to meet the idea of a rational capital city. Piecemeal, the historic center of Rio de Janeiro gained monumental, functional cityscapes that functioned as grand civicscapes at regular intervals timed to the civic calendar. By the 1940s, the city's civicscape reached toward the north zone, along the Avenida Presidente Vargas, a megaboulevard originating downtown that had been projected by Agache as a key transportation artery. Vargas and Federal District mayor Henrique Dodsworth invested heavily in the rhetoric that the new avenue was the physical embodiment of the new Brazil. Although not precisely following the plan laid out by Agache, the Vargas regime had, by 1945, urbanized a functional cityscape that doubled as a spectacular "theater of power."[9]

The Revolution of 1930 Comes to Rio de Janeiro

It is somewhat ironic that the military-civilian coalition that took up arms in support of Vargas in 1930 came to deploy a language of revolution and its attendant destructive impulses, while demonstrating restraint in committing actual violent acts against the capital's built environment. When president Washington Luís lost the support of the military high command and was forced from office, the insurrectionary troops heading toward the capital lost their motive to conquer Rio by force. Public buildings, such as the presidential palace and congress buildings, were taken easily. Denied the pretext of an armed seizure of the capital, the newly installed Vargas regime turned to symbolic violence against the deposed republicans. In advance of Vargas's arrival, rebel troops hitched their horses to the obelisk built at the end of Avenida Rio Branco, laying claim to a well-known symbol of urban and ideological "civilization" built during the Pereira Passos reforms. In the following days, Vargas's military and civilian allies took literal and symbolic control of other spatial, symbolic, and temporal monuments associated with the old regime.

The targets of such symbolic violence rapidly shifted from monuments associated with the old regime to the larger civic landscape of the deposed republicans. On November 15, the new Provisional Government organized a military parade along the Avenida Beira-Mar to celebrate the anniversary of the republic and its new leaders. The parade included not only members of the regular armed forces, but also contingents from the Federal District police and fire departments, as well as a militarized women's aid society from Minas Gerais, named after João Pessoa. Photos of the day indicate a very significant turnout of spectators for an event (mistakenly) reported to be the first of its kind. The *Correio da Manhã* informed its readers that a brigade of 300 men had been charged with a symbolic cleansing of public spaces—"a toilette do Rio"—stretching from Botafogo, in the South Zone, to São Cristóvão, in the north.[10] The newly empowered rebel forces seemed to share an urbanist's vision for public sanitation.

Four days later, the new regime commemorated Flag Day. Francisco Campos, the incoming minister of education, delivered a speech at Rio's city hall in which he envisioned a future of national renewal that flowed from the martyrdom of soldiers felled in the recent "Revolution," the *tenente* mutinies, and other struggles. Campos spoke of a time when Flag Day events would incite pride in the citizenry, especially youth, and not merely serve as an empty backdrop to long-winded speeches and uninspired parades.[11] The public was invited to join the new regime in remaking the genealogy of republican legitimacy.

The Provisional Government took a systematic approach to the temporal underpinnings of the public sphere on December 5, 1930, when Vargas signed off on Decree 19.488, trimming six of the twelve national holidays celebrated by the deposed republican regime. Gone were the dates commemorating the constitution of 1891, the precursors to Brazilian Independence, May Day, the discovery of Brazil, national fraternity, independence and republicanism in the Americas, and the discovery of the Americas. The official civic calendar remained republican, but it lost much of the historical specificity of the early years of the Republic, when embattled republican factions tried to shore up their tenuous hold on political legitimacy by marginalizing monarchists, jacobins, and labor radicals from civic time and memory.[12] The pared-down calendar became the temporal template in which the Vargas regime would begin to remake the Brazilian nation and its capital city.

Of course, intervention into the civic calendar had deep historical precedents. The civic calendar revised in 1930 had been modified on several occasions since the January 14, 1890, decree establishing the Republic's official civic clock. November 15 and 19 may have appeared to be timeless, but they were, in fact, invented traditions intended to help provide a regular chronological pretext for the imagination of the national community.[13] The legal changes of December 1930, then, were neither the first nor the last manipulation of civic time to meet immediate political needs as well as the larger goal of nation-building (see table 3.1).

Table 3.1   The Federal Civic Calendar, 1889–1960*

Old Republic (1889–1930)

January 1	Universal Fraternity
February 24	Promulgation of the Constitution of 1891 (1891–)
April 21	Precursors to Brazilian Independence (Tiradentes Day)
May 1	Workers' Day (1924–)
May 3	Discovery of Brazil
May 13	Brazilian Fraternity (Abolition of Slavery)
July 14	Republic, Liberty, and Independence in Americas (Bastille Day)
September 7	Independence
October 12	Discovery of America (Columbus Day)
November 2	Finados (Memorial Day)
November 15	Anniversary of the Republic
December 25	Christmas (1922–)

Provisional Government (1930–34)

January 1	Universal Fraternity
May 1	Universal Fraternity of the Working Classes
September 7	Independence
November 2	Finados
November 15	Anniversary of the Republic
December 25	Spiritual Unity of Christian Peoples

Constitutional Government (1934–37)

January 1	Universal Fraternity
April 21	Tiradentes Day
May 1	Universal Fraternity of the Working Classes
May 3	Discovery of Brazil
July 16	Promulgation of the Constitution of 1934
September 7	Independence
October 12	Discovery of America
November 2	Finados
November 15	Proclamation of the Republic
December 25	Christmas

Estado Novo (1937–45)

January 1	Universal Fraternity
April 19	Vargas's Birthday (1940–)
April 21	Tiradentes Day

Continued

Table 3.1 Continued

May 1	Workers' Day
August 25	Caxias' Day (Soldier's Day)
September 7	Independence
October 12	Dia da Raça (Children's Day)
October 28	Public Employees' Day (1939–)
November 2	Finados
November 10	Anniversary of the Estado Novo
November 15	Anniversary of the Republic
November 19	Flag Day
November 27	Anniversary of the Intentona Comunista (1936–)
Constitutional Regime (1945–60)	
January 1	Universal Fraternity
May 1	Universal Fraternity of the Working Classes
September 7	Independence
November 15	Anniversary of the Republic
December 25	Spiritual Unity of Christian Peoples

Note: *Key laws include: Decree 155-B (January 14, 1890), Decree 3 (February 28, 1891), Decree 4.497 (January 19, 1922), Decree 4.859 (September 26, 1924), Decree 19.488 (December 5, 1930), Law 108 (October 29, 1935), Law 622 (April 6, 1949); Additional information on the civic calendar has been culled from: Reis Carvalho, *Os feriados brasileiros* (Rio de Janeiro: Pimenta de Mello, 1926); Francisco Cintra Assis, *Os feriados da República, explicação histórica dos feriados nacionais* (Rio de Janeiro: Irmãos Pongetti, 1934); and, Letter from Lourenço Filho to Gustavo Capanema, February 20, 1942, AGC, GC 38.08.09Ag XVIII-2, FGV/CPDOC.

If the young regime was immediately drawn to the remaking civic time, the Provisional Government's treatment of civic space, especially in the capital, was initially timid and unimaginative. In 1931, for example, Independence Day (September 7) ceremonies included a military parade at the Quinta da Boa Vista, a presidential tour of naval installations, and a naval parade on the Enseada de Botafogo.[14] The reported attendance at the military parade—7,000—was unimpressive; the choice of location had little impact on how the city might be reengineered to fit the needs of the new regime, as the Quinta da Boa Vista was an isolated park, with limited possibilities for commercial, administrative, or civic improvement. In 1932 and 1933, federal agents again drew on past precedent to mark September 7 and November 15. Independence Day ceremonies involved a military procession at the equestrian monument to D. Pedro I located on Praça Tiradentes, while the anniversary of the republic was marked at the monument to Benjamin Constant, on the Praça da República. The deposed republicans had used both sites.

Under the constitutional government, the civicscape of the capital took on a more discernible face of the "revolutionary" regime. The armed forces and paramilitary organizations, for instance, began to take a much more decisive role in Independence Day commemorations. In 1934, under the supervision of the Conselho da Segurança e Defesa Nacional (National Security and Defense Council), the day's events included a large morning parade along Avenida Rio Branco, which Vargas and other dignitaries watched from a dais erected in front of the National Library. In the early afternoon, composer Heitor Villa-Lobos led an youth choral song (*canto orfeônico*) program at the Praia do Russell (alternatively spelled Russel), located in Glória. The day ended with a public pledge of allegiance, the *Hora da Independência* (Hour of Independence), on the Esplanada do Castelo, and a nighttime gala at the Teatro Municipal.[15] Newspaper accounts of the day identify the members of the proto-fascist Integralist movement as enthusiastic participants. The Integralists, in fact, would be one of the most active agents of the period, turning the civic calendar into a public asset, experienced through large-scale public ceremonies of disciplined, patriotic citizens who took to the streets of the capital.

In the following years, spearheaded by the ministry of education, the municipal government of the Federal District, and the Departmento de Propaganda e Difusão Cultural (Department of Propaganda and Cultural Diffusion) and its more notorious successor, the Departmento de Imprensa e Propaganda, the commemoration of Independence Day gradually stretched into a multiday celebration, the *Semana da Pátria* (Week of the Fatherland). It typically included a military parade from the Praça Paris toward Avenida Rio Branco, youth parades along Avenida Rio Branco or inside the Estádio Vasco da Gama, performance of choral song and flag-raising ceremonies at the *Hora da Independência*, and a black-tie gala at the Municipal Theater. Gustavo Capanema, an intellectual-politician from the state of Minas Gerais who assumed the post of minister of education in 1934 believing deeply in the transformative power of organized civic culture, must be credited for the federal government's intensified interest in civic culture generally, and especially the combination of military and youth processions that came to be a distinguishing feature of the *Semana da Pátria* during the first Vargas regime.[16]

If the general direction was toward making better, more intensive, more regulated use of the capital's civic space in the making of a new state, state-sponsored civism had yet to fully reflect the rising authoritarian underpinnings of the Vargas regime. In 1934—the year of a series of innovations in Independence Day ceremonies—the anniversary of the republic offered little novelty. The day's primary event took place at the Benjamin Constant monument and included speeches delivered at the base of the monument and performances of the Brazilian and French national anthems. The universalist underpinnings of liberalism and humanism endured even as conservative ideologues and reactionary political movements, such as Integralism, tried to delink Brazilian culture from the Western liberal tradition.[17]

The key shift appears to come between 1935 and 1936; when the scale of civic ceremonies grew significantly, public works were integrated into the festivities, and the physical and rhetorical mobilization of the citizenry took on greater urgency, especially in relation to clashes between government forces and the Left. September 7 commemorations included the traditional events at the monument to D. Pedro I on the Praça Tiradentes as well as ever-larger parades for youth, athletes, and the armed forces, organized by federal authorities in concert with the Liga da Defesa Nacional (League of National Defense) for the Avenida Rio Branco–Avenida Beira-Mar axis. Although the figures must be treated with some skepticism, the 1936 September 7 ceremonies reportedly included 14,660 schoolchildren at the *Hora da Independência* held on the Esplanada do Castelo in addition to the 35,000 regular troops and cadets assembled for the military parade held at the Avenida Beira-Mar.[18] Similar figures would be reported through the end of the Estado Novo.

The civic calendar for the remainder of the year expanded and intensified, with the October commemoration of the anniversaries of the Revolution of 1930, the traditional November celebrations of the republic and Flag Day, and the introduction of the new civic date: November 27, anniversary of a 1935 mutiny among left-wing military troops, known as the *Intentona Comunista*. November 27 would remain a peculiar date in the civicscape of the capital: date of the most infamous of all civic ceremonies of the Estado Novo, the *Queima das Bandeiras* (Burning of the Flags) ceremony held on the Praia do Russell in 1937, as well as occasion for an annual gathering of the president and the highest military authorities from 1937 through 1990.[19]

What is striking in the general intensification of civic culture during the constitutional interregnum is how a diverse cross-section of the capital's government and civic associations took part in the planning and execution of civic events even as the constitutional system grew unstable. The 1935 events, for example, were officially coordinated by a government commission, headed by president of the Chamber of Deputies Antônio Carlos Ribeiro de Andrada, but events were also planned by the army, navy, and air force, the ministries of war and

education, private patriotic leagues and sports clubs with close connections to the government, such as the Liga da Defesa Nacional and
the Liga de Sports da Marinha (Navy Sports League), as well as
unions and trade associations. In 1935, the main lawyers' association,
the Instituto da Ordem dos Advogados (Brazilian Bar Association),
was reported to have made a special appeal to "intensify to the farthest
extent possible the enthusiasm among the Brazilian people for the
passage of the great date in our nationality."[20] School principals and
teachers, and to a more limited degree parents of schoolchildren,
would become important facilitators in making grand civic events,
which required significant logistical coordination and public collaboration, a success. Although the evidence does not necessarily indicate
a truly *popular* culture of civism in the mid-1930s, the civic calendar
did carry certain expressive meanings for certain sectors of *carioca*
society.

An intensified regime of urbanism provided the context in which
civic culture took on a more monumental and massive, if not always
popular, scale in the city. The 1935 Independence Day ceremonies
included the laying of the cornerstone of an emergency clinic for naval
personnel and their families. Undoubtedly small in the larger scheme
of the growing city's urban life, the event, nonetheless, set the tone
for the flurry of cornerstone-laying ceremonies and public works
inaugurations. Often set in front of large disorderly worksites, these
civic events exerted their physical mark on the national capital, while
encouraging the city's residents to interact with changing public space
in new ways. The constitutional government was also the period during which the general plans for one of the most audacious public
works—the headquarters for the ministry of education—was refined
from the "original sketch" made by the high-priest of interwar modernism, Le Corbusier.[21] A short distance from the Esplanada do
Castelo, on a large lot adjacent to lots reserved for the ministries of
labor and finance, the controversial building, elaborated by a team of
Brazilian architects-urbanists led by Lúcio Costa and Oscar Niemeyer,
put the strong stamp of modern architecture and urban planning onto
a monumental edifice of public administration, which uncoinciden-
tally was led by a minister whose stated intent was to remake Brazilian
culture—body, mind, and soul.

The Estado Novo and Rio de Janeiro

The Estado Novo dictatorship (November 10, 1937–October 29,
1945) brought the idea of the rationalized city into the practice of

state-regulated civic culture. In the temporal plane, the Vargas regime made an indelible mark on the civic calendar within days of the proclamation of the Estado Novo, first somewhat quietly on November 15, the anniversary of the republic, and then in spectacular fashion on November 27, the second anniversary of the *Intentona Comunista.* The day's *Queima das Bandeiras* was an especially singular event, in that it married together a traditional republican holiday, Flag Day, with a new commemorative date, the anniversary of the *Intentona Comunista* to articulate a ritual language of the new regime.

The day's program grew out of plans for a conventional Flag Day celebration, scheduled for the Praia do Russell. The ministry of education, which had assumed an aggressive stance toward civic education, worked closely with various branches of the federal and municipal government in planning a schedule of events that centered largely on ritual pledges of alliance. The weather proved to be uncooperative, and the November 19 program was suspended.[22] Rescheduled for November 27, a revised program counted upon the presence of some 3,000 students from Rio's municipal schools as well as 21 female students from the Instituto de Educação, the highly-regarded normal school that was turning out a teacher corps that represented a white, female, and middle-class ideal of racial order.[23] Joined by Vargas and other authorities, these youth watched as Cardinal Sebastião Leme celebrated a mass on a giant flag-draped stage, named the *Altar da Pátria* (Altar of the Fatherland). The mass was followed by a flag-hoisting ceremony, led by Vargas, and then a ceremonial flag-burning, in which the flags of each state of the Brazilian Federation were placed in a large urn and set afire.[24] Following a rendition of the National Anthem, led by Villa-Lobos, Minister of Justice Francisco Campos delivered a speech that linked the singularity of the national flag to the sacrifice of soldiers killed in 1935, making clear that all Brazilians had to unite against the threat of internal dissention and discord.[25] The day concluded with a funerary pilgrimage to the graves of the officers and regular troops killed in the *Intentona*, at the São João Batista and São Francisco Xavier Cemeteries, respectively (the remains would later be consolidated at a mausoleum at São João Batista, inaugurated in 1940). The ashes of the state flags, in the meantime, were sent to the National Historical Museum, an institution that was developing an intimate relationship with the Vargas state.[26]

The burning of soiled or tattered flags was not unheard of during previous Flag Day ceremonies, but the 1937 Flag Day ceremonies were a watershed moment in the political history of the Brazilian republic. In Bahia, Flag Day was marked by the *interventor's* directive to burn hundreds of books of fiction considered favorable to communism. This event anticipated an even larger ceremonial incineration of books seized from the Editorial Paz.[27] In Rio, on November 27, the sacralization of national martyrs and the explicit incorporation of Catholic rituals—representatives of the Ligas Católicas (Catholic Leagues), the Confederação Católica do Rio de Janeiro (Catholic Confederation of Rio de Janeiro), and the Ação Católica Brasileira (Brazilian Catholic Action) joined the Cardinal in renditions of various religious songs—sharply departed from the secular civicism that had been a hallmark of republican traditions. Most importantly, the day's admixture of traditional republican iconography, Roman Catholicism, anticommunism, hypernationalism, and a militarized youth parade marked a new direction for the ritualization and sacralization of *estadonovista* authoritarianism.[28] Out of the events of November 27, the Estado Novo attained the symbolic energies to aggressively pursue an agenda of statist, antiregionalist, antiliberal, eugenicist politics of national modernization. In practice, the process of state-led modernization was contested and self-contradictory. The "authoritarian democracy" exalted in state propaganda was hampered by compromise, internal debate, and outright resistance. But in symbolism, the *Queima* was the essence of the authoritarian state.

By June of 1938, when the authoritarian state apparatus was fairly well secure, the regime made yet another adjustment to the federal civic calendar, official (re)recognizing May 1 as a national holiday, while reaffirming the recognition of January 1, April 21, September 7, November 2 and 15, and December 25.[29] Gustavo Capanema, the ideologically heterodox minister of education who cast his lot with Vargas following the authoritarian turn of the Estado Novo, drafted legislation to fold November 10 into the national civic calendar.[30] A specific law to this effect was never passed but, in practice, November 10 was perhaps the most important holiday of the Estado Novo calendar, especially so in Rio, where large civic commemorations accompanied inaugurations of the regime's major public works in Rio and elsewhere.

Even as the dictatorial regime afforded itself wide latitude in limiting free assembly, civil society was invited to make public observations of a wide range of anniversaries and commemorative dates. For the schoolchildren of Rio de Janeiro, attendance was often required. The size and scope of public assemblies—coordinated by the ministries of education and labor, in collaboration with the DIP, the armed forces, authorities from the government of the Federal District, and private patriotic leagues—increased dramatically after 1937, with intensive scheduling in mid-April through May 1 (Vargas's birthday, Tiradentes Day, and May Day), September (the *Semana da Pátria*), and November (the anniversaries of the Estado Novo and the Proclamation of the Republic, Flag Day, and the anniversary of the *Intentona Comunista*).

The urbanist underpinnings for the intensification of civic culture in the capital were notable. With portions of the *Agache Plan* resurrected in municipal building codes passed in 1935 and 1937 (particularly aspects of the plan dealing with the volume, massing, and setbacks of large constructions downtown), municipal and federal officials commissioned urban planners, engineers, and architects to imagine and build a capital city capable of hosting large assemblies of mobilized citizens, and more importantly, capable of imposing an urbanist order on public life. Federal District mayor Henrique Dodsworth and his secretary of transportation and public works, Edson Passos, played especially instrumental roles in working with the federal government and private construction firms to complete massive public works projects, including the Avenida Presidente Vargas, completed in stages between 1941 and 1944.

Never reaching the singular grandeur of the Porta do Brasil, a spectacular civicscape still emerged downtown, within a roughly shaped quadrilateral bounded by the Avenida Rio Branco, the Avenida Beira-Mar and its continuation along the Avenida Presidente Wilson, the Avenida Arparicio Borges (today's Presidente Antonio Carlos) and its continuation along the edge of Praça XV and the Rua Primeiro de Março, and the large traffic circle surrounding the Igreja Nossa Senhora da Candelária. A second, linear axis stared at the rear of the Candelária Church and continued along Avenida Presidente Vargas to Praça Onze. Within this large swath of historic Rio, specific nodes of civicscape development concentrated in the stretch of Avenida Beira-Mar between the Praça Paris and the Deodoro da Fonseca Monument; the lower stretch of Avenida Rio Branco, especially the area in front of the National Library; the Esplanada do Castelo; and, the section of the Avenida Presidente Vargas between the Ministry of War and the Campo Santana.

In its attraction to the concentration of state power in this quadrilateral, the federal government built anew or remodeled six ministerial headquarters (Navy, 1933; Transportation and Public Works, 1936; Labor, Industry, and Commerce, 1938; War, 1941; Treasury, 1943; Education and Health, 1945), and financed the construction of the 26-story clocktower atop the Central do Brasil railway headquarters (1937), located on Avenida Presidente Vargas.[31] The Senate and House of Deputies—both shuttered in the coup of

November 1937—were retrofitted to house the ministry of justice and the DIP, respectively. New state regulatory agencies, such as the Instituto de Alcool e Açúcar (Alcohol and Sugar Institute, 1942) and the Instituto de Resseguros do Brasil (Reinsurance Institute of Brazil, 1943), won new downtown headquarters. New public statuary paying homage to Deodoro da Fonseca (1937), the Barão de Rio Branco (1943), and Brazilian Youth (1947), among others, provided additional opportunities for the spectacle of the commemorative acts as well as the more permanent reconfiguration of the cityscape as a civic lesson in stone, concrete, bronze, and glass.[32]

The architectural styles of these interventions into the city core were extremely diverse, with a jumble of eclectic, modernist, art-deco, classicizing, and rationalist edifices inserted among older colonial, neoclassic, and vernacular architecture.[33] Privately financed constructions followed similarly diverse styles, with major commercial firms generally choosing a look of modernity in construction engineering and decorative languages that could not be reduced to a single architectural-urbanist message or school. Downtown Rio ca. 1945 had won a certain volumetric monumentality that Agache might have admired, but it lacked the aesthetic coherence of the plan turned over to Prado Junior in 1930. The city center, nonetheless, structured an imposing self-image for the Vargas state. Minister of Labor Alexandre Marcondes Filho commented in 1944 that "the epoch that fails to distinguish itself by its architecture and the value of its [public] constructions is barren . . . a community that has failed to perpetuate itself through the eloquent symbolism of monuments raised through a collective effort."[34] The Vargas regime had committed itself to ensuring that its "collective efforts" would indeed be distinguished by the capital's public architecture and urban plan.

The rationalization of public administration was an important byproduct of urbanization. Civil service reformers at the Departamento Administrativo do Serviço Público (DASP) were especially pleased to report that the new structures, owned wholly by the federal government, freed the federal government from burdensome rent payments and the vicissitudes of the private real estate market.[35] They were also pleased to see that the new buildings provided an architectural basis for workplace discipline. The physical concentration of public dependencies, then, provided the state with better conditions to internally rationalize public administration as public administration rationalized the surrounding city.[36] Urbanism was, then, the underpinning of a new kind of state—a state that enjoyed autonomy and efficiency in function and form.

Vargas himself linked aesthetics, urbanism, and state functionality for the post-1930 regime at the inauguration of the headquarters of the Ministry of the Treasury, built upon one of the large lots zoned around the Esplanada do Castelo. Vargas commented:

> [T]he new Ministry of the Treasury building reflects our present state. . . . The old structure on Avenida Passos, which was insufficient and colonial, corresponded to our position as a debtor nation, when we were weighted down by interest payments, loans, and bailouts [*fundings*] which were ruinous to the national economy . . . until the Revolution of 1930 modified the general panorama of our finances.
>
> The provisional housing on Avenida Rio Branco marked an era of transition, in the same manner that this monumental building shows the prosperity achieved, that will only increase with our hard work to guarantee Brazil the position of independence and dignity that it has conquered in the concert of civilized nations.[37] (Italics in the original).

The new ministry, then, served to reorganize, relocate, and most importantly, rebuild Brazilian history such that the Vargas regime was the concrete incarnation of the public good.

The civicscape repercussions of state-led urbanism were indeed most evident downtown, but their impact was to be seen throughout the city. Residential and industrial patterns changed in relation to the general growth of the city population—planned and unplanned—as well as in relation to the resignification of the downtown as an administrative and commercial megacenter increasingly emptied of its historical functions. The demolition work that made way for the Avenida Presidente Vargas forced many small-scale factories and petty commercial establishments to relocate to areas on the fringes of the central district or further away, toward the suburban areas along the Central do Brasil and Leopoldina rail lines. This displacement, in turn, was accompanied by residential displacement, with poorer downtown residents migrating toward the northern suburbs, and middle-class property owners settling in and around Tijuca or the South Zone. The waterfront neighborhoods in the south, particularly Flamengo and Copacabana, experienced a process of rapid verticalization, as one and two-story homes were replaced with high-rise apartment buildings destined for the rising middle class. Ironically, as the city center became more rationalized, the urban spread to the north and south created chaotic infrastructural conditions, due to the loose regulation of land use and building codes as well as the precipitous proliferation of *favelas*.[38]

Despite the chaos at the "periphery," the downtown civicscape was indeed more integrated and rationalized by the close of the Estado Novo. It was more Agachian in its functionality and look. The ceremonial dedication of public works and the annual civic ceremonies provided the pretext upon which the Vargas state was able to include the citizens of Rio into a process of urbanization that was otherwise disruptive and for some residents, unwelcome.

Of course, the federal civic space failed to capture the entirety of urban occupation, civic sociability, and memory in the Federal District. The feast days of the Catholic Church, the commemoration of the city's patron saint, Saint Sebastian, and, of course, Carnival processions, were occasions in which the streets were filled by *cariocas* marking spaces and times that fell outside of federal and municipal controls. Neighborhoods untouched by reurbanization—some quite close to downtown—changed more slowly. The middle-class beach neighborhoods, such as Copacabana, moreover, developed to a rhythm that was quite distinct from downtown.[39] The civicscape described here cannot capture, even in its idealized form, the variety of civic and social relations in the streets of Rio de Janeiro during the first Vargas regime. However, if the gaze is focused onto the city center, the main civicscape, we do catch a glimpse of how the residents of Rio—the majority living outside the monumental civicscape of downtown—used downtown to make their own sense of the Estado Novo, ultimately contributing to its downfall through acts of symbolic violence not unlike those practiced by the Vargas regime back in 1930.

This point reminds us that in spite of the intense disciplining that accompanies civic ceremonies, the occupation of the city often fell outside of state regulation, even in moments explicitly marked as civic or patriotic in nature. The Avenida Presidente Vargas—site of many of the Estado Novo's most grandiose civic ceremonies—was scene of episodic popular protest against the avenue's construction and the authoritarian politics of urbanism.[40] On August 18, 1942, downtown streets were invaded by large numbers of *cariocas* enraged by the news that several Brazilian merchant marine vessels had been sunk by Nazi torpedoes. Flooding many of the same downtown streets used during Independence Week ceremonies, tens of thousands of Rio residents occupied civic spaces without the careful coordination and disciplining of the central state and municipal authorities.[41] Although this public occupation of the civicspace apparently took municipal security officials by surprise, the Vargas regime deftly used the spontaneous demonstrations of patriotism as immediate justification for the declaration of war on the Axis, and the continuation of an intense regime of civic commemoration.

By early 1945, the schedule of civic culture started in the constitutional regime and intensified during the Estado Novo showed signs of internal destabilization. This should not be especially surprising as the Estado Novo regime itself was experiencing an internal dissolution. In 1944, the September 7 *Parada da Juventude*, alternatively known as the *Parada da Raça* or the *Parada da Mocidade*, counted upon the presence of 30,000 schoolchildren for the youth parade organized since 1934. By mid-August 1945, the Rio press, released from the strict censorship restrictions imposed at the outset of the Estado Novo, freely circulated rumors that the youth parade, planned for Avenida Rio Branco, might be disrupted by students who refused to participate in protest of the participation of the Juventude Brasileira, the Estado Novo's paramilitary youth organization, founded in 1940. The *Correio da Manhã* published an open letter by General Manuel Rabello, president of the Sociedade Amigos da América (Society of the Friends of America), to the Brazilian people that likened the annual youth parade and its complementary public acts honoring Vargas to "nazi-fasci-integralist" parades.[42] Abgar Renault, director of the Departamento Nacional de Educação (National Department of Education) and key collaborator in Gustavo Capanema's vision of a mobilized and healthy youth culture, received notification that Sindicato dos Estabelecimentos do Ensino (Trade Union of Educational Institutions) had joined the Congresso dos Estudantes Secundários (Congress of Secondary School Students) in manifesting its opposition to the realization of the annual parade, amidst the uncertainties surrounding the *queremista* rallies (which, significantly, began in the Largo do Carioca and ended in front of the Palácio Guanabara in Flamengo— two sites that did not receive much attention by *estadonovista* urbanists), the repatriation of the Força Expedicionária Brasileira (Brazilian Expeditionary Force), and the presidential campaign.[43] João Alberto, chief of police in the Federal District, had to put down rumors that the September 2 event, planned for 15,000 participants, might incite direct civil disobedience.[44]

The 1945 youth parade was indeed postponed by the ministry of education, citing bad weather and a flu outbreak. The September 7 military parade took place, as planned, and the turnout for the *Hora da Independência* ceremonies in the Vasco da Gama stadium were still quite impressive, drawing some 30,000 children to sing various songs in homage of independence, the Republic, military troops, Brazilian workers, and peace.[45] The ceremonies also included a "spontaneous" demonstration of *queremista* support for Vargas. One month later, on the fifteenth anniversary of the outbreak of the Revolution of 1930, the ministry of education headquarters was officially inaugurated. The day's events included a speech by Capanema, delivered in front of a bust to Vargas, that detailed the work of the ministry in the formation of Brazilian culture.

The public ceremony of October 3, 1945, closed a cycle of civic urbanism that began in late October 1930 with symbolic interventions into the Rio cityscape and evolved into permanent interventions into the urban configuration of the national capital. Vargas was deposed in a bloodless military coup on October 29. Capanema also lost his post. The Vargas state would face the same kind of symbolic violence that it exacted upon the republicans in 1930; busts of Vargas were removed from public squares and the *estadonovista* civic calendar was eviscerated by early 1946.

The larger city would experience tremendous growth in the period between the fall of the Estado Novo and the transfer of the capital to Brasília in April 1960, fueled by population increase, massive public works (e.g., tunnel and freeway construction; street widening; hillside razing and bayside landfill; the construction of Maracanã Stadium), private residential construction, and unregulated land occupations. Ironically, the downtown core changed relatively little in the 1940s and 1950s, as the federal government settled into dependencies built during the Estado Novo and private capital was invested elsewhere. The Avenida Presidente Vargas, for instance, failed to become the monumental banking-commercial-automotive corridor imagined in 1944.[46]

The downtown would remain largely a product of Estado Novo urbanism until the 1960s, when the Superintendência de Urbanização e Saneamento (SURSAN; Superintendency of Urbanization and Sanitation, founded 1957) began to implement a comprehensive overview of urban development and public works that tended to build around or above urban areas prized by federal and municipal planners during the first Vargas regime. By the mid-1970s, the city's loss of political power to Brasília and economic power to São Paulo, in conjunction with the explosive growth of outlying areas and *favelas*, propelled SURSAN and its successors to essentially abandon the civicscape of the first Vargas regime in favor of a much different kind of urban planning and its attendant ideas of social moralization.[47]

Memoryscapes of the First Vargas Regime

The Estado Novo as a built environment dissolved gradually, but never wholly disappeared in Rio. The Avenida Presidente Vargas remains a major thoroughfare in and out of the downtown. Nearly all of the federal ministries and regulatory agencies to gain new headquarters during the first Vargas regime remain in their place. The region around the Esplanada do Castelo remain largely urbanized as it was in 1945, with the imposing regional offices of the ministries of labor, education, and finance still towering over the smaller colonial-era churches and the 1943 monument to Rio Branco, sadly abandoned. Surely, there are many newer buildings on the Esplanada, owned by the city of Rio, the judiciary, and private commercial interests, and the main thoroughfare has been renamed. Highways and parking lots have severed the connection to Guanabara Bay. Nevertheless, the Castelo district still gives us a sense of what Agache and his Estado Novo counterparts had in mind when trying to create a monumental civic space, dedicated to public administration, social control, and moralization though civic pageantry.

The built environment of the first Vargas regime can still be discerned, but the competing civicscapes of other epochs in Rio's history—Praça XV de November and the cultural corridors in Lapa and along the Rua Primeiro de Março being quite successful examples of revitalization through the valorization of cultural heritage—cloud the view. These memory sites breath new life into Rio's historic core, which suffered a serious degradation in physical upkeep and quality of life in the 1980s. But, with the exception of a few isolated buildings such as the refurbished ministry of education building, now named after Gustavo Capanema, downtown Rio's built environment no longer speaks an architectonic and urbanist language that might be directly related to the first Vargas regime. The language of civism that the Vargas regime imprinted upon downtown is even more difficult to hear, as Rio's civic celebrations have largely abandoned all spaces utilized by the Vargas regime with the exception of the area fronting the Praça da República, site of September 7 military parades.

The passage of the fiftieth anniversary of Getúlio Vargas's suicide, in August 2004, occasioned a possible shift in the architectural-ceremonial dissolution of the Vargas era civicscape. The anniversary of Vargas's suicide had been marked by various forms of private and public ceremonies for decades, including various rallies, processions, and vigils in the Praça Floriano, where a bust of Vargas stands, and at the Palácio do Catete, the former presidential palace.

The events for 2004 included a number of reflections on Brazilian society during the Vargas era, the legacies of the Vargas state, and more prosaically, Vargas as statesman. Most major newspapers and newsweeklies published special retrospective editions about Vargas and his era. The Museu da República (Museum of the Republic), in the Catete palace, hosted a three-day major symposium, one of the several organized in Rio and elsewhere, and inaugurated a new exhibition, *Getúlio: Presidente do Brasil*. One of the exhibit's galleries included artistic rendering of municipal maps, taken of various Brazilian cities, showing streets, plazas, and thoroughfares named after Vargas. The gallery served as a reminder that Vargas and his era made their mark on urban space throughout Brazil. A map of Rio was, curiously, not included in the gallery, but it is indubitable that the physical likeness of Vargas or some memory of his presence can be found throughout the city, with an especially intense concentration of busts, plaques, and inscriptions downtown. The Museu da República, of course, continues to be the most compelling memory site—the *mise-en-scène* of Vargas's death by suicide.[48] Like the busts scattered throughout the city, the blood-stained pajama top and the fatal bullet on display on the third floor of the former presidential palace form part of the memoryscape of an era.

The peculiar innovation to the 2004 Vargas commemoration—one that raises the question of the civicscape of the first Vargas regime— was the dedication of the Memorial Getúlio Vargas. Located below the Hotel Glória, at the foot of the Rua do Russell, the memorial has two dimensions: above-ground, two triangular planes rise out of a circular reflecting pool, curving toward one another. Nearby, an oversized bust of Vargas, looking slightly aged, sits on a large pedestal. Below ground, a 1,800-square meter space houses an exhibition hall, auditorium, visitor center, and café. Inaugurated on August 24, the memorial is the municipal government's first official memorial to a *gaúcho* who lived in Rio for the better part of four decades.

The memorial is sited in an oval-shaped park officially named after Portuguese epic poet Luís de Camões. Known in the nineteenth century as the Praia do Russell or the Praia do Dom Pedro I, the area was associated with religious ceremonies held at the Glória do Outeiro church and the public sanitation works installed nearby. The construction of the Avenida Beira-Mar, started during the Pereira Passos administration (1902–06) and expanded under Prado Junior (1926–30), made a misnomer of the name *praia* (beach), as access to the water was rather difficult by the early 1930s. Set back from the bay, and lacking the appeal of the nearby pleasure gardens at the Praça Paris and the upscale commercial establishments along the Rua do Catete, the Praia do Russell faded to semiobscurity by the mid-twentieth century, although the grassy area, surrounded by trees, served as a nice staging ground for public gatherings. The "beach's" transformation into a landlocked neighborhood would be complete with the construction of the Aterro do Flamengo, which left the area an isolated urban park situated between a large marina, a hillside, and mass transportation arteries. The plaza's privileged locale right below the landmark church, and the installation of the statue of patron saint São Sebastião, in 1965, afforded the park a certain feel of "postcard Rio." Nevertheless, the general economic and social decline of the Glória-Catete corridor, when combined with the physical isolation, emptied the park of civic meaning.[49] This void would become an asset for the construction of the Vargas memorial.

The Vargas memorial was originally to be sited downtown—within the civicscape built by the Vargas state. In 1984, Leonel Brizola, then governor of the state of Rio and the heir to Vargas style populism, announced a public competition to locate a memorial where the Palácio Monroe once stood, before it was torn down for the construction of the Rio subway. Aside from its primate location at the end of the Praça Floriano and the theaters of Cinelândia, there was a certain historical logic to situating the memorial on the site of the former senate chamber: on November 16, 1937—six days after the proclamation of the Estado Novo and the closure of the senate—the small street in front of the palace was named after Vargas. After Vargas's death, in 1954, a bust of the fallen president inscribed with the *Carta-Testamento* was installed in the Praça Floriano, within sight of Palácio Monroe. The bust had been a favorite destination for public remembrances of the president-dictator-populist, and Brizola's Partido Democrático Trabalhista frequently used the bust in the invocation of Vargas's legacy of *trabalhismo*.

Convened in late 1984, a blue-ribbon committee selected 3 of the 95 submissions for further review. All three finalists—whose lead members were Henock Freitas de Almeida, Cêça Guimaraens, and Albert Katayama and Edson Kawashima—worked within variants of modern architecture to propose memorials that include above-ground monuments and below-grade interpretation centers. The Almeida design, described later, was the cleanest in its above-ground monument, whereas the Guimaraens and Katayama–Kawashima teams proposed more architecturally complex structures, with large steel beams and swooping concrete, respectively. The Guimaraens project included plans to move the bust in Praça Floriano into the new memorial, with the specific intention of making the memorial into a site of ritual.[50] The selection committee, chaired by Oscar Niemeyer, awarded first prize to the Rio-born Almeida.[51] In its plasticity, the winning design was indeed quite Niemeyer-like, graced by sinuous, unadorned white planes rising out of a reflecting pool surrounded by an empty plaza. The design made virtually no reference to Vargas, but it did manage to evoke the architectural language of Brazilian modernism that got its start during the first Vargas regime. Almeida, Brizola, and others would have to wait nearly 20 years to see the memorial actually built. Early delays stemmed from the controversy surrounding the selection of Almeida's design, on both procedural and aesthetic grounds, as well as Rio's fiscal insolvency.[52]

The municipal administration of Cesar Maia, a second-term mayor whose urbanist designs have an air of Pereira Passos and Prado Junior, rescued Brizola's plan, announcing in mid-2003 that it hoped to rebuild the Palácio Monroe on its original site, which had been renamed to honor Indian statesman Mahatma Gandhi. The rebuilt senate chamber was to house a municipal memorial to Vargas. This was an ideologically curious move for Maia, whose political convictions had migrated decisively from the populist Left à la *brizolismo* to the center-right. Nevertheless, Maia found a place for the memorial into his larger public works politics. The mayor reportedly contemplated Brizola, under whom Maia had once served as finance secretary, as the memorial's director.[53] The idea of reconstructing the old senate building quickly proved unviable, especially in Maia's zeal for breakneck public works timetables, and the mayor instead opted to resurrect Henock de Almeida's 1984 design. The memorial's new locale was the Largo do Russell, Glória's forgotten urban park. Work for the project, estimated to cost 4 million reais (approximately US$1.3 million), began in December 2003.

The Associação dos Moradores e Amigos da Glória (AMA-Glória; Association of Residents and Friends of Glória), a residents' association that dated from 1981, vehemently opposed the monument's new location. Led by association president Wilson Guedes, local residents lodged a number of protests that criticized the size of the Almeida monument, its incompatibility with other monuments located in the park, the possible elimination of a children's recreation area, and the historic designations granted to nearby Parque do Flamengo. Distraught that the decision to move the monument to Glória had been taken without citizens' input, the residents also made the case that Vargas effectively had a memorial just one kilometer away, at the Museu da República. AMA-Glória launched a media, web, and direct action campaign, targeting public opinion as well as the Ministry of Culture, preservation agencies, local legislators, and, finally, the mayor. Construction temporarily stopped for review by federal, state, and local preservation agencies, which found no legal reason to halt the project (there was a perverse irony in this decision, as the legislation intended to protect historical zones from modern constructions originated during the first Vargas regime). Maia and the municipal public works agency, well-versed in locals' complains against his ambitious reurbanization projects (Rio-Cidade and Bairro-Favela being the most well-known), prevailed in their plan to pay homage to Vargas, hoping to use the memorial as an opportunity to reurbanize and beautify the region from Glória to Lapa. The residents had to take solace in winning the city's concession to lower the height of the monument from 25 to 17.5 meters.[54] Construction proceeded throughout 2004, and the memorial was dedicated by Maia on August 24, 2004, on the eve of his successful bid for reelection. Maia likely did not see (or choose to ignore) a larger banner hanging from a nearby building expressing the locals' continued indignation at the monument.

The curious aspect of the memorial's localization was how city planners, politicians, and even local residents tended to forget the *Queima das Bandeiras*, held on the Praia do Russell on November 27, 1937, even as they struggled to give meaning to the location of the memorial. The memorials' visitor literature makes passing reference to the Russell site as a scene of "civic events that counted upon the presence of Getúlio Vargas" and recognizes that Vargas frequented the nearby Hotel Glória. In their protests against the memorial, local residents made it clear that they were aware that Vargas was no stranger to their neighborhood. However, no one seems to recall the November 27, 1937, event cited by the regime as proof of its unwavering commitment to national unification and scorned by regime opponents as the embodiment of the antiliberal, antiregionalist, fascistic impulses of the Estado Novo state. Somewhere quite near Almeida's placid reflecting pool, the nation's civicscape experienced a purification-through-fire that was truly unique. However, in a city in which other notorious acts of political violence are memorialized, the Praia do Russell is a memory site to constructive aspects of the Vargas era.

The forgetting of the *Queima das Bandeiras* does not imply that the memorial is simply a memory site emptied of all disagreeable or discomforting facts. The below-ground interpretation center, curated by the well-known historian José Murilo de Carvalho, assembles documentary, photographic, and material objects that tell the basic storyline of Vargas's political trajectory from his lawyer origins in Rio Grande do Sul through his various guides as chief executive in Rio. These interpretive texts make it clear that Vargas ruled as a dictator and the Estado Novo was an authoritarian state. The exhibit's multimedia terminal, in fact, contains a 1937 film short documenting the November 27 ceremony.[55]

However, the principal axis of memorializaton is Vargas's personal and political relationship to Rio de Janeiro, capital of the Brazilian republic. The opening panel is entitled "Getúlio Vargas and Rio de Janeiro," and the general narrative thread tells a story of how Vargas lived 31 of his 45 years of public service in Rio de Janeiro. One of the panels is specifically dedicated to the theme "Getúlio Vargas and the Urban Renewal of Rio de Janeiro." It is a double-process of memory-making and homage-paying, as the memorial documents Rio as a capital city, transformed by the Vargas state as it transformed Brazil, as it makes Vargas into an honorary *carioca*. Murilo de Carvalho describes how "the Vargas governments changed Brazil as they changed the face of Rio de Janeiro," whereas Secretary of Cultures Ricardo Macieira described settling of the city's "old debt" in paying its homage to Vargas.[56] Vargas returns to the city as the city invests itself in Vargas.

When we consider how the memorial has been described by city planers as an opportunity for civic beautification and reurbanizaton of a historic neighborhood, we see reflections of the *carioca* civicscape of the 1940s, in which patriotic civism, the cult of Vargas, and urbanism were imagined to work in unison. These reflections tend to mystify the most blatantly authoritarian aspects of the Vargas state, and its impact on the daily lives of *cariocas*. They also tend to obscure the strategies in which *cariocas* took to the public arena not merely to celebrate and venerate the Vargas state, but also to protest and subvert it. Nonetheless, we see in the Memorial Getúlio Vargas elements of the civic-inspired urbanism that Agache envisioned for Rio in 1930 and the Vargas state implemented, in its own style, during the first Vargas regime. What remains to be seen is whether the memorial will have any measurable impact on the civicscape and memoryscape of contemporary Rio de Janeiro, a city whose population has quintupled since Vargas's first arrival.

Notes

Portions of this chapter have been adapted from my doctoral dissertation, *Making Brazil Modern: Political Culture and Cultural Politics Under Getúlio Vargas, 1930–1945* (Stanford University, 1995). I thank Mark Kehren for sharing his doctoral research on the history of urban planning in Rio de Janeiro, which proved to be extremely useful in framing the argument for this chapter. I thank Cleube Ana dos Santos, who served as my research assistant in 1998, gathering information on civic ceremonies. Finally, I thank Hendrik

Kraay and the members of his 2004 IFCS/UFRJ graduate seminar for reading a preliminary draft of this text.

1. The plan's formal title was *Cidade do Rio de Janeiro: extensão, remodelação, embellezamento* (Rio de Janeiro: Foyer Bresilien, 1930).
2. See Jaime Benchimol, *Pereira Passos, um Haussmann tropical: a renovação urbana da cidade do Rio de Janeiro no início do século XX* (Rio de Janeiro: Secretaria Municipal de Cultura, Turismo e Esportes, Departamento Geral de Documentação e Informação Cultural, Divisão de Editoração, 1990) and Jeffrey Needell, *A Tropical* Belle Époque: *Elite Culture in Turn-of-the-Century Rio* (Cambridge: Cambridge Univ. Press, 1987).
3. David Underwood, "Alfred Agache, French Sociology, and Modern Urbanism in France and Brazil," *Journal of the Society of Architectural Historians* (June 1991): 130–166.
4. I choose the term *civicscape* as a way to capture the overlapping categories of cityscape and civic space. A search of the term in various academic databases indicates that my use is original among historians. The term does appear to have some limited usage among construction contractors and professional city planners in the United States and the United Kingdom. I discovered one possible proprietary use of the term, in relation to city services available in the town of Saxonburg, PA. See: http://www.saxonburg.net/, accessed November 1, 2004.
5. The Agache Plan is discussed in detail by David Underwood and Norma Evenson, *Two Brazilian Capitals: Architecture and Urbanism in Rio de Janeiro and Brasília* (New Haven: Yale Univ. Press, 1973).
6. Underwood, "Alfred Agache," 158.
7. Maurício de A. Abreu, *Evolução urbana do Rio de Janeiro* (Rio de Janeiro: IPLANRIO and Jorge Zahar Ed., 1987), 86–90.
8. Underwood and Evenson, *Two Brazilian Capitals*, 46.
9. The Avenida Presidente Vargas as a disciplining "theatres of power" is developed in Evelyn Furkin Werneck Lima, *A Avenida Presidente Vargas: uma drástica cirurgia* (Rio de Janeiro: Biblioteca Carioca, 1990), esp. chapter 5.
10. *Correio da Manhã* (Rio), November 16, 1930.
11. *Correio da Manhã* (Rio), November 21, 1930.
12. Lúcia Lippi Oliveira, "As Festas que a República manda guardar," *Estudos Históricos* 4, no. 2 (1989): 172–189.
13. Here, I am obviously drawing upon title-phrases from classic works on the cultures of nationalism and nation-state formation.
14. *Correio da Manhã* (Rio), September 8, 1931.
15. *Correio da Manhã* (Rio), September 8, 1934.
16. For the origins of Capanema's interest in civic mobilization, see the discussion of the Legião de Outubro in the classic work, Simon Schwartzman, Helena Maria Bousquet Bomeny, and Vanda Maria

Ribeiro Costa, *Tempos de Capanema*, 2nd ed. (Rio de Janeiro: Paz e Terra, 2000). Capanema's public life is treated in: Ângela Maria Castro Gomes, ed., *Capanema: o ministro e seu ministério* (Rio de Janeiro: Ed. da FGV; Bragança Paulista: Universidade São Francisco, 2000).

17. The conservative ideological underpinnings of the Vargas era are profiled in Lúcia Lippi Oliveira, Mônica Pimenta Velloso, and Ângela Maria Castro Gomes, eds., *Estado Novo: ideologia e poder* (Rio de Janeiro: Jorge Zahar Ed., 1982).

18. Superintendência de Educação Musical e Artística (by Heitor Villa-Lobos?), "Relação dos Participantes da Concentração (Grande Desfile)," AGC, GC 35.09.26g I-72, FGV/CPDOC. For a more extended discussion of the history of the *Semana da Pátria*, see: Maurício Parada, "Educando corpos e criando a nação: cerimônias cívicas e práticas disciplinares no Estado Novo" (PhD diss., Programa de Pós-graduação em História Social/Instituto de Filosofia e Ciências Sociais, Universidade Federal do Rio de Janeiro, 2003).

19. Celso Castro, *A invenção do Exército Brasileiro* (Rio de Janeiro: Jorge Zahar Ed., 2002) esp. 49–67.

20. *Correio da Manhã* (Rio), September 1, 1935.

21. The history of the ministry of education headquarters is well documented in Schwartzman, Bomeny, and Costa, *Tempos de Capanema*, and Maurício Lissovsky and Paulo Sérgio Moraes de Sá, orgs., *Colunas da educação: a construção do Ministério da Educação e Saúde* (Rio de Janeiro: MinC/IPHAN/FGV-CPDOC, 1996).

22. *Correio da Manhã* (Rio), November 19–20, 1937.

23. Jerry Dávila, *"Diploma of Whiteness": Race and Social Policy in Brazil, 1917–1945* (Durham: Duke Univ. Press, 2003), chapter 4.

24. The day's schedule-of-events went as followed: Vargas arrived by open car at 10:00 a.m., to join various political, military, and ecclesiastical authorities. At 10:20 a.m., Cardinal Sebastião Leme stepped up to the *Altar da Pátria* and led a mass that included songs praising Rio's patron saint, St. Sebastian, and prayer. Heitor Villa-Lobos led a group of assembled schoolchildren in a rendition of the National Anthem. As the anthem played on, Vargas hoisted a single national flag atop a large flagpole set up alongside the *Altar da Pátria*, while 21 female students from the Instituto de Educação, dressed in white skirt-suits and carrying a flag of each Brazilian state, place the flags in a large urn that was then set afire. Balloons flying overhead released a cascade of several hundred miniature national flags onto the heads of the audience below. The speech by Campos was followed by a parade along the Praia do Russell, which included students, union delegations, and soldiers. Later in the day, a mass is held for the loyalist troops killed in the *Intentona*. *Correio da Manhã* (Rio), November 27–28, 1937.

25. See Francisco Campos, *O Estado Nacional: sua estructura, seu conteúdo ideológico*, 3rd ed. (Rio de Janeiro: José Olympio, 1941), 247–252.

26. See my *Culture Wars in Brazil: The First Vargas Regime, 1930–1945* (Durham and London: Duke Univ. Press, 2001), chapter 5.
27. Maria Luiza Tucci Carneiro, "O Estado Novo, o Dops e a ideologia da segurança nacional," in *Repensando o Estado Novo*, org. Dulce Pandolfi (Rio de Janeiro: Ed. da FGV, 1999) 330–331.
28. See Alcir Lenharo, *Sacralização da política* (Campinas: Papirus and Ed. da UNICAMP, 1986).
29. Decreto-Lei 486, June 10, 1938.
30. Doc. III-7 Handwritten draft, in Capanema's hand, 1938, AGC, GC 35.09.26g, FGV/CPDOC.
31. On the Ministry of the Treasury headquarters, see "O novo edifício do Ministério da Fazenda," *Revista do Serviço Público* III:II:3 (June 1940): 97–100; "O novo edifício do Ministério da Fazenda," *Revista do Serviço Público* VI:IV:3 (December 1943): 122–123. On the Ministério da Guerra, see: "O novo edifício do Quartel Geral do Exército," *Revista do Serviço Público* I:IV:2 (November 1938): 105–115; on the Central do Brasil headquarters, see Lima, *A Avenida Presidente Vargas*, 84–91.
32. *Monumentos da Cidade* (Rio de Janeiro: Diários de Notícias, 1946).
33. The diversity of styles and the history behind individual buildings on the Esplanada do Castelo are treated in Lauro Cavalcanti, *As preocupações do belo: arquitetura moderna brasileira nos anos 30/40* (Rio de Janeiro: Taurus Ed., 1995).
34. Adalberto Mário Ribeiro, "A Exposição de Edifícios Públicos," *Revista do Serviço Público* VII:III:3 (September 1944): 90–113.
35. See: Lucílio Briggs Brito, "Localização de serviços públicos na Capital Federal," *Revista do Serviço Público* IV:I:3 (March 1941): 56–68.
36. *Correio da Manhã* (Rio), August 2, 1944; Joaquim Bertino de Moraes Carvalho, "A centralizacão e o controle das construções de edifícios públicos," *Revista do Serviço Público* VI:IV:3 (December 1943): 27–35; "Localização—fator de organização," *Revista do Serviço Público* VII:II:3 (June 1944): 43–48; Jorge Oscar de Melo Flores, "Edifícios Públicos," *Revista do Serviço Público* VII:III:3 (September 1944): 5–19.
37. *A Manhã* (Rio), November 16, 1943.
38. Rio's overall growth patterns in 1940s and 1950s is treated in Abreu, *Evolução urbana do Rio de Janeiro*, chapter 5.
39. On this subject, I look forward to the future publication of Bert Barickman's current research on the social history of beach-going in Rio de Janeiro.
40. Lima, *A Avenida Presidente Vargas*, 33–34.
41. Parada, *Educando corpos e criando a nação*, chapter 3.
42. *Correio da Manhã* (Rio), September 2, 1945.
43. *Diário Carioca* (Rio), August 31, 1945.
44. *Correio da Manhã* (Rio), August 31, 1945.

45. *Jornal do Commercio* (Rio), September 8, 1945.
46. This point is made in Lima, *A Avenida Presidente Vargas*, chapter 6, and Abreu, *Evolução urbana do Rio de Janeiro*, 114–115.
47. These issues are discussed in Mark Edward Kehren's dissertation, under development at the Univ. of Maryland, *The Building of a City-State: The Urban Transformation of Rio de Janeiro, 1960–75*.
48. On the history of this gallery, see Daryle Williams and Barbara Weinstein, "Vargas Morto: The Death and Life of a Brazilian Statesman," in *Death, Dismemberment, and Memory: Politics of the Body in Latin America*, ed. Lyman Johnson (Albuquerque: Univ. of New Mexico Press, 2004), 273–315.
49. The neighborhood's history and decline is described in the historical section of Rio's Strategic Plan, available at: http://www.rio.rj.gov.br/planoestrategico/, accessed November 1, 2004.
50. I thank Cêça Guimaraens, of the Faculdade de Arquitetura e Urbanismo at the Universidade Federal do Rio de Janeiro, for sharing her original design and other materials related to the competition.
51. The other members of the selection committee were historian Maria Yedda Linhares, architect Ítalo Campofiorito, plastic artist Adriano de Aquino, and engineer J. C. Sussekind.
52. The controversies are detailed in *Renovando: Jornal do Sindicato dos Arquitetos do Rio de Janeiro* 4, no. 37 (January 1985): 1, 5–6.
53. *O Globo* (Rio), June 24, 2003.
54. *O Globo* provided regular coverage of the controversy surrounding the memorial's construction. See the issues for March 5, March 31, April 4, and August 5.
55. The film short, *Queima das Bandeiras*, was produced by A. Botelho Filho. The original is credited to the Cinemateca Brasileira.
56. Rio de Janeiro, Secretaria Municipal das Culturas, *Memorial Getúlio Vargas* [visitor pamphlet], 2004.

Chapter 4

"All for São Paulo, All for Brazil": Vargas, the *Paulistas*, and the Historiography of Twentieth-Century Brazil

James P. Woodard

In the ten years since the last decimal-divisible anniversary of Vargas's pajama-clad martyrdom, scholarly understanding of the mid-twentieth century—the so-called "Vargas Era"—has advanced markedly. We now know a great deal more about these decades, including about issues that historians in Vargas's day would have never thought to inquire of. New *getuliana* arrives in bookstores every year; while the 1995 publication of Vargas's long-lost diary (or, more accurately, diaries) of the years 1930–42 stands out as the most spectacular example of this kind of material, there exists a great deal more that should be of interest to scholars and nonspecialists alike. Entries in the 2001 edition of the multivolume biographical dictionary published by the Centro de Pesquisa e Documentação de História Contemporânea do Brasil now allow us to trace the lives of all but the youngest of Vargas's contemporaries on through to their respective eternal rewards. CPDOC itself, as the research institution that serves as repository of Vargas's papers, regularly elicits the benediction "*primeiro mundo*" from admiring visitors. And while we still lack a first-rate life-and-times of the man himself, we have been given an idea of what one might look like in Fernando Morais's 1994 biography of media magnate Assis Chateaubriand, arguably the second-most-important civilian figure in the pantheon of Brazilian public life during these years.[1]

For all of these signs of advance (dare one call it progress?), there remain areas in which our understanding of the period lags and the reigning historiographical wisdom bears more than a passing resemblance to *getulista* catechesis.[2] One such area is Vargas's relationship with the state of São Paulo, Brazil's economic giant.[3] In looking at this tortuous relationship, it becomes clear that an accurate rendering of what was at stake during the 1930s demands closer attention to the knotty issues of regional politics rather than to the oft-studied, but obviously ephemeral attempts at mass mobilization on the green-shirt Right and the red-flag Left. Likewise, it is time that historians ceased their solemn recitation of the old canard that *varguismo's* most consistent opponents in the abortive 1937–38 presidential campaign were reactionaries unseated by the coup d'etat of October 24, 1930. Brief explications of these two initial arguments are followed by three further arguments sure to spark debate among the faithful; these arguments span the 1930s, 1940s, and 1950s.

São Paulo was Vargas's Greatest Political Concern during the 1930s

This point is one of the few incontrovertible conclusions that one can draw from the Vargas *Diário*. Vargas spilt more ink over São Paulo than over any other unit in the Brazilian federation during this period; he was more concerned with news from São Paulo than with developments in any other state, including his home state of Rio Grande do Sul, in which his former allies gave him plenty to worry about during the years 1931–37.

Vargas was particularly concerned with events in São Paulo in 1936–37, at precisely the moment at which the existing historiography would lead one to believe that any Brazilian statesman would be more concerned by "extremism," in the form of Integralism and Communism.[4] Instead, Vargas was focused on São Paulo's preparations for the presidential elections to be held in early January 1938.[5]

An unavoidable corollary of this argument is that a serious study of the abortive 1937–38 presidential campaign is sorely needed.[6] There is not a single historical monograph, or if there is it has eluded my searching over the years, on the Partido Constitucionalista (Constitutionalist Party) of São Paulo (1934–37), the ruling party of São Paulo during Armando de Salles Oliveira's tenure as governor, or on the União Democrática Brasileira, the national coalition formed in part by the Constitutionalist Party to support Salles Oliveira's bid for the presidency.[7]

When one reflects on the relative abundance of books, articles, and essays on the Ação Integralista Brasileira, the Aliança Nacional

Libertadora, and the Communist-led revolt of 1935, this historio-graphical lacuna is even more striking. While easily explicable, even understandable, it is something that continues to profoundly affect scholarly understandings of the 1930s, as evidenced by Robert M. Levine's *The Vargas Regime*, the earliest English-language interpreta-tion of these years, and the relevant portion of Brian P. Owensby's recent *Intimate Ironies*.[8]

Scholars' tendency to gravitate toward the AIB and the ANL stems largely from a fascination with the Far Right and Left. Levine, as a young, North American liberal in the 1960s, apparently set out, full of purpose, to explore the "extremism" that he believed the two groups represented.[9] Since then, scholars more decidedly of the Left have tended to be drawn to the ANL and the Partido Comunista Brasileiro as subjects through some variety of ideological affinity, or at least some sympathy with these groups' stated ideals, and to the AIB by a corresponding enmity, while for the most part ignoring *paulista* con-stitutionalism, the UDB, and the Salles Oliveira campaign.[10]

This absence also has to do with the place from which scholars are looking at Brazil and thus approaching the Brazilian past. That the Arquivo Nacional and the Biblioteca Nacional have remained in Rio de Janeiro after most of the rest of the federal apparatus has moved on to that former speck of Goiás now known as Brasília has been won-derful for sun-and-sand-loving researchers, but it has contributed to a certain degree of myopia, among other problems of perception, on the part of historians, particularly foreign historians. Put succinctly, there is an overwhelming tendency to look at Brazil during these years from the point of view of Rio de Janeiro and, in some cases going still further, from the point of view of the various national governments housed there down to the transfer of the capital to Brasília in 1960.

This perspective is inseparable from the problem of sheer scholarly inertia. When Levine looked back at the 1930s later in his career, there was little desire evident on his part to approach his earlier work critically. If anything, there was a greater tendency on his part to iden-tify with Vargas's Rio-based government: "He had become adamant that only he could move Brazil forward to national integration, and the election campaign between Armando de Sales Oliveira and José América [*sic*] de Almeida dismayed him as a choice between a *paulista* restoration and uncontrolled radical populism."[11] Similarly, drawing in part on Levine's *The Vargas Regime*, Owensby dedicates three sen-tences to the 1936–37 campaign in a chapter dominated by discussion of the AIB and the ANL: "Two other contestants remained in the race: José Américo, Vargas's hand-picked man, and Armando de Salles

Oliveira, the candidate of the liberal, largely fraudulent constitutionalism that had been practiced by the oligarchy during the Old Republic. The campaign ran fairly smoothly through early 1937 until Vargas and his advisors began to worry that Salles might actually win. Such a victory would have allowed the political forces that had been defeated in the Revolution of 1930 to realize their dream of gaining power."[12]

As suggested by these quotes, the lack of scholarly attention to the 1936–37 conjuncture and to the forces at play in the run-up to the aborted 1938 election points to a broader problem with the existing historiography. This problem is the degree to which scholarly production has mirrored the *getulista* reading of this period in Brazilian history.

Armando de Salles Oliveira's 1937 Campaign Was No Mere Bid for a Return to the *Ancien Régime*

That the *paulista* Constitutionalists and their allies in the UDB (or at least some of their allies in the UDB) aimed at more than just a return to the status quo ante of 1930 should be apparent to anyone with even the most rudimentary knowledge of the balance of political forces in 1937. After all, the rump of the Constitutionalist Party came from the Partido Democrático of São Paulo (1926–34), which had backed the "Revolution of 1930." The Partido Republicano Paulista, on the other hand, that had lost power in 1930, backed José Américo, widely seen as Vargas's candidate (and, for that matter, the PRP supported the 1937 coup and was the party of nearly all of the senior *paulista* figures involved in the Estado Novo government from 1937 down to 1945). A look beyond São Paulo makes this fact even more plain. For example, in the city of Rio de Janeiro, the Salles Oliveira campaign received the support of Pedro Ernesto Batista, the reformist former mayor who had been jailed as a subversive by Vargas's henchmen.[13]

But one need not stop there. Indeed, looking more closely at Salles Oliveira's program and his tenure in government in São Paulo, and at contemporary portrayals of his candidacy, the fact that his candidacy did not represent a bid for a return to the politics, policies, and practices of the 1920s becomes even more clear.

As *interventor*, then governor of São Paulo, Salles Oliveira was first and foremost an administrator. The state's educational system underwent significant expansion during his tenure, at every level, from the public primary schools of the interior through the University of São Paulo, founded in 1933. As a supporter of the further diversification of the economy, Salles Oliveira promoted pluriculture and industrialization; he even made statements advocating the breakup of unproductive latifundia. Although his government did not banish clientelism, nepotism, and corruption—no government could have, at this point—it was probably relatively more honest and meritocratic than the PRP governments that had ruled the state down to 1930.[14]

During the 1937 campaign, in which his slogan was *Para que o Brasil continue* [So That Brazil May Carry On], he sounded various appeals that belie the image of him as representing the status quo ante. Campaigning in Juiz de Fora in August, for example, he addressed the charge that he was a "banal reactionary," calling the attention of the "workers of Juiz de Fora" to his government's achievements in the areas of popular education and worker protection, and promising to enforce the social provisions of the constitution of 1934.[15]

Writing in September, Oswald de Andrade, at that point a member of the PCB, noted: "The two legitimate candidates for the presidency of the Republic are of the 'left,' for both of them struggle against the threat of dictatorships, for the primary human value that is liberty." This "left," he went on state, "represents the defense of national independence. . . . Beyond which, it is the call of liberty and the path of democracy."[16] Earlier in the year a leading figure in the local branch of the PCB had even explored the possibility of an alliance with Salles Oliveira and his supporters.[17]

Furthermore, the *paulista* intellectuals who supported the Salles Oliveira campaign wholeheartedly were profoundly influenced by the issues and ideologies of the 1930s; they were not engaged in an attempt to recreate the cultural, social, and political status quo of the 1920s.[18] Much the same could be said of Salles Oliveira himself.[19] Once again, however, the dominant historiographical perspective is more than a little reminiscent of *getulista* myth.

Vargas Was as Skillful a Manipulator of Brazilian Regional Identity, Regional Symbolism, and Regional Alliances As He Was of His Friends, Foes, and—Eventually—His Followers among the Brazilian People

This assertion may at first glance appear to be more than a little off, given the abundance of instances in which Vargas and those around him appeared to trample on regional brio. These cases have reached the status of national legend, but a quick review remains useful.

First of all, there was the rather gauche manner in which his con-
federates from Rio Grande do Sul entered the city center of Rio de
Janeiro following the overthrow of Washington Luís, on horseback,
clad in ponchos, wide-brimmed hats, and red bandanas, proceeding
to tether their mounts to a downtown monument. Performances like
this one hardly seem designed to assuage disquiet among Brazilians
from other states in the federation.

Second, there was the rebellion of 1932, which is often assumed to
have been sparked by Vargas's inattention to regional demands, in
particular an inadvertent delay on his part in appointing a civilian,
paulista governor, a sin of omission rather than of commission.
Joseph L. Love, for example, writes that "Vargas's major political
error during this period was turning São Paulo over to the *tenentes*,
thereby alienating and uniting the *paulistas*."[20]

Third, there was Vargas's alienation of his fellow *gaúchos* at points
throughout the 1930s. Vargas was never so brusque that he led Rio
Grande do Sul to outright rebellion, but he did alienate many former
supporters and was apparently deeply concerned by the question of
the state's loyalty in 1936–37.[21]

Finally, and most famously, there was the Flag Day ceremony held
a little more than two weeks after the declaration of the Estado Novo.
On November 27, 1937, at an "altar of the Pátria" constructed on the
shore of Guanabara Bay, each of the state flags was burned, beginning
with the São Paulo state flag, in a ceremony presided over by Vargas
himself. The spectacle was accompanied by a mass given by Cardinal
Sebastião Leme and a speech by Justice Minister Francisco Campos in
which the author of the Estado Novo constitution praised the new
order as the achievement of Brazilian national unity.[22]

These examples might seem to indicate that Vargas had a tin ear
when it came to Brazilians' regional loyalties, which one observer
writing in 1931 noted were "probably the only common sentiment[s]"
that linked people in Brazil together across lines of class and culture,
but a closer look suggests that he had a pretty good sense of what he
was doing.[23] This was the case not only in 1937, when he was firmly
in power, backed by the military, and clearly making a statement, but
also in his earlier relationship with São Paulo.

From the very beginning, the Liberal Alliance campaign of 1929–30
was dogged by accusations that it was directed against São Paulo as a
whole, rather than Washington Luís, Júlio Prestes, and the PRP. It was
in this context, on September 24, 1929, that Republican relic Cândido
Motta took to the floor of the São Paulo Senate and declared that the
Liberal Alliance was directed "against our beloved and glorious State of

São Paulo" and was motivated by "Sãopaulofobia," resulting from "certain petty spirits' undying envy of our dazzling progress that when all is said and done should be a source of pride for all of Brazil." Motta followed this declaration with an overview of São Paulo's *história pátria*, coupled with statistical evidence emphasizing the *paulista* contribution to the national economy.[24]

Vargas, however, seems to have done his best to assuage the concerns of proud *paulistas*. Two weeks before Motta's speech, he wrote João Neves:

> The perrepista newspapers of São Paulo are very much attacking Rio Grande do Sul. . . .
>
> We should not respond in the same tone. On the contrary, we should praise São Paulo, its progress, its values, etc., accentuating that we are not campaigning against a [single] State, because São Paulo is not the P. R. P., nor the personal policies of the President of the Republic.[25]

Vargas instead argued that *perrepista* attacks on Rio Grande do Sul worked to their advantage. These attacks stirred up "the spirit of our [*gaúcho* followers]," he noted, before warning again that "if we attack São Paulo, we will awaken the *bairrista* spirit of those from there who are sympathetic to us." In another letter to Neves, he reminded him, "we must not forget that the paulistas are very touchy about the things of their land," and instructed that a *paulista* ally, preferably congressman José Adriano Marrey Júnior, should be entrusted with speaking on "the matter of coffee" in the national legislature, so as "to prevent possible exploitations."[26]

Although apparently reluctant to campaign in São Paulo, whether out of respect for the "rules" of intraelite politics, or due to the fact that he had given his word to Washington Luís that he would not, or for simple effect, Vargas did visit São Paulo in early January 1930.[27] On the stump, he delivered precisely the kind of performance suggested by these letters.

On January 4, 1930, Vargas addressed 100,000 people in the state capital's Praça do Patriarca. Attuned to the peculiarities of the *paulistas*, Vargas indulged their local pride, opening his speech with appeals to some of São Paulo's most beloved invented traditions:

> Paulistas! Glorious paulista people! Fortunate land that made possible the rise of the bandeirantes, a privileged race, which tamed the land and laid the bases of a new civilization. From here came the cry of independence, on the symbolic slope of Ipiranga, [and in] the words of the orators and the civic enthusiasm of the rallies were prepared the campaigns for abolition and the Republic.

All of the dynamic forces of the nationality, all of the great movements that agitate the spirit of the race, when they do not actually come
from São Paulo, find in its bosom a vibrant and decisive echo.[28]

Continuing in the same vein, he cited native sons Diogo Antônio
Feijó, Prudente de Moraes, Campos Salles, Francisco de Paula
Rodrigues Alves, and Antônio Prado as exemplars of the *paulista* spirit
before moving on to the Liberal Alliance program, which he summa-
rized as "the more direct involvement of the people in the choice of
their rulers" and "reforms necessary for the restoration of democratic
practices." But he never strayed too far from the subject of regionalism, denying that there were any "regional candidates" on the field
and explaining that the federal government had the duty of supporting *paulista* production—"agricultural, commercial [*sic*], and
industrial"—as the economy of São Paulo was central to the Brazilian
economy. Along the way he mixed criticism of the existing system
with the claim that his stance was "personal" rather than "political."[29]

Even under the Estado Novo, in the years following the ceremonial
burning of the state flags, appeals were made to markers of regional
identity on behalf of the national state and its leader. It was in this
context that Cassiano Ricardo published an essay entitled "O Estado
Novo e o seu sentido bandeirante" [The Estado Novo and its
Bandeirante Significance] in the inaugural issue of the official
estadonovista organ *Cultura política*.[30]

Vargas himself was not above approximations with regional tradition during the Estado Novo years. In 1938, he visited São Paulo for
the first time since 1930, touring some of the larger cities of the interior before arriving in the state capital, in which he presided over the
inauguration of the Ninth-of-July Tunnel.[31] An Estado Novo propa-
gandist, writing of the visit, argued that his reception afforded him by
the "paulista people" was "indubitable proof of the support, of the
solidarity of the bandeirante land with the Chief of the Nation."[32]
When Vargas returned to São Paulo the following year for the inauguration of a bridge over the Tietê River, he lauded São Paulo's
progress, which he linked to the *bandeirante* tradition.[33]

Vargas Actively Alienated the *Paulistas* during the Years 1931–32

If Vargas did not actually manipulate the *paulistas* into outright
rebellion in 1932, he certainly aimed to flush them out and clearly
benefited from their failed gambit. This assertion relies on the

evidence that the main issue at play leading up to the Constitutionalist Revolt—particularly in rallying the people of São Paulo against the national government headed by Vargas—was regional identity, as Barbara Weinstein's work has begun to show and as was apparent to Brazilians at the time.[34]

Hugo Borghi, who would later help to found, fund, and lead the *queremista* movement, explained that support for the 1932 revolt, including his own as a young volunteer, resulted from regional loyalty: "Now, the motivation was São Paulo. All of São Paulo, the paulista politicians came together, there was a United Front, and this United Front gave the state a complete unity. And this political unity was propagated, evidently, by all newspapers and radio stations. The population was convoked and there was political unity for the Revolution of 32." More personally, it was "paulista solidarity" and fear of being considered a coward that led Borghi himself to sign up.[35]

Jorge Duque Estrada, who fought on the side of the national government, remembered the years leading up to the revolt in a similar fashion: "The revolution was not skillful in relation to São Paulo. The paulista . . . felt like [he was in] an occupied state. The propaganda that the revolution had made against São Paulo reached all . . . and the paulista became offended."[36]

While I agree with Estrada that the regional brio of the state's population had been wounded, I part ways with his description of the provisional government's treatment of São Paulo as somehow inadvertent, resulting from a lack of skill or grace on the part of its personnel. Given Vargas's earlier sensitivity to regional *amour propre*, this conclusion falls somewhat short. Rather, I would argue that flushing out revolt, if not outright civil war, was a goal of the national government headed by Vargas during these years and that it was accomplished by the most characteristic of Vargas's tactics, prevarication.

For well over a year, Vargas successfully put off the increasingly insistent demands of his erstwhile allies in the Partido Democrático of São Paulo. It was in this context, on January 9, 1932, that he received a delegation of senior PD leaders. These leaders claimed that the population of São Paulo, in the absence of a "civilian and paulista" *interventor*, was on the verge of revolt. In effect, it was an ultimatum: either Vargas withdrew his support from the military faction that sought to maintain Colonel Manuel Rabello as *interventor* or the PD would break with the federal government. Vargas responded by counseling patience, asking PD leaders to work "to contain the just disquiet of the paulista people" and promising that "the case of São Paulo will soon be resolved."[37] At least that is how one of the delegates remembered it. Vargas himself, in his diary, noted laconically: "Paulo de Morais Barros, on behalf of the Democratic Party, came to talk to me about the substitution of interventor Rabelo. We agreed that, on his return to São Paulo, he would address General Miguel Costa and, if the latter rejected the agreement [Morais Barros] would write me letting me know and indicating some names. . . . He returns to São Paulo, tells me nothing, and the democratic directorate publishes a manifesto breaking with me."[38]

Two months later, when Vargas read the decree that elections for a national constitutional assembly were to be held, few *paulistas* believed him. As one later remembered, "that announcement sounded like a diversionary strategy" to the "politicians, intellectuals, students, workers, all already caught up in the revolutionary spirit."[39]

On March 14, Vargas received a telegram from his *interventor* in São Paulo suggesting a new state cabinet, one that would include members of the PD and the PRP. He apparently took no action, writing a few days later: "The *démarches* for the resolution of the case of São Paulo continue. I do not recognize nor negotiate with the [United Front of São Paulo] that, together with the [United Front of Rio Grande do Sul], conspired against the government."[40]

Two months later, on May 22–23, mass mobilization in the city of São Paulo forced the formation of a new state government, amid "morras" for Vargas. Four young men were killed in an attack on the headquarters of the Partido Popular Paulista (Paulista Popular Party): a planter, a clerk, a pharmacist's assistant, and a commercial employee. As the social profile of the fatalities indicates, the rioters that spearheaded this "extraordinary victory of São Paulo public opinion" came from a broad swath of the state's *classes cultas*.[41]

By late July, at which point the new state government was at war with the federal government, "[e]very city" in the state had its own unit "embracing the blue blood of São Paulo's planters and aristocracy, as well as farmers, laborers, business men, and all classes of society." This "extraordinary and unusual unity of the people" was clear in the "enthusiasm . . . evident everywhere, among bankers, newsboys, manufacturers, waiters, planters, laborers, artisans, black and white, rich and poor, and the women are fanatic."[42]

But this broad-based support should not lead one to believe that the movement was not directed from above; it was a movement supported by the people, but it was not a movement for the people.[43] As one observer explained, "São Paulo . . . has an extraordinary morale engendered by 20 months of humiliation and the realization that it is fighting for its political position, its white man's culture, and the wealth, the lives, and the homes of its citizens."[44] By this point, the defense of these values was profoundly connected to the struggle against Vargas. In the words of one chant popular among volunteers: "*São Paulo não é Changai/Desta vez o Getúlio/Cai! Cai! Cai!*"[45]

Vargas, as Populist, Was Known by His Enemies

A large part of Vargas's appeal to the ordinary men and women of São Paulo, from the *queremista* movement of 1945 onward, was the ire that he provoked among their supposed social betters, the "better class *paulistas*" who had formed the leadership of the 1932 revolt.[46] It was not Vargas's popular appeal that made the upper classes of São Paulo hate him, it was the fact that the upper classes hated him that allowed him to appeal to the people of São Paulo. Put more succinctly, Vargas was not hated by the *classes cultas* because he was a populist; he was a populist because he was hated by the *classes cultas.*

Júlio Mesquita Filho embodied this abiding hatred of Vargas on the part of the *paulista* upper class. He was publisher of *O Estado de S. Paulo*, a position he inherited from his father, from 1927 down to 1969, except for the early 1940s, when the Estado Novo government took over the newspaper, and the times (not infrequent in the 1930s) when he was in exile or jail. While his father, the well-married son of modest Portuguese immigrants, had something of the common touch and had even lent his newspaper's support to striking workers in the early twentieth century, Mesquita Filho was an aristocrat through and through.[47]

Mesquita Filho was also an unrepentant racist, as evidenced by his response to a questionnaire at an unspecified point in the post–World War II period, by which time "racial democracy" had established itself as the predominant way in which Brazilians talked about race relations:

> There is a constantly increasing desire to see Brazil, through racial intermarriage, approach more and more closely the pure white type. The aesthetic canons which have always inspired our country are those which have governed the other so-called Western nations. Even the most superficial observation will affirm that we are withdrawing further and further from African values. There is no other way to account for the desperate effort made by mulattos to appear white and, at all cost, whenever, to disguise all characteristics of their race. . . . For all these reasons, it is obvious that I would never willingly accept the marriage of any member of my family with anyone who was clearly a person of color.[48]

In matters political, Mesquita Filho was a liberal constitutionalist, one who clung to his father's nineteenth-century liberalism well into the twentieth century. His newspaper supported the PD during the late 1920s (younger brother Francisco was a party leader) and he personally, alongside some of the most celebrated of the rebellious junior military officers now known as *tenentes*, participated in plotting that aimed at overthrowing the Washington Luís government. In 1930, he backed Vargas's Liberal-Alliance campaign for the presidency and took part in the plotting that led up to the outbreak of revolt on October 3. In late October, he committed *O Estado de S. Paulo* wholeheartedly to welcoming Vargas to the city of São Paulo as rebel columns made their way to Rio de Janeiro from the south.[49]

By 1931, Mesquita Filho was conspiring against the Vargas-backed government of São Paulo state (though not yet the federal government itself); in April, he was jailed for his participation in a failed revolt. In 1932, he was among the most important leaders of the Constitutionalist Revolt. With the failure of the revolt, he was exiled to Portugal. Upon his return, he backed the Constitutionalist Party and the presidential campaign of Armando de Salles Oliveira, his brother-in-law. In the wake of the Estado Novo coup d'etat, he went into European exile once again. In 1945, he was a strong supporter of the anti-*varguista* União Democrática Nacional and of *udenista* presidential candidate Eduardo Gomes.

Years later, in the months leading up to Vargas's suicide, Mesquita Filho recalled his role in the events of 1930: "The Democrats and us, the *paulistas* of the so-called 'Estado' group, who then agreed to participate in the revolutionary movement, did so in the belief that we were carrying out a mission that had been left to us by our forbears. . . . We were certain that, once the splendid movement was victorious, we would see that for which all of the great ones of São Paulo had struggled, the Andradas, Feijó and Prudente, the great benefits of democracy, extend throughout all of Brazil. We were wrong when we assumed that the Andradas, Feijó, Prudente and Brazil were one and the same, when, in reality, [Brazil] was much closer to Getúlio Vargas and his kind."[50]

As this quote from Mesquita Filho indicates, the visceral reaction to Vargas on the part of the most snobbish, most socially and culturally conservative elements of the *paulista* upper class set in quite early in the 1930s, mixed with a deep sense of resentment and betrayal, and continued to manifest itself over the course of the following decades. Indeed, it outlived the former dictator himself.

In 1932 and after, anti-Vargas sentiment came to find its most radical expression in São Paulo's small separatist movement, made up of advocates of an independent *paulista* republic. One observer, not himself a separatist, later remembered "that all of that separatist fervor was the natural effect of a romantic tremor," adding that "paulista separatism was never a *political* movement, in the true sense of the word. It was no more than a reaction of rage against Getúlio."[51]

Under the Estado Novo, in the pages of the antiregime *Brasil*, the image of the state flag burned in November 1937 was paired with text lauding the 1932 struggle to bring "order and liberty to the entire country" and decrying Vargas as a "third-class dictator." Though its first issue, which also "asserted that treason was [Vargas's] only principle, and administrative, political and intellectual dishonesty his only program," bore the dateline of "Terra-de-Ninguem, January 3, 1938," it was published clandestinely in São Paulo by Paulo Duarte in collaboration with Júlio Mesquita Filho.[52]

When Vargas visited São Paulo in mid-1938, for the first time since 1930, the most prestigious student group at the traditional São Paulo Law School (an institution that was itself closely identified with the established upper classes of São Paulo) declared him persona non grata. Law students also set off stink bombs to disrupt a banquet held to honor Vargas.[53]

It was likewise students of the São Paulo Law School who on May 23, 1939, the seventh anniversary of the 1932 uprising, put out the first issue of the anti-Vargas publication *Folha Dobrada*. Among the *Folha's* feature articles was one authored by the son of *paulista* exile Paulo Nogueira Filho; this article referred to the state flag as "a symbol of liberty and autonomy" that "continues, proud and lofty, dominating the spirit of millions of *bandeirantes*!"[54]

Paulista law students also commemorated the seventh anniversary of the May 1932 uprising with speeches condemning "the wrongs and humiliations that irresponsible men have thrust upon this much-sacrificed land." On the evening of May 23, they gathered portraits of Vargas, required by law to be on display in commercial establishments, and set them aflame in two bonfires.[55]

In September 1941, word that Vargas would be given an honorary degree by the University of São Paulo sparked outrage among politicized *paulista* students. In John Dulles' words: "Anti-Vargas activists at the law school screamed to protest giving Vargas the same honor that the university had in the past bestowed on such figures as Francisco Morato, Júlio de Mesquita Filho, and Armando de Sales Oliveira. Protests also arose at the Grêmio Politécnico, alma mater of Armando de Sales Oliveira." Speeches were again the order of the day, answered with cries of "down with Vargas," and law students draped the Law School's monuments to José Bonifácio and the fallen of 1932 in black crepe.[56]

Dutra's election in 1945, and the degree to which it reflected Vargas's personal popularity, was cause for further bitterness on the part of likeminded *paulistas*, who had backed Eduardo Gomes. As one wrote years later, "the first elections, characterized by demagoguery . . . proved disappointing. The people . . . revealed that they were not prepared to use the right to vote. . . . It was as difficult for them to sign the sheets of the electoral justice system and place the ballots in the envelope as to distinguish authentic statesmen from ordinary demagogues."[57]

During the 1950 presidential race, *O Estado de S. Paulo's* writers were ordered not to mention Vargas by name; rather, he was to be referred to as "the former dictator." When he visited the city of São Paulo on campaign, the University of São Paulo was decked out as if in mourning: "the façade . . . was draped with black crepe and the University flag flown at half mast."[58]

The university, founded in part by Júlio Mesquita Filho in the mid-1930s, was one of the key institutions of the *paulistano* upper class, the self-described aristocracy of "*paulistas* of 400 years" (*paulistas de quatrocentos anos*) or "four-hundred-ers" (*quatrocentões*), in that most invented of regional traditions. In decking the university's façade with black cloth, anti-Vargas *paulistas* were echoing the earlier symbolic protest of the law students.

When Jânio Quadros won the Brazilian presidency in 1960, anti-Vargas *paulistas* chose to interpret it as a victory over Vargas, who had been dead for six years. *O Estado de S. Paulo* proclaimed that "the victory of Democracy has turned into a defeat of unprecedented proportions for the remains of Getulismo. . . . Brazilian labor has ended up by learning its lesson. The people's late but real discovery of the truth is the best reward we could have received."[59]

As late as the early 1990s, the events of 1930 were remembered in certain well-bred *paulista* corners as the "short, little Getúlio Vargas's betrayal." Such was the case, at least, for Heloisa Alves de Lima e Motta, whose three surnames indicate her descent from some of São Paulo's leading "traditional families," though she was not above reminding those who might not be up on their *paulista* genealogy.[60]

In some corners (though not among former supporters of the Liberal Alliance like Mesquita Filho) anti-*varguismo* could come to merge with an idealized vision of the pre-1930 period, as in one *paulista's* assertion in 1941 that before Vargas "we had a democracy based upon an agricultural economy led by a cultured elite. . . . It was reflected in the law schools of São Paulo and Pernambuco and it was inspired first by the British parliamentary system[,] then, after the end of the monarchy, by the American Constitution."[61]

As many of these examples make clear, anti-*varguismo*, regionalist identity, and various other forms of chauvinism (ranging from aristocratic snobbery to out-and-out racism) became entangled in the thinking of São Paulo's *classes cultas*, in the ways they understood, wrote of, and talked about history, society, and politics.[62] While these very ideas were being created and rehearsed, however, São Paulo was undergoing tremendous changes as it was increasingly peopled by men and women who had little stake in the *paulista* reading of Brazilian history and no place in *quatrocentão* institutions like the São Paulo Law School—many of whom suffered racial discrimination at the hands of São Paulo's self-proclaimed "élite" and the junior members of the *paulista classes cultas* who formed the native middle class.[63] It is impossible that ordinary folks living in São Paulo—working women and working men who had been born in São Paulo and considered themselves to be *paulistas* of a sort, immigrants and those of sufficiently recent immigrant stock to still identify with the old country, migrants from the interior of Brazil, and the interior of northeastern Brazil in particular—did not sense this condescension and did not resent it.

An oral history interview with Octávio Brandão, a pharmacist's son from a town in the interior of Alagoas, provides a humorous example of a non-*paulista* bristling at *paulista* chauvinism: "I met a paulista at the Livraria José Olímpio. And the paulista begins to sing the praises of São Paulo. That São Paulo is a locomotive, twenty empty boxcars. . . . São Paulo produces this and that. Brazil doesn't produce anything, I don't know what else, and a bunch of [other] things." When Brandão replied that São Paulo had created Brazilian misery through the valorization of coffee to benefit its planters, the paulista became agitated: " 'O senhor sabe com quem está falando? . . . O senhor está falando com um paulista de quatrocentos anos." Brandão wryly replied that he was a "Caeté de dez mil anos."[64]

Brandão's response was of course nothing short of perfect, but we should not let his irrepressible comic sense to stop us from drawing further conclusions regarding *paulista* identity in the context of *varguismo*. It is my sense—my hunch—that the very fact that São Paulo's *classes cultas* found Vargas to be so horrid was a source of his appeal to ordinary folks.

Vargas's victory in 1950 led at least one member of the *paulista* intelligentsia to begin to wade through his *Nova política do Brasil*.

Oswald de Andrade wrote at the time: "I was surprised the other day by a friend going through the bulky collection of *Nova política do Brasil*, by Sr. Getúlio Vargas. And he said to me: 'I never believed in this man. I was allergic to him. But [now] I see him return to the Catete on the plebiscitarian arms of the Brazilian people. I'm going to read this guy!' "[65] But Vargas's popular appeal to the men and women of São Paulo—his "populism"—was not to be found in books or even in his speeches; it had to do, at least in part, with the reaction that he elicited from their supposed social betters. These were years in São Paulo when to be *culto* was to be "non-populist" in style, to be anti-Vargas and (though space precludes a separate discussion of this important additional point) to be anti-Adhemar de Barros.[66]

Though one cannot measure "style," impressionistic evidence indicates that the correlation of racism, regionalism, snobbery, and anti-*varguismo* among upper-class *paulistas* contributed to Vargas's ability to reinvent himself as a "populist." Carlos Lacerda, writing of his comrades in the UDN, complained that "the group from São Paulo . . . had to our eyes a very reactionary coloring." They were, he continued: "folks [who were] very reactionary. . . . [Their] position . . . was very conservative, very regional. They struggled against Getúlio less for the harmful effects that he could have nationally, than for the fact that to the paulistas the Revolution of 1930 was remembered as an attempt to destroy the influence of São Paulo in the Federation."[67] Ernani Silva Bruno would have agreed, writing years later: "The old 'paladins of public liberties,' who before 1930 had not won elections because they were fraudulent, after 1930 continued not to win them because, in the eyes of the immense majority of the people, they were representatives of an elite that—although possibly honest—could not look kindly on the rising tide of popular demands."[68] In a similar vein, Carlos Castilho Cabral noted the "aversion of the working masses for the '*cartolas*,' the *grã-finos* of the UDN."[69]

Some might see the resulting political alignments as nothing short of tragic. Those *paulistas* who were most committed, at least theoretically, to the rule of law, civil liberties, and liberal democracy, were precisely those least possessed of the qualities that would allow them to appeal to the people. At worst, they were racists, regional chauvinists, and snobs, as many of the liberal constitutionalists in the UDN were.[70] At best, they were clubby and lacked "*garra*," to quote from Boris Fausto's description of the leadership of the São Paulo chapter of the Brazilian Socialist Party, which generally sided with the UDN against Vargas.[71]

Discriminated against, snubbed, and otherwise slighted, ordinary folks in São Paulo were instead drawn to figures like Vargas, who infamously declared that, in Brazil, "quem não tem um pé na cozinha, tem no mato," and who were not above clasping hands with them or slapping them on the back. After all, Vargas had to have something going for him if he so enraged the *quatrocentões*.[72]

Notes

1. Getúlio Vargas, *Diário*, 2 vols. (Rio de Janeiro: Ed. da FGV/São Paulo: Ed. Siciliano, 1995); *DHBB*, ed. Alzira Alves de Abreu, Israel Beloch, Fernando Lattman-Weltman, and Sérgio Tadeu de Niemeyer Lamarão, 2nd ed., 5 vols. (Rio de Janeiro: Ed. da FGV, 2001 [1984]); Fernando Morais, *Chatô: o rei do Brasil* (São Paulo: Companhia das Letras, 1994). The benediction translates as "first world."

2. For a small, English-language sample of the latter, see José Barbosa, "Catechism of a Getulista," trans. Michael Conniff, in *Problems in Modern Latin American History: A Reader*, ed. John Charles Chasteen and Joseph S. Tulchin (Wilmington, DE: Scholarly Resources, 1994), 120–122.

3. Another such area, one that goes undiscussed below, is the framing of the years 1930–45 as "the Vargas regime" or "the first Vargas regime." The idea that the various Brazilian governments that existed between the October 24, 1930 coup d'etat that cleared the way for Vargas to be made a "revolutionary" provisional president and the October 29, 1945 coup that overthrew the philofascist father figure as he seemed to be completing his reinvention as a man of the people constituted a single "regime"—a single governmental and administrative system—is no less risible for being so widely accepted.

4. See esp. Robert M. Levine, *The Vargas Regime: The Critical Years, 1934–1938* (New York: Columbia Univ. Press, 1970). Cf. Vargas, *Diário*, 2:67: "The struggle over the presidential succession exploits and aggravates dangers that don't have the significance that [some] would like to attribute to them. Thus, the communist [and] integralist phenomena and the question of Rio Grande [do Sul] awaken the champions of democracy, who come forward alarmed as if they had discovered something new."

5. Vargas, *Diário*, 1:549, 552–553, 556–557, 559–562, 564, 568–573, 2:13–19, 21–25, 27, 31–33, 35–38, 43, 46–48, 50, 65, 67, 69, 74–77. Even in mid-to-late 1935, amid serious politicking involving the states of Rio Grande do Sul and Rio de Janeiro, Vargas demonstrated a marked interest in events in São Paulo; one gathers that this interest was motivated in part by the presumed presidential succession. See esp. ibid., 1:404, 422, 432, 442.

6. Given his successful demolition of so many enduring myths and mis-conceptions regarding the Constitutionalist Revolt of 1932, Jeziel De Paula would be an ideal candidate for the job. See his *1932: Imagens construindo a história* (Campinas: Ed. da Universidade Estadual de Campinas, 1998).

7. The only book-length treatment of the political history of São Paulo in these years is journalist Plínio de Abreu Ramos's *Os partidos paulistas e o Estado Novo*, which—its title notwithstanding—is an introductory survey of the period between the 1870 founding of the Republican Party and the proclamation of the Estado Novo in 1937. Ilka Stern Cohen's unpublished doctoral thesis, entitled " 'Para onde vamos?': alternativas políticas no Brasil, 1930–1937," is an intellectual history that does deal at some length with aspects of Salles Oliveira's program and with support for his candidacy in certain circles of the *paulista* intelligentsia. Plínio de Abreu Ramos, *Os partidos paulistas e o Estado Novo* (Petrópolis: Ed. Vozes, 1979); Ilka Stern Cohen, " 'Para onde vamos?': alternativas políticas no Brasil, 1930–1937" (Tese de doutorado, Universidade de São Paulo, 1997), see esp. chapters 3–4.

8. Levine, *The Vargas Regime*; Brian P. Owensby, *Intimate Ironies: Modernity and the Making of Middle-Class Lives in Brazil* (Stanford: Stanford Univ. Press, 1999), 135–158.

9. Levine, *The Vargas Regime*. In August 1965, according to an acquaintance, Levine was "doing research . . . on the extremist movements of the 1930's. He has not yet decided how to orient the subject, whether to deal with it from the point of view of the Alianca Libertadora Nacional and the Açao Integralista themselves, from their relationship with the Vargas government, or in terms of being the end of one epoch and the beginning of another in Brazilian history." Robert J. Alexander, notes on a conversation with Robert Levine, Rio de Janeiro, August 5, 1965, Robert J. Alexander Papers (microfilmed collection; original at Rutgers University), reel 3, frame 259 [original spelling].

10. For example: Hélgio Trindade, *Integralismo: o fascismo brasileiro na década de 30*, 2nd ed. (São Paulo: Difel, 1979 [1974]); idem, "Integralismo: teoria e práxis política nos anos 30," in *História geral da civilização brasileira*, ed. Sérgio Buarque de Holanda, tome 3, *O Brasil republicano*, ed. Boris Fausto, vol. 3, *Sociedade e política, 1930–1964* (São Paulo: Difel, 1981), 297–335; Leôncio Martins Rodrigues, "O PCB: os dirigentes e a organização," in ibid., 361–443; Paulo Sérgio Pinheiro, *Estratégias da ilusão: a revolução mundial e o Brasil, 1922–1935* (São Paulo: Companhia das Letras, 1991); Marcos Chor Maio and Roney Cytrynowicz, "Ação Integralista Brasileira: um movimento fascista no Brasil, 1932–1938," in *O Brasil republicano*, ed. Jorge Ferreira and Lucília de Almeida Neves Delgado, 4 vols., vol. 2, *O tempo do nacional-estatismo: do*

início da década de 1930 ao apogeu do Estado Novo (Rio de Janeiro: Ed. Civilização Brasileira, 2003), 39–61; Marly de Almeida G. Vianna, "O PCB, a ANL e as insurreições de novembro de 1935," in ibid., 63; Vitor Manoel Marques da Fonseca, "A ANL na legalidade" (Tese de mestrado, Universidade Federal Fluminense, 1986); Wilson Montagna, "A Aliança Nacional Libertadora e o Partido Comunista Brasileiro, 1934–1935" (Tese de mestrado, Pontifícia Universidade Católica de São Paulo, 1988). See also the bibliographies of the essays by Marcos Chor Maio and Roney Cytrynowicz on the AIB and Marly de Almeida Vianna on the ANL and the PCB (in Ferreira and Delgado, eds., *O Brasil republicano*, 2:59–61 and 2:104–105, respectively).

11. The quote is from *Father of the Poor?: Vargas and his Era* (Cambridge: Cambridge Univ. Press, 1998), 51. See also his "Perspectives on the Mid-Vargas Years, 1934–1937," *Journal of Interamerican Studies and World Affairs* 22, no. 1 (February 1980): 57–80.

12. Owensby, *Intimate Ironies*, 150. The assertions made in the first sentence, after the colon, are demonstrably false, as is the entire third sentence, unless one assumes that Salles Oliveira intended to hand over power to his foes in the Paulista Republican Party.

13. Michael L. Conniff, *Urban Politics in Brazil: The Rise of Populism, 1925–1945* (Pittsburgh: Univ. of Pittsburgh Press, 1981), 157; Paulo Brandi, "Pedro Ernesto," in *DHBB*, 2:2011.

14. Vilma Keller, "Armando Salles," in *DHBB*, 5:5175–5180; Antônio Carlos Pacheco e Silva, *Armando de Salles Oliveira* (São Paulo: Martins, 1966); Joaquim A. Sampaio Vidal, *Synthese do pensamento político de Armando de Salles Oliveira* (São Paulo: n.p., 1937). Salles Oliveira's technocratic, modernization-driven administration was also probably more elitist than earlier PRP governments.

15. Armando Salles Oliveira, *Para que o Brasil continue* (Rio de Janeiro: José Olympio, 1937), 37–58 (quotes on 38).

16. Oswald de Andrade, "O divisor das águas modernistas," originally published in the rotogravure supplement of *O Estado de S. Paulo*, [date missing] September 1937, 4. It is reprinted in the posthumously published collection *Estética e política*, ed. Maria Eugenia Boaventura (São Paulo: Ed. Globo, 1992), 53–56 (quotes on 55, 56).

17. Paulo Duarte, *Memórias*, 10 vols. (São Paulo: Hucitec, 1974–1980 [vol. 10 published in Rio de Janeiro by Paz e Terra]), 5:96–105, 110–116, 146–155.

18. Cohen, " 'Para onde vamos?,' " chapters 3–4; Dalton Sala, "Mário de Andrade e o anteprojeto do Serviço do Patrimônio Artístico Nacional," *Revista do Instituto de Estudos Brasileiros* 31 (1990): 19–26.

19. Pacheco e Silva, *Armando de Salles Oliveira*; Cândido Motta Filho, *Dias lidos e vividos* (Rio de Janeiro: José Olympio, 1977), 120–121, 124–125.

20. Joseph L. Love, *Rio Grande do Sul and Brazilian Regionalism, 1882–1930* (Stanford: Stanford Univ. Press, 1971), 252.

21. For his perspective, see the *Diário* entries through 1937.
22. John W. F. Dulles, *Vargas of Brazil: A Political Biography* (Austin: Univ. of Texas Press, 1967), 178; idem, *The São Paulo Law School and the Anti-Vargas Resistance, 1938–1945* (Austin: Univ. of Texas Press, 1986), 41; Duarte, *Memórias*, 6:90; Vargas, *Diário*, 2:87; Daryle Williams, *Culture Wars in Brazil: The First Vargas Regime, 1930–1945* (Durham and London: Duke Univ. Press, 2001), 9–10, 177.
23. The quote is from Vivaldo Coaracy, *O caso de São Paulo* (São Paulo: Irmãos Ferraz, 1931), 12.
24. Cândido Motta's speech is discussed in Affonso Henriques, *Vargas, o maquiavélico* (São Paulo: Palácio do Livro, 1961), 171–172 (quotes on 172).
25. [Getúlio Vargas] to João Neves, Porto Alegre, September 9, 1929, AGV, GV 1929.09.09/6, FGV/CPDOC.
26. [Vargas] to João Neves, Porto Alegre, September 9, 1929; [Getúlio Vargas] to João Neves, Porto Alegre, November 20, 1929, AGV, GV 1929.11.20/2, FGV/CPDOC.
27. Aureliano Leite, *Páginas de uma longa vida* (São Paulo: Martins, 1966), 48–49; Paulo Nogueira Filho, *Ideais e lutas de um burguês progressista: o Partido Democrático e a revolução de 1930*, 2 vols. (São Paulo: Anhembi, 1958), 2:401–404; Percival de Oliveira, "Outras causas," *Diário de S. Paulo*, January 14, 1930, reprinted in the same author's *O ponto de vista do P. R. P.* (São Paulo: São Paulo Ed., 1930), 231–232; Hélio Silva, *1930: a revolução traída* (Rio de Janeiro: Ed. Civilização Brasileira, 1966), 36–37; Delegacia de Ordem Social e Política (hereafter DOPS-SP) transcript of telephone conversation between Paulo Nogueira Filho (São Paulo) and Francisco Morato (Rio de Janeiro), 15 [December 1929], Fundo Paulo Duarte (hereafter FPD), pasta DET.61, Universidade Estadual de Campinas/Centro de Documentação Cultural Alexandre Eulalio (hereafter CEDAE); DOPS–SP transcript of telephone conversation between Paulo Nogueira Filho (São Paulo) and Paulo de Moraes Barros (Rio de Janeiro), 30 [December 1929], FPD, pasta DET.61, CEDAE; DOPS–SP transcript of telephone conversation between José Carlos de Macedo Soares (São Paulo) and José Eduardo de Macedo Soares (Rio de Janeiro), January 1 [1930], FPD, pasta DET.61, CEDAE.
28. "Como foram recebidos os candidatos liberaes," *O Estado de S. Paulo*, January 5, 1930, 6. In another speech, apparently never delivered, he was to have expressed his delight at being "in the great metropolis of coffee, in the formidable producing center of the country that is, at the same time, the regulator and the exponent of the national economy" and to have declared "[c]offee represents two thirds of the total value of our exports. It is, thus, the axis of the greatness and prosperity of Brazil. . . . To defend it, to support it, is to support and defend Brazil itself." "Discurso proferido por Getúlio Vargas . . . ," in *A revolução de*

30: textos e documentos, ed. Manoel Luiz Lima Salgado Guimarães, Paulo Sérgio de Sá, Silvia Ninita de Moura Estevão, and Vera Lúcia Ascenção, 2 vols. (Brasília: Ed. da Universidade de Brasília, 1982), 2:262–263 (quotes on 262).

29. "Como foram recebidos os candidatos liberaes," *O Estado de S. Paulo*, January 5, 1930, 6. It is needless to add that this address was not among the speeches selected for publication in his *Nova política do Brasil*, the official, multivolume, Estado-Novo-era collection of his pronouncements from the Liberal Alliance onward.

30. Cassiano Ricardo, "O Estado Novo e o seu sentido bandeirante," *Cultura política* 1, no. 1 (March 1941), 110–132.

31. Vargas, *Diário*, 2:147; Motta Filho, *Dias lidos e vividos*, 145.

32. Editor's comments in Getúlio Vargas, *Ideário político de Getulio Vargas*, ed. Raul Guastini (São Paulo: n.p., 1943), 100.

33. Vargas, *Ideário político de Getulio Vargas*, 121–123. Other speeches and images included in this volume manipulate regional traditions from elsewhere in Brazil in ways apparently designed to heighten support for Vargas's rule (see esp. 17, 52–53, 149–168).

34. Barbara Weinstein, "Racializing Regional Difference: São Paulo vs. Brazil, 1932," in *Race and Nation in Modern Latin America*, ed. Nancy Appelbaum, Anne Macpherson, and Karin Rosemblatt (Chapel Hill: Univ. of North Carolina Press, 2003), 237–262.

35. Hugo Borghi, interviewed by Lucia Hippolito and Israel Beloch, Rio de Janeiro, June 1977, Programa de História Oral (hereafter PHO), FGV/CPDOC.

36. Jorge Duque Estrada, interviewed by Israel Beloch, Rio de Janeiro, June 21, 1977, PHO, FGV/CPDOC.

37. Paulo Nogueira Filho, *Ideais e lutas de um burguês progressista: a guerra cívica de 1932*, 4 vols. in 6 (Rio de Janeiro: José Olympio, 1965–1981), 1:331.

38. Vargas, *Diário*, 1:88. In any case, the manifesto had already been drafted when Morais Barros and his comrades met with Vargas. Nogueira Filho, *A guerra cívica*, 1:332.

39. Goffredo Telles Junior, *A folha dobrada: lembranças de um estudante* (Rio de Janeiro: Ed. Nova Fronteira, 1999), 61.

40. Vargas, *Diário*, 1:104.

41. De Paula, *1932*, 88–95; telegram, C. R. Cameron to the Secretary of State, São Paulo, May 24, 1932, Record Group 59 (hereafter RG59), 832.00/791, NARA; Leite, *Páginas de uma longa vida*, 66–67; quote from C. R. Cameron to Edwin V. Morgan, São Paulo, May 25, 1932, RG59, 832.00/799, NARA. A gently sarcastic account of an encounter with one of the *exaltados* of May 23, who rails "against the slavery of S. Paulo" and shouts "Long live the 13th of May of the august race of the Bandeirantes," can be found in Belmonte [pseud., Benedicto Carneiro Bastos Barreto], *Assim falou Juca Pato: aspectos divertidos de*

uma confusão dramática (São Paulo: Ed. Nacional, 1933), 144–147. The term *classes cultas*, which indicated the upper classes and respectable middling folks, translates literally as "cultured classes."

42. C. R. Cameron to Edwin V. Morgan, São Paulo, July 30, 1932, RG59, 832.00/810, NARA. See also Leite, *Páginas de uma longa vida*, 68.

43. Cf. Aureliano Leite, *Martírio e glória de São Paulo* (São Paulo: n.p., 1934), in which the author, who was a leader of the São Paulo opposition in 1932 and was forced into exile following the revolt, explains that his party's program represented "the beautiful American trichotomy of government of the people, by the people and for the people" (19).

44. C. R. Cameron to Walter C. Thurston, São Paulo, August 9, 1932, RG59, 832.00/11, NARA.

45. "São Paulo is not Shanghai/This time Getúlio/Falls! Falls! Falls!" Quoted in Leite, *Páginas de uma longa vida*, 79.

46. The reference to "better class paulistas" is from C. R. Cameron to Edwin V. Morgan, São Paulo, July 30, 1932.

47. Marieta de Morais Ferreira, "Júlio de Mesquita Filho," in *DHBB*, 4:3789–3791; Maria Helena Capelato, *Os arautos do liberalismo: imprensa paulista, 1920–1945* (São Paulo: Ed. Brasiliense, 1989); Maria Helena Capelato and Maria Lígia Prado, *O bravo matutino. Imprensa e ideologia: o jornal "O Estado de S. Paulo"* (São Paulo: Ed. Alfa-Omega, 1980); Barbara Weinstein, "Impressões das elites sobre os movimentos da classe operária: a cobertura da greve em *O Estado de S. Paulo*, 1902–1907," in ibid., 135–176; Antônio Figueiredo, *Memórias de um jornalista* (São Paulo: Ed. UNITAS, 1933), 219–233; Paulo Duarte, *Júlio Mesquita* (São Paulo: Ed. HUCITEC, 1977); Maurício Goulart, "Julio Mesquita," in Aureliano Leite, Affonso E. de Taunay, Fernando Góes, Victor de Azevedo, Rubens do Amaral, Cândido Motta Filho, et al., *Homens de São Paulo* (São Paulo: Martins, 1955), 304–365; Roberto de Abreu Sodré, *No espelho do tempo: meio século de política* (São Paulo: Ed. Best Seller, 1995), 28–29. *O Estado de S. Paulo* was referred to as "the most trusted organ of paulista public opinion" in Leven Vampré, *São Paulo, terra conquistada* (São Paulo: Sociedade Impressora Paulista, 1932), 74.

48. Quoted in Gilberto Freyre, *Order and Progress: Brazil from Monarchy to Republic*, trans. Rod W. Horton (New York: Knopf, 1970 [1959]), 207–208.

49. "S. Paulo recebe triumphalmente o presidente Getulio Vargas," *O Estado de S. Paulo*, October 30, 1930, 1–2.

50. Mesquita Filho, "Os ideais democráticos na revolução brasileira," in his *Política e cultura* (São Paulo: Martins, 1969), 118–119. This chapter was originally published in serial form in *O Estado de S. Paulo* in 1954, amid commemorations of the four hundredth anniversary of the founding of São Paulo.

51. Telles Junior, *A folha dobrada*, 101 (original emphasis).

52. Dulles, *The São Paulo Law School*, 41.

53. Ibid., 45–46. Vargas, true to form, described his reception as "difficult to describe, it not being really necessary as it concerns a subject broadly divulged by the press." The newspapers of the day, subject to *estadonovista* censorship, did not report on the disruption of the reception. Vargas, *Diário*, 2:147; Dulles, *The São Paulo Law School*, 46.

54. Dulles, *The São Paulo Law School*, 53.

55. Ibid., 54–55.

56. Sodré, *No espelho do tempo*, 37–39; Dulles, *The São Paulo Law School*, 85–88 (quotes on 86, 87). Dulles's spelling of Armando de Salles Oliveira's name reflects the orthographic reforms of the mid-twentieth century. I have maintained the earlier spelling of the proper name Salles, as Armando himself did.

57. José Bonifácio Coutinho Nogueira, quoted in Dulles, *The São Paulo Law School*, 192.

58. Dulles, *Vargas of Brazil*, 295. In his memoir, published in 1966, Aureliano Leite usually refers to Vargas as "the Dictator" or the "ex-dictator" as well. See his *Páginas de uma longa vida*, passim.

59. *O Estado de S. Paulo*, October 6, 1960, quoted in Dulles, *The São Paulo Law School*, 195.

60. Heloisa Alves de Lima e Motta, *Uma menina paulista* (São Paulo: Ed. Totalidade, 1992). The quote regarding Vargas is on 77.

61. Quoted in Harold Callendar, "Brazilians' Unity a Defense Need," *New York Times*, July 13, 1941, 12. As early as 1924, the law schools in São Paulo and Recife were referred to as "two great foci of regionalism." See Jorge Americano, *A lição dos factos: revolta de 5 de julho de 1924* (São Paulo: Saraiva, 1924), 34.

62. This kind of regionalist *saudades* for a largely imaginary vision of the pre-1930 period, or even of the early 1950s, often combined with an attitude of at the very least condescension toward subsequent arrivals, is not entirely something of the past, though it is a tradition whose most unabashed proponents are of advanced age. It was something that I could pick up on as a researcher at certain institutions in São Paulo and something that—it was clear to me—elicited a corresponding resentment on the part of the descendants of immigrants and internal migrants.

63. On racial prejudice in São Paulo during these years, see, for example, Carl N. Degler, *Neither Black Nor White: Slavery and Race Relations in Brazil and the United States* (New York: Macmillan, 1971), 99–100, 127–137, 145–146, 149–152, 155–157.

64. The *paulista*: "Do you know who you're speaking to? You're speaking with a paulista of four hundred years" (i.e., a proud *paulista* of the oldest stock—see also above). Brandão's reply indicated that he was a Caeté Indian of ten *thousand* years. Octávio Brandão, interview by Maria Cecília Velasco e Cruz and Renato Lessa, Rio de Janeiro,

February 10, 1977, PHO, CPDOC. In their mania for standardization, CPDOC has indexed this interview under the more modern spelling of Brandão's first name (Otávio), which he never himself adopted.

65. Oswald de Andrade, "Velhos e novos livros," reprinted in *Estética e política*, 215–230 (quote on 216–217). I am inferring that Andrade's friend was a fellow member of the *paulista* intelligentsia.

66. As should be clear from my discussion thus far, I understand Vargas's "populism"—and, as importantly, his opponents' "non-populism"—to have been a matter of "style," in a manner similar to that outlined by Alan Knight in a recent article in the *Journal of Latin American Studies*. Those scholars "who believe that . . . Latin American history is best avoided by foreigners working from foreign sources," will be at least partially relieved to learn that Afonso Arinos de Melo Franco, a Brazilian, conceptualized "populism" similarly as a "state of mind." Alan Knight, "Populism and Neo-populism in Latin America, especially Mexico," *Journal of Latin American Studies* 30, no. 2 (May 1998): 223–248; the quote regarding the practice of Latin American history is from idem, *The Mexican Revolution*, 2 vols. (Cambridge: Cambridge Univ. Press, 1986), 1:x; Afonso Arinos is quoted in Maria Victoria de Mesquita Benevides, *A UDN e o udenismo: ambigüidades do liberalismo brasileiro, 1945–1965* (Rio de Janeiro: Paz e Terra, 1981), 261, 271.

67. Quoted in Maria Lígia Coelho Prado, *A democracia ilustrada: o Partido Democrático de São Paulo, 1926–1934* (São Paulo: Ed. Ática, 1986), 197.

68. Ernani Silva Bruno, *Almanaque de memórias: reminiscências, depoimentos, reflexões* (São Paulo: HUCITEC, 1986), 114.

69. ". . . the '*top-hats*,' the *elegant grandees* of the UDN." Carlos Castilho Cabral, *Tempos de Jânio e outros tempos* (Rio de Janeiro: Ed. Civilização Brasileira, 1962), 8 (my emphasis).

70. See above. Goffredo Telles Junior described the goals of the *paulista* liberal constitutionalists who had supported the "Revolution of 1930" (and founded the UDN) as "the implantation of a liberal democracy, in which the authentic results of universal suffrage would be respected, and in which such results would inevitably be favorable to them." He continued: "What distinguished them from those that they called *carcomidos* [their 'worm-eaten' opponents in the PRP] was, more than anything else, a certain state of mind, a certain mentality, a set of ideals or convictions and an air of superiority, acquired in urban life, a disdain for the dirt-farmers of the interior [*roceiros dos campos do interior*], an amusing arrogance of those who are convinced that they are the sole owners of the truth." Despite all of these (negative) characteristics, Telles Junior asserted that their "idealism" was undeniably deeply held. Telles Junior, *A folha dobrada*, 98.

71. Interview with Boris Fausto, March 2000, in José Geraldo Vinci de Moraes and José Marcio Rego, *Conversas com historiadores brasileiros* (São Paulo: Ed. 34, 2002), 102. Garra: literally, "claw," its figurative equivalent in English is guts; in the same colloquial sense, hence to "lack 'garra' " may translate to "lack 'guts.' "

72. "He who doesn't have a foot in the kitchen, has one in the jungle." Vargas's one-liner is quoted, among other places, in Leite, *Páginas de uma longa vida*, 253.

Chapter 5

The Military and the Dictatorship: Getúlio, Góes, and Dutra

Frank D. McCann

On November 10, 1937, the government of Brazil declared a new constitution and began eight years of dictatorship. Scholars have given vague explanations as to why the constitutional regime of 1934 fell into dictatorship. The standard explanation was the president's lust for power. The frustrations of the complicated presidential election process were not sufficient to force the dramatic changes. And why would the army's top generals concern themselves with the political struggle? Long available but overlooked documents provide a close behind-the-scenes view of the motives of the three main actors: President Getúlio Vargas, and Generals Pedro de Góes Monteiro and Eurico Dutra.[1]

The Military Actors

When Dutra took over the Ministry of War from General João Gomes in December 1936, he had no intellectual or emotional links with *tenentismo* or with the Revolution of 1930, rather his military thinking was rooted in the institutional reformism of the Young Turks and *A Defesa Nacional.*[2] He felt gratitude to Getúlio Vargas for his promotions to colonel and to brigadier general. His long ministry and his partnership with Góes would fortify the centralization of the national government, modernize the army, take it to war against Germany, eliminate political regionalism as a threat to the *Pátria*'s integrity, and make the armed forces the moderator of the political system for the next half century. At that crucial juncture of Brazilian history he had the power to influence the future of Brazil.

Góes became chief of the general staff, because Dutra insisted on his appointment, and Vargas's first choice, his wife's uncle, General Valdomiro Castilho de Lima, proved to be an embarrassment, and maybe a threat.

Dutra wanted tighter control over the officer corps. One of his first steps as minister was to call back officers serving outside the ranks. On January 21, 1937 he sent to the congress a report on officers who were serving on detached duty with federal ministries and at the disposition of state governors. In all there were 60 officers assigned outside the army, some of whom had been away for years. This strange situation existed because the army had long been trying to control the militarized police forces of the states, some of which were armed and configured to hold the federal army at bay. Some of the officers loaned to the state forces were more loyal to them than to the army. Dutra's recall was to correct this problem. In the mid-1930s some general officers, such as Góes and Dutra, were particularly worried about Rio Grande do Sul, where independent-minded Flores da Cunha held sway as governor. Three of the officers Dutra ordered to return were military advisors to Flores. In the first half of 1937 Góes directed troop movements to checkmate Rio Grande's state units.

Several generals, alarmed that the pressure on Flores could cause civil war, drafted a condemnation of Góes's maneuvers in the south. These "pacifying generals" met individually with Dutra, who on May 19 had issued a proclamation to the army insisting that the troop movements had nothing to do with the presidential succession. All of the measures he had taken as minister, he declared, were to put the army in position "to fulfill its mission of maintaining internal order and of carrying out the decisions of the legally constituted government." But it also was a public admission that federal military preparations had been made "to forestall any resistance by Rio Grande do Sul." Regarding the presidential campaign, Dutra wrote that the army should be "a vigilant and dispassionate spectator, willing and able to give its cooperation so that the succession could be carried out by legal means, within constitutional norms and according to electoral law." He charged his "comrades" to remember that "now and forever, the honor and integrity of the *Pátria*, the prosperity of the Nation and the tranquility of the Brazilian Family" rested on "our unity of vision, on our firm cohesion and on our conscious and unyielding discipline." Despite the high-sounding language, the proclamation was the "first indication that [there were] any fears . . . for the morale of the army."[3]

Góes was angry because the generals' protest had deflated his plans to invade Rio Grande; so he sent a letter to all the generals in the Rio area, demanding to know who had attended the meeting that drafted the protest. This was an odd situation, Góes had no legal authority to query his fellow generals, but their respect or fear made them answer. Fifteen general officers replied swiftly and thoroughly; a few were brief, but most responded carefully.[4] However, the incident showed that Góes and Vargas did not have absolute power; several generals had warned the most powerful men in the country that their support had limits. It also showed that perhaps a sizeable portion of the army could have been provoked to mutiny over what would have been, until less than a decade earlier, fairly common practice, that is federal intervention in a state. The incident emphasized, as well, the special regard officers had for Rio Grande do Sul. There had been no similar reaction when the government intervened in Rio de Janeiro and Mato Grosso. Finally, it offers evidence of the anxiety Góes was suffering; to have sent the original letter to the generals was startling enough, but his troubled replies showed that the undoing of his plans affected him deeply.

The public façade of army unity began to crumble as the press got wind of the generals' meeting. "Poor guys!" Vargas wrote in his diary, "It seems that Flores is more a general than they are. It would be preferable, instead of sabers, to give them pillows to embroider."[5] General Valdomiro denied that the generals were conspiring, but Góes Monteiro told Vargas that his wife's uncle had been carrying on secret communications with Flores. Getúlio turned to Dutra, who had come with Góes, saying that the government had to take vigorous measures to prevent the political scene from "dissolving into military anarchy."[6]

In the midst of this back stage crisis, what the public saw was the minister of justice releasing 300 and some political prisoners—in reality, as Vargas admitted, pick pockets and street toughs arrested during the state of war. Dutra added to the peaceful façade by telling the press that the army had no objections to ending the oft-renewed state of war. So, censorship ended, constitutional rights returned. But beyond public view the drama continued. Vargas met General Valdomiro on June 11 to tell him that the government knew what he was up to and that he could no longer be considered for chief of staff and, in fact, Góes would assume that position. The general denied involvement in political maneuvers and said he would resign as commander of the First Military Region if Góes became chief. Indeed, Dutra had already made clear that Góes's appointment was required for him to stay on as minister. After a public confrontation, he removed Valdomiro from command of the First Military Region and attached him to the president's military staff. There, outside his jurisdiction, he would be the president's problem.[7]

General José Pessoa weighed in with an "energetic" letter to Vargas defending himself against the conspiracy charge and lamenting that "certain elements" (i.e., Góes) had reached "high posts of responsibility, where they may more easily gratify their morbid thirst for fostering contention and disorder." He bound himself to resign from the army immediately if the charges proved true, and asked that his accuser "proceed with like dignity" if the reverse be the case. In response, the president ordered him imprisoned for six days. General of Division Firmino Borba, now head of the First Military Region, opened a military inquiry into the two generals' charges against Góes Monteiro. The American military *attaché* worried that the quarrel could split the army into rivaling factions.[8]

Rather than splitting the army it solidified the general officers. The Góes-Valdomiro struggle came to an end with charges and counter charges before the Supreme Military Tribunal and the arrests and brief imprisonments of Valdomiro and Pessoa. General Borba's inquiry report "attempted to place all of the officers involved in as favorable a light as possible." However, the sidelining of these two prominent generals served as an object lesson to other senior officers who might think of opposing the unfolding course of events. Valdomiro was given some minor military judicial inquiries to conduct and died of a stroke in February 1938. Pessoa was left without assignment until March 1938, when he was sent to command the Ninth Military Region in Mato Grosso, the army's traditional banishment posting.[9] The "politics of the generals," as Vargas called the episode, ended with the army under the command of the Dutra-Góes duo. They would be the longest-serving minister and chief of staff in Brazilian history.

While these events claimed the officer corps' attention, the politicians had come up with two candidates for the January 1938 elections. Armando de Salles Oliveira formally launched his candidacy in São Paulo. Vargas's man, Governor Benedito Valladares dramatically announced in a radio address that "Minas Gerais will not lend itself to any movement of coercion or violence." Some commentators wondered if the address meant that Valladares had broken with Vargas. A convention of *políticos* from around the country, which Valladares organized in Belo Horizonte, raised as their candidate José Américo de Almeida of Paraíba. Fascinating though it is, the ill-fated electoral campaign is the backdrop for the main drama and need not take our attention away from the march to dictatorship.[10]

With the army secure, the government moved against Flores. For Vargas, he represented the keystone of potential state-level political opposition to centralization; politicians in other states were not likely to move without his leadership. Góes had pushed military preparations close to completion in the first three months of 1937. Indeed, there were so many reports of *paulista* and *gaúcho* arms purchases abroad that Vargas noted in his diary that it seemed as if the two states were arming "for a war to conquer Brazil."[11]

With public attention focused so intently on political figures, it is not surprising that some "normal" military events escaped scrutiny. The annual cycle of training in the army of that time began in May and ended in the following March. Individual recruits and draftees moved from manual of arms through small unit tactics to ever larger configurations until they could function in combined divisional operations. Such large training operations depended on funds being available to regional headquarters. In March 1937, the Third Military Region received the necessary funds and staged maneuvers in the Santa Maria area and at Portão, near Novo Hamburgo. The plans of the two maneuvers seemingly aimed at defending against forces attacking along the rail line from Uruguaiana and from Santa Catarina, but because Brazilian units played both offensive and defensive roles, the training had immediate application in case of confrontation with the state's Brigada Militar and provisionals. The two weeks of maneuvers involved about 10,000 infantry, cavalry, and artillery troops, included use of observer aircraft, and practiced "the organization in troop movements and supply."[12] Surely Flores was well aware of this training and what it portended.

Oswaldo Aranha, passing through Brazil for the Pan-American meeting in Buenos Aires, had tried to reconcile Flores and Getúlio. For the president the solution was simple, Flores should keep quiet, not stir things up, and he would not be hostile to him. Effectively that would mean that Flores would stop his newspapers from attacking the federal government, or sending circular telegrams to other state governors, or negotiating resistance agreements with them. He had even tried to get Uruguay to pledge neutrality in the event of conflict between Rio Grande and Rio de Janeiro. Oswaldo convinced the two former friends, now protagonists, to meet. On April 2, Flores and Getúlio talked alone about the presidential succession. They agreed that neither of them was committed to a particular candidate, in fact Flores said he was willing to try to convince Salles to withdraw his name. In what would be their last meeting, both were cordial and conciliatory. Flores said he would remain for 15 days in Rio at Vargas's disposition, but five days later, unexpectedly, he telegraphed that he had to return to the south immediately. The power balance in the *gaúcho* state assembly was by a precarious one-vote margin that had shifted against him. Getúlio's brother Benjamin led the opposition state deputies against Flores. The Vargas brothers crafted a strategy that they hoped would provoke Flores to some hostile response that would justify federal military intervention. On April 25, the opposition deputies requested that for peace and security in the state the administration of the special state of war powers be transferred from Flores to General Emílio Lúcio Esteves, the Third Military Region commander. To the surprise of all, the normally explosive Flores restrained himself. Esteves, or his staff, had convinced Flores to accept the slap peacefully. Even so Dutra canceled the leaves of all officers and urged Esteves to concentrate army units in Porto Alegre. The general replied that such troop movements could provoke an unnecessary confrontation. In effect Esteves, a *gaúcho* from Taquara, in the eastern Serra, and for several years chief instructor of the state Brigada Militar who made no secret of opposing federal intervention, acted as a buffer between Flores and authorities in Rio de Janeiro. In any case the national state of war expired on June 18 and so was no longer a tool to irritate Flores.[13]

However, the struggle against Flores was not over. Góes sent his assistants Colonel Gustavo Cordeiro de Farias and Major Arthur Hescket Hall to Rio Grande to be his eyes and ears. They radioed assessments of the political and military situations, as did General Esteves, who stayed until July to oversee the continuing disarming of provisional units. On June 29, Esteves telegraphed that the provisionals had been disarmed and disbanded completely. And as of mid-July, regiments and battalions sent south in preceding months were still there awaiting further orders.[14]

On that same day the Ministry of War circulated a warning to all commanders that in adjusting to the return to constitutional status they should be alert to inflamed political passions arising from the presidential election campaign. Some civil authorities, it noted, would likely "confuse liberty with license and justice with tolerance. The army must be calm, exact and vigilant so as not to be taken by surprise." The most dangerous enemy continued to be communism, because it is "organized and persistent subverting the results of centuries of civilization and endangering our sacred homes." Góes Monteiro, who most likely wrote this inflated prose, concluded by recalling the tragic events of November 1935 and the vandalism that they must never forget![15]

On July 2, after his seriously ill friend, General Pais de Andrade, had resigned as chief of staff, Góes succeeded him. While Góes shuffled regional commanders, Dutra flew to inspect units in Rio Grande. On July 5, he and Vargas had discussed the trip and for the first time the two spoke openly of federal intervention. Vargas was concerned that the troops must carry out "any order of the government." Dutra conferred with officers in Curitiba, Paraná, and further south with those of some reinforcement units in Tuberão on the narrow coastal plain of Santa Catarina. In Porto Alegre, Flores staged a "grandiose" reception at the airport, and had his official car carry the minister to the headquarters of the Third Military Region to meet General Esteves. The latter was saddened at the news that he was to be moved to another military region. Dutra met Flores, who took the opportunity to stress his peaceful intentions, but noted that, if necessary, "he would know how to defend the dignity of the state." He asserted that he had dissolved the provisionals, except for about 1,800 who were engaged in essential services. Flores provided a special train to carry Dutra and Esteves to the key military center of Santa Maria. In conversations with Brigadier General José Joaquim de Andrade and the officers of the Fifth Infantry Brigade, Dutra perceived that they wanted to stay out of local politics and placed restrictions on federal intervention. Andrade and Esteves were agreed that they should avoid armed conflict. Officers in Cruz Alta expressed similar restrictions regarding intervention. Dutra and Esteves made the circuit of Uruguaiana, Alegrete, São Gabriel and Bagé. At each stop on this circuit, Dutra emphasized the need for "unconditional obedience." On July 14, at the Ninth Independent Cavalry Regiment in São Gabriel, in which he had served as a major in 1927–28, Dutra gave a brief speech in which he reminded officers that "it was not up to us to debate [the government's] decisions, but only to carry them out, with loyalty and with the impartiality that ought to characterize us."[16]

Meanwhile, back in Rio de Janeiro, Góes had been rearranging the top commanders. General Guedes da Fontoura, who had been such a headache during the salary controversy in mid-1935 and had been posted to command the Fifth Military Region in Curitiba, was moved to a supposedly higher post as inspector general of the First Group of Military Regions (South). As had been shown during Góes's tenure, the inspector general was only as powerful as the president, the minister of war, and now the chief of staff wanted him to be. For Guedes, who was made a general of division, it was an empty post. He would be retired in November. Góes had placed the Fifth Military Region in the capable hands of one of his trusted men, Bahian General of Division Manoel de Cerqueira Daltro Filho. He had been commanding the invasion forces that were poised to strike Rio Grande had

Flores resisted. Now he awaited new orders. Esteves would be transferred to the Fourth Military Region in Minas Gerais, whose state troops would ensure that he did not give into any sudden impulses to aid Flores. In early August, Góes and Dutra reshuffled the commands once more to gain even tighter control. Amongst the five generals who moved was Daltro Filho. This time he went to the Third Military Region. Esteves stayed in Minas, while Brigadier General José Meira de Vasconcellos took over the Fifth Military Region. As the generals moved, their lower-ranked trusted officers also shifted.[17]

At the same time Dutra turned the screws tighter on Flores by demanding that Rio Grande return all of the weapons that the army had loaned the state as far back as 1930! No consideration was to be given for worn out material, nor for normal losses and disappearances. The state could either return the arms or pay for them. Flores made a conciliatory reply and requested that the army and his state seek an impartial judge to reach a settlement. But Dutra asserted that was not acceptable because the question was an army matter and only the army and the national government had authority to resolve it.[18]

August, the darkest of Brazilian months frequently marred by political crises and problems, lived up to its reputation in 1937. At the end of July, "official" candidate José Américo gave a fiery address to a political rally in Rio's Esplanada do Castelo laying out his sweeping reform priorities if elected. On July 31, Minister Dutra issued a stern circular message to the military regions cautioning that the presidential campaign could turn violent, because "we are not accustomed to political clashes of such vast proportions." Left to themselves, "the masses could easily slide into aggressive violence and disorder, with nothing to keep them within reasonable limits. . . . It is then that the national Armed Forces exercises its most legitimate and elevated mission . . . as guardian of internal order. . . ." The army, he emphasized, must "stay aloof from the political struggle" and "be impartial." Therefore, the officers must keep their eyes on national interests that must supersede "political aspirations, regional ambitions [and] ideological concerns."[19]

On August 4, Plínio Salgado, *integralista* candidate for the presidency, gave a radio address warning of a Communist coup plot. That same day José Américo told Getúlio that he and Edmundo Bittencourt, founder of Rio's *Correio da Manhã*, were trying to persuade Flores to resign. He also cautioned the president that there was danger of a coup; Góes had told him that, if the politicians did not reach an understanding, the army would act. During August there were almost daily rumors of either a Communist uprising, an *integralista* putsch, or a military coup d'état, which, according to the U.S. embassy, was causing uneasiness in the government and in business circles. On August 7, a rally in São Paulo against Armando de Salles was broken up with gunfire. Rumors of conspiracies and warlike preparations in Rio Grande continued to run hot. The death, on August 8, of recently resigned chief of staff General Pais de Andrade added to the somber mood. On 15, in Campos, state of Rio de Janeiro, an *integralista* rally ended in a riot that left 13 dead and several injured. On August 18, Dutra instructed regional commanders to be set for public disturbances. He also ordered the Central do Brasil railroad to be prepared on short notice to transport troops. And the next day Daltro Filho telegraphed Vargas that officers in the Third Military Region were saying that they would oppose any assault on Rio Grande's autonomy, and that Flores was determined to resist intervention. Daltro discovered that his own headquarters staff included a number of officers allied with Flores and so gradually he arranged orders for the dubious ones to be sent elsewhere. To underscore the precariousness of the situation, he sent by courier a report with photographs of 16 groups of road workers, who were provisionals paid by the state Brigada Militar. Daltro also reported that discipline in the Paraná garrisons was shaky. Moreover, Flores was communicating with São Paulo regarding a broad movement against the national government and, according to Daltro's report, intended to place General Valdomiro in command. Once again the specter of civil war hung over Brazil.[20]

It should be no surprise that, with all these complicated matters, Vargas did not feel very well and grew even more anxious when Argentina, England, and Germany opposed the agreement that he had worked out with Roosevelt to lease six old American destroyers for naval training purposes. Brazilian newspapers, regardless of their sentiments toward the federal government, rose to defend the acquisition of the vessels as a matter of national honor and expressed disappointment and exasperation with Argentina, which was then building seven destroyers.[21] On August 19, Vargas's frustrations caused him to wonder if "perhaps they'll push me to get out of this with a brisk and unexpected decision." Was he having thoughts of resigning, or of suicide?[22]

Did Vargas's dark mood reflect that of the country or was he projecting his own perceptions? Indeed, what was he thinking? His diary entries grew more cryptic. Certainly presidential candidate José Américo's speeches were discouraging his political backers. However, Vargas, in a diary entry on 23, seemed to minimize the dangers that the campaign was stirring up, writing that "the communist, *integralista*, and . . . Rio Grande phenomenons did not have the significance" that "the champions of democracy" wanted to give them. He thought that Américo's extreme positions were mainly a "candidate's pose" and that he did not have "the same misgivings" as alarmed political leaders.[23]

The Mysterious Cohen Plan

Soldiers certainly needed a lot of faith in the future of the *Pátria* at this juncture in history. All the ink that has been spilled over the Cohen Plan episode has not clarified why a fake document was used to justify the re-imposition of a state of war. It is well known that the document was written by Captain Olímpio Mourão Filho, an *integralista* since 1932, organizer of the party's paramilitary militia, member of its Council of Four Hundred, and, in 1937, chief of its secret service. He was also serving in the intelligence section of the army's general staff! He wrote the document that became the Cohen Plan, as an *integralista* defensive exercise against a supposed Communist coup d'etat. Plínio Salgado rejected it for party use as too fantastic. But Góes used a portion of the document as justification for a government request to the congress to re-impose the state of war.

The episode raises questions the current state of research does not provide answers. The fact that Mourão was not charged under National Security Law 48 of April 1935 for organizing an unapproved militia is likely the most glaring evidence that the law was selectively applied. If the government needed Communist documents why did it not use some of those captured with Prestes and the other Moscow agents? Who knew it was fake? General Mariante, Góes's mentor in the 1920s, and in 1937 president of the Supreme Military Tribunal, obtained a copy from Mourão, who explained exactly what the document was. General Góes, who seems to have gotten a copy from Mariante, also knew. Major (later general) Aguinaldo Caiado de Castro, who encountered Mourão typing the document in a general staff office, certainly knew as well. Mourão asserted that, when he heard that such a document was about to be made public, he hurried to Góes's office to protest; the chief of staff curtly told him to shut up. Did Góes tell Vargas or Dutra that the Cohen Plan was false? The former's memoir and the latter two's diaries provide no answer. If there was no Communist plot that demanded a salvationist military response to safeguard Brazil, why did the generals support the coup of November 10?

Vargas-Goes Monteiro-Dutra-Alliance

A constant theme that ran through the army's postimperial history had been its worry about the poor state of its arms and equipment, the difficulties of mobilizing and training sufficient soldiers to have adequate armed forces to defend the country against internal and external enemies. In 1903, Sergeant Getúlio Vargas had seen first hand the precariousness of mobilization on the Mato Grosso frontier; the Revolution of 1930, the *paulista* rebellion of 1932, and the Communist barracks revolt of 1935 each revealed weaknesses in Brazil's army and navy. With the world stumbling toward some terrible, yet still unknown, crisis, Vargas linked the solution to Brazil's political predicament, with national defense. Governments in France, the United States, not to speak of Germany, Italy, Poland, and Portugal, were solidifying their control over national policy formation and execution. Why should Brazil not do so too?

Vargas and Dutra's worries about the army's possibly negative response to orders to intervene in Rio Grande do Sul, let alone to a change of regime, were behind the new code of military discipline imposed by executive order. The extremely detailed code cited, in the words of the American attaché: "everything a soldier or officer has been known to do, everything it might occur to him to do, and quite a number of acts it probably never would enter his mind to do." Various provisions aimed at keeping a social distance between officers and troops. The new rules would be subject to severe testing in the next few months.[24]

For most of the 1930s Góes Monteiro had been trying to make Vargas understand the desperate need for basic reforms. Brazil's fleet and its army had human talent and a full array of schools, but scarcely any arms or munitions. This was not news, but the world panorama in 1937 was exceptionally frightening. The Spanish civil war indicated that Brazil had been lucky in 1932 not to have attracted foreign intervention, but it likely would not have such good luck twice. The Soviet Union's involvement in the 1935 fiasco raised fears that it would try again, if the chance presented itself; and Nazi Germany had already been much too attentive to the status of German communities in southern Brazil. Argentina had just shown in the Destroyers' Affair that it was a "false friend." Old fears of losing rich, untapped, and often undiscovered natural resources gave Brazilian officers and knowledgeable politicians nightmares.

Back in March 1935, Ambassador Oswaldo Aranha had written from Washington to Góes that he had fallen in love with democracy.

> But my friend, it is necessary not to confuse this ideal form of government with its deformed examples. Our problem, my dear friend, consists only in giving military organization to the military to safeguard authority, maintain the unity and to defend the integrity of the country and, more, to improve the race and the land, to educate the people and to give liberty to Brazil. . . . Russia, Germany, [and] Italy are in perpetual economic convulsions, stuck in unstable situations that will toss those peoples into war or anarchy. We should not drag Brazil down such mistaken paths. *I confess that it seems that a regime of force would be useful to us. . . . The military organization of Brazil is an internal and external necessity. . . .* The world is getting mixed up and our continent is growing nervous (emphasis added).[25]

And he concluded: "Brazil can and should equip itself, if it does not, it will pay more than we can calculate."[26] Similarly, in June 1937 Aranha wrote Vargas that "my opinion is that we must arm ourselves, making purchases abroad, whatever it costs. If we don't do so quickly and immediately, it will cost much more, materially and morally." He suggested a strategy to create a special defense fund.[27]

Vargas, Dutra, Góes, and Aranha agreed that Brazil had to modernize its armed forces. A modern army would hold the country together against the centrifugal forces of regionalism, and defend it against foreign enemies. It would also set an example of educated modernity for the Brazilian people. By September 1937 the first three were more or less in agreement as to the course they were following. In a sense Vargas had become a captive, he would have to carry out their plans or risk being deposed. The two generals could back down, but Vargas could not.

The arrangement was straightforward. Góes and Dutra were to give Vargas internal peace and security, and he would get them the arms and the modern industries that would support continued military development. On September 1, 1937, Vargas presided over a meeting of the National Security Council, which included the cabinet ministers and the chiefs of staff of the army and navy. This was only the third time it had met since its formation in 1934, so it was an unusual event.[28] They discussed the equipping of the armed forces and the need to create a source of revenue to pay for it.

As Stanley Hilton has shown, during 1934–36, the army had been negotiating with the German Krupp Corporation and with the Swedish Bofors company for modern artillery to be paid for with natural resources.[29] The navy engaged in similar activity with the Italian government for submarines and with the American government for destroyers. In his annual report to the president in May 1937, Minister Dutra had written, "it would be to lie to the Nation to say that we are armed, in condition to guard it and to defend its enormous patrimony. . . . It is sad but true to confess that we do not possess sufficient material resources to deal with even our internal requirements. . . . We can not stand still while the rest of the world advances."[30]

Vargas committed himself to arming and equipping the military and building a national steel complex in return for military backing of extending his presidency with dictatorial powers that would eliminate politics. The public implementation of this arrangement proceeded in the hesitant, indirect way in which Getúlio usually maneuvered. The signals that he flashed were certainly mixed. It is most common for historians to see his contradictory moves as deliberate diversions intended to confuse. It is more likely, however, recalling his behavior in 1930, that such moves really indicated his indecision and caution. In his September 7 address to the nation he asserted that it would be the last time he would commemorate Independence Day as chief of state. Was he serious or trying to lull opponents? Over the next few days, politicians, including Valladares, who had been supporting José Américo, became dismayed by the candidate's speeches and attitudes, and wanted to drop him in favor of a third or conciliatory candidate.[31]

Then on September 13 the political scene exploded. Former Mayor of Rio, Dr. Pedro Ernesto, acquitted by the Supreme Military Tribunal, was released from jail. Rio de Janeiro erupted into an impromptu, out-of-season carnival. The city government declared a holiday and the crowds swelled with city workers. Praça Onze, the traditional gathering spot for samba groups, was so full of people that Ernesto's car could not enter. To reach the Esplanada do Castelo, where he was to speak, his car was pushed along by the cheering throngs. They passed directly in front of the Ministry of War, from whose windows officers, soldiers, and civilian employees watched the spontaneous outpouring of affection and loyalty. The doctor had stayed neutral in the presidential race so both Américo and Salles backers had organized demonstrators. In his talk in the Esplanada he stressed that he had not been involved in the 1935 revolts, and he added: "I am not, was never, and will never be a Communist." Only days later, on September 29, he announced his backing for Armando Salles. The outpouring for Ernesto "inadvertently precipitated" action by the coup planners.[32]

During the next few days Vargas met with Valladares and Dutra. They agreed that a substitute third candidate was impossible to arrange. Extending Vargas's mandate legally was also not possible. To this point it is likely that Vargas and his collaborators had been moving toward a congressionally approved extension of his term, but from here onward they pursued an extra legal solution. Such an interpretation would explain why Dutra could say that their discussion on September 18 was the first time Vargas had spoken openly with him about reacting "against the situation that was developing, by staging a revolution from the top down, that is, unleashed by the government itself." The president complained that the congress had done nothing useful and opposed the executive's initiatives. The only solution was to change the regime and reform the constitution. But the general said Vargas commented that "he would make the revolution" only if Dutra collaborated with him; Dutra was silent for a few moments and then replied that "he could count on him, but he could guarantee nothing regarding the army." They would begin by eliminating Flores. Feelers went out to Plínio Salgado that gave him the idea that, by collaborating with a change of regime, Integralism would have a major place in the new Brazil.[33]

Curiously, even as Vargas was moving to break the back of regionalism, he was willing to use, and thereby strengthen, a proponent of regionalism in the person of Governor Benedito Valladares. Because the conspirators assumed that there would be some resistance in São Paulo and Rio Grande, they had to have *mineiro* state troops on their side. Valladares demanded two conditions in return for his support, namely that the army accept the revolution; and that the Força Pública of Minas, except for two battalions, not be federalized and remain under his command.[34]

On September 19, Valladares called on Dutra saying that Vargas had asked Salgado to join the movement and offered him a ministry in return. The governor suggested that they limit the participation of Salgado and Góes. In another conversation the following day, Valladares lamented the impossibility of finding a third candidate, and affirmed strongly that their only path was "revolution" headed by Getúlio. He gave Dutra rough drafts of a suggested presidential manifesto and of the constitution that Francisco Campos was preparing. He pointed out that the latter would extend Vargas's term for another six years.[35]

In what has often been described as a cold and calculated series of events, there was actually considerable emotion. On September 22, the government declared a holiday, complete with the closing of commerce, and held a commemoration for the dead soldiers of November 1935. Vargas and the generals gathered at the grave site in Rio's São João Batista cemetery for prayers and speeches. The event was odd in its timing and likely would have been forgotten except for what happened next. The Chamber of Deputies entered a prolonged debate over entering the grave side speeches into the official record of the chamber, which led General Newton Cavalcanti, commander of the First Infantry Brigade at Vila Militar, and key enthusiast in the army for Integralism, to charge that there was "a Communist current or grouping within the National Congress itself."[36] The debate expanded to examine the crisis in Brazilian democracy and rumors that Góes was plotting a coup. He issued a formal denial and asserted that in serving the *Pátria* his greatest desire was to put the army in condition to face any danger to national integrity.[37]

On the morning of September 27, Dutra convoked a crucial meeting in his office.[38] Those invited were Góes, Almério de Moura (First Military Region), José Antônio Coelho Neto (Director of Aviation), Cavalcanti, and Filinto Müller (police chief of Federal District). They had received copies of the report on the Cohen Plan from Góes, which Dutra assured them was "not a government fantasy." The ministry of justice's actions were "fomenting" rather than repressing "the energies that are ready to explode." Our laws, Minister Dutra asserted, were not working. "The armed forces, particularly the army, constitutes the sole element capable of saving Brazil from the catastrophe ready to erupt. . . ." He concluded that "it is necessary to act and to act immediately." Cavalcanti, referring to the Cohen Plan document, declared that the Communist intention was "to liquidate the army itself." The undermining of the congress was shown by its refusal to include in its record the speeches of a few days ago. The looming of a new Communist threat, he asserted, "required immediate action in defense of the army, of democratic institutions, of society, of the very family threatened with death . . . *it is necessary to act, even outside the law*, but in defense of the corrupted law and institutions" (emphasis added). General Coelho Neto, the newest of that rank, observed that they had to involve the navy and Vargas himself. Several generals stated that the Chamber of Deputies must be purged of its reactionary, weak, and incapable members. Dutra and several of the others insisted that "the constituted authorities should be maintained. The movement will carry with it the President of the Republic, whose authority will be strengthened."

In an aside, Góes charged that José Américo was bankrolling the fellow traveler newspaper *O Popular* (Rio), and Coelho Neto recalled that the candidate had not attended the grave side ceremony. He noted the Communist plans required "a military movement that amounted to a coup d'etat." However, he added, their plans should be "a generals' secret." They should sign an agreement that "they did not want a military dictatorship." Müller insisted "that the Armed Forces, conducting this movement, stay outside the government, to guarantee the operation and the constituted government." He also suggested that arrests be summary with no right of defense and that forced labor camps be established. Cavalcanti declared that the two service ministers should direct the operation, at the side of the president, to secure for him, with force, the exceptional powers required. Success, he went on, "demanded an immediate return to a state of war without any restrictions, as well as declaring of Martial Law in all of its fullness." Dutra chimed in that it should apply to the whole country. They should, he said, involve the entire army, and especially the air arm.

Cavalcanti defended himself against the charge of being an *integralista*. "I am not," he said, he opposed political influence, even *integralista*, in the army. "Only use them, if needed, as enlisted troops, but never as [*integralista*] militia." Góes and Cavalcanti, seemingly summed up the group's feelings: "We only wish to work for the Army and for the salvation of the Pátria." The next day they all signed the minutes pledging themselves to the "exclusive purpose of saving Brazil and its political and social institutions from the disaster that was about to occur . . . excluding from their intentions any personal gain or any idea of military dictatorship." It is ironic that on that day the Chamber of Deputies approved entering the celebrated speeches into the record of its debates.

The next day General Dutra and Vice Admiral Henrique Aristides Guilhem (naval minister) went to Guanabara Palace to speak with Vargas about the need to resume the state of war. The two ministers agreed to provide an explanation that the president could send to the congress. Later, at his office, Dutra told his colleagues that this would be the "most viable way" for them to have some legal basis to attack communism, arrest congressmen, and other such acts. On 29, Vargas sent the ministers' petition to the congress. It is curious that in his diary Getúlio's references to the request distanced him from it. He wrote that he was forwarding the document "in accord with the request of the military ministers."[39]

The ministers' document was addressed to Vargas and was so lacking in detail that it is difficult today to see it as a serious request for extra constitutional powers. The ministers evoked the ghosts of the

Intentona by declaring "just as in 1935 the threats are evident . . . [and] many people do not believe, attributing the ostensive preparations to maneuvers of biased politics, fantasies of salaried authorities." Despite the ministers' efforts to counter the Communist threat, the "crime against the *Pátria* committed in 1935 is about to be repeated with greater energy and more certainty of success."

> The armed forces can not be silent. For them not to act is a crime. . . . The Armed Forces are the only element capable of saving Brazil from the catastrophe ready to explode. . . . The struggle will be violent without quarter. . . . We have the example of Spain. . . . Thus it is necessary to act, and to do so immediately, without stopping for any considerations. Above everything is the salvation of the *Pátria*. . . . speaking for the generals and admirals of the armed forces of Brazil . . . speaking for all of Brazil . . . [we] ask for an immediate return to the state of war.[40]

On September 30, the government radio program *Hora do Brasil* (Hour of Brazil) featured an announcement about the general staff's "discovery" of the Cohen Plan, and the next day's headlines took the story, and the government's appeal to restore the state of war, to the streets and byways. During the previous days Daltro Filho had reported shipments of arms from abroad into Porto Alegre, information on the location of secret arms caches, and Flores's expanding the numbers of Brigada Militar troops. As Vargas had commented in his diary on September 27, "things were becoming clearer."[41]

On October 1, debates in the congress centered on the legitimacy of the supposed dangers. Some deputies and senators naturally wanted to see the documents mentioned but not submitted. Others said that to ask for the documents would be to question the honesty of the armed forces chiefs, who would be held responsible by their colleagues in uniform and by history. The Chamber approved the measure 138–52 and the Senate 21–3. That night Vargas signed the decree re-imposing a state of war on Brazil. For the first time it was to be supervised nationally by a commission, named on October 7, made up of the Minister of Justice Macedo Soares, General Cavalcanti, and Admiral Dário Pais Leme de Castro. In the states the governors were in charge, except in São Paulo, Rio Grande do Sul, and the Federal District, where the authority rested with Generals of Division César Augusto Pargas Rodrigues and Daltro Filho, and with Captain Filinto Müller, respectively. The attitudes of the national commissioners were extreme. Pais told reporters that "anyone not against communism is

a Communist," and Cavalcanti concurred saying that "the enemies of
the Pátria" were "the Communists and the indifferent." The commission's plan called for summary judgments, the detention "of all
Communist sympathizers" and the creation of a "Federal Police."
Even Masonic Lodges and spiritist centers were to be closed.[42]

The decision not to have the governors in the two suspect states
implement the state of war required that the Força Pública in São
Paulo and the Brigada Militar in Rio Grande be placed under the
commands of the two military regions. In the previous weeks considerable negotiation and maneuvering had placed army sympathizers in
key positions. Dramas large and small took place as police officers
weighed their options, loyalties, and futures. Neither police force was in
the mood for civil war. But even so, tensions mounted and uncertainty
hung in the air. São Paulo showed no resistance.

What would Flores do? Gaúchos were born and bred loyal to Rio
Grande, could the governor marshal those sentiments? The Archbishop
of Porto Alegre Dom João Becker discussed the impasse with Flores
seeking an honorable way out short of violence. Flores recognized
that the Brigada had gone over to the army, and that the provisionals
were listening to their Brigada officers. In a symbolic gesture of
gallantry, he donned his uniform on Sunday morning, October 16,
and made the rounds of the Brigada barracks in Porto Alegre to make
his farewells. Then in defiance and pride, he refused to sign a decree
giving the Brigada over to the army. Instead the next day he resigned
and took the waiting Varig aircraft to the Uruguayan frontier. There
would be no more gaúcho caudilhos like him. On 19, Vargas decreed
federal intervention in his home state and named Daltro Filho as
interventor. For a short time, until the general fell to a fatal illness in
December, Rio Grande had an outsider, a Bahian, at its head. Worried
that the paulistas might react against the intervention in Rio Grande,
Dutra ordered his old Fourth Cavalry Regiment in Três Corações
(Minas Gerais) to a position closer to the São Paulo line and requested
Valladares to concentrate police in similar fashion. The paulistas kept
quiet. But in Rio Grande there were sufficient problems with arms
that Flores had ordered abroad and suspicious behavior by some
Brigada officers. Daltro Filho's chief of staff, Colonel Cordeiro de
Farias, commented that it took 30 days to get the situation under
control.[43]

Back in Rio de Janeiro, Góes and Cavalcanti were showing Vargas
documents accusing the governors of Bahia and Pernambuco of
having plotted with São Paulo and Rio Grande against the federal
government. Cavalcanti also complained that Minister of Justice

Macedo Soares was not cooperating on running the state of war commission with Admiral Pais and him. One can imagine Vargas groaning to himself as he wrote in his diary: "A crisis is created, or rather a new crisis."[44]

From October 20 onward, Dutra met or spoke with Vargas on a daily basis. Curiously, Vargas did not note all of these conversations, but Dutra, who was now using the fateful term "coup d'etat," kept a record. On 21, they talked about replacing Macedo Soares with Francisco Campos, and on 23, they disagreed about intervening in São Paulo; Dutra was afraid that it could cause a widespread reaction, even in the army. He preferred leaving São Paulo alone, and intervening instead in Pernambuco and Bahia. In the end all three were intervened. In these days too, in addition to the federalization of two battalions of *mineiro* troops, the military police forces of the other states were taken over by federal authority.[45]

The next major step was to delude Salgado and his green shirts into thinking that they would have an important function in the new regime. Campos, who was writing the new constitution on the model of the Polish and Portuguese documents, had developed a friendly relationship with the ostensible Brazilian *Führer* and went so far as to get his comments on the draft document. On Sunday, October 24, in his Guanabara Palace residence, Vargas met with the core conspirators, Minister of Justice Macedo Soares, Minister of Labor Agamemnon Magalhães, Governor Valladares, and Generals Dutra, Góes, and Cavalcanti, to discuss how to carry out the "constitutional reform." They talked about military measures to control Pernambuco, Bahia, and São Paulo, the likely "nonconformist states." They did not reach consensus regarding how to legalize the new constitution. Cavalcanti contended that the congress should approve it. Others preferred that the government declare it effective and subsequently submit it to a plebiscite. Dutra noted in his diary (perhaps referring to a separate conversation) that he and Vargas had agreed to present the draft constitution to the National Security Council, followed by a presidential manifesto to the nation. Two days later, Vargas met with Salgado in the home of a mutual friend. They got on well, Vargas regarding him as "shrewd and intelligent hick." The president gave Salgado to understand that in the reorganized government the education ministry would be his.[46]

Emissaries from Valladares and Vargas winged their way to get agreement of the state governors for the change of regime. They skipped Pernambuco and Bahia whose governors would be deposed. Some unidentified generals were "conspiring" to mount a counter action. Such plotting, which unfortunately for historians has left few traces, may have motivated Dutra to take the precaution of face-to-face meetings with certain generals and to do some shifting of regional commanders. On October 26 he visited artillery units getting ready to proceed to Pinheiros, São Paulo, then he went to Villa Militar to be assured that Cavalcanti was convinced of the necessity of their moves and would cooperate fully. On Sunday, October 31, he was in Juiz da Fora talking with Fourth Military Region commander Esteves whom he found securely committed to the government. While in Minas, Dutra stopped by some army units and two state police units. The tension he felt exploded when General Valdomiro flagged down his car on the highway back to Rio. Vargas and uncle Valdomiro had been at a barbecue at a *fazenda* near Petrópolis and the general had made some suggestions of measures he might take as inspector general of the group of regions that included São Paulo. Vargas told him to submit the ideas to Dutra. Instead, in their beside-the-road conversation, Valdomiro presented them as if they were the president's orders. The minister got so upset that he wanted to resign then and there. Getúlio had to return to Rio the next day to "put things back in place." One can imagine that he and Dutra must have had an interesting exchange about uncle Valdomiro![47]

The next day, All Soul's Day, was a public holiday, but even so it was a busy one at Guanabara Palace. Vargas met with *gaúcho* allies, federal deputies João Neves da Fontoura and João Baptista Lusardo, bringing them up-to-date. Lusardo then left for Rio Grande, where he told political colleagues that the coup was set for November 15 and that Vargas wanted them to behave as if nothing was about to happen. Finance Minister Souza Costa was arguing for an end to the artificial support of coffee prices via government purchase and burning or dumping into the sea of millions of tons. Months before, in May, he had negotiated an agreement with the Roosevelt administration that allowed Brazil to separate United States and European foreign-debt negotiations, thereby facilitating a repayment plan, and he had obtained guarantees of US $60 million to finance a Brazilian central bank. Because an important part of the plan for regime change involved suspending foreign-debt payments to allow arms purchases, Souza Costa's views carried considerable weight with the conspirators. Müller and Campos put in appearances, and with the latter the president went over some changes in the language of the constitution and of the accompanying manifesto. Generals Dutra, Cavalcanti, Deschamps, and Daltro Filho made their reports and heard the latest on the "coming political and constitutional reform."[48]

On November 5, *Correio da Manhã* broke the news that serious intrigues involving the government and the armed forces were afoot. Vargas wired Valladares, who had sent Deputy Negrão de Lima to inform the northeastern governors of the impending coup, to put out the story that Negrão's mission had been to search out possible "legal political solutions." After trying to calm worried congressmen, he received a letter from Macedo Soares wanting to resign his post. The generals had long been impatient with his efforts to maintain a liberal attitude toward human rights and the regime's façade of the rule of law. The day before, Cavalcanti had complained to Vargas that he could no longer work with the minister. And later Macedo Soares came by the palace to say that he was worn out and suggested that either the general be removed or new commissioners named. Thinking on it for a night, he had decided to quit. Significantly, in the afternoon of November 5 Vargas met with the two service ministers, Góes and Müller, with whom he discussed the day's events. "After hearing them, I resolved to accept the resignation of the minister of justice" telling them that Campos would replace him. That night Campos accepted the post.[49]

On the afternoon of November 8, opposition leaders met at the home of candidate Salles who told them that he was sending a letter to the military chiefs "denouncing the sinister conspiracy that was being hatched in official circles against [national] institutions." "If some powerful force," he warned, "does not intervene in time . . . a terrible blow suddenly will shake the nation to its deepest foundations. . . . A long prepared plan is about to be executed by a small group of men, so small that they can be counted on one hand, intending to enslave Brazil. . . . The nation turns to its military leaders: in suspense, awaiting the killing blow or the saving word." Apparently, Américo had declined to sign the manifesto, on the advice of friends, who thought it would likely hurt him more than do any good in stopping the coup. Ironically, at about the same time, Generals Dutra and Góes and Admiral Guilhem were at Campos's home going over the text of the new constitution.[50]

The next day, in the Chamber of Deputies, João Carlos Machado, an ally of Flores, read to the deputies Salles's appeal to the military to resist the coup. In the Senate, Paulo de Morais Barros, the nephew of President Prudente de Morais (1894–98), did the same. Lusardo, who had returned quickly from Porto Alegre, was on hand to witness the scene in the chamber. The "atmosphere was," he thought, "revolutionary." He hurried to the Catete Palace to inform Getúlio. He warned that "tomorrow the Nation will know everything. . . . Either you stage the coup today, gaining the upper hand, or their revolution will be in the streets. Call Dutra and Góes. It has to be today." In the meantime the Salles manifesto was reaching the barracks and the lower officer ranks. As Dutra left his home he told his family: "Either Dr. Getúlio unleashes the coup today, or he won't be able to." In trying to stop the plot Salles succeeded in precipitating it.[51]

In the course of the planning, Dutra and Góes strove to lower the profile of army involvement, perhaps due to what Getúlio called "the intrigue and division of the military." It was to that division and because D-Day was known to be November 11 that it was "necessary to precipitate the coup, taking advantage of surprise." With Müller, Campos, and Dutra, Vargas arranged the final steps. Dutra ordered the First, Second, and Third Military Regions to stand ready, and alerted the other regions that highly important political events were about to occur and that they should be ready to act. However, it would not be federal troops stationed outside the closed houses of congress, but the Federal District's military police. At 6 a.m. Müller informed the acting president of the Senate that the congress was dissolved, but *mineiro* Pedro Aleixo, president of the Chamber of Deputies, suffered the embarrassment of being turned away by the police. Also in the early hours Dutra went to the São Cristóvão district to check on the readiness of the First Cavalry Regiment and the Guard Battalion. Vargas had Lusardo inform José Américo of the coup. Awakened very early by the head of his campaign committee, the candidate accepted the inevitable: "It wasn't I who failed; it was Brazil itself that was deaf."[52]

On that overcast November 10 at ten in the morning, the cabinet, save for the dissenting minister of agriculture, signed the new constitution. During the day, 80 members of congress sent congratulatory messages. Those associated with Salles were under house arrest. In the afternoon, the foreign minister called in the American ambassador to assure him that there would be no changes in foreign policy and that the government would be very liberal toward "foreign capital and foreigners who have legitimate interests in Brazil." That night at 8, Vargas addressed the nation by radio. The political parties, infected by regionalism, he claimed, were subverting order, threatening national unity, and endangering Brazil's existence with their polarizing rivalries and encouragement of civil disorder. To avoid Brazil's disintegration he had decided to restore the national government's authority. He reviewed the country's economic and military needs: suspension of foreign debt payments, construction of railroads and highways into the vast interior, and reequipping of the armed forces, all of which he linked directly to "the important problem of national defense." He emphasized that it was "urgently necessary to provide the armed forces with efficient equipment that will make them capable of assuring the country's integrity and independence. . . ." For those reasons there had been no other alternative to "installing a strong regime of peace, justice and labor."[53]

Dutra's Proclamation

The afternoon newspapers of November 10 gave front page space to Dutra's statement that was also circulating in the barracks. In the odd military prose that characterized such pronouncements he explained the army's mission:

It was up to the army, to the armed forces not to permit that the people's aspirations be frustrated. . . . The army did not shape the internal political scenario, it did not foment the discord among the competing factions. What it did do, and would continue to do, was to contain explosions, to constitute a barrier to partisan ambitions, expelling from its ranks undesirable elements, snuffing out immediately the smallest outbursts of disorder. . . .

As everyone knows, today a new Federal Constitution was proclaimed. . . . Perceiving the lacunas and defects in the statute of 1934 . . . new directions were set for our democratic regime, better suited to its federative continuity. . . . Any disturbance of order will be a breech through which might rush the enemies of the Pátria, the adversaries of democratic rule. We must avoid this, carrying out with calmness and with firmness our mission. If we proceed thus, Brazilian society will continue to be confident in us . . . the Pátria and the regime will be under our guard . . . in defence of internal order, of political integrity, of national sovereignty. This is our mission.[54]

What did Vargas get from this army support? Clearly he kept the presidency until October 1945, but this meant more work and personal sacrifice. He may have loved power, but surely his motivations were more complex than enjoying being president. His thirst for power had other elements driving it. He and the generals shared a dream, perhaps not with the same details, but they dreamed of an important, flourishing nation spread over a splendidly magnificent portion of the earth, living and producing in security and happiness. Vargas was dedicated to the improvement of Brazil and was confident in his ability to make the right decisions for his country. However, he was careful to seek advice and not to get too far ahead of elite opinion.

He did not rob the treasury, and after his demise his family was not markedly wealthy. The evidence available does not make clear, whether the dictatorship was Getúlio's idea or that of the generals. Getúlio once joked with a friend, who was also a high-ranking officer: "In 1930 I made the revolution with the *tenentes*, in 1937 with the Generals." His daughter said that he acted to prevent a military dictatorship, but the minutes of the generals' meeting of September 27 stated that they did not want one.[55] Does it matter who first expressed the idea? Perhaps not, but it does matter why the army supported dictatorship. On a personal and institutional level the coup insured that Dutra and Góes would remain in charge of the army, allowing them to shape its continuing professionalization according to their ideas.

The army, represented by its top generals, wanted to safeguard the country. They believed that the army could not do so under the regime of 1934, so they toppled the constitutional government in the name of the higher good of the security of the *Pátria*. Vargas made a pledge, or *compromisso*, that he would equip and arm the armed forces so that they could carry out their assigned duty, in return they would provide the muscle for a regime of force and national development. On November 17 Vargas wrote Aranha to explain why he had changed the constitution and to say that he needed him in Washington to obtain American capital for a great reform and development program centering on "large acquisitions of material for our military and railroads."[56] In a series of speeches in early 1938 he repeated the quid pro quo in various ways. In his New Year's radio address he said that Brazil had "a mission in America and in the world" of mobilizing the riches of half a continent, which "we can not leave undefended. We are stubbornly working on the equipping and preparation of the armed forces, which bring together thousands of Brazilians disposed to sacrifice everything for the integrity of the Pátria." In Porto Alegre, a week later, he told an elite audience that he was happy to be back in his native Rio Grande, now safe from the dangers of civil war. Even more pointedly, in his address at the banquet offered to him by the Second Independent Cavalry Regiment in his hometown of São Borja, he declared that he had "tried always to enhance the prestige of the army, because the greatness of the country is founded on the army. . . . I have counted on the army, principally, to put down the 'political bosses,' who were attempting to set up a regional hegemony to supercede the authority of the central power, weakening Brazil. Today, all this is assured." The mission of the armed forces was to guarantee order, so that there would be public confidence. And then he stated the *compromisso* succinctly: "Give me order and tranquility and I will restore the finances, develop the economy, construct all that which our raw materials could give us; . . . the iron necessary for our industries and for our progress, from locomotives to aero-planes. . . . For this . . . I need order. But I trust in you who are the Nation."[57]

The clearest statement of this *compromisso* was that of Góes in his general staff report for 1937. Góes charged that the 1934 law specifying that army reorganization was to be completed within three years had not been fulfilled. The army was, he said, "fragile, more fictitious than real," its big units were "dismantled . . . incapable of being mobilized in reasonable time and employed in any situation. . . ." The general staff's worries about Brazil's military weaknesses, he wrote, had intensified with the news that Chile was renewing its army's equipment and that Argentina was improving its armament, expanding its weapons industry, and generally developing its military capabilities. In the United States, Roosevelt was calling for the "prompt and intensive equipping of its armed forces." The nations of the globe were preparing for war. "The violence in Abyssinia, China, and Spain were," Góes asserted, "true practice wars to test the means of destruction and protection" in rehearsal for a great and decisive struggle. Neither pacifist illusions nor Brazil's turn-of-the-century Krupp artillery would be able to protect it. On Brazil's very borders the "ex-belligerents of the Chaco, despite the interminable peace conference in Buenos Aires, had returned to the path of complete rearmament, in expectation of another appeal to arms." Góes warned that "the moment, in which we are living, imposes a radical transformation of [our] military organism . . . [because] we remain paralyzed, about a decade behind." These circumstances motivated Góes and Dutra "to solicit insistently from the President of the Republic all the measures required for the reform of our [army's] structure. . . ."[58]

He ended the report with a review of the "internal situation" in which he cast the struggle with Flores as the "extermination of *caudilhismo*." He said that he had battled "with all of his soldier's soul for inviolable national unity and for the prestige of authority." In November 1935 "subversive elements . . . following instructions from Moscow," he declared, had threatened that prestige. And finally, "the secret document captured last year" (Cohen Plan) had led "all the country's classes, through their legitimate representatives, to agree that exceptional powers, in such emergency, should be given to the Sr. President of the Republic." The need for the declaration of a state of war amounted, in his mind, to a condemnation of the 1934 regime as incapable of "promoting the happiness of the *pátria*."[59] The country's peaceful atmosphere after November 10, he warned,

> should not delude us. Brazil, today more than ever, needs to be a militarily strong power, able to neutralize, on any field, the aggressions of our internal and external enemies. The army, in whose soul resonates, in a special way, the yearnings of the purest sentiments of *Brazilianess, places its hopes in the promises of the Government that, without doubt, will not stop championing its complete restoration*, in the very favorable situation that we are traversing. If this rare opportunity is not taken, it would be reason for the army to give up believing that it would ever be possible to carry out its high purpose. I already said, and I repeat, that the military problem can not allow incomplete, unilateral solutions. . . . All Brazilians must contribute to, and be responsible for, the common task of National Defense.[60]

Góes had the "firm conviction that the action of November 10 responded to an inevitable national necessity and, at least, [was] a barrier against the political-military decomposition that had progressed to a well advanced degree." The constitution of 1934 was proof, Góes lamented, that Brazilian statesmen had turned their backs on the "politics of reality." They had evoked the ideas of other countries without paying attention to how those countries actually solved their problems. The 1934 regime had the trappings of constitutional rule without the mechanisms, mentality, and traditions that made such a government work. The army would do its part and "the government will do the rest, fulfilling the *compromisso* it assumed to equip the Armed Forces so that they can carry out the roles reserved to them."[61]

In May 1938, Dutra stated the *compromisso* more succinctly, writing that the government "only wished peace and tranquility to develop the country economically and financially. In order to carry out its program of national renewal the government depends on the army." In his annual report to the president he affirmed that "the army no longer is interested in questions of party politics." And clarifying somewhat, he assured Vargas, that, if any rare intervention occurred, it would be "under the command of authorized chiefs to assure liberty, maintain law and order. . . ." As a mere spectator of the political scene, following unfolding events from outside, the army, every day more," the minister assured the president, "constitutes the support on which the Government can count, anytime that noxious elements try to subvert order or attack the integrity of the *Pátria*."[62]

This moment changed the way the army thought of itself.[63] From 1937 onward, the army, in the persons of its senior officers, asserted the institution's right to be national moderator. Vargas's "*compromisso*" opened the gate and the generals marched in.

Throughout the 1930s the general staff had pointed repeatedly to the United States as the best source of arms and of investments in industry. But just as Brazil was taking the turn toward more centralized and authoritarian rule, Germany was becoming an important market for Brazilian goods, particularly cotton and food stuffs, and an enthusiastic arms supplier. The famous pre-World War II American-German competition for Brazil had its origins not in ideology, but in the need of the Brazilian armed forces to arm themselves.

In June 1935, the Vargas government had arranged an informal compensation trade arrangement with Germany that through elaborate exchange mechanisms allowed Brazil to use its natural or agricultural products to obtain German manufactures. The United States objected strenuously to this closed system that removed Brazilian-German trade from the broader international system based upon gold and convertible currencies. As a result of the close linkage between obtaining arms and Brazil's international trade, the military were more than interested observers of foreign commerce, they were direct participants in the debates that shaped the government's policies.

The Brazilian government's attitude toward the United States prior to the turn of events discussed was to see the northern republic as a natural ally. After their cordial meeting in late 1936, Vargas proposed to Roosevelt that their representatives discuss full military and naval cooperation, including building of a naval base in Brazil for American use in the event of a war of aggression against the United States.[64] But Washington did not act and Brazilian leaders turned to their own needs and solutions. The high American prices, unfavorable payment conditions, and neutrality laws led the Brazilians to turn to Europe, ordering artillery in Germany, light infantry arms in Czechoslovakia, and warships in England and Italy. In the United States they ordered aircraft and material to lay down some destroyers.[65]

The Brazilian generals were painfully aware that their coastal artillery guarding entrances to the country's ports could not stop an Argentine, let alone a German, naval attack. According to Chief of Staff Góes Monteiro, it would take five years to make their defense plans operational.[66] It was to remedy the vulnerability of the ports and land frontiers that the army placed an order in Germany for US $55,000,000 in artillery and accessories in March 1938. The weapons were to be paid for mostly in compensation marks earned in the trade arrangement outlined earlier. From at least June 1936, Vargas had been worried about how to pay for the armaments. On June 15,

1936 he had noted in his diary that the only way to make the necessary purchases would be "a great reduction in payment of the foreign debt" and that could not be done under "the political regime that we are following."[67] Ultimately, defense policy drove the Vargas-Dutra-Góes alliance that resulted in the authoritarian Estado Novo.

Notes

Adapted from *Soldiers of the Pátria: A History of the Brazilian Army, 1889–1937* by Frank McCann, © 2004 by the Board of Trustees of the Leland Stanford Jr. University, by permission of the publisher.

1. Getúlio Vargas, *A nova política do Brasil* (Rio de Janeiro: José Olympio, 1938–47), 5:32; Estado-Maior do Exército (hereafter EME), *Relatório dos trabalhos do Estado-Maior . . . 1937 . . . pelo General de Divisão* [Major General, hereafter GD] *Pedro Aurélio de Góes Monteiro* (Rio de Janeiro: Imprensa do EME, 1938), 4–5, 8–9.

2. The "Young Turks" were 32 officers sent for training in Germany between 1906 and 1913. In the latter year they founded the military journal *A Defesa Nacional* to spread their reform and professional ideas throughout the army.

3. Maj. Lawrence C. Mitchell, Rio, May 20, 1937, "Pre-election Activities, Army and Politics," Rpt. No. 1869, 2657-K-74, 6000, G-2 Report, War Department (of the United States; hereafter WD), Record Group (hereafter RG) 165, NARA. This report by the American military attaché contains the proclamation text. See also Getúlio Vargas, *Diário*, 2 vols. (Rio de Janeiro: Ed. da FGV/São Paulo: Ed. Siciliano, 1995), 2:41–50, entries for May 4, 14, 17, 28–29, 31; "Valdomiro Lima," in *DHBB*, ed. Alzira Alves de Abreu, Israel Beloch, Fernando Lattman-Weltman, Sérgio Tadeu de Niemeyer Lamarão, 2nd ed., 5 vols. (Rio de Janeiro: Ed. da FGV, 2001), 3:1869; "José Pessoa," in *DHBB* 4:2706; Luiz Gonzaga Novelli Junior and Mauro Renault Leite, eds., *Marechal Eurico Gaspar Dutra* (Rio de Janeiro: Ed. Nova Fronteira, 1983), 195–196.

4. Correspondence with 15 generals, June 5–7, 1937: Góes Monteiro Papers (hereafter GMP), Arquivo do Exército, Rio de Janeiro (hereafter AE). The replies were dated June 7 or 8. For names see Frank D. McCann, *Soldiers of the Pátria: A History of the Brazilian Army, 1889–1937* (Stanford: Stanford Univ. Press, 2004), 542n6.

5. Vargas, *Diário*, 2:50, entry May 31, 1937.

6. The conversation with Generals Valdomiro, Dutra and Góes took place on June 2; Vargas used the term "military anarchy." Ibid., entry June 2, 1937.

7. Ibid., 2:53, entry June 11, 1937.

8. Lourival Coutinho, *O General Góes depõe* (Rio de Janeiro: Ed. Coelho Branco, 1956), 294–295; Maj. Lawrence C. Mitchell, Rio, June 16, 1937: "Army Feud," Rpt. No. 1900; the quote is from Pessoa's press release that appeared in June 17, 1937: "Army Feud Developments," Rpt. No 1901; June 24, 1937: "Further Developments in Army Feud,"

Rpt. No. 1909, 2006-128 6200d, Military Intelligence Division (hereafter MID), WD, RG165, NARA.

9. Elected president of the Military Club in 1944, he was active in the events of October 1945 that led to the deposition of Vargas. "José Pessoa," in *DHBB*, 4:2705–2706; Maj. Lawrence C. Mitchell, Rio, June 15, 1937: "Changes in High Command," Rpt. No. 1897; July 1, 1937: "Army Feud Approaches Settlement," Rpt. No. 1916, 2006-128, 6200d, MID, WD, RG 165, NARA (the quote is from this report).

10. José Américo de Almeida told his view of the campaign in *A palavra e o tempo (1937–1945–1950)* (Rio de Janeiro: José Olympio, 1965), 5–83.

11. Vargas, *Diário*, 2:13, entry January 18.

12. Maj. Lawrence C. Mitchell, Rio, May 11, 1937: "Maneuvers, 3rd Region (Rio Grande do Sul)," Rpt. No. 1858, 2006-151, 6700g, LCM/B, G-2 Regional, WD, RG165, NARA.

13. Vargas, *Diário*, 2:13–32; Carlos E. Cortés, *Gaúcho Politics in Brazil: The Politics of Rio Grande do Sul, 1930–1964* (Albuquerque: Univ. of New Mexico Press, 1974), 78–82; "Emílio Lúcio Esteves," in *DHBB*, 2:1205–1206; GV 37.04.28/2, AGV, FGV/CPDOC.

14. It would be a mistake to assume that the whole affair had been merely trumped up against Flores. See for example the 71 pages of correspondence on the crisis in GV 37.05.01, AGV, FGV/CPDOC. General Esteves to Eurico Dutra, Porto Alegre, June 29, 1937, teleg., GV 37.06.29/1, AGV, FGV/CPDOC. For a factual report by a foreign observer: Maj. Lawrence C. Mitchell, Rio, July 15, 1937: "Visit of Minister of War to Southern Brazil," Rpt. No. 1929, 2657-k-74, 6940c; August 17, 1937: "Displacement of Troops," Rpt. No. 1951, 2657-K-74, 6180 LCM/B, both G-2 Regional, WD, RG165, NARA.

15. Circular, Ministro de Guerra to Commandantes de Regiões e Diretores de Serviços, Rio de Janeiro, June 29, 1937, GMP, AE.

16. Quotes are from Dutra's diary, entry July 9, as in Novelli Junior and Renault Leite, eds., *Marechal Eurico Gaspar Dutra*, 199–205 (for Dutra's statement about duty, see esp. 202); and from "José Joaquim de Andrade," in *DHBB*, 1:139–140. The trip was from July 7 to 19.

17. Maj. Lawrence C. Mitchell, Rio, August 1937: "Changes in High Commands," Rpt. No. 1941, 2006-128, 6180a, MID, WD, RG165, NARA; documentary evidence regarding movement of lower ranks was not available.

18. The exchange of telegrams dated July 28, August 2, 5, and 9, 1937, are in Novelli Junior and Renault Leite, eds., *Marechal Eurico Gaspar Dutra*, 199–202; Eurico Dutra to Flores da Cunha, Rio, August 9, 1937, telegram, GV 37.08.09/2, AGV, FGV/CPDOC.

19. Novelli Junior and Renault Leite, eds., *Marechal Eurico Gaspar Dutra*, 209–212.

20. José Américo, *A palavra e o tempo*, 17–22; Hélio Silva, *1937: Todos os golpes se parecem* (Rio de Janeiro: Ed. Civilização Brasileira), 372. Vargas, *Diário*, 2:58–65. Col. Oswaldo Cordeiro de Farias, who was

Gen. Daltro's chief of staff, told how the suspected officers were removed from the regional staff: Aspácia Camargo and Walder de Góes, *Meio século de combate: Diálogo com Cordeiro de Farias* (Rio de Janeiro: Rio Fundo Ed.), 230–232. Daltro Filho to G. Vargas, Porto Alegre, August 19, 1937, GV 37.08.19, AGV, FGV/CPDOC.

21. On the destroyer deal, that would soon be torpedoed by Argentina and U.S. congressional objections, No Name, Naval Attaché's Report, Rio, August 18, 1937: "Brazil-Navy; Ships, Destroyers," Rpt. No. 912-800, Brazil 5900, G-2 Regional, MID, WD, RG165, NARA; file GV 37.08.13, AGV, FGV/CPDOC; Frank D. McCann, *Brazilian-American Alliance 1937–1945* (Princeton: Princeton Univ. Press, 1973), 113.

22. On his state of mind: Vargas, *Diário*, 2:64–67.

23. Vargas, *Diário*, 2:67, entry for August 27.

24. Executive Decree No. 1899, August 19, 1937; Maj. Lawrence C. Mitchell, Rio, September 8, 1937: "New Discipline Regulations," Rpt. No. 1973, 2006-161, 6300b, MID, WD, RG165, NARA.

25. O. Aranha to P. Góes Monteiro, Washington, March 9, 1935, AOA, FGV/CPDOC.

26. Ibid.

27. O. Aranha to Getúlio Vargas, Washington, June 4, 1937, AOA, FGV/CPDOC.

28. Vargas, *Diário*, 2:189 (Letícia crisis), 347 (Chaco War and "nossa completa falta de recursos para enfrentar uma situação"), 427 ("precariedade do nosso material bélico").

29. Stanley Hilton, *Brazil and the Great Powers, 1930–1939: The Politics of Trade Rivalry* (Austin/London: Univ. of Texas Press, 1975), 117–129.

30. EME, *Relatório dos trabalhos do Estado-Maior . . . 1936 . . . pelo GD Arnaldo de Souza Pais de Andrade* (Rio de Janeiro: Imprensa do EME, 1937), 4. Ministério da Guerra (hereafter MG), *Relatório apresentado ao Presidente da República dos Estados Unidos do Brasil pelo General de Divisão Eurico Gaspar Dutra, Ministro de Estado da Guerra em Maio de 1937* (Rio de Janeiro: Imprensa Militar, 1937), 37–38.

31. Vargas, *Diário*, 2:68–69, entries for September 7–13.

32. Michael L. Conniff, *Urban Politics in Brazil: The Rise of Populism, 1925–1945* (Pittsburgh: Univ. of Pittsburgh Press, 1981), 156–158.

33. Novelli Junior and Renault Leite, eds., *Marechal Eurico Gaspar Dutra*, 228–229 (quotes); Vargas, *Diário*, 2:70, entry for September 15–18. Dutra told Hélio Silva this version in 1959, see Silva, *1937: Todos os golpes se parecem*, 390–391.

34. Benedicto Valladares, *Tempos idos e vividos: Memórias* (Rio de Janeiro: Ed. Civilização Brasileira, 1966), 157–166. Regarding the federalization of the states' military police forces, see MG, *Relatório . . . Dutra . . . 1937*, Quarta Parte, 13–14.

35. Silva, *1937: Todos os golpes se parecem*, 455–456.

36. Vargas, *Diário*, 2:71.

37. Aspásia Camargo, Dulce Chaves Pandolfi, Eduardo Rodrigues Gomes, Maria Celina Soares d'Araújo, and Mario Grynszpan, *O golpe silencioso: As origens da república corporativa* (Rio de Janeiro: Rio Fundo Ed., 1989), 213.

38. The minutes of the meeting, which are cited in this and the next two paragraphs, appear in both Silva, *1937: Todos os golpes se parecem*, 391–399, and Novelli Junior and Renault Leite, eds., *Marechal Eurico Gaspar Dutra*, 231–238.

39. Vargas, *Diário*, 2:72, entry for September 28, 1937; Novelli Junior and Renault Leite, eds., *Marechal Eurico Gaspar Dutra*, 239. Dutra did not want to act without legal cover.

40. Dated September 29, 1937, the text is in both Silva, *1937: Todos os golpes se parecem*, 403–409; Novelli Junior and Renault Leite, eds., *Marechal Eurico Gaspar Dutra*, 239–244. For various details: "José Carlos de Macedo Soares," in *DHBB*, 4:3227–3233. Macedo was the minister of justice, March 6–September 11, 1937, who formally sent the document to the congress. On 28, according what Dutra told Hélio Silva in 1959, Vargas told the service chiefs that, if Macedo Soares did not agree with request for state of war, he would remove him. Silva, ibid.

41. Vargas, *Diário*, 2:72.

42. Camargo, Pandolfi, Gomes, d'Araújo, Grynszpan, *O golpe silencioso*, 219.

43. Silva, *1937: Todos os golpes se parecem*, 414–425, and Novelli Junior and Renault Leite, eds., *Marechal Eurico Gaspar Dutra*, 246–256 (in the midst of these events the army seized arms from Germany that arrived at Porto Alegre, see p. 254); Camargo and Góes, *Meio século de combate*, 232.

44. Vargas, *Diário*, 2:75–76.

45. Ibid., 2:74. Paulo Brandi, *Vargas: da vida para a história* (Rio de Janeiro: Jorge Zahar Ed., 1983), 119; Novelli Junior and Renault Leite, eds., *Marechal Eurico Gaspar Dutra*, 257–258.

46. Vargas, *Diário*, 2:77–78, 574. John W. F. Dulles, *Vargas of Brazil: A Political Biography* (Austin: Univ. of Texas Press), 165 wrote that Vargas told Salgado that "the Armed Forces had decided to 'change the regime' and that he had agreed with them." His source is not clear.

47. Novelli Junior and Renault Leite, eds., *Marechal Eurico Gaspar Dutra*, 258–259; Vargas, *Diário*, 2:79.

48. Vargas, *Diário*, 2:80; Glauco Carneiro, *Lusardo: o último caudilho*, 2 vols. (Rio de Janeiro: Ed. Nova Fronteira, 1978), 2:208–210; "Artur Ferreira da Costa," in *DHBB*, 2:962.

49. Vargas, *Diário*, 2:80–81; on Negrão de Lima's mission see Carneiro, *Lusardo: o último caudilho*, 2:208–210. Lusardo was Chair and Negrão was secretary of José Américo's election committee.

50. The manifesto's text appears in many places, I used Carneiro, *Lusardo: o último caudilho*, 2:210–211. See also Scotten, Rio,

November 20, 832.00/1111 and /1106, RG 59, NARA and, on
Américo's refusal to sign, Novelli Junior and Renault Leite, eds.,
Marechal Eurico Gaspar Dutra, 267.

51. "João Carlos Machado," in *DHBB*, 3:1989–1991; "Paulo de Morais
Barros," in *DHBB*, 1:331; Novelli Junior and Renault Leite, eds.,
Marechal Eurico Gaspar Dutra, 269; Vargas, *Diário*, 2:82–83.
Originally the plan was to stage the "reform" on Republic Day,
November 15.

52. Vargas, *Diário*, 2:82–83; Carneiro, *Lusardo: o último caudilho*,
2:211–212.

53. McCann, *The Brazilian-American Alliance, 1937–1945*, 46–47;
Vargas, *A nova política do Brasil*, 5:19–32, quotations from 28.

54. Novelli Junior and Renault Leite, eds., *Marechal Eurico Gaspar
Dutra*, 271. Only Generals José Pompeu de Albuquerque Cavalcanti,
commander of Coast Artillery, and Pantaleão Pessoa protested against
the new regime, both were summarily retired. Paulo Brandi said there
were five generals who were relieved for protesting, but only mentions
the two above and Guedes da Fontoura, who was likely marked for
retirement in any case; Brandi, *Vargas: da vida para a história*, 125.

55. Nélson de Mello quoted in Valentina da Rocha Lima, ed., *Getúlio:
uma história oral* (Rio de Janeiro: Ed. Record, 1986), 204; "Nélson
de Mello," in *DHBB*, 3:2191–2194. Vargas's daughter Alzira Vargas
do Amaral Peixoto told me this in an interview on August 10, 1969.
There is a discussion of this question in my *Brazilian-American
Alliance, 1937–1945*, 43.

56. Getúlio Vargas to O. Aranha, Rio, November 17, 1937, AOA,
FGV/CPDOC. He also stressed that he wanted to use American
capital "so that we would be able to avoid accepting offers from
other countries [read Germany?], that I have resisted and intend to
resist."

57. Vargas, *A nova politica do Brasil*, 5:127–128 (New Year), 145 (Porto
Alegre); rest is from Robert M. Scotten, Rio, January 19, 1938,
Dispatch 272, 832.001 Getúlio Vargas 10/47, RG59, NARA.

58. EME, *Relatório dos Trabalhos do Estado-Maior . . . 1937*, 4–5, 8–9.
"Heredamos . . . um Exercito quasi que apenas nominal, desprovido
do essencial e, portanto, imprestável para o campo de batalha" [5].

59. Ibid., 37–39.

60. Ibid., 39.

61. Ibid., 40–41.

62. MG, *Relatório . . . Dutra . . . 1938*, 6–8.

63. It has been the view of scholars that with the overthrow of the empire
in 1889 the armed forces "assumed the function of the moderating
power." See, for example, Ronald M. Schneider, *"Order and
Progress": A Political History of Brazil* (Boulder: Westview Press,
1991), 9.

64. Sumner Welles to F. D. Roosevelt, Washington, January 26, 1937, PPF 4473 (Vargas), Franklin Delano Roosevelt Library. This contains Vargas's message, which said in the event of an attack upon the United States "the vital interests of Brazil would necessarily be involved."

65. Oswaldo Aranha to Sumner Welles, Rio, November 8, 1938, AOA, FGV/CPDOC.

66. EME, Relatório *dos Trabalhos do Estado-Maior . . . 1937*, 10–11; BG Allen Kimberly (chief of American Military Mission) to Eurico Dutra, Rio, September 19, 1938: "Defense of Rio de Janeiro," 2667-K-4, Brazil 6800, G-2 Regional, RG165, NARA.

67. Vargas, *Diário*, 1:523–524.

Chapter 6

Vargas Era Social Policies: An Inquiry into Brazilian Malnutrition during the Estado Novo (1937–45)

John J. Crocitti

Social policies were key elements in the Brazilian corporatist state constructed after Getúlio Vargas assumed power in 1930. Although he did not commit the state to sweeping social policies until the Estado Novo's inception in late 1937, a perceptive Vargas would have recognized that Brazilian sentiments increasingly leaned in that direction after 1930. Scholarly articles, journalistic reports, and newspaper editorials regularly broached social issues as diverse as nutrition, education, housing, labor, physical fitness, and the family. At the same time, political extremists often justified their actions with calls for social reforms. After declaring the Estado Novo, Vargas strengthened his dictatorship by appropriating his political opponents' mantra of social reform and endorsing social policies advocated by political moderates. The wedding of social policies to a corporatist state constituted one of Vargas's most important legacies and remains controversial in the current period of neoliberalism. This study assesses Estado Novo social policies directed at one of Brazil's most serious and persistent ills, malnutrition.

A fuller appreciation for Vargas's social policies will result by first situating them in their global, historical context. During the 1930s and 1940s, leaders in Europe and the Americas retreated from liberalism to adopt a variety of political alternatives that thrust the state into daily life on an unparalleled scale. Liberalism appeared ascendant in 1900, but turbulent events and political movements—among these, Italian and Portuguese Fascism, the Mexican and Bolshevik

Revolutions, and World War I—soon warned that material depriva-
tion and cultural despair might corrode support for the liberal state.
The Depression brought liberalism's weaknesses into full view for
political leaders, raising concerns about popular discontent and forcing a reassessment of people's commitment to the liberal state. The
German turn toward Nazism not only confirmed common people's
weak allegiance to liberalism, but also warned those leaders still nominally embracing liberalism to reconsider their laissez-faire policies if
they hoped to steer their countries away from fascist and Bolshevik
solutions. These leaders responded by reforming their political
systems and social policies in a manner that would not only relieve
unrest among the popular sectors, but also benefit those private enterprises most able to comply with costly regulations and engage in
gigantic, publicly financed projects. Balancing the interests of both
popular sectors and private enterprises required a degree of state
intervention previously unimagined by liberalism's advocates. World
War II, by demanding coordinated economic activity and uninterrupted labor productivity, put the final touches on the institutionalization of state intervention into social reforms and economic policies.
By 1945, little doubt remained that economic crisis and global war
had transformed the state into a dominant force in everyday life.

The social reforms and economic policies emerging from the 1930s
and 1940s often wore, and continue to wear, a nationalist and populist garb. Leaders regularly reminded their compatriots that the time
had come to put aside class and regional differences in the spirit of
national unity. Working and fighting in union, people would move
their nations farther along the path to prosperity, modernity, democracy, and international status. As these goals became realities, an
impartial government would monitor the nation's social and economic health and, if necessary, intervene in order to guarantee everyone a rightful share of a plentiful bounty. This scenario, if brought to
fruition, represented a radical departure in favor of laboring classes.
Prior to the 1930s, governments in the Americas sometimes enacted
limited reforms on behalf of common people, for example Argentina's
Sáenz Peña Law of 1912 that expanded the franchise and the United
States' Progressive Reforms of the late nineteenth and early twentieth
centuries. Generally, however, they entirely neglected common people
when not leveling heavy doses of police repression against them such
as during Argentina's *La Semana Trájica* (The Tragic Week) and the
United States' Palmer Raids, both events occurring in 1919. During
the 1930s and 1940s, a reversal appeared in the making as governments
publicly committed themselves to ensuring the material well-being of

the entire polity. How well one government, Brazil's Estado Novo under Getúlio Vargas, lived up to that commitment is the focus of this chapter.

Brazil felt the aftershocks of global economic crisis and war as much as fully industrialized nations. Coffee exports, the country's primary means of foreign exchange, had already been in dire straits prior to 1929 while industry had progressed somewhat because of international market disruptions caused by World War I. After the Crash of 1929, little doubt remained that the heyday of Brazilian coffee exports had passed. The new Vargas regime's efforts to revive coffee prices and exports bestowed a fiscal windfall on producers, but failed to alleviate Brazil's external debt crisis. The combination of government-subsidized coffee incomes and external-debt-induced curtailment of imported manufactured products created a political and economic climate favorable to import substitution industrialization.[1] Thus, upon declaration of the Estado Novo dictatorship in late 1937, Vargas made industrialization a focal point of both policy and propaganda. Laws, such as the Industrial Property Code that dealt with patent and trademark registrations, offered guarantees necessary to lure industrial investment.[2] In other cases, the most famous being the steel mill at Volta Redonda, the government directly administered economic development.[3] Wartime exigencies gave Vargas further reason to emphasize industrialization as Brazil supplied both material and men to the Allied effort. Vargas cleverly fashioned industrialization and war into an epic undertaking that promised to modernize Brazil and assure common folk "the right to collaborate in the renovation of political and economic order."[4] Thus, when Vargas was forced to relinquish power in 1945, strong reasons existed for the public to associate industrialization, modernization, and social reform with the Estado Novo.

Official propaganda actively promoted that association while portraying it in nationalist and populist terms. Although much of the Estado Novo industrialization represented quantitative rather than qualitative growth, officials never demurred in glorifying the process as essential for the collective welfare. Workers played a special role in this process because their actions transcended the mere exchange of labor for wages. Individual workers not only toiled for themselves, but also on behalf of all other Brazilian workers who would eventually share the rewards of nationalist industrialization. Estado Novo propaganda relentlessly identified Vargas with this noble endeavor, going so far as to label him "the number 1 worker of Brazil" and "the incomparable guide who is going to be carrying Brazil to its exalted destiny."[5]

Social policy was an essential ingredient in the industrialization effort. If industrialization were to be successful, then Brazil would need healthy, skilled workers willing to submit to workplace discipline. Social reforms promised to meet that requirement by developing a modern workforce that would not upset social order. Such reforms had interested Brazilian policymakers as early as World War I, but only after Vargas's seizure of power in 1930 did authorities address social issues as anything other than a police matter.[6] Vargas accelerated the pace of reform during the Estado Novo by promulgating and codifying sweeping laws dealing with issues as diverse as labor, the family, education, a youth corps, and sports.[7] The bulk of the Estado Novo program survived Vargas's fall in 1945 and, at the least, forced the state to acknowledge its responsibility for the welfare of Brazil's common folk.

Nutrition figured prominently in Vargas's social package and, perhaps, offers a means to test the Estado Novo's actual impact on common people. Nutritional studies had begun to interest reformers only as a result of the calamities brought on by World War I.[8] By the 1930s, national and international organizations were devoting full-time attention to nutrition.[9] Economic crisis and war interrupted global food supplies after 1930, forcing increasing numbers of people to go hungry on a regular basis. Although altruism cannot be totally discounted, a number of practical considerations directed policymakers' attention to the underfed. In a depressed economy, food-relief might stimulate agricultural production and produce a positive ripple throughout the industrial sectors.[10] Above all else, a hungry population threatened political stability, perhaps especially so during the 1930s when competing ideologies stood ready to win converts and destabilize established governments.[11] Therefore, policymakers who disregarded their hungry countrymen risked losing them to subversive organizations. Wartime placed greater urgency on the food problem, not only because armies needed well-nourished soldiers, but also because better nutrition might boost morale on the home front and contribute to uninterrupted production.

Although Brazil shouldered the same political and strategic exigencies as industrialized nations during the 1930s and 1940s, its peripheral economic and cultural status acted as additional prods toward nutritional reform. Interest in nutritional reform came at a time when intellectuals were reassessing Brazil's racial and cultural heritage, on the one hand, and turning to economic nationalism, on the other. Together, these intellectual trends endowed Brazilian nutritional reform with a flavor that differed significantly from that of industrialized, or core, countries. For the idealists among Brazil's policymakers, reforms such as nutritional programs formed part of a larger project whose ultimate goal was a modern race of Brazilian workers fully in charge of the productive traits attributed to their counterparts in North Atlantic countries.

Nutritional theories fit well with nationalist intellectual sentiments that redeemed Brazil's racial and cultural heritage. Prior to 1930, racial theorists set the terms for intellectual debate by blaming Brazil's racial composition, particularly among the laboring classes, for the country's social and economic problems.[12] In a major shift after 1930, the initiative passed to intellectuals who cited colonialism and economic underdevelopment as sources of Brazil's malaise.[13] Steadfast in their belief that "nutrition makes the race," nutritionists helped debunk earlier racial theories that portrayed Brazilian laborers as inherently lazy, weak, and feebleminded.[14] Rather than shamefully indolent, Brazilian workers simply functioned at the maximum energy level allowed by their abysmal diets. Likewise, their susceptibility to disease and high mortality rates did not reflect racial flaws, but rather the inadequate intake of protective nutrients. As for intellect, if Brazilians indeed possessed reduced aptitudes for modern technology, then culpability rested in social factors such as diet instead of natural inferiority.[15]

A strong relationship also existed between nutrition and economic nationalism. From their vantage, 1930s intellectuals felt that true Brazilian independence meant graduation from an agricultural export economy to one based on modern industry. Reformers emphasized that modern machinery alone could not ensure such progress since "the worker in the factory is a living cell who acts in collaboration with the machine for the attainment of advantageous results."[16] Just as machines required lubrication, workers needed proper nutrition in order to operate at maximum efficiency and contribute fully to national progress.[17] At the same time, well-fed workers would have less reason to engage in social protests that might interrupt Brazil's march toward progress. Unquestionably, these propositions bonded food policies with social control and cooption of the working class. Nevertheless, the idealist element within Brazilian reform never ceased to present these concepts as credible steps toward nationalist development. These cynical and idealist currents blended almost imperceptibly so that an enigmatic aura surrounded Estado Novo nutritional policies.

Whether motivated by a reassessment of Brazil's racial and cultural heritage or by economic nationalism, by the end of the 1930s, nutritionists had certainly issued powerful indictments against the eating habits prevalent among Brazil's urban residents. In many cases, families "were unable to obtain the number of calories usually considered necessary."[18] In general, however, Brazilians avoided dramatic scenes of starvation, suffering, instead, from chronic malnutrition that remained hidden and misunderstood as it debilitated the popular classes. Urban workers ate especially poorly, routinely living in a condition of undernourishment despite spending over half their wages on food.[19] Experts and pundits recognized that food production and distribution, and consequently affordability and quality, were critical to nutritional reforms. At the same time, however, nutritionists directed much of the blame for undernourishment toward the workers, themselves, claiming that their miseducation and outmoded traditions led to improper food selection. By defining the problem in that manner, nutritionists partially deflected attention away from the root of Brazil's food problem, a lack of resources available to popular classes and, in particular, inadequate real wages earned by workers.

Nutritional studies and anecdotal accounts unanimously described the normal urban diet as monotonous and woefully deficient. Milk consumption, even in families with children, hardly merited serious measurement. Working-class meals almost never included green vegetables and fruit other than an occasional fried banana. Eggs occasionally entered the urban diet, but usually only at well-stocked restaurants catering to the wealthy or foreigners. Rice and fresh meat seemed more common among higher-paid workers, although consumption remained spotty at best. Only bread and beans, flavored with dried or salted meat and garnished with the ubiquitous manioc flour, consistently found their way onto working-class palates. In many instances, however, substandard bakery practices and overage beans diminished even these meager rations' salutary effects. Corn meal mixed with water, seasoned with lard or bacon grease and cooked until thick, completed working-class meals. Known as *polenta*, the dish provided the bulk necessary to fill empty stomachs and quell hunger pains, perhaps in this way masking consumers' nutritional deficiencies. Sweetened coffee might serve as a lunchtime and dinnertime aperitif or as a morning stimulant.[20]

Nutritionists routinely blamed malnutrition on popular ignorance that relegated eating "simply to the imperium of hunger or the caprice of appetite."[21] Failing to understand the value of a balanced diet, Brazilian workers sated themselves on carbohydrates and fats at the expense of nutritionally rich dairy products, green vegetables, and fruit. The Brazilian taste for manioc, a starchy root, especially riled reformers who found considerable truth to the northeastern lament, "Manioc flour fills the belly with ease, deceiving the stomach!"[22] Reformers also complained about working-class restaurants and bars, perhaps, because their public nature and location near centers of employment allowed easy scrutiny. Able to intrude on these gathering spots with both cameras and notebooks, reformers skillfully framed their pictures to include beer bottles or wall posters advertising alcohol. Consequently, photographs accompanying journal articles usually portrayed these establishments as notorious places where workers compounded their nutritional misdeeds by drinking alcoholic beverages. With proper information and guidance provided by reformers, workers would shed these bad habits in favor of nutritionally correct meals served either in the home or the workplace. Only then, asserted reformers, would Brazilians effectively confront the scourge of malnutrition.[23]

Although reformers never ignored economic factors behind Brazilian malnutrition, their strong condemnation of popular miseducation and habits drew attention away from structural problems such as low real wages, the country's weak infrastructure, and deficiencies in food production and distribution.[24] A common-sense approach immediately reveals that subtle pressures influenced how urban popular classes ate. With only 0.8 percent of their monthly salary available for the purchase of miscellaneous merchandise other than clothing, urban workers in 1930s Brazil could hardly afford refrigerators or ice boxes.[25] In 1939, a bottom-line Montgomery Ward refrigerator cost 3:400$000 in Rio de Janeiro, putting it out of reach for the majority of working people throughout Brazil.[26] In many cases, Brazil's infrastructure further complicated food storage for urban consumers by rendering electrical appliances useless. According to the 1940 census, approximately one-half of urban residential buildings in the state of Rio de Janeiro lacked electricity.[27] Even for those urban folk who could afford refrigerators and had electrical service, the onset of World War II reduced Brazilian imports of such consumer durables as foreign suppliers geared up for military production.[28] Without refrigeration, the purchase of perishable items such as milk, fresh meat, and green vegetables would be unwise unless they were consumed immediately. Nevertheless, people often miscalculated when purchasing groceries, forcing them to decide between throwing out expensive meat or fish, whether uncooked or leftovers, and risking food poisoning by eating the suspect food. Children, such as 6-year-old Maria Lopes of Rio de Janeiro, who knew hunger but nothing of food poisoning, often required medical treatment after sating themselves with spoiled food found in their household kitchen.[29] Institutional kitchens, where refrigeration was available, also sometimes neglected sanitary procedures, resulting in cases of food poisoning such as that suffered by more than 160 patients and employees at Rio de Janeiro's Guilherme da Silveira Hospital, who ate contaminated *bacalhau* (salted cod fish).[30] Even when purchased for immediate consumption, fresh meat and fish posed a risk since vendors frequently sold spoiled goods rather than take a loss. Consumers, whom experience had taught to be suspicious, commonly accused suppliers and vendors of selling rotten meat or fish, as occurred in 1944 when an outbreak of food poisoning in Niterói led to allegations against a supplier of beef to a local butcher shop.[31]

Unable to store perishable foods at home and suspicious of food vendors, urban working-class families assumed diets that minimized the risk of spoilage and food poisoning. Of nine items included in a diet moderately above subsistence level, only fresh meat risked spoilage without refrigeration.[32] The others were either dried, cured, precooked, or refined foods requiring no refrigeration. In a similar fashion, the rhythm of working-class life in the city dictated much about culinary practice. Eight-hour and longer shifts, plus substantial commuting time, meant that workers rose early, hurried to work, and returned exhausted at mid-evening. With economic conditions pushing working-class wives and daughters into the workplace, the image of a well-cooked supper waiting for the tired husband who is rushing home matched reality only for households solidly within the middle class. The cost of a gas stove and shortages of gas further discouraged working-class families from healthy cuisine that featured relatively greaseless baking and broiling. Stovetop burners, fueled by a small amount of charcoal and kerosene, could sizzle grease and boil water quickly, in contrast to the larger amounts of precious fuel and time required to heat an oven for baking. Less affluent households reliant on tabletop kerosene burners did not even have the option of baking and broiling.[33] For lower income groups, whose needs were better fulfilled by an expedient meal than a well-prepared one, frying was preferable to longer, more costly procedures involved with baking or broiling, thereby creating a reliance on lard and fatty bacon despite their low nutritional value.[34]

If urban workers spent all or most of their incomes to meet subsistence needs, then modern conveniences related to food preservation and preparation clearly stood out of reach. Lacking refrigerators or even an obsolete icebox in which to store perishables, working-class families had to consume fresh meat, greens, and milk shortly after the bi-weekly or tri-weekly *feira livre* visited their neighborhood. Local grocery stores existed, but their higher prices made housewives reluctant to abandon the *feira livre* despite the latter's reputation for fraudulent practices, such as cheating on weights and measures, and evasion of governmental price controls.[35] With housewives preferring the *feira livre*, even the lucky minority of households earning more than the cost of a subsistence diet could only enjoy fresh foods two or three times weekly. It is also obvious that one family member, alone, could not provide the household's subsistence intake. Husbands, wives, single parents, and older children all had to contribute toward meeting food expenses. Time spent away from home meant that meals had to be rushed. Even when wives stayed at home and took in laundry or sewing, time available for cooking diminished.[36] With cooking time limited, frying and boiling made sense and, thereby, helps explain the prevalence of potatoes, manioc, lard, and bacon in the working-class diet.

Although the most prestigious nutritional experts emphasized education as central to improved Brazilian nutrition, their poignant descriptions of working-class diets left little doubt of the poverty plaguing working-class Brazilians. Journalists and politicians, who possessed fewer academic credentials and defined the problem more colloquially than the experts, tended to see improved nutrition in terms of increasing the food supply and regulating markets, policies that might lower prices, or seen from another perspective, raise real wages. The experts and nonexperts did not seriously disagree. Instead, they simply addressed the problem with different emphases and terminologies, perhaps since the experts spoke to Brazil's intellectual and political elite whereas nonexperts, including those influenced by the experts, communicated to a broader audience.[37]

A campaign to encourage milk consumption illustrated how nutritional education advocated by experts might overshadow structural problems cited by pundits. In 1938, the milk industry intensified promotional efforts with its "Drink More Milk" campaign. Designed to encourage sales, the campaign nevertheless possessed an academic aura by stressing milk's nutritional value in a manner that mimicked expert studies. Texts of one or two paragraphs appearing in newspapers and movie theaters under titles such as "Milk Is the Basis for Excellent Health," "Milk in the Feeding of the Poor," "What a Liter of Milk Furnishes Us," and "We Should and Can Drink More Milk!" extolled milk consumption with an air of scientific authority similar to that expressed by the nutritional experts quoted in governmental communiqués. Moreover, these texts never revealed a link to commercial interests. With the Estado Novo's climate of controlled news releases, knowledgeable commentators mistakenly attributed the campaign to the government's Serviço de Propaganda e Educação Sanitária (SPES; Hygiene Education and Propaganda Service) and to nutritionists lending their expertise to the government. National regulations dealing with milk's inspection, purity, healthfulness, and nutritional content had indicated the Vargas government's interest in dairy consumption as early as 1934, thereby adding to speculation that the government was behind the "Drink More Milk" campaign. Despite their error, commentators correctly understood that improved milk consumption depended on more than clever propaganda and a new dairy code:

"Drink more milk" is the refrain. *It is all very fine to say that!* Drink it how, if in Rio it costs an exorbitant price, inaccessible even to those least abandoned by fate? Since the propaganda started, its price has risen in the same proportion that the cubic centimeters of each liter have diminished. And, will the value of the product—the water-milk that is imposed on the public—be the same as the food of proclaimed excellence? . . . Make the propaganda. But, without the complementary action that imposes the product's purity and lowers its cost to a reasonable level, the torture will increase for whoever already cannot drink even the "less milk"—the watered milk.[38] (Italics in original and italics originally written in English)

Laws ensuring product quality were important steps toward solving malnutrition, as were efforts to educate the public by experts, political leaders, and commercial interests. Well-publicized arrests of vendors who sold adulterated milk, such as a Rio de Janeiro gang that used stolen government dairy inspection seals in their scheme to water down milk, also improved product quality and increased consumer confidence.[39] Nevertheless, commentators who derided the "Drink More Milk" campaign understood that, more than anything else, the relationship between wages and food prices shaped Brazil's nutritional problem as Vargas put together the Estado Novo's social programs. Most Brazilians could not afford to provide each member of their family with a sample food basket, containing little more than a moderate subsistence diet (table 6.1) In 1938, the Estado Novo's first year, less than a third of blue- and white-collar workers sampled in the Federal District earned enough to pay for these modest household rations (table 6.2). Viewed from the opposite perspective, approximately 70 percent of workers earned monthly salaries less than the cost of a sample monthly diet for an average family of four. Those workers who could purchase the sample hardly overfed their families since the sample monthly ration for each person included only 1.20 liters of milk while totally omitting eggs, green vegetables, and fruit. Figures for 1939 painted an even more dismal picture since they included samples from urban areas outside the capital. Nationally,

Table 6.1 Sample Food Basket for a Moderate Subsistance Diet Plus "Luxury" Items

Food	Monthly Consumption
1. Dry Beans	4.80 kg
2. Manioc Flour	3.60 kg
3. Dried/Salted Meat	0.80 kg
4. Coffee	1.35 kg
5. Sugar	4.20 kg
6. Bread	9.00 kg
7. Rice	4.20 kg
8. Corn/Corn Meal	1.20 kg
9. Fresh Meat	2.70 kg
10. Lard	0.60 kg
11. Bacon	1.60 kg
12. Milk	1.20 L
13. Potatoes	3.00 kg
14. Onions	3.00 kg
15. Butter	0.60 kg

Note: Items 1–6 comprised a common minimum subsistence diet. The addition of items 7–9 yielded a common moderate subsistence diet. Items 10–15 were considered common "luxury" foods.

Table 6.2 Approximate Percentage of Industrial and Commercial Workers in Brazil Earning At Least Four Times Food-Basket Total Cost

Year	Industrial Workers	Commercial Workers
1938	29.78[*†]	—
1939	19.17[†]	—
1944	24.64	42.03
1945	26.99	41.97
1946	33.31	46.01
1948	32.18	51.71
1949	37.60	53.98
1950	43.32	59.30

Note: * Federal District only; † Blue- and white-collar workers.

only a fifth of sampled urban workers could supply their families with the sample food basket (table 6.2). Of six major urban areas surveyed in 1939, workers fared best in the Federal District, São Paulo, and Porto Alegre where around one-fourth of sampled workers earned the market basket's cost (table 6.3). Conditions deteriorated considerably in Belo Horizonte and Salvador, while in Recife less than one in ten workers sampled could afford luxuries such as milk, potatoes, and onions for their families.

Table 6.3 Approximate Percentage of Industrial Workers of Six Urban Areas Earning At Least Four Times Food-Basket Total Cost

Município	1939	1944	1949
Federal District	26.34[†]	61.23	53.56
São Paulo	23.48[†]	41.57	52.51
Porto Alegre	27.29[†]	44.71	59.43
Belo Horizonte	18.49[†]	14.47	27.06
Salvador	11.62[†]	08.07	13.33
Recife	06.39[†]	08.37	11.40

Note: [†] Blue- and white-collar workers. Given that tables 6.2–6.4 indicate consistently higher wages and salaries for commercial workers, industrial workers probably fared worse in 1939 than indicated in table 6.3.

The wage-food price relationship illuminates several important facets of daily life faced by urban, popular classes as the Estado Novo commenced. Foremost, with incomes so low that acquisition of subsistence needs became problematic, hunger avoidance and not nutritional theory influenced workers' dietary habits. Critics might deride the monotonous use of beans and bread in popular cuisine, but, in 1939, a meal consisting of one kilogram of each item cost 30.7 percent less than two kilograms of perishable fresh meat (table 6.1).[40] Similarly, although experts recommended milk for children, an equivalent expenditure on nonperishable corn meal allowed mothers to cook a porridge that, when liberally thinned with water, could sate young bellies for a longer period (table 6.1).[41]

Despite the fanfare accompanying policy statements and projects, undernourishment remained widespread among urban, popular sectors throughout the Estado Novo. The nuances of popular, urban cuisine all flowed from one factor: the depressed level of working-class wages relative to food prices. Estado Novo leaders might have failed to understand that relationship's significance or purposely sidestepped the problem because its solution would have meant the redistribution of wealth toward popular classes. Some might have believed that, in the long term, Brazil's industrialization would elevate real wages and agricultural production, thereby obviating stronger measures to contain food prices. Whatever their reasoning, Estado Novo officials publicized the need to raise workers' nutritional awareness, but left unanswered questions about affordability of proper nutrition.

Implementation of food policies also lacked comprehensiveness as a few, highly publicized projects improved conditions for only a fraction of Brazil's urban working class. Vargas enacted a variety of laws and programs dealing with nutrition and food-relief throughout the Estado Novo. In some cases, laws regulated market conditions in an attempt to increase supplies and limit prices. In 1941, after severe floods struck southern agricultural regions, Vargas prohibited rice exports and authorized strict measures against speculation in the commodity. Also in 1941, he approved resolutions by the Commission for Defense of the National Economy that imposed price controls on basic foodstuffs.[42] Other laws sought improved domestic food production and distribution. Thus, in a 1943 decree, Vargas not only mandated government manipulation of food supplies and prices, but also allowed government operation of slaughterhouses, flourmills, and storage facilities.[43] Food occupied such a high priority among Estado Novo policymakers that nutritional policy sometimes found its way into seemingly unrelated laws. For example, the 1940 decree creating the Brazilian Youth Corps contained an obligatory acknowledgment of the role of food in proper child rearing.[44]

Planners also made food-relief an integral part of state-run developmental projects. The National Motor Works, located on the national capital's outskirts, maintained its own agricultural lands as a means to augment food supplies for its workers and their families. Workers and students at the National Agricultural Research College, also near Rio de Janeiro, enjoyed similar benefits at the facility's well-stocked cafeteria. Architects also remembered the importance of food when planning important bureaucratic structures such as the grandiose building of the Ministry of Labor, Industry, and Commerce. The restaurant perched atop the ministry surely impressed provincial labor and management officials conducting negotiations in the capital. Gazing over the beautiful panorama while enjoying a delicious meal, many of them would have sensed that great things were in store for Brazil. It mattered little that their unsophisticated hometowns had yet to undergo such renovation. *Cariocas* dined in a "workers' palace," and that was the message these provincial leaders would deliver to the people back home.[45]

The Estado Novo's most ambitious and publicized nutritional program was the Serviço de Alimentação da Providência Social (SAPS; Social Welfare Food Service). Created in 1941, SAPS promised to improve Brazilian workers' nutrition through a combination of hygienic, affordable central restaurants and workplace lunchrooms operated in conjunction with educational campaigns designed to alter dietary habits.[46] Right from the start, however, SAPS bore several defects that belied its high-profile concern for workers. First, only those workers contributing to the government sanctioned pension institutes would be eligible for SAPS benefits, thus skipping over the multitude who labored in the informal economy or for employers not complying with pension laws.[47] Lunchroom provisions also left many workers unaffected since a 1939 law, upon which SAPS's responsibilities would later be based, required lunchrooms only in workplaces with over 500 employees.[48] Finally, while the provision of workers' restaurants and lunchrooms might appear a generous government offering, much of the money for these projects came out of workers' own pockets. Fiscal regulations obliged official pension funds, into which insured workers donated up to 8 percent of their salaries, to finance SAPS's central administration and related services.[49] Set up as an autonomous service, SAPS also levied a 10-percent markup on meals in order to cover operating costs. Instead of offering food handouts to the needy, therefore, SAPS redirected relatively well-off workers and, perhaps more importantly, their funds to operations directly under official bureaucratic control.

SAPS's educational aspects answered nutritionists' complaints about Brazilian dietary habits by making it incumbent upon the state to alter workers' mealtime behavior. SAPS's nutritionists were to fan throughout the country, analyze regional dietary practices and needs among workers, and draw up appropriate nutritional guidelines. Concentrating on workplaces, officials would then disseminate propaganda urging adoption of nutritionally correct meals. Meanwhile, SAPS's restaurants and lunchrooms would change workers' eating habits by introducing them to proper foods. When not engaging workers collectively, SAPS's officials were to intervene intimately in working-class family life by visiting individual homes and reorienting the daily kitchen routine. In a glaring omission, however, the SAPS law never explained how working-class families would pay for improved diets or find time for healthy culinary practice.

SAPS successfully maintained several highly publicized restaurants for workers in Rio de Janeiro. In 1942, restaurants began service at the National Press and the National Student Union, the latter serving

600 students daily. Vargas personally sampled the first lunches served at the National Porcelain Works, not coincidentally, on May Day in 1943. Located in Inhaúma, a working-class neighborhood, this restaurant served local residents and 500 workers at a nearby textile mill in addition to the porcelain workers. Two hundred of the workers' school-aged sons and daughters also received daily meals. The July 1943 opening of a fourth restaurant, located at the Stevedores' Union hall, blended politics and food-relief into a spectacular propaganda offering. In addition to Vargas, dignitaries present at the 500-seat restaurant included: Ernani do Amaral Peixoto, Vargas's son-in-law who was appointed *interventor* for the state of Rio de Janeiro during the Estado Novo and elected as the state's governor during Brazil's postwar democracy; Marcondes Filho, Brazil's labor minister; SAPS Director Edison Cavalcanti; Colonel Alcides Etchegoyen, police chief for the city of Rio de Janeiro; Colonel Jonas Correa, the city's secretary of education; Stevedores' Union President Manoel Fonseca, along with the union's entire directorate; and high-ranking civilian and military authorities. Extracting maximum propaganda value from the event, Vargas and his coterie arrived at the restaurant at 1 o'clock, the busy lunchtime. After being greeted with applause from the stevedores, Vargas and the other dignitaries patiently passed through the restaurant's food line, carrying the same aluminum trays as workers did while awaiting service, and then dined among workers on a lunch composed of roast beef, carrot soup, rice, beans, milk, bread, butter, and bananas. During the gathering, Vargas, Cavalcanti, and Fonseca delivered speeches in which they enthusiastically praised each other and the entire Estado Novo administration. Since Rio de Janeiro was Brazil's capital and a cosmopolitan media center, national and international wires undoubtedly relayed flattering propaganda similar to that contained in a flyer distributed to stevedores as they ate:

Worker:
The State complies with what it promises and achieves what is necessary. It remains vigilant in defense of the rights and interests of the collectivity, and its anxieties are also the ordeals of the popular classes—for a more prosperous Brazil, for a greater Brazil. This banquet in which you participate, and which marks a new stage in the efforts for the bettering of the Brazilian Man, is an utmost example of the certainty with which we walk forward, leaving behind difficulties perhaps judged insuperable. Alongside each of us, at this instant, is President Getúlio Vargas, a worker who is, also, of national greatness—our leader and our friend, lending prestige to the work that is now being inaugurated, and which

represents a gesture of true and democratic collaboration between SAPS and the country's labor organs.[50]

As with much of the rhetoric of nutritional reform, the message to the stevedores glorified the state and its personification, Getúlio Vargas, as defenders of social harmony and national greatness. For stevedores in the national capital whose union leaders had privileged access to political leaders, the message might have rung true, especially as they ate a nutritious meal in SAPS's new restaurant. For other workers, however, such as those in the informal economy and those residing in political backwaters, such public relations events did little to assure the affordability of proper nutrition.

SAPS's foremost restaurant, Central Restaurant, located at Rio de Janeiro's Bandeira Plaza, daily served low-cost lunches to 2,500 people under regimented conditions. Although the restaurant provided convenient propaganda for the government's *Hora do Brasil* (Hour of Brazil) radio program, officials openly admitted that demand for its services outstripped its capacity.[51] Those who did dine at Central Restaurant, however, followed a regime that anticipated their conversion into proper industrial workers. After paying an entrance fee, they scrubbed up at the washroom and, then, climbed a spiral ramp to the dining room. Continuing their regimented route and procedure, they collected utensils and various entrees at the serving area before sitting at one of over 300 tables so that "everything runs under the greatest order and discipline."[52] After bringing their dirty utensils to the disposal area, customers went to a special exit that separated them by sex and registered "the number of each one for control."[53] Attendants then allowed an equal number to enter, thereby producing a continuous, well-regulated flow of people whose movement resembled a smoothly operating assembly line. As with other SAPS projects, Central Restaurant was a showpiece, not only of improved nutrition, but also of a dining environment and routine appropriate for a modern, well-disciplined working class.

At best, the Estado Novo's nutritional policies resulted in mixed success. At worst, they represented cynical instruments of control, cooption, and propaganda that conferred meaningful benefits only to participants in modernized industrial, commercial, or bureaucratic sectors. In either case, by 1945, even government officials recognized that Brazil's food problem persisted despite a variety of relief measures. A family allowance program granted money to families with eight or more children. However, the majority of these grants went to rural families, a group that Vargas substantially excluded from working-class rights and protections through Article Seven of the Consolidação das Leis do Trabalho (CLT).[54] Institution of a minimum wage, partially calculated from the cost of food, promised to alleviate malnutrition in working-class households, but failed in several respects since enforcement was problematic and companies sometimes responded to the minimum wage by withdrawing voluntary benefits such as free lunches.[55] In addition, employers who provided meals, housing, or other benefits to their employees could legally discount the minimum wage by up to 30 percent.[56] Thus, rural workers housed in rudimentary cabins by landowners, and service workers given a cheap lunch by restaurateurs and hoteliers received monetary salaries less than the minimum wage even though minimum-wage laws covered both groups. In January 1945, Vargas tacitly conceded the government's failure to end malnutrition by encouraging companies employing over 300 people to open low-cost grocery stores for their workers.[57] As with other Estado Novo policies, company stores offered a degree of food-relief, but never enough to match the magnitude of Brazilian malnutrition. Thus, when the military terminated the Estado Novo in October 1945, Brazilian nutritional consumption remained "among the world's lowest."[58]

The wage-food price relationship demonstrated that malnutrition still plagued Brazilians in 1945. During the Estado Novo's final two years, only one-fourth of sampled industrial workers earned salaries greater than the sample food basket's cost (table 6.2). While this represented a statistical improvement from 1939, three-fourths of those industrial workers lacked the purchasing power necessary to supply their families with a limited diet. White-collar workers sampled in wholesale commercial establishments, such as clerks and salespeople, faired better than industrial workers, but the majority of them still earned less than the sample food basket's cost when the Estado Novo ended (table 6.2). Under such circumstances, the Estado Novo can hardly be considered a victory over Brazilian malnutrition.

Regional variations in the wage-food price relationship imply that people living in industrial, commercial, and bureaucratic centers had greater reason for optimism. São Paulo's impressive gains between 1939 and 1944 probably reflected the growth of large-scale industry in the area (table 6.3). SAPS targeted large enterprises, thereby placing São Paulo's workers in a better position to receive food benefits than their counterparts in less developed regions. By helping to make up the difference between industrial wages and food prices, SAPS allowed industrialists to pay their workers less than was required to reproduce their labor. This represented a subsidy that favored São Paulo's industrialists over their rivals in less developed regions. At the same time, SAPS expanded the market for efficient producers of nutritionally correct foods such as wheat, rice, and meat. Porto Alegre, its hinterland consisting of fertile grasslands, boasted important commodity markets and food processing operations. As a result, workers in this southern city also registered substantial improvements in the wage-food price relationship during the Estado Novo (tables 6.3 and 6.4).

Table 6.4 Approximate Percentage of Commercial Workers of Six Urban Areas Earning At Least Four Times Food-Basket Total Cost

Município	1939	1944	1949
Federal District	26.34[†]	74.12	76.86
São Paulo	23.48[†]	54.53	68.62
Porto Alegre	27.29[†]	64.44	64.96
Belo Horizonte	18.49[†]	33.39	38.24
Salvador	11.62[†]	32.89	41.63
Recife	06.39[†]	30.75	42.78

Note: †Blue- and white-collar workers. Given that tables 6.2–6.4 indicate consistently lower wages and salaries for industrial workers, commercial workers probably fared better in 1939 than indicated in table 6.4.

By far, the Federal District's workers benefited most from the Estado Novo. Several factors, in addition to those affecting *paulistas*, acted in favor of the national capital's workers. First, bureaucratic expansion and its attendant rise in patronage jobs, many of them connected to social programs such as SAPS, helped drive up nominal wages. At the same time, the bureaucracy acted as an influential political constituency whose satisfaction depended, in large part, on reasonable food prices. Fully grasping the bureaucracy's strategic political position, Vargas tried to capture its support through popular programs such as SAPS and by keeping food prices tolerable. In addition, Rio de Janeiro's bureaucratic prominence meant that national and international attention automatically focused on the city's living conditions, thereby encouraging officials to head off embarrassing complaints over food prices. Finally, proximity to the Labor Ministry buttressed *cariocas'* tradition of labor activism, forcing employers to concede relatively better wages and benefits to their employees.[59] These factors led to a dramatic improvement in the wage-food price relationship for the Federal District's workers sampled during the Estado Novo (tables 6.3 and 6.4). Nevertheless, more than one-third of the capital's industrial workers still could not purchase this study's sample food basket for their families in 1944.

The improvements felt by workers sampled in Rio de Janeiro, São Paulo, and Porto Alegre never occurred in less developed regions. Despite modest improvements in their ability to purchase food, approximately two-thirds of sampled commercial workers in Belo Horizonte, Salvador, and Recife still lacked the earnings necessary to ensure proper nutrition as the Estado Novo entered its final year. Industrial workers sampled in those cities fared even worse, struggling simply to stave off hunger since their wages remained abysmally behind local food prices throughout the Estado Novo (tables 6.3 and 6.4). To some degree, the Estado Novo's limited successes came at the expense of these unfortunate regions. Without large industries or bureaucratic interest groups that might grab policymakers' attention, these regions simply languished. Unable to feed their families, many workers migrated to Rio de Janeiro and São Paulo in search of the progress advertised in government propaganda. These migrants provided the labor pool necessary for continued economic development in Rio de Janeiro and São Paulo while augmenting these cities' populist political base. As a result, Vargas's policies reinforced regional economic disparity well beyond the Estado Novo's duration. As the 1940s drew to a close, therefore, national statistics pointed to continued gradual improvement in the wage-food price relationship (table 6.2) while statistics from the six cities in this study indicated persistent regional gaps in food's affordability (tables 6.3 and 6.4).

The data on commercial and industrial workers' wages warns that conditions were worse than officially indicated. According to official statistics, employees at wholesale commercial establishments consistently earned more than industrial workers, perhaps encouraging the conclusion that all commercial workers enjoyed that advantage. However, the data omitted thousands of commercial workers who commonly received a free meal in lieu of the minimum wage's complete monetary value. The omission would have been significant in the national and major state capitals because of their proliferation of cafés, luncheonettes, bars, restaurants, recreation clubs, hospitals, monasteries, convents, and pensions that employed kitchen staffs, counter help and servers.[60] Statisticians, therefore, skewed the wage data, giving greater weight to employees at wholesale commercial establishments that, in addition to not offering meals coupled with wage discounts, were more inviting sites for collective bargaining and higher wages than small businesses, medical facilities, recreational clubs, and religious institutions. Similarly, the data on industrial workers probably overstated wages since workers benefiting from Brazil's industrial growth and labor activism, such as those in the São Paulo suburb of Santo André, received more bureaucratic and statistical attention than nonunionized workers in less dynamic locales.[61] Underpaid and underemployed workers in the informal economy likely were missing from the data entirely.

There was also another form of inequality that complicated Brazil's food problem. When the Estado Novo ended in 1945, urban families in the popular sectors probably fed themselves as they had during the early 1930s. As many family members as possible sought employment because the household head, alone, could not feed the family. Unfortunately, this survival strategy produced diminishing returns. Women normally earned less than men, as was the case in 1942 when monthly industrial salaries for women averaged only 58 percent of those for men. Teenagers entering the industrial workforce faired no better, with substantial declines in earning power for younger workers.[62] Even when mothers and teenagers supplemented the fathers' income, proper nutrition might not be attainable. For single mothers and independent teenagers, survival itself could not be taken for granted.

The Estado Novo's nutritional policies reflected a global trend toward state involvement in social reforms and economic development. While concepts and policies resembled those in core countries, the Estado Novo never produced the same results for common Brazilians. Starting from a lower economic base than core countries, the Estado Novo had much more difficult obstacles to overcome. Furthermore, after 1945, North Atlantic countries, the United States in particular, but also those whose economies had been weakened by the war, resumed their economic leverage over industrializing nations by providing the capital necessary for the latter to maintain their pace of nationalist development.[63] As a result, core countries could partially pay for social programs with profits made in the periphery. Brazilians lacked such a luxury and had to finance their social programs either by recirculating workers' own funds or by condemning certain regions in their country to abject poverty. The only other alternative would have been some form of revolutionary social change. Given Vargas's predilection toward control and manipulation of workers during the Estado Novo, the latter option clearly was not on the table. Thus, while improvements in nutrition occurred during and after the Estado Novo, they never eliminated malnutrition as a fact of everyday life for a large sector of the population. By the 1960s, even modest nutritional gains stopped coming so that Brazilians, such as the São Paulo slum dweller, Carolina Maria de Jesus, still "fought against the real slavery—hunger!"[64]

Methodological Appendix

All wage and price data were derived from absolute numbers supplied by the *Anuário Estatístico do Brasil*. The *Anuário Estatístico* divided blue- and white-collar workers separately into wage brackets, listing the absolute number of workers in each bracket. From these absolute numbers, calculations derived the percentages of workers in each wage bracket. These wage calculations were of two sorts. First, blue- and white-collar workers in the *municípios* of all state capitals plus the Federal District were separately totaled to calculate national percentages of workers from each group that fell within each wage bracket. Second, separate calculations produced the percentages of blue- and white-collar workers in each wage bracket for six selected cities: the Federal District, São Paulo, Porto Alegre, Belo Horizonte, Salvador, and Recife. For 1938 and 1939, workers receiving benefits such as food and housing were not counted because employers deducted their value from money wages. Calculation of percentages in each wage bracket was a straightforward process without tricky mathematics.[65]

Determining the cost of a sample food basket required a more complex process. First, a determination of popular dietary patterns for 1930s and 1940s Brazil was made on the basis of factors described in the text. This diet reflected popular tastes and usage, not nutritional value. Once a list of food was drawn up, the author assigned daily rations to each item based on army, navy, and police recommendations of the early 1930s.[66] The author always selected the lowest ration recommended for an item from among the three standards, thus favoring a low-cost sample food basket, but not necessarily a nutritious one. Daily rations were multiplied by 30 to arrive at monthly figures that could be used in conjunction with monthly wage data. In some years, the *Anuário Estatístico* calculated national average prices for food items. For other years, the author performed the calculations by averaging each item's price in state capitals plus the Federal District.[67] Monthly ration was multiplied by average price to arrive at the monthly cost for each item. These costs were then totaled and multiplied by four, assuming a slightly optimistic household size.[68] As is obvious at this point, selection of data and methods generally favored higher wages and lower total food costs, thus biasing the wage-food price relationship toward a best-case scenario. The only significant deviation from this routine involved the use of bacon instead of lower costing fish because data for the latter was unavailable.

To arrive at the percent of industrial workers earning more than the food-basket cost, a linear interpolation became necessary. For example, the total food-basket cost on a national level in 1950 was Cr$1235.44. For 1950, the *Anuário Estatístico* divided workers into the following monthly wage brackets: Cr$0–299, Cr$300–399, Cr$400–599, Cr$600–799, Cr$800–999, Cr$1000–1499, Cr$1500–1999, Cr$2000 and above, and those earning commissions. Nationally, 29.06 percent of industrial workers earned monthly salaries in excess of Cr$1499 and, thus, could afford the sample (those earning commissions were also considered able to purchase the sample). Linear interpolation within the Cr$1000–1499 income bracket followed in this manner:

(Cr$1499 − Cr$1235)/Cr$500 × 27.01 percent = 14.26 percent, with 27.01 percent representing the percentage of workers within the Cr$1000–1499 income bracket

The 14.26 percent derived from this linear interpolation was added to the previous figure of 29.06 percent to determine that 43.32 percent of industrial workers nationally could afford the sample in 1950 (table 6.2).

Notes

1. Werner Baer, *The Brazilian Economy: Growth and Development*, 3rd ed. (New York: Praeger, 1989), 24–47; Warren Dean, *The Industrialization of São Paulo 1880–1945* (Austin: Univ. of Texas Press, 1969), 83–239; Celso Furtado, *The Economic Growth of Brazil: A Survey from Colonial to Modern Times*, trans. Ricardo W. de Aguiar and Eric Charles Drysdale (Berkeley: Univ. of California Press, 1965), 193–239; Nelson Werneck Sodré, *História da burguesia brasileira*, 3rd. ed. (Rio de Janeiro: Ed. Civilização Brasileira, 1976), 247–308; John D. Wirth, *The Politics of Brazilian Development, 1930–1954* (Stanford: Stanford Univ. Press, 1970), 1–68.

2. Decree-Law N. 7903, August 27, 1945, in *Lex Coletânea de Legislação*, vol. 9 (São Paulo: Lex Ltda. Editôra, 1945).

3. Werner Baer, *The Development of the Brazilian Steel Industry* (Nashville: Vanderbilt Univ. Press, 1969), 68–79; José Ricardo Ramalho, *Estado-Patrão e Luta Operária: o caso FNM* (Rio de Janeiro: Paz e Terra, 1989), 17–141; Wirth, *The Politics of Brazilian Development*, 71–129.

4. Getúlio Vargas, speech, September 7, 1942, in *Boletim do Ministério do Trabalho, Indústria e Comércio* (hereafter BMTIC) 9, no. 98 (October 1942).

5. Marcondes Filho, "Volta Redonda e o trabalhador nacional," speech at Volta Redonda, 1944, in *BMTIC* 10, no. 117 (May 1944): 134–135.

6. Two examples of pre-1930 attempts at social reforms dealt with apprenticeship programs and workers' retirement plans in 1918 and 1923, respectively. See: Decree N. 13064, June 12, 1918, in *Coleção das Leis da República dos Estados Unidos do Brasil de 1918*, vol. 2 (Rio de Janeiro: Imprensa Nacional); Decree N. 4682, January 24, 1923, in *Coleção das Leis de 1923*, vol. 1.

7. For example, see laws regulating unions, organization and protection of the family, industrial education, the Brazilian Youth Corps, and sports. Decree-Law N. 1402, July 5, 1939, in *Coleção das Leis de 1939*, vol. 6; Decree-Law N. 3200, April 19, 1941, in *Coleção das Leis de 1941*, vol. 3; Decree-Law N. 4073, January 30, 1942, in *Coleção das Leis de 1942*, vol. 1; Decree-Law N. 2072, March 8, 1940, in *Coleção das Leis de 1940*, vol. 1; Decree-Law N. 3199, April 14, 1941, in *Coleção das Leis de 1941*, vol. 3.

8. Josué de Castro, "Alimentação racional," *O Observador* 4, no. 47 (December 1939): 25–27; Lincoln de Freitas Filho, "A alimentação no Brasil," *O Observador* 8, no. 87 (April 1943): 30; Francisco de Assis Guedes de Vasconcelos, "Fome, eugenia, e constituição do campo da nutrição em Pernambuco: uma análise de Gilberto Freyre, Josué de Castro e Nelson Chaves," *História, Ciências, Saúde-Manguinhos* 8 (julho–agosto 2001): 316–317.

9. During the 1930s and 1940s, the *International Labour Review*, published by the International Labour Office, regularly carried feature articles and short notices from around the globe concerning dietary conditions. During the same period, the United States Department of Labor frequently addressed American nutrition in its journal, *Monthly Labor Review*.

10. Castro, "Alimentação racional," 27.

11. For the Latin American perspective, see Thomas C. Wright, "The Politics of Urban Provisioning in Latin American History," in *Food, Politics, and Society in Latin America*, ed. John C. Super and Thomas C. Wright (Lincoln: Univ. of Nebraska Press, 1985), 24–45. For an overview of the extreme right and left in 1930s Brazil, see: Robert M. Levine, *The Vargas Regime: The Critical Years, 1934–1938* (New York: Columbia Univ. Press, 1970).

12. Among the best known of the racial theorists, Nina Rodrigues linked Afro-Brazilians to criminality; see Nina Rodrigues, *Os africanos no Brasil*, revised and preface by Homero Pires, 4th ed. (São Paulo: Companhia Ed. Nacional, 1976), especially chapter IX. Another racial theorist was Oliveira Viana who employed eugenics in his analysis of Brazilian history. For a sample of Viana's eugenic theories, see Oliveira Viana, *Evolução do povo brasileiro*, 2nd ed. (São Paulo: Companhia Ed. Nacional, 1933), 161–194. For an excellent review of Viana's work, see Jeffrey D. Needell, "History, Race, and the State in the

Thought of Oliveira Viana," *Hispanic American Historical Review* 75 (February 1995): 1–30. During the Great Drought in the Brazilian Northeast of 1877–79, policymakers disparaged food relief to victims, preferring, instead, work relief as a means to educate and discipline victims. The Brazilian elite's embrace of Social Darwinism and their perception that rural Brazil was failing to modernize buttressed such responses to hunger during the Great Drought. Although racial theories fell out of vogue after 1930, modernizing, educating, and disciplining working people remained important threads. On elite thought during the Great Drought, see Gerald Michael Greenfield, "The Great Drought and Elite Discourse in Imperial Brazil," *Hispanic American Historical Review* 72 (August 1992): 375–400.

13. Caio Prado Junior was among the leaders of the new intellectual trend that accused Brazil's colonial heritage and foreign imperialism for contemporary problems, including economic underdevelopment; see Caio Prado Júnior, *História econômica do Brasil*, 27th ed. (São Paulo: Ed. Brasiliense, 1982); Caio Prado Júnior, *The Colonial Background of Modern Brazil*, trans. Suzette Macedo (Berkeley: Univ. of California Press, 1971). For the classic vindication of Brazil's racial composition written during the 1930s, see Gilberto Freyre, *The Masters and the Slaves: A Study in the Development of Brazilian Civilization*, trans. Samuel Putnam, 2nd English-language ed., rev. (Berkeley: Univ. of California Press, 1986). For a review of Freyre's views on nutrition and race, plus a comparison of his ideas to leading post-1930 nutritionists from Pernambuco, see Guedes de Vasconcelos, "Fome, eugenia e constituição do campo da nutrição," 315–339.

14. Dante Costa, "A alimentação e a raça," *BMTIC* 10, no. 118 (June 1944): 220.

15. Ladario de Carvalho, "A alimentação do operário," *BMTIC* 2, no. 15 (November 1935): 86–90; Castro, "Alimentação racional," 27; Costa, "A alimentação e a raça," 219–228; A. Carneiro Leão, "O Brasil rural e o problema de sua educação," *BMTIC* 10, no. 115 (March 1944): 232–243; Jorge Queiroz de Morais, "O problema alimentar no Estado de São Paulo," *BMTIC* 7, no. 82 (June 1941): 246–255; Alexandre Moscoso, "A alimentação do trabalhador nacional," *BMTIC* 3, no. 30 (February 1937): 120–124, 131; Alexandre Moscoso, "O problema alimentar," *BMTIC* 3, no. 33 (May 1937): 118–122.

16. Carvalho, "A alimentação do operário," 89.

17. Plínio Reis de Cantanhede Almeida, "Restaurantes para operários," *BMTIC* 9, no. 98 (October 1942): 224–232; Moscoso, "A alimentação do trabalhador," 133–134.

18. Horace B. Davis and Marian Rubins Davis, "Scale of Living of the Working Class in São Paulo, Brazil," *Monthly Labor Review* 44 (January 1937): 249.

19. Ibid., 249–250; Castro, "Alimentação racional," 27–28, 34; "Alimentação para os operários," *O Observador* 6, no. 64 (May 1941): 34; Antonio de Oliveira and Eulalia Maria Lahmeyer Lobo, "O Estado Novo e o sindicato corporativista 1937–1945," in *Rio de Janeiro operário: natureza do Estado e conjuntura econômica, condições de vida e consciência de classe 1930–1970*, ed. Eulalia Maria Lahmeyer Lobo (Rio de Janeiro: Access Ed., 1992), 108–123; Robert Morse Woodbury, "Food Consumption and Nutrition in the Americas," *International Labour Review* 46 (September 1942): 250.

20. BMTIC and *O Observador* throughout the 1930s and 1940s commented on dietary habits. Also: Josué de Castro, *A alimentação brasileira à luz da geografia humana* (Porto Alegre: Ed. Globo, 1937), 130–144. Travel accounts also provided important information. See: Peter Fleming, *Brazilian Adventure* (London: Reprint Society, 1940), 93, 96–97, 127; Bertita Harding, *Southern Empire Brazil* (New York: Coward-McCann, Inc., 1948), 171–177; Jack Harding, *I Like Brazil: A Close-up of a Good Neighbor* (Indianapolis: Bobbs-Merrill Company, 1941), 309–315. On substandard products, see comments in Carolina Maria de Jesus, *Child of the Dark: The Diary of Carolina Maria de Jesus*, trans. David St. Clair (New York: New American Library, 1962); Paulo Seabra, "As condições alimentares do trabalhador em Campos," *BMTIC* 7, no. 81 (May 1941), 227; Joel Wolfe, *Working Women, Working Men: São Paulo and the Rise of Brazil's Industrial Working Class, 1900–1955* (Durham: Duke Univ. Press, 1993), 10, 90, 105. Consumers who could afford milk often found that it had been watered down, thereby reducing its nutritional content. Of more concern than nutrient deficient bread and beans were disease and food poisoning caused by contaminated or spoiled food. Although the Vargas government had issued regulations to ensure proper sanitation and inspection in the dairy industry, accusations persisted that milk was contaminated with tuberculosis. Especially in Brazil's tropical and subtropical zones, working-class families that could not afford a refrigerator often faced the dilemma of discarding expensive food that had been sitting in their kitchens for a long time or risking food poisoning. In other cases, children left unattended might sample leftovers that had gone bad. In addition, unscrupulous venders sometimes sold spoiled food. Food poisoning and the sale of contaminated, spoiled, adulterated, and improperly processed food frequently were mentioned in the back pages of leading newspapers. See for example: *Correio da Manhã* (Rio de Janeiro), March 29, April 3, 1936, September 9, October 14, November 10, 1937, July 29, 1938, June 1, October 14, 1939, September 7, October 1, November 6 and 8, and December 1, 1940.

21. Moscoso, "A alimentação do trabalhador," 124.

22. Paulo Seabra, "Almoço proletário e defesa nacional," *BMTIC* 7, no. 84 (August 1941): 212. In Spanish America, manioc is known as yuca or yucca. In the British West Indies and Africa, it is cassava.

23. "Alimentação para os operários," 37–38, 40; Freitas Filho, "A alimentação no Brasil," 31; Morais, "O problema alimentar no Estado de São Paulo," 252; Moscoso, "A alimentação do trabalhador," 121–132; Moscoso, "O problema alimentar," 125, 129–140.
24. Castro, "Alimentação racional," 37–38; Freitas Filho, "A alimentação no brasil," 34; Moscoso, "A alimentação do trabalhador," 128; Moscoso, "O problema alimentar," 127–140.
25. Davis and Davis, "Scale of Living," 253.
26. For price of refrigerator, see advertisement in *Correio da Manhã*, December 24, 1939. For wage data, see: *Anuário Estatístico do Brasil Ano V—1939/40* (Rio de Janeiro: IBGE, n.d.), 491, 493. Herein, *Anuário Estatístico do Brasil* will be *Anuário*. For an explanation of the author's calculations using the wage data found in the *Anuário*, see "Methodological Appendix." The price, 3:400$000, was in *mil-réis*. One thousand *mil-réis* equalled one *conto*. Thus, the price was 3,400 *mil-réis* or 3.4 *contos*. In 1942, the *cruzeiro* replaced the *mil-réis* so that the price would have read Cr$3,400.
27. *V Recenseamento Geral do Brasil*, Série Regional, Parte XV—Rio de Janeiro (Rio de Janeiro: IBGE, 1951), 180.
28. To get an idea of the effect of World War II on Brazilian imports, see *Anuário Ano VI—1941/1945* (Rio de Janeiro: IBGE, 1946), 264–267.
29. *Correio da Manhã*, August 16, 1940.
30. Ibid., November 25, 1939. The salt is soaked out of the *bacalhau* before cooking so that a delay in cooking or mishandling might contaminate the food.
31. Ibid., November 5, 1944.
32. In this study, the nine items included in a diet moderately above subsistence level were dry beans, manioc flour, dried/salted meat, coffee, sugar, bread, rice, corn/corn meal, and fresh meat. See "Methodological Appendix" for an explanation of how food items and their daily/monthly rations were determined for this study.
33. On the shortage of cooking gas, see *Correio da Manhã*, February 8, 1944. On continued use of charcoal, wood, and kerosene stoves, see advertisements in ibid., June 16 and August 18, 1940. Aware that many housewives did not have gas ovens, one pre-Christmas culinary article featured advice for baking cakes on a charcoal-fueled stovetop; see ibid., November 19, 1939. Kerosene and alcohol fueled stovetops sometimes exploded, as when four people were burned in Rio de Janeiro in 1940; see ibid., June 13, 1940.
34. Moscoso, "A alimentação do trabalhador," 132; Moscoso, "O problema alimentar," 133; John Wells, "Industrial Accumulation and Living Standards in the Long-Run: The São Paulo Industrial Working Class, 1930–75, Part I," *The Journal of Development Studies* 19 (January 1983): 164–168; Joel Wolfe, " 'Father of the Poor' or 'Mother of the Rich'?: Getúlio Vargas, Industrial Workers, and

Constructions of Class, Gender, and Populism in São Paulo, 1930–1954," *Radical History Review* 58 (Winter 1994): 89.

35. *Correio da Manhã*, August 5 and 26, September 10, 1936, December 24, 1937, July 28, 1938.

36. Davis and Davis, "Scale of Living," 248; Wolfe, *Working Women*, 91–92.

37. One of the most influential nutritional experts, Josué de Castro, participated in several Estado Novo nutritional programs, including the Social Welfare Food Service (SAPS); see Guedes de Vasconcelos, "Fome, eugenia e constituição do campo da nutrição," 323–324.

38. *Correio da Manhã*, May 10, 1938. For examples of the "Drink More Milk" texts, see *Correio da Manhã*, March 8, 22, 25, 29, 30, 31, April 2, 14, 23, May 10, and June 4 1938. For other commentaries, see *Correio da Manhã*, April 7, June 5, 7, and July 1, 1938. For the dairy code, see Decree N. 24549, July 3, 1934, in *Coleção das Leis de 1934*, vol. 4, part 1. The dairy code and stricter enforcement of milk's quality in part represented the culmination of longstanding concern over the transmission of tuberculosis from infected cows; see Mirtes de Moraes, Maria Gabriela Haye Biazevic, Eliseu Alves Waldman, and Marcelo Oswaldo Alvares Corrêa, "Tuberculose e leite: elementos para a história de uma polêmica," *História, Ciências, Saúde-Manguinhos* 9 (setembro–dezembro 2002): 609–623.

39. *Correio da Manhã*, December 12, 1944.

40. In 1939, one kilogram each of beans and bread cost 1$130 and 1$848, respectively, for a combined cost of 2$978. Two kilograms of fresh meat cost 4$300. Rice cost 1$095 per kilogram, so that when added to a kilogram of beans, a meal cost 2$225, or 48.3 percent less than two kilograms of fresh meat. Data on 1939 food prices from: *Anuário Ano IV—1938* (Rio de Janeiro: IGBE, 1938), 335, 339; *Anuário Ano V—1939/1940*, 462–485. For an explanation of how food prices were calculated, see "Methodological Appendix."

41. Data on 1939 prices for milk and corn meal from: *Anuário Ano IV—1938*, 335, 339; *Anuário Ano V—1939/1940*, 462–485.

42. See *Lex*, vol. 5: Decree-Law N. 3378, June 30, 1941; also in same volume, Resolution 7, May 5, 1941 and Resolution 9, May 18, 1941.

43. See *Lex*, vol. 7: Decree-Law N. 5220, January 22, 1943.

44. Decree-Law N. 2072, March 8, 1940, in *Coleção das Leis de 1940*, vol. 1.

45. "Estrada Rio-S. Paulo—km. 47," *O Observador* 8, no. 85 (February 1943): 36; Dulphe Pinheiro Machado, "A construção do Palácio do Trabalho," *BMTIC* 6, no. 65 (January 1940): 127–152; Ramalho, *Estado-Patrão*, 49–57.

46. Decree N. 8067, October 16, 1941, in *BMTIC* 8, no. 87 (November 1941): 65–82.

47. On the limited reach of Vargas's corporatist social structure, see Joel Wolfe, "The Faustian Bargain Not Made: Getúlio Vargas and Brazil's

Industrial Workers, 1930–1945," *Luso-Brazilian Review* 31 (Winter 1994): 77–95.

48. Castro, "Alimentação racional," 34–35; Decree-Law N. 1238, May 2, 1939, in *Coleção das Leis de 1939*, vol. 4.

49. Law N. 367, December 31, 1936, in *Coleção das Leis de 1936*, part 1.

50. "O S.A.P.S.," *BMTIC* 11, no. 131 (July 1945): 270–276; "Um restaurante do S.A.P.S. para os estivadores," *BMTIC* 9, no. 108 (August 1943): 320–327.

51. "Alimentação para os operários," 38–39; Marcondes Filho, "Alimentação e previdência social," radio speech on *Hora do Brasil,* June 1942, in *BMTIC* 8, no. 95 (July 1942): 363–4.

52. "Alimentação para os operários," 36.

53. Ibid.

54. *Anuário Ano VI—1941/1945,* 366; Decree-Law N. 3200, April 19, 1941, in *Coleção das Leis de 1941,* vol. 3. Article Seven of the original Consolidation of Labor Laws of 1943 reads: "The continuous precepts of the present Consolidation, except, when in each case, are expressly stipulated to the contrary, do not apply . . . to rural workers, thus considered those who, exercising functions directly linked to agriculture and livestock, are not employed in activities that, by the methods of execution of the respective jobs and by the product of their operations, would be classified as industrial or commercial." See: *Consolidação das Leis do Trabalho* (Rio de Janeiro: Imprensa Nacional, 1943).

55. *Consolidação das Leis do Trabalho,* Art. 81; Seabra, "As condições alimentares," 225; Wolfe, "Faustian Bargain," 80–88.

56. *Consolidação das Leis do Trabalho,* Art. 76, 82.

57. Decree-Law N. 7249, January 16, 1945, in *Coleção das Leis de 1945,* vol. 1; Wolfe, *Working Women,* 105–106.

58. Josué de Castro, "Política alimentar no Brasil de após-guerra," *BMTIC* 12, no. 136 (December 1945): 175.

59. Wolfe, "Faustian Bargain," 86. On Rio's populist politics, see: Michael L. Conniff, *Urban Politics in Brazil: The Rise of Populism, 1925–1945* (Pittsburgh: Univ. of Pittsburgh Press, 1981).

60. The Retirement and Pension Institute for Commercial Workers defined commercial workers to include, among others, those employed at the above mentioned establishments and institutions. See: Decree-Law N. 5493, April 9, 1940, in *Coleção das Leis de 1940,* vol. 4.

61. Thus, in 1944, wage data for São Paulo suddenly includes Santo André. See *Anuário Ano VI—1941/1945,* 328–329.

62. Ibid., 327–328.

63. Celso Furtado, *Economic Development of Latin America: Historical Background and Contemporary Problems,* trans. Suzette Macedo, 2nd ed. (Cambridge: Cambridge Univ. Press, 1976), especially chapter 18. On the question of profit remittances to the United States from Brazil after 1945, see Moniz Bandeira, *Presença dos Estados Unidos no Brasil (Dois séculos de história)* (Rio de Janeiro: Ed. Civilização

Brasileira, 1973), especially chapter XLI. Immediately after World War II, Brazil held sterling balances as a result of Britain's wartime indebtedness, but was unable to use its creditor status to avoid a deteriorating balance of payments; see Marcelo de Paiva Abreu, "Brazil as a creditor: sterling balances, 1940–1952," *Economic History Review*, 2nd series, XLIII (Part 3, 1990): 450–469.

64. Jesus, *Child of the Dark*, 34; John Wells, "Industrial Accumulation and Living Standards in the Long-Run: The São Paulo Industrial Working Class, 1930–75, Part II," *The Journal of Development Studies* 19 (April 1983): 311–319.

65. Wage data taken from following: *Anuário Ano IV—1938*, 340; *Anuário Ano V—1939/1940*, 491, 493; *Anuário Ano VI— 1941/1945*, 328–329; *Anuário Ano VIII—1947* (Rio de Janeiro: IBGE, 1948), 354; *Anuário Ano XII—1951* (Rio de Janeiro: IBGE, 1952), 326–327.

66. Moscoso, "A alimentação do trabalhador," 125–127.

67. Price data taken from following: *Anuário Ano IV—1938*, 331–339; *Anuário Ano V—1939/1940*, 460–485; *Anuário Ano IX—1948* (Rio de Janeiro: IBGE, 1949), 337–341; *Anuário Ano XII—1951*, 313–317. Prices for 1938 are from Federal District only. In 1939, data from Acre reflect prices in Sena Madureira.

68. Davis and Davis, "Scale of Living," 248; Wells, "Industrial Accumulation . . . Part II," 160–161.

Chapter 7

Defending *Ordem* against *Progresso*: The Brazilian Political Police and Industrial Labor Control

Oliver Dinius

Introduction

Since the mid-1990s, historians have gained access to a wealth of documentation on political policing in Brazil from the 1930s to the 1980s. The newly opened archives of the federal political police, the Departamento de Ordem Política e Social, and its counterparts in the states have revealed the full scale and scope of police operations against individuals and associations deemed subversive to the established social and political order. The targets of political policing, above all militants of the Partido Comunista Brasileiro, were always aware of the police's reach and denounced it at the time in the critical press. Historians, however, paid little attention to the political police until recently and displayed much greater interest in the Serviço Nacional de Investigações (SNI; National Service for Investigations), the intelligence service of the military regime (1964–85), because of its unsavory role in the violent repression of the opposition. As long as the Brazilian armed forces successfully resist pressure to open their archives, however, those of the political police serve as the best proxy to understand the role of intelligence services in national politics during the Vargas era. Research on political policing during the Estado Novo (1937–45) and the Populist Republic (1945–64) has revealed a high degree of ideological continuity in Brazil's intelligence community: the logic of political policing foreshadows the military regime's National Security Doctrine. It suggests, moreover, that the SNI's work in the service of repression could not have been as effective were it not for the intelligence gathered by the political police since the 1930s.

This chapter focuses on the significance of political policing for the developmentalist state created under the Estado Novo, the last eight years of Getúlio Vargas's first presidency. Specifically, it analyzes the role of political policing for industrial labor control in Volta Redonda, home to the Companhia Siderúrgica Nacional. Volta Redonda is particularly relevant to a reassessment of Vargas's political legacy because the three tiers of his modernization project intersected there: fostering rapid industrialization, expanding labor rights, and maintaining order in an increasingly complex industrial society. The government created the CSN in 1940 as a state-owned enterprise that was to be at the core of Brazil's industrialization drive. From its completion in 1946 to at least the 1960s, the Volta Redonda steel mill was the country's single most important industrial facility and a symbol of Brazil's state-led modernization. The Estado Novo planners wanted Volta Redonda to serve as model for social development under Vargas's new labor legislation, the Consolidação das Leis do Trabalho, signed into law by Vargas on May 1, 1943. It guaranteed workers welfare benefits and the right to unionize, although it also afforded the state extensive bureaucratic control over labor unions. CSN workers were among the first to experience the benefits of the CLT, whose application would—so reasoned the Estado Novo's social engineers—turn Volta Redonda into a haven of social peace. To maintain order in the short term, however, the state established a strong police presence as tens of thousands of workers flocked in to build and then populate this "City of Steel." The political police in particular shaped the relations between CSN management and the workers as it became a tool for the state to forestall labor organization under Communist leadership.

The Estado Novo government conceived of the creation of state-owned enterprises, the promulgation of the CLT, and the strengthening of the political police as complementary parts of an agenda to usher Brazil into its industrial future. Under the Populist Republic, however, it proved more difficult to reconcile the ideals of fostering economic progress and defending social order. State-employed managers, labor militants, and police officers rarely agreed in their priorities. The history of Volta Redonda illustrates that the political police stood for an ideologically rigid defense of order, while union leaders insisted on the most progressive implementation of Vargas's social legislation. CSN managers, in their majority ideologically conservative military officers, took a pragmatic approach depending on operational goals and the political balance of power. The history of political policing in Volta Redonda therefore serves as a reminder that the political legacies of the Estado Novo did not form a coherent whole.

The case study illuminates the institutional and ideological trajectory of the political police as well as its shifting strategies and tactics for labor control. Volta Redonda was among the first cities in the interior for the political police to establish an effective presence: the close cooperation with the CSN served as model for the policing of state-owned enterprises. The city also became a site of interagency competition. Both the political police for Rio de Janeiro state and the federal political police claimed authority, the latter because the CSN was a federally administered company. Occasionally the respective agents coordinated operations, but most often they worked independently, and sometimes they competed outright. The situation was more complicated still because the CSN had its own force to police mill and town, including undercover agents who worked closely with the federal agents. Last but not the least, Volta Redonda had regular Polícia Militar (Military Police) and Polícia Civil (Civil Police) units that supported the political police upon request.[1] What emerges is the picture of a city under a tight web of policing, which became a powerful instrument of social control.

It is useful to divide the history of political policing in Volta Redonda from the early 1940s to 1964 into five phases. During World War II, the CSN was an important test case for the shift from the reactive to the preemptive policing of industrial labor. The company relied on police intelligence to prevent infiltration and sabotage, especially by Axis nationals, and enjoyed the freedom to implement repressive measures upon the mere suspicion of a "subversive" labor movement. The dynamics changed with the clandestine reorganization of the PCB and the founding of a local metalworkers union in 1944. The CSN tolerated the Communists' presence and respected union rights, but nevertheless welcomed the political police's preventive measures against the PCB in order to contain its influence on the workers and prevent a potential capture of the union. In 1947, the government of President Eurico Gaspar Dutra used a legal charade to break the union, a move that was part of a national crackdown on leftist militants and marked the beginning of the third and most repressive phase. Until late 1950, the political police used all its might to neutralize the remaining Communist militants in Volta Redonda. This intense repression only ended with Getúlio Vargas's return to the presidency in 1951. His government revitalized unions, a measure that shifted the balance of power in industrial relations and diminished the role of the political police for labor control. Consequently, police agents began to treat all labor mobilization as a threat to the established order in Volta Redonda and gathered intelligence even on militants allied to Vargas's Partido Trabalhista Brasileiro. A failed attempt to purge the metalworkers union in October 1955 sharpened the political police's antilabor stand. The union's political alliance with the labor-friendly governments of Juscelino Kubitschek (1956–61) and João Goulart (1961–64) shielded local union leaders from repression, but the intelligence gathered in those years would serve as evidence in purges and tribunals after the 1964 military coup.

The political police was obsessed with "communism" and warned persistently of the threat the PCB allegedly posed to social peace in Volta Redonda. The PCB did target the city in the mid-1940s as part of its effort to rebuild a working-class base and enjoyed moderate electoral success there in 1945 and 1947. It was only legal and eligible to participate in elections for that two-year window, however, too short a time to build the organizational strength to present the sustained threat the police made it out to be. The 1947 crackdown crushed the local party and effectively ended the possibility of a Communist-led unionization of the CSN workforce. Still, the police kept the few remaining PCB militants under constant watch and clamped down at the slightest sign of "subversive" activity. The state-sanctioned revival of the metalworkers union in 1951 legitimized non-Communist labor organizers and limited the freedom of the political police to use repressive tactics. Subsequently, police officers began to apply the label "*comunista*" (Communist) to any militant who adhered to a supposed "communist" ideology and used allegedly "communist" tactics.[2] After the failed union intervention in 1955, the terms "*comunista*" and "*vermelho*" (red) became effectively synonyms for "militant," complementing the always popular "*subversivo*" (subversive), "*perturbador da ordem*" (disturber of order), and "*elemento radical*" (radical element). By the late 1950s, police agents used "*comunista*" for all militants that did not share their narrow vision of the proper order for Brazil.

This chapter provides great detail on the day-to-day operations of the political police for two reasons. First there is the nature of the sources. Unfortunately, the documentation that Rio de Janeiro's state archive received from the federal police in the early 1990s included no police manuals or other instructional materials.[3] Therefore a narrative of police operations serves to illustrate police strategy and tactics. Secondly, it is valuable to provide detail on police operations to illuminate the day-to-day practice of preemptive policing. Often, tactics evolved as events unfolded, officers' momentous decisions deviated from standard practice, and political expedience shaped policing priorities. The narrative is as important as attention to institutional structure for understanding the political police's historical role in industrial labor control at the CSN. The picture that emerges from this narrative of political policing in Volta Redonda corresponds to the general recollections of Cecil Borer—a high-ranking officer with DPS's labor section recently interviewed by historians at the Arquivo Público do Estado do Rio de Janeiro.[4]

From Reactive to Preemptive Policing

Before the 1930s, the policing of industrial labor in Brazil was primarily a matter of crowd control. After World War I and throughout the 1920s, militant labor movements rocked Brazilian cities, above all São Paulo, Santos, and Rio de Janeiro, and the government used regular police forces and army units to break strikes and club down protests.[5] The civil police was clearly not prepared for the challenges posed by rapid industrialization, but it would be left to Vargas's government to restructure the police forces. In 1933 the regime created a specialized force to "protect the political and social order," the Delegacia Especial de Segurança Política (DESPS; Special Delegacy for Political Security), whose tasks included the monitoring of civic organizations such as unions.[6] The DESPS replaced reactive crowd control with the preemptive policing of militant labor organization, a shift that complemented, rather than contradicted, the parallel drive for comprehensive social welfare legislation. To the police reformers, the repression of the "uprisings" by the left-wing Aliança Nacional Libertadora in 1935 and the right-wing Ação Integralista Brasileira in 1938 showed both the necessity and the promise of preemptive policing.[7] The operations against the ANL and the AIB had relied on DESPS's intelligence gathering, and they further increased the quantity and quality of information available to the political police. Seized archives, interrogation records, and transcripts of trials against militants generated a wealth of new documentation on "subversives" that DESPS organized into an extensively cross-referenced file system.[8] This archive—constantly updated with intelligence from field agents and other state agencies—became the backbone of the national security apparatus under the Estado Novo and beyond.[9]

The political police expanded further in the early 1940s. Brazil's civil service agency, the Departamento Administrativo do Serviço Público (DASP), revamped the country's security apparatus and created the Departamento Federal de Segurança Pública (DFSP; Federal Department for Public Security) that assumed control over all federal police forces, including DESPS.[10] In order to strengthen the continent's defenses against potential sabotage of military and industrial installations by Axis nationals, the United States began cooperation with DFSP even before Vargas declared war on the Axis. The U.S. Special Intelligence Service (SIS) provided extensive technical assistance that helped to transform DESPS into a secret police with greater reach for its mission to prevent "crimes against the state" and "crimes against the social order."[11] The SIS-assisted reforms culminated in the extinction of DESPS and the creation of the Divisão de Polícia Política e Social (DPS; Division of Political and Social Police) in 1944. This paved the way for a further expansion of the force, as Brazilian administrative law empowered a *Divisão* to establish subordinate *Delegacias*.[12] The DPS created the (1) Delegacia de Segurança Política (DSeP; Delegacy for Public Security) to prevent "crimes against the political order, meaning acts carried out against the structure and the security of the state," and the (2) Delegacia de Segurança Social (DSS; Delegacy for Social Security) to prevent "crimes against the social order, in accordance with the stipulations of the constitution and the laws establishing the individual rights and guarantees and their civil and penal protection."[13] The Serviço de Investigações (SIv; Investigation Service) and the Serviço de Informações (SI; Information Service) supported the *Delegacias*. The SIv maintained the archive on suspicious individuals and organizations and prepared new dossiers on "topics which in their complexity [went] beyond the capacities of the regular file system."[14] It also operated the "secret service," coordinated all clandestine operations, and condensed intelligence into a daily bulletin on the security situation for key government officials, including the president. The SI's most important subdivisions were the Fiscalização Trabalhista (Labor Control) and Ordem Pública (Public Order). Both had mandates that left much room for interpretation by the supervising government and the political police: the Fiscalização Trabalhista "carr[ied] out the investigations concerning labor," while Ordem Pública "execute[d] all services of prevention against the disturbance of public order and of personal rights of interest to the political police."[15]

Volta Redonda became an early testing ground for the preemptive political policing of large industrial enterprises. DESPS (and its successor DPS) worked closely with the CSN in the implementation of its policy to employ only men and women with an *atestado ideológico*, a document issued by the political police to certify that she/he did not adhere to an ideology opposed to Brazil's social and political order. To obtain the *atestados* the CSN personnel department submitted the names of potential employees to DESPS headquarters, where the archival staff checked the files for *antecedentes ideológicos* (ideological past). The CSN made ideological screenings a standard procedure, although it was often impractical to await final police approval as the company hired dozens of workers every day during construction. In 1943, for example, the DESPS obtained a list of all the workers employed in the construction of the coke plant and checked every single one of the more than 1000 names against its files.[16] For the CSN, cross-checking personnel records against DPS files and sharing information about employees with federal authorities became an important tool of industrial security and labor control. DPS agent Milton Brandão praised the meticulous file keeping and noted that the "different archives of the company are all joined together in one to allow better control and security for future consultations."[17]

Another important field of cooperation between the CSN and the political police was the persecution of men who abandoned work without company authorization. Under decree-law 11.087 (10/12/ 1942), the construction site was a military installation of "national security interest" and workers there had the legal status of soldiers. They were considered "deserters" if they quit working, and the equivalent charge for workers of foreign nationality was "sabotage."[18] DESPS regularly assisted the CSN in tracking, arresting, and returning such perpetrators. In March 1943, for example, five Portuguese employees committed "sabotage" by leaving Volta Redonda unauthorized: upon CSN request, the DESPS officers detained three of them in the Federal District and arranged for the Delegacia de Ordem Política e Social—Estado de Rio de Janeiro (DOPS-RJ; Delegacy for Political and Social Order for the State of Rio de Janeiro) to arrest the other two in Niterói.[19] This wartime cooperation helped the CSN to retain labor and established procedures the political police's Setor Trabalhista (Labor Sector) would continue to use after the war. The exchange of information between the DPS, the CSN, and the Ministério do Trabalho, Indústria e Comércio (MTIC, Ministry of Labor, Industry, and Commerce) went hand-in-hand with on-site intelligence gathering as part of an increasingly coherent strategy for industrial security.

Policing the "Democratic" Transition (1944–47)

The much-celebrated promulgation of the CLT in 1943 altered the parameters of industrial labor control in Brazil. It granted benefits and strengthened the position of industrial workers vis-à-vis their employers by guaranteeing the right to unionize and establishing labor courts.[20] The wartime regime limited the new legislation's reach, however, as many of the most progressive provisions remained suspended, including the right to vacation, the eight-hour day, and the progressive pay scale for extra hours.[21] The CLT nevertheless had an immediate impact in Volta Redonda.

In 1943 still, workers organized the Associação Profissional dos Trabalhadores nas Indústrias Metalúrgicas, Mecânicas e de Material Elétrico de Barra Mansa (Professional Association of Workers in Metallurgical, Mechanical, and Electrical Industries in Barra Mansa) and soon filed an application to have it recognized as the local metalworkers union.[22] The political police, however, was in a position to delay or even block union recognition under the CLT's highly bureaucratized rules. The CLT required the association to submit to the Delegacia Regional de Trabalho (DRT; Regional Labor Delegacy), among other documents, an *atestado ideológico* and an *atestado de bons antecedentes* (certificate of good conduct) for each of its directors—and those had to be issued by the state political police, the DOPS-RJ.[23] Labor Minister Alexandre Marcondes Filho approved the recognition of the Sindicato dos Trabalhadores nas Indústrias Metalúrgicas, Mecânicas e de Material Elétrico de Barra Mansa (STIMMMEBM; Union of Workers in Metallurgical, Mechanical, and Electrical Industries in Barra Mansa), on April 14, 1945, but the role of the political police did not end there. The DPS and DOPS-RJ were responsible for monitoring the union's political activities.[24] The STIMMMEBM's statutes obliged its directorate to "collaborate with the state in the development of class solidarity" (Article 3a), "rigorously observe the law and the principles of morals and the understanding of civic duties" (Article 4a), and "abstain from any [political] propaganda, including not only doctrines incompatible with the national institutions and interests, but also candidacies for electoral office outside the union" (Article 4b). The political police controlled whether the union adhered to these statutes and had the right to intervene and preserve social order in case of violations.[25]

The police warned about Communist influence immediately. Several of STIMMMEBM's founders had ties with Socorro Vermelho (Red Rescue), an antifascist organization founded by the clandestine PCB in 1943 as cover for rebuilding.[26] The PCB began campaigning openly in February 1945 once Vargas had announced national elections for November. By mid-1945, the PCB had a Comitê Regional (Regional Committee) for the Sul Fluminense and Comitês Municipais (Municipal Committees) in Barra Mansa, Barra do Piraí, and Resende. The local cadre Alcides Sabença organized a

Comitê Distrital (District Committee) in Volta Redonda.[27] Several PCB members held supervisory positions in the CSN, most prominently Gentil Noronha, the party's Secretário de Propaganda (Propaganda Secretary) and the company's head of the press office.[28] In January of 1945, the DPS arrested Noronha and brought him to Rio de Janeiro for interrogation. He assured the officers that he had never seen political propaganda in Volta Redonda, but they were not convinced.[29]

[T]his delegacy [*Delegacia*] believes that his [Noronha's] statements to the effect that he had not seen Communist texts or symbols at the company where he works are wrong to the absurd, because his occupation forces him to go through the company grounds regularly. We do not mean to suggest that the Communist propaganda—muffled, discreet, and thus dangerous—that appeared at the company was instigated by this outcast [*marginal*]; but neither do we wish to declare him innocent, in the face of his past, not only here, but also in the state of Minas Gerais.[30]

The language revealed just how much subversive energy the political police attributed to the Communists, but there was little evidence that they exercised a strong influence in Volta Redonda. One undercover agent reported that he "[could] not detect even the smallest wave stirring up the existence of men dissatisfied with the country's regime."[31] The political police also interviewed an ex-CSN employee, who acknowledged that many workers talked about communism, but dismissed the notion that they were ideologically committed.[32] Yet the police warned of a growing threat of communism as the elections came closer. In August 1945, one agent reported that "almost all workers in the city favor[ed] the communist creed," and CSN security expected the Communists to carry 60 percent of the city's working-class vote.[33] The actual election results fell far short of these dire predictions. The PCB received 11.5 percent of the vote in the municipality of Barra Mansa, much less than in old industrial centers such as Duque de Caxias (29.4 percent) and São Gonçalo (25.3 percent).[34] The only success for the local PCB was the election of Alçides Sabença to the constituent assembly.[35]

However, the election did afford the PCB political legitimacy and that was reason enough for the security forces to step up repression. In May 1946, the CSN prohibited political propaganda on factory grounds and forbade the establishment of any association or sports clubs in the company town without previous authorization.[36] That spelled the end for the successful literacy courses offered by the PCB's Comité Popular Democrático (Democratic Popular Committee).[37] The political police accused STIMMMEBM of being under undue influence from the PCB, which was tantamount to charging that the union endangered the social order under the new decree-law 9.502 (23/07/1946).[38] Tension mounted in November 1946 when the union joined the Confederação dos Trabalhadores do Brasil (CTB; Confederation of Brazilian Workers), an organization the labor ministry branded as "Communist conspiracy."[39] The political police also undermined the PCB's perfectly legal campaign for state elections in January 1947. The state's Secretaria de Segurança (Secretariat for Security) regularly refused permission for PCB rallies in Volta Redonda citing danger to public order. When a PCB rally was authorized, DPS deployed its agents and requested units of the military police as well as municipal guards; for the largest rallies, DOPS-RJ's Polícia Especial (Special Police) supplied additional shock troops to assure the police of overwhelming force in case of disturbances.[40] Ironically, it was the local police that stirred up the crowds at a PCB rally on December 1, 1946, when their overzealous chief, Italo Baroni, forced his way through the crowd in a car, pulled his gun on the speakers, and insisted that they abandon the stage.[41] The PCB accused the police of provoking a "state of civil war" as pretext for further repression, and the police response to the incident warranted that claim. The DOPS-RJ "refined" its methods to avoid a "repetition of events": it sent half a dozen officers and shock troops for two PCB rallies in Barra Mansa in mid-December and asked for additional support by the CSN and local police. The goal, in police language, was systematic control and professional repression to achieve the "essential objective" [*desideratum*], the "absolute maintenance of order."[42]

The PCB retained its strength in the January elections, but the political scenario looked less and less favorable. Former CSN Technical Director Macedo Soares was elected governor of the state of Rio de Janeiro, and PCB militants who had praised him as defender of national industry soon learned that he was only too willing to crack down on the Communists to "protect" the CSN. Tension was high since the CSN had begun to fire large numbers of workers in late 1946 as part of the transition from a construction workforce to an operational workforce for the mill.[43] In March 1947, the company refused to renegotiate the union contract, even though the level of inflation justified the call for a wage adjustment under a previous agreement.[44] Company guards broke up the gatherings whenever PCB cadres or labor militants carried their political "agitation" onto

CSN grounds; consequently rallies had to be held off company grounds, which reduced attendance and facilitated the police's task to disperse the crowd.[45] To make matters worse, the union was under close scrutiny by an increasingly hostile labor ministry because it had been mired in a financial crisis for months.[46]

On April 5, 1947, STIMMMEBM was the first union in the country to suffer government intervention as part of a sweeping government crackdown on "communism." The MTIC had granted the Departamento Nacional de Trabalho (DNT; National Labor Department) expanded powers over unions: it had to approve budgets and certify election results.[47] The DNT refused to approve STIMMMEBM's 1947 budget and invoked Article 528 of the CLT to authorize an intervention because of "circumstances that disturbed the functioning of the union."[48] It installed a Junta Governativa (Governing Board) and designated an MTIC officer to lend the new directorate assistance in developing and implementing measures necessary to "normalize the functioning of the union." The government preserved the appearance of legal procedure under the CLT and cloaked its political motives for the intervention in the police's language of order, citing *irregularidades* (irregularities) and *graves perturbações* (severe disturbances).[49] The legal charade was necessary because links to the PCB, still a legal party, did not constitute sufficient cause for intervention. That changed after May 7, 1947, when the Tribunal Superior Eleitoral (TSE; Superior Electoral Court) outlawed the PCB. That decision served as justification for the government to close down the CTB and decree intervention for more than 170 unions allegedly under Communist influence because of their affiliation with the CTB. Congress voted in October to remove all Communists from public offices and cancelled the mandates of all PCB parliamentarians on January 7, 1948.[50] In Volta Redonda, police seized the PCB's records and used its membership lists and detailed descriptions of party activities to root out remaining cells. The CSN fired workers with links to the PCB.[51] Although the PCB link was not cited in the intervention of STIMMMEBM, the case would have been difficult to make without the detailed intelligence provided by DPS and DOPS-RJ obtained between 1945 and 1947—often illegally.

Repression by Overwhelming Force

Despite the devastating success of the strike against the Left and the apparent ease of its execution, the political police requested more resources for the struggle against the "communist" specter. The director of DPS, Major Adauto Esmeraldo, laid out the challenges and explained the need for more personnel in his annual report for 1947.

> It is obvious that we waged our most important struggle against Communism. We were always in the offensive, with determination, but without boasting, confronting the ploy of the opponents and the incomprehension of the pseudo-democrats. . . . An intense wave of propaganda, disguised in various colorings, followed upon the banning of the PCB, which obliged us to engage in a prolonged campaign of counterespionage. . . . Although the situation now appears to be under control, the struggle has to continue, because the Bolsheviks began to operate almost exclusively in the shadow, as was to be expected. Because we have to adapt to any kind of struggle, it is only logical that our means need to be readjusted. The staffing is insufficient, more so than ever before, because inquiries multiply in the subterranean world, requiring a greater number of officers. The costs, on the other hand, are increasing as a consequence of the forced necessity to step up the number of infiltrations, not only in Rio de Janeiro, but also in some states.[52]

Rather than proclaim victory, Esmeraldo argued in characteristic secret service logic that greater resources were needed to find and destroy a weakened enemy. Federal and state governments were apparently receptive for this reasoning. The DPS and the DOPS-RJ received significant budget increases to expand their forces in the fight against the remnants of the PCB.[53] The DOPS-RJ assigned a full-time officer to Barra Mansa and Barra do Piraí, one Austricliano da Silva, who would remain stationed there for over ten years and develop great familiarity with local conditions. The CSN also reorganized its security forces in late 1947 and greatly increased the number of guardsmen.[54] Last but not the least, the army took on a more prominent role. The First and Second Batalhão da Infanteria Blindada (BIB; Armored Infantry Battalion) had been stationed in Barra Mansa since 1944 with orders to protect the CSN against sabotage. The first mission under those orders came only in April 1948, however, when BIB units occupied strategic points inside the mill and throughout Volta Redonda in response to reports about subversive activity.[55] In July 1950, the regional army command ordered BIB to execute the standard emergency plan in response to a CSN request for military support to contain a protest march and rally against the Lei da Segurança (Security Law). One battalion occupied the mill and secured the surrounding area, while the second took up positions in Barra Mansa to prevent the rally and control the city. The troops only returned to the barracks four days later.[56]

The force the state brought to bear stood in no relation to the strength of the remnants of the PCB. The CSN security chief Assis Gomes could only name half a dozen known Communists still on the payroll, but warned nevertheless that "communist" cells still existed in the coke plant, the rolling mill, the steel works, the blooming mill, the blast furnace, and the mechanical shop, and according to his informants also in the neighborhoods of Jardim Paraíba, Vila Santa Cecília, Vila Operária, and Casas de Blocos. Assis Gomes further cited *comícios relâmpagos* (literally "lightning rallies") on the shop floor as evidence for continued "communist" presence and reminded his superiors that the apparent quiet could well be the "calm before the next storm."[57]

The political police expressed concern about the PCB militants' new disguises. Reports stressed that Communists dismissed by the CSN often remained in Volta Redonda and earned their living as petty merchants, trying to recruit former coworkers as they sold them their merchandise.[58] DPS and DOPS-RJ also accused two long-time PCB militants, Henrique Ferreira and Benjamin Marques, of engaging in partisan propaganda under the mantle of two seemingly nonpartisan causes: the nationalist "O Petróleo é Nosso" (The Oil is Ours!) movement, and the campaign "Em Defesa da Paz and Contra a Bomba Atómica" (For the Defense of Peace and against the Nuclear Bomb).[59]

The security forces' response was to intensify preemptive policing. The DPS and DOPS-RJ deployed agents and special squads to rallies staged by suspected Communists and intervened readily at the slightest sign of disturbances.[60] Police broke up the 1948 Carnival parade in Volta Redonda because known PCB militants wore costumes that protested the government's disregard for the 1946 constitution. The chief of the local civil police reported with apparent disdain on their characteristically "communist" tactics:

[T]hey . . . by means of their costumes, not only dishonored the country's Constitution, which they had transformed in tattered newspaper pages, but also criticized . . . municipal authorities in an obscene, vile, and shameless manner. . . . always trying, in their partisan sadism, to cause confusion, be it at rallies, be it at meetings, or at whatever other event that they use to appear in public, always meaning to take advantage, with notorious disrespect for the law, the order they plan to subvert, and the society they wish to destroy.[61]

DPS agents arrested the perpetrators and took them to Rio de Janeiro for interrogation.[62] Such arbitrary arrests and the physical intimidation of suspected "communists" was common in those years, and the DPS in particular gained a reputation for abuses against prisoners. After the arrest of three Volta Redonda militants in March 1950, *Imprensa Popular* wrote that the CSN police "handed [them] over to the roughnecks of the *Rua da Relação*"—the address of the DPS.[63]

No police operation illustrates the full arsenal of repressive techniques and the imbalance of power better than the one against an alleged strike movement in July 1949. DOPS-RJ received word that local "communists" were planning a strike for early August, and the Setores Trabalhistas of DOPS-RJ and DPS responded immediately by deploying special squads to Volta Redonda.[64] They "carried out several raids" and arrested seven "communist" militants whom DPS detained for over a week in Rio de Janeiro without informing the families.[65] Some officers stayed in Volta Redonda to monitor further developments and intercepted a "communist" pamphlet with a "program of demands" that denounced the CSN's handsome profits and the exorbitant increase in the cost-of-living, up 150 percent since 1946.[66] The DPS and DOPS-RJ carried out more raids in the days before the suspected strike date, August 12, and made five more arrests.[67] The great coup was the arrest of one Ruben Santos de Oliveira, recently hired by the CSN, whom DPS identified as a "Communist infiltrator" with the "codename 'Menelik.'" He aroused the agents' suspicion because he wore a "bigode tipo Stalin" (moustache à-la-Stalin), and his fate was sealed when they found a letter from PCB leader Luís Carlos Prestes in his house.[68] The anti-Communist newspaper *O Globo* played its part running a sensationalist article that identified him as the "brain of the Volta Redonda Communists" and asserted that he was a paid PCB organizer.[69]

Subsequent interrogations by the DOPS-RJ revealed just how thoroughly the security forces had penetrated "communist" circles. Two workers admitted that they had attended a meeting with Menelik in late July at the home of one Antônio Pereira to discuss the wage campaign and develop a strategy to gain control of the union. Both had informed CSN security of the meeting and denied any intention of getting involved in politics.[70] Pereira himself testified that Menelik had visited workers' homes to "lecture" them on labor issues, invite them to join a wage commission, and rally support for the Communist party, and that he had supplied the men at the meeting with pamphlets addressed "To the Workers of the Companhia Siderúrgica

Nacional."[71] A fifth man who had attended the meeting, "Socata"—a pseudonym for José Nunes—revealed that he was a CSN spy. Even if Pereira was on Menelik's side, as Nunes claimed, police informants were in the majority at the conspiratorial meeting! This would explain why "Captain Oswaldo [de Assis Gomes]" was, in Nunes's words, "well informed regarding the most active elements among the Communists in Volta Redonda."[72] The CSN's secret police was so well informed that it seized the files of the PCB's Municipal Committee, which included a "plan of national action," a list of card-carrying members, and documentation concerning the transfer of organizers.[73] The company used that intelligence to dismiss the remaining militants on its payroll for "openly expressing 'communist' ideas."[74] Legal challenges against these political dismissals stood little chance of success. The labor courts consistently ruled that spreading propaganda on company premises or inciting a strike were *faltas graves* (serious misconduct), backing the CSN's case that links to a "communist" campaign was a *justa causa* (just cause) for dismissal.[75]

That the political police portrayed Menelik as the single greatest threat to social order in Volta Redonda since 1947 spoke to the success of state repression against an overmatched ideological enemy. The security forces targeted "communists" long before their "contagious" ideology could "infect" others and strengthen the ranks of the "subversives." The effective cooperation with other state agencies further enhanced the power of the political police. The labor ministry depended on police intelligence to learn about the political leanings of potential union leaders and assess whether grievances filed under the CLT were "legitimate" or "political." The labor courts relied on the political police to screen plaintiffs for their ideological past, which indicates that judges treated "communists" differently.[76] Legal action was therefore not a viable alternative for labor militants in Volta Redonda in the face of the overwhelming repression against direct action. The CSN management welcomed the strong police presence because it minimized labor organization at a time when the company organized production—a volatile process that required strict labor discipline and regular reassignments that would likely have met greater resistance had workers had the freedom to organize. Managers were not so concerned with ideology, but they valued the freedom to administer the company without interference by labor.

Ideologically, the anti-Communist crusade of the Dutra regime reinforced the political police's predisposition. The language of internal reports shows that its officers felt a deep-rooted aversion to "communism," too strong to be attributed to indoctrination or an

institutional interest to exaggerate the "communist" threat. A DOPS-
RJ report on the political situation in September 1950 alerted the
state governor to a "feverish activity of the 'communist' bosses in the
entire territory of the state, where they held secret meetings." It
noted that two former PCB militants from Volta Redonda were candidates for the Partido Trabalhista Nacional (National Labor Party)
and portrayed their campaign rally as an attempt by the Communists
to "undermine the efforts by federal and state governments to guarantee elections in an environment of freedom and confidence." "After
all," the agent reasoned, "they attacked everything and everybody,
giving the clear impression that they want either confusion or else the
great *Satalin* to govern our endangered republic."[77] This linguistic
hybridization of "Satan" and "Stalin" was no spelling error: for this
agent the leader of world communism was a manifestation of the
greatest evil. The officers of the political police adhered to an ideology
of *Ordem e Progresso* (Order and Progress) steeped in Catholic corporatism; they believed that their anti-Communist crusade in Brazil
helped to defend the Christian world. It was indicative of the depth of
these convictions that one agent signed a report with "Leão XIII," the
pope whose encyclical *Rerum Novarum* (1891) called on the faithful
to halt the advance of communism and socialism among the working
classes.[78] Officers saw it as their duty to prevent militants from organizing workers in support of an inherently "communist" agenda such
as the demand for basic labor rights. Social reformers, not least those
who had written the CLT, conceived of labor unions as advocates of
progress; the political police championed the defense of the established order over progressive reform whenever a choice had to be
made between *Ordem* and *Progresso*.

Populist Politics and Police Ideology (1951–55)

The ideology of the political police no longer corresponded to government policies after Getúlio Vargas's victory in the 1950 presidential election. The leadership of the clandestine PCB instructed its
supporters to abstain, but many Communist militants voted for
Vargas because they expected him to grant labor more freedom to
organize. Once Vargas was in power, they began forging alliances with
petebistas (members of the PTB) in the official unions, even though
the PCB's official line called for building independent unions under
Communist control.[79] These new alliances disoriented the political
police: labor militancy no longer meant opposition to the government
and adherence to the Communist dogma. From 1945 until early

1951, the DPS and DOPS-RJ had operated under the assumption that only card-carrying Communists would profess to "communist" ideology and employ "communist" tactics, but now that was no longer true. The political police had to reconsider the nature of its "communist" enemy in a fast-changing political and institutional environment.

Most importantly, the CLT now applied without emergency legislation limiting its reach. The consequent revival of the state-sanctioned industrial unions made direct bargaining central to industrial relations and provided militants with political space to organize labor. The labor judiciary could rule on grievances according to the letter of the law, and recourse to the labor courts became key to the unions' industrial relations strategy. Filing a grievance could lead to a court victory, but often the mere threat of legal action was sufficient as bargaining lever to extract concessions from companies. The revival of the CLT also meant that bureaucrats in the MTIC and its regional offices established themselves as major power brokers in the fast-industrializing society of the 1950s. The strengthening of unions and the labor bureaucracy went hand-in-hand with a diminished role for the political police in industrial labor control. It had been one of Vargas's campaign promises to abolish the *atestado ideológico* as requirement for candidates to union office, which threatened to deprive the political police of its primary tool to manipulate union elections: it would no longer be able to bar leftist candidacies and stall the investiture of victorious tickets. Labor Minister Danton Coelho announced at the national Labor Day parade on May 1, 1951, that the government had sent legislation to congress to eliminate the *atestado*, and two days later the MTIC decreed that candidates could substitute for the *atestado* by filing a signed declaration that their candidacy conformed to the rules of the CLT. On September 1, 1952, Vargas finally signed the new union law, which revoked Article 530 of the CLT and explicitly stated that it was "forbidden, under any pretext or condition, to require the *atestado de ideologia* or any other [certificate] that aims to judge or scrutinize the political, religious, or philosophical convictions of the unionized."[80]

Industrial relations in Volta Redonda changed radically in this new political and institutional environment. The Chapa Proletária—an independent ticket led by Allan Cruz—won STIMMMEBM's elections on December 13, 1950.[81] Cruz's had run on a reformist platform demanding that the CSN comply fully with the CLT and improve working conditions: on the agenda were the introduction of the paid rest day (Lei n.° 605), a significant wage increase to compensate for high inflation, and the payment of the constitutionally guaranteed participation in profits.[82] The CSN tried to stonewall Cruz's inauguration in a last ditch effort to retain control over industrial relations. The state-appointed union president, José Maria Pimenta (1947–51), refused to hand over power "without the explicit permission of the CSN," but pressure by a worker delegation finally made him acquiesce to Cruz's investiture (*investitura*) on May 1, 1951. The DRT still tried to engineer an intervention, citing Cruz's failure to submit minutes of assemblies and budgets for 1947 and 1948, and it delayed final approval for STIMMMEBM's 1951 budget until mid-1952.[83] Under the Dutra administration, this technicality might well have served as pretext for the DRT to annul the elections and appoint an administrator. Under the new regime, however, Cruz cleared this bureaucratic obstacle by enlisting Vargas's personal support. The president instructed the labor minister to recognize the new directorate and convene a round table with CSN and STIMMMEBM representatives to discuss the union's wage demands.[84]

The political police's stand toward the revived metalworkers union was ambiguous. It welcomed that Cruz ran on an anti-Communist platform and acknowledged that he kept his distance from known Communist militants. In fact, the local DOPS-RJ agent relied on Cruz and his fellow director Walter Millen da Silva for information about the activities of more radical labor organizers.[85] The CSN security assured the DPS that the PCB exercised no influence over STIMMMEBM and emphasized the union's cooperative attitude.[86] On the other hand, police reports warned about the union's aggressive bargaining strategy and raised the specter of a strike. STIMMMEBM's new lawyer Aarão Steinbruch filed a collective grievance in the local courts, and the police promptly accused him of a "defamation campaign" against the CSN that culminated in a public rally in which PTB politicians allegedly "called on the workers to revolt and to expel the current [CSN] directorate." This was the first time that DPS agents associated the governing PTB with PCB militants and accused them of making common cause in a movement that threatened social order.[87] In that context, the CSN's Assis Gomes reminded his superiors that the local Communists were critical of Cruz's union leadership not because they disagreed with his platform, but because he was too slow implementing it.[88]

Police reports acknowledged, however, that there was still a clear ideological divide between the PCB and the Vargas regime. The CSN security reported in late August 1951 that PCB militants had painted slogans on walls in Volta Redonda and Barra Mansa that read

"Getúlio, father of the profiteers—Bread and Peace" and "Getúlio returned, but the cost-of-living went up."[89] Ahead of Vargas's visit to Volta Redonda for the Labor Day parade in 1953, the "reds" distributed fliers that urged the workers to protest the high cost-of-living and the excessive profit participation for CSN directors.[90] The PCB pamphlets always included divisive national political demands that overshadowed areas of agreement with *petebistas* on workplace grievances and local bread-and-butter issues. One such pamphlet in July 1954 addressed local education and health care, the cost of living, public works, transportation, telephone service, and local roads, but tacked on a call for democratic liberties under the 1946 constitution, the struggle for peace, and the struggle against American imperialism. As late as mid-1954, the political police was still clear on the divide between prominent local "communists," on the one hand, and PTB or PSD-affiliated labor organizers on the other. DOPS-RJ's list of the "main agitators" in Volta Redonda and Barra Mansa included almost exclusively men who had been members of the PCB in the mid-1940s.[91] The ideological dividing line was no longer as clear among the union rank-and-file, however. A police brief on STIMMMEBM's general assembly stressed that two "communist" agitators spoke out in favor of demands for a new wage scale. Neither Euclydes Mendes de Souza nor José Bonifácio, though, had established links with the PCB.[92] The ideological differences between "communist" agitators and legitimate union leaders began to blur in the eyes of the police, a process that would accelerate after Vargas's suicide in August 1954.

Trabalhismo as Threat to "Order" (1955–64)

Vice President João Café Filho (PSP) assumed as interim president after Vargas's death. Café Filho performed a political U-turn and enlisted the support of the UDN and conservative factions within the PSD to restore order to Brazil. The new government took an openly hostile stance toward organized labor and justified that line with a recent wave of strikes (1953) and rising inflation, which conservatives blamed on increases in the minimum salary. Labor Minister Napoleão de Alencastro Guimarães clamped down on major strikes in São Paulo, Rio de Janeiro, and Minas Gerais. He decreed an intervention in the Leopoldina Railway workers union, ordered arrests of workers at the São Paulo Tramway, Light and Power Co., and outlawed the União Geral dos Trabalhadores (UGT, General Workers Union).[93] Communist organizers responded by seeking to forge closer alliances with *trabalhistas* who enjoyed support in the PTB-controlled labor bureaucracy, a strategic shift made possible by the PCB's ideological reorientation after the death of Joseph Stalin in 1953.[94] Police reported from Volta Redonda that known Communists closed ranks with *petebistas* and campaigned actively for Juscelino Kubitschek (PSD) and João "Jango" Goulart (PTB) ahead of the presidential elections in October 1955.[95] In response to this electoral alliance between *pecebistas* (members of the PCB) and *petebistas*, the political police decided to cast its net for alleged "communists" wider—with profound implications for STIMMMEBM's elections that year.

The union elections were held in February 1955, but the political dust would not settle until after the national elections in October. The race for STIMMMEBM'S presidency was wide open, which nurtured hopes in the Café Filho government that it could rein in an increasingly independent and powerful union—with a little help from the DPS, DOPS-RJ, and the CSN. STIMMMEBM president Walter Millen da Silva expected to secure victory for a handpicked successor, but he had squandered much of his once solid support with political gaffes. He had fired Aarão Steinbruch, he belonged to an establishment party (the PSD), and he maintained close relations with the CSN administration—too close in the eyes of many workers.[96] The opposition rallied behind José Claudio Alves, about whom it was rumored that he sympathized with the *integralistas*. For DOPS-RJ, however, the real "brain behind the ticket" was Mendes de Souza, whose police file categorized him as "professional 'communist' agitator."[97] Merely by raising the suspicion that "communists" tried to gain control of the union, the political police assured itself a prominent role in the election process. Candidates had to submit two documents to the DRT to be eligible: a signed declaration that their candidacy was legal under the CLT and an "*atestado de ideologia política para fins sindicais*" to certify that he had "no ideological past."[98] The latter had to be issued by the DOPS-RJ; it was effectively the old *atestado ideológico* under a new name. Mendes de Souza learnt that he had a police file in time to withdraw his candidacy and thereby prevent the DOPS-RJ from disqualifying Alves's ticket.

There were rumors that it swarmed with "communists," though, and attempts to exploit the issue continued. Two weeks before the elections, the DRT received a letter from a worker who demanded that several tickets be barred from the elections because they supposedly violated the rules of the CLT.[99] Millen supported the request arguing that Alves's ticket in particular "provided cover" for "subversive elements selected by Mendes de Souza." The DRT was quick to issue the impugnation.[100] When a successful appeal by the barred candidates threatened to leave the entire election in limbo, all parties agreed to count all votes and declare a winner only after the MTIC had passed its final verdict on the impugnation. With Alves's ticket won, Millen promptly tried to make the case that the DRT should uphold the impugnation to save the union from the election of "communist elements" and a "red adventure." He argued that Alves's ticket violated Article 530 of the CLT, the very Article that Vargas's reform in 1952 had abolished.[101]

The political police took center stage in the attempt to overturn the election results. The DRT asked DOPS-RJ to (re)assess the ideological past of the winning candidates—with surprising results. The same officer who had signed off on the original *atestados* now concluded that Alves and several of his running mates did indeed adhere to a "communist" ideology. He cited "trustworthy sources" to assert that they were involved in subversive activities under the guidance of Mendes de Souza, who allegedly stirred trouble in the union and "threatened Walter Millen da Silva with death."[102] The *antecedentes ideológicos* had become a self-fulfilling prophecy. The DPS and DOPS-RJ routinely created files on candidates that stood for union elections, files that could be (re)interpreted after the elections as a preexisting "communist" past. The DOPS-RJ file of Alves's vice-presidential candidate Nestor Lima, for example, had no record of any political activities until 1956—the year *after* the election.[103] The DRT endorsed the "new" police report and warned in its memo to the MTIC that the elected leadership included people "antagonistic to the harmony of classes and the democratic order—adherents of the Marxist ideology."[104] Alves and his running mates were fortunate that interim Labor Minister Waldir Niemeyer had the final say: he overturned the impugnation and ordered the DRT to proceed with the "investiture" of Alves's victorious ticket.[105] The case was reopened, though, when the new STIMMMEBM directorate went on a collision course with the CSN. Alves asked for a 12 percent salary increase and more rigid compliance with the CLT's "equal pay for equal work" provision, both demands the CSN rejected.[106] With political tension high in the last weeks of a closely contested national campaign between Kubitschek and the conservative presidential candidate Juarez Távora, the losing candidate in STIMMMEBM's elections asked the MTIC once more to reconsider the impugnation of Alves's ticket. There was no new evidence in the legal opinion (*parecer*), however: it relied on the old police report and cited the danger of "communist" infiltration.[107] Still, Labor Minister Alencastro Guimarães overturned the earlier decision, annulled STIMMMEBM'S elections, and ordered the DRT to appoint a temporary union president with a mandate to call new elections within 60 days.[108]

This triggered a showdown between the political police and the CSN's unionized workers. STIMMMEBM's directors called a general assembly and vowed that it would remain in session until the crisis was resolved. Workers denied the state-appointed intervener access to the union building and thereby prevented him from assuming power, while militants rallied STIMMMEBM's members against this "act of state arbitrariness" and raised funds to sustain the resistance.[109] The fronts hardened the next day when police and army sent reinforcements. Although the political police made every effort to present the resistance as a "communist" plot, it clearly had broad support among the workers and in the local population. The spokesmen of the local commercial association publicly denounced the intervention, and mayor Sávio Cota de Almeida Gama (PSD) distributed a leaflet opposing the MTIC's decision. The CSN's Director of Social Services, Paulo Monteiro Mendes, personally assured the workers of the company's full support.[110] However, the DOPS-RJ insisted on installing the DRT-appointed intervener, and its chief officer Sílvio Solon Ribeiro led the operation personally. Police vehicles protected by special squads with machine guns made their way to the union premises, but the officers were unable to breach a human wall of workers that protected the union office. One of Solon's assistants took several kicks and punches, and a worker even "attacked him with an umbrella." The police retreated and waited for reinforcements. The workers, in the meantime, called on their families to reinforce the human shield—a move the DOPS-RJ agent condemned as "*tática comunista*" (communist tactics). Workers also set up checkpoints to search cars and pedestrians for weapons, and they were so effective that DOPS-RJ chief Solon no longer considered the streets of Volta Redonda safe for police.[111] Force was the only remaining option for the DOPS-RJ to break the resistance, but former governor Ernani do Amaral Peixoto (PSD) extracted a guarantee from the Secretário de Segurança (Minister for Security) that the conflict would be settled peacefully. The DRT admitted defeat and revoked the intervention.[112]

The events drove a wedge between STIMMMEBM and the political police. The local DOPS-RJ agent believed firmly that the actions of the "communist" militants, above all Mendes de Souza, had been decisive for the outcome.[113] The divide grew deeper over the question which direction the CSN should take under the new federal government. PTB militants expected the victorious Kubitschek-Goulart ticket to appoint a new CSN president who would be more conciliatory toward workers' demands. To their surprise Kubitschek asked Macedo Soares to stay on, although he was politically close to the conservative UDN. The resentment over this decision led to an embarrassing incident during the president's inaugural visit to Volta Redonda. PTB activist Othon Reis Fernandes confronted Kubitschek—who was in the company of U.S. Vice President Richard Nixon and Macedo Soares—and demanded emphatically: "Your Excellence has to remove this man from here."[114] Macedo Soares was not amused. He demoted Reis Fernandes from head of the personnel department to office clerk, but that only redoubled his drive to strengthen the union.[115] Reis Fernandes quickly came to occupy a leadership role in the local PTB and maintained good relations with "communist" militants such as Mendes de Souza and STIMMMEBM's Vice President Nestor Lima. They worked together to impeach Alves in July 1956 and cooperated closely on the successful campaign for higher salaries in October 1956.[116] In 1957, Reis Fernandes won a relatively close victory over Lima to become STIMMMEBM's next president.[117] His charisma and administrative skill united the different groups within STIMM-MEBM, greatly strengthened the union's position vis-à-vis the CSN, and ultimately led to Macedo Soares's resignation from the company presidency in 1959.

By the late 1950s, the political police no longer cared to draw a distinction between *pecebista* and *petebista* labor militants. For all the officers concerned, the militants used "communist" tactics that endangered the social and economic order both locally and nationally. Othon Reis Fernandes became the archetype of the political police's imagined "communist." Reports described him as a "practitioner of demagogic and subversive politics" and as the "characteristic type of the famous *pelego*, communist, or democrat, whatever serves the purpose at the time." He supposedly used " 'communist' techniques" to lead strike movements, and one file even identifies him as a *"fascista-comunista"*—the ultimate subversive.[118] The DPS and DOPS-RJ continued to gather intelligence on Reis Fernandes and his fellow union leaders throughout the early 1960s, at a time when STIMMMEBM was one of Brazil's bastions of independent unionism.

The accumulated allegations about "communist" activities were too tenuous to justify police action under the labor-friendly governments of the late 1950s and early 1960s, but they would come back to haunt the militants after the 1964 coup.[119] The Inquérito Policial Militar (IPM) against Reis Fernandes in 1964 built its case largely on intelligence from DPS and DOPS-RJ files citing, for example, his 1958 speech in honor of Luís Carlos Prestes, which "established him perfectly well as a 'communist' and practitioner of demagogic and subversive politics." The military investigators also denounced him as an "agitator disguised as union leader" and as "constant inciter of strikes." Even the Supremo Tribunal Militar (Supreme Military Tribunal) recognized in Reis Fernandes's 1966 habeas corpus trial that the denunciations presented in the original IPM were "irritating, ineffective, and legally invalid."[120] Still, Reis Fernandes was stripped of his political rights by the IPM and had to live in exile within Brazil, away from his political base, Volta Redonda.

Conclusion

Unfortunately, the doubt that the Supremo Tribunal Militar cast very belatedly on the credibility of evidence used against alleged "communists" could not erase the effects of the work of the political police. Such tenuous intelligence had been used in the years since the CSN's construction in order to justify and legitimize operations against individual labor organizers and the entire metalworkers union. Questionable allegations of a commitment to the "communist" cause resulted in much individual suffering, and the police operations clearly tilted the balance of power in industrial relations in favor of the CSN. The consequences of the political police's obsession with "communism" were particularly apparent in the crackdowns in 1947 and 1964, but the threat of an intervention was always present. Had it not been for political support in high places, Vargas personally in 1951 and senior PSD leaders in 1955, STIMMMEBM and the workers it represented might have lost those struggles, too, against a security apparatus obsessed with the specter of communism.

Researching the files of the political police, one does sometimes wonder whether its presence actually affected the balance of power in industrial relations in Volta Redonda. Maybe the officers merely played an inconsequential cat-and-mouse game with a handful of "communists," artificially inflating the threat to justify the continued policing? That the political policing did matter for industrial relations becomes readily apparent when its history is placed in the context of the CSN's operational needs. Initially, management valued the preemptive policing because it helped to suppress resistance to the strict discipline imposed by the CSN in order to facilitate the organization of production and the establishment of work routines. The police undermined labor organization during the peak years of mill construction (1943–46) and the subsequent transition to full production (1947–49). In those years, STIMMMEBM remained much weaker than militants had hoped given the size of the workforce and the strenuous working conditions. The CSN's priorities shifted in the early 1950s, once the maximization of output became paramount: management had to weigh the benefits of repressive action against the potential impact on labor productivity and took a more conciliatory stand. The revitalized metalworkers union was well-organized and enjoyed sufficient political support to demand a fuller implementation of the labor law and less state interference in industrial relations. The primary arena for the political police to affect labor control under those conditions was the cooperation with other state agencies to create bureaucratic obstacles for worker mobilization, for example by providing intelligence that served as pretext to cancel union elections.[121] A radical change in political conditions, however, such as the 1964 military coup, could quickly return aggressive policing to a prominent role in industrial labor control.

Notes

1. Throughout this paper, I refer to specific police forces by their acronym or an unmistakable description such as "CSN's police" or "local (civil) police." "Political police" refers to either federal and/or state political police whenever the distinction is not crucial.
2. Portuguese spelling does not distinguish between the terms "Communist" for card-carrying party members and "communist" for an alleged ideological orientation. I translated "*comunista*" as "Communist" whenever the respective individual was clearly a member of the PCB and " 'communist' " in all other cases.
3. There is evidence that the proper political police, the federal police, and the state government all removed incriminating documentation before the files were handed over to the Arquivo Público do Estado do Rio de Janeiro (hereafter APERJ).
4. APERJ, "Ação e investigação: comunismo e polícia política no Brasil, 1945–64. Entrevistas com Cecil Borer, Hércules Corrêa dos Reis, José de Moraes e Nilson Venâncio" (unpublished manuscript, Rio de Janeiro: APERJ, 2002).
5. On the labor movement before 1930, see Paulo Sérgio Pinheiro and Michael M. Hall, org., *A classe operária no Brasil: documentos, 1889 a 1930* (São Paulo: Ed. Alfa Omega, 1979); Claudio H. M. Batalha, *O movimento operário na Primeira República* (Rio de Janeiro: Jorge Zahar Ed., 2000). John French's recent book shows that the leaders of the First Republic conceived of labor control as a "police matter" (*caso de polícia*), an aphorism attributed to President Washington Luís (1926–30). French emphasizes the role of policing for industrial labor

control in both the First Republic and the 1930s, but pays no attention to the shift from reactive to preemptive policing. John D. French, *Drowning in Laws: Labor Law and Brazilian Political Culture* (Chapel Hill: Univ. of North Carolina Press, 2004), 122–133.

6. The first police force with the task to "protect the social order" was created in the Federal District as early as 1907. Police legislation in 1920 identified the working class as threat to social order but targeted primarily anarcho-syndicalists and workers of foreign nationality. Thomas Jordan, "Policing the Unions: Social Police and Workers in Rio de Janeiro, 1930–64" (unpublished paper presented at the Midwest Association of Latin American Studies meeting, Charleston, IL, November 7, 2003).

7. On the Communist split over the COMINTERN's strategic shift towards the Popular Front and its significance for the ANL uprising, see Paulo Sérgio Pinheiro, *Estratégias da ilusão: a revolução mundial e o Brasil, 1922–1935* (São Paulo: Companhia das Letras, 1991), 287–297.

8. An internal memo stated, not without pride, that the archive contained 20,211 well-organized files and address information on an additional 102,000 people as of 1941. Dossiê 1, Estados 20, Departamento de Ordem Política e Social/Departamento Geral de Investigações Especiais (hereafter DOPS/DGIE), APERJ.

9. Leila Menezes Duarte and Paulo Roberto de Araújo, "História administrativa: DFSP—DPS" (unpublished manuscript, Rio de Janeiro: APERJ, 1998).

10. APERJ, "Ação e investigação," 13–14.

11. On the inter-agency fight for control of the SIS, see Leslie B. Rout and John F. Bratzel, *The Shadow War: German Espionage and United States Counterespionage in Latin America during World War II* (Frederick, MD: University Publications of America, 1986), 36–45.

12. APERJ, "Ação e investigação," 15.

13. Duarte/Araújo, "História Administrativa: DFSP—DPS," 3.

14. Ibid., 8. All translations by the author unless otherwise noted.

15. Ibid., 9.

16. Dossiê 1, folhas 32–139, Geral 21, DOPS/DGIE, APERJ. The file contains correspondence between CSN and DPS on dozens of ideological screenings and the list of the coke plant workers with all the annotations by DESPS.

17. Milton Brandão to DPS/DF, 04/1943, Dossiê 1—CSN, folha 146, Geral 21, DOPS/DGIE, APERJ.

18. The decree built on earlier legislation. Decree-Law 4.309 (May 18, 1942) had made the CSN a project of military interest, while decree-law 4.937 (November 9, 1942) "assure[d] the full operation of civil and military factories that produced war matériel" and established legal restrictions for their employees. Edmundo Macedo Soares e Silva to Ernani Amaral Peixoto, February 19, 1945, Arquivo Edmundo

Macedo Soares e Silva, EMS f-publ 39.05.12, Pasta 2, FGV/ CPDOC. The government revoked the CSN's status as a military installation in January 1946. "Decreto-Lei 4.937," *Boletim de Serviço de Volta Redonda* (hereafter *BSVR*) 011 (January 16, 1946), 92.

19. Guilherme Guinle to Chefe de Polícia do Distrito Federal, March 2, 1943; and Chefe da Secção de Segurança Social to Delegado Especial, March 20, 1943, Dossiê 1, folhas 26–30, Geral 21, DOPS/DGIE, APERJ.

20. Brasil. *Consolidação das Leis do Trabalho. Decreto-Lei n. 5.542, de 1.° de maio de 1943* (Rio de Janeiro: Imprensa Nacional, 1943).

21. The laws overriding these provisions were Decree-Law 4.868 (October 23, 1942) and Decree-Law 6.361 (March 22, 1944).

22. The documentation on the recognition of *sindicatos* is part of the poorly organized labor ministry records in the National Archives in Brasília. The closest to a proper citation would be MTIC, 413.126/46, DNT 51.001/44, Reconhecimento Sindical, 1945, Caixa 120, Arquivo Nacional do Brasil, Brasília (hereafter ANdoB-B).

23. Estado do Rio de Janeiro, Secretaria de Justíça e Segurança Pública, Instituto de Criminologia, Serviço de Identificação, *atestado de bons antecedentes*, and Estado do Rio de Janeiro, Secretaria de Segurança Pública, Delegacia de Ordem Política e Social, *atestado ideológico* for president José Calaça Gomes, secretary Elpídio Antônio da Costa, and treasurer Hélio Leão Velasco. The DRT later reconfirmed with DPS that none of them "professed ideologies incompatible with the institutions or interests of the Nation [*nação*]," Mr. Xavier Sobrinho, head of the DRT, to Dr. Alvim de Souza, head of the DOPS-RJ, November 20, 1944. All in MTIC, 413.126/46, DNT 51.001/44, Reconhecimento Sindical, 1945, Caixa 120, ANdoB-B.

24. Commissão do Enquadramento Sindical, Resolução, March 20, 1945, MTIC, 413.126/46, DNT 51.001/44, Reconhecimento Sindical, 1945, Caixa 120, ANdoB-B.

25. *Estatutos do Sindicato dos Trabalhadores nas Indústrias Metalúrgicas, Mecânicas e de Material Elétrico de Barra Mansa*, Capítulo I, Articles 3, 4 and 5. MTIC, 413.126/46, DNT 51.001/44, Reconhecimento Sindical, 1945, Caixa 120, ANdoB-B. The labor law established these obligations in very specific terms. CLT, Article 518 in Brasil. *Consolidação das Leis do Trabalho e legislação complementar: prejulgados do TST na íntegra, súmulas do STF e do TST; textos revistos, anotados e atualizados até setembro de 1973*, ed. Adriano Campanhol, 35th ed. (São Paulo: Atlas, 1973), 138.

26. Regina Lúcia de Moraes Morel, "A ferro e fogo. Construção e crise da família siderúrgica: o caso de Volta Redonda (1941–1968)" (Tese de Doutoramento em Sociologia, Universidade de São Paulo, 1989), 123.

27. Relatório Interno: "Atividades do PCB," Estados 20, folhas 134–135, DOPS/DGIE, APERJ; Ficha Interna, D529, folhas 1–2, Caixa 530, DPS, APERJ.

28. Relatório Interno, November 3, 1945, D155, folha 13, Caixa 421, DPS, APERJ.

29. Relatório Interno: "Atividades do PCB," Estados 20, folhas 134–135, DOPS/DGIE, APERJ; Termo de Declarações, January 6, 1945, Prontuário P. 9.814—Gentil Noronha, DOPS/GB, APERJ.

30. Ficha Verde—Biografia, Prontuário P. 9.814—Gentil Noronha, DOPS/GB, APERJ.

31. Report from Investigator Lívio Fleury Curado to DPS/DF, April 10, 1943, Dossiê 1, folha 144, Geral 21, DOPS/DGIE, APERJ.

32. Interview with ex-CSN-worker, 1943, 50-B-0 1, Departamento Estadual de Ordem Política e Social de São Paulo (hereafter DEOPS), Arquivo Público do Estado de São Paulo (hereafter AESP).

33. Comunicação, D155, folha 1, Caixa 421, DPS, APERJ; Internal Memo, November 3, 1945, D155, folhas 12–14, Caixa 421, DPS, APERJ.

34. Dossiê 1, folha 163, Estados 20, DOPS/DGIE, APERJ; and TSE, *Dados estatísticos: eleições federal, estadual e municipal—realizadas no Brasil a partir de 1945*, vol. 1/II (Rio de Janeiro: DIN, 1950), 19.

35. Relatório Interno, June 17, 1946, Prontuário P. 9.308—Alcides Sabença, DOPS-GB, APERJ.

36. "Propaganda política," *BSVR* 005 (January 8, 1947), 37; "Organização," *BSVR* 086 (May 7, 1946), 655.

37. "Fechada, pelos agentes do Fascismo, a escola do Comitê de Volta Redonda," *Tribuna Popular*, August 8, 1946, D155, folha 28, Caixa 421, DPS, APERJ.

38. This was part of the Dutra government's first offensive against organized labor and the PCB. Decree-law 9.070 (March 15, 1946) limited the recourse to *dissídios coletivos* (collective grievances) and declared strikes illegal, while decree-law 9.502 (July 23, 1946) altered union election rules and restricted unions' political freedom. Mônica Kornis, "Movimento Unificador dos Trabalhadores (MUT)," in *DHBB*, eds. Alzira Alves de Abreu, Israel Beloch, Fernando Lattman-Weltman, and Sérgio Tadeu de Niemeyer Lamarão, 2nd ed., 5 vols (Rio de Janeiro: Ed. da FGV, 2001) (Rio de Janeiro: Ed. da FGV, 2001), 4:3991.

39. "Aderem a CTB os metalúrgicos de Volta Redonda," *Tribuna Popular*, November 7, 1946, Pasta 2, Caixa 650, DOPS-RJ, APERJ. A major reason for the conspiracy charge was that CTB affiliated with the Confederação dos Trabalhadores da America Latina (CTAL; Confederation of the Workers of Latin America) and the World Federation of Trade Unions (WFTU), even though it was illegal for Brazilian unions or federations to join international labor organizations. Leslie Bethell, "Brazil," in *Latin America between the Second World War and the Cold War, 1944–1948*, ed. Leslie Bethell and Ian Roxborough (Cambridge: Cambridge Univ. Press, 1992), 56–60.

40. For the state's right to grant or deny permission for rallies, see §11 do Art. 141 da Constituição Federal; Art. 128 da Constituição do Estado

do Rio de Janeiro. On police procedures, see Pasta 1, Caixa 640, DOPS-RJ, APERJ.

41. Parte do Serviço—Barra Mansa, December 11, 1946, Pasta 1, Caixa 651, DOPS-RJ, APERJ.

42. Boletim—Comité Distrital de Volta Redonda, December 1946, Pasta 1, Caixa 651, DOPS-RJ, APERJ; Telegrama Interno Volta Redonda—Niteroí, December 12, 1946, Pasta 7, Caixa 643, DOPS-RJ, APERJ.

43. The order to end the CSN's practice of hiring all able-bodied men who wanted employment came in "Admissão de serventuários," *BSVR* 198 (October 17, 1946), 1626. The union challenged the dismissals in the labor courts, ultimately unsuccessfully. "Dispensa de empregados— Recurso Extraordinário (Proc. T.S.T. 5.028/47)—Parecer do Procurador do T.S.T.," *BSVR* 176 (September 12, 1947), 1563–1565.

44. "Aditamento ao Acôrdo para o Aumento Coletivo," *BSVR* 015 (January 22, 1947), 142–143; CSN, Resolução da Diretoria 260, Rio de Janeiro, March 26, 1947.

45. For an example of a dissolved gathering, see the episode with the PCB candidate Benedito Maranhão. Recorte de Jornal, *Tribuna Popular*, January 7, 1947, Pasta 4, Caixa 643, DOPS-RJ, APERJ. A rally in March ended with brawls between *pecebistas* and *petebistas* and gunshots fired at a PCB speaker. Relatório, March 26, 1947, Pasta 2, Caixa 671, DOPS-RJ, APERJ.

46. MTIC, 465.612/46, DR 5265/46, Previsão Orçamentária, 1941/47, Caixa 5, ANdoB-B.

47. MTIC, Portaria (March 20, 1947), published in *Diário Oficial da União* (hereafter D.O.), March 25, 1947, 4042. To approve election results for unions, federations, or confederations under intervention, it took a directive from the labor ministry.

48. MTIC, Portaria N.35 (April 5, 1947), published in *D.O.*, April 10, 1947, 4874.

49. MTIC, 465.612/46, DR 5265/46, Previsão Orçamentária, 1941/47, Caixa 5, ANdoB-B.

50. Decreto 23.046 (May 7, 1947) outlawed the PCB. For an example of the reasoning to justify the union closings, see the case of the Sindicato de Carregadores e Transportadores de Bagagens do Porto do Rio de Janeiro (Union of Porters and Stevedores of the Port of Rio de Janeiro) on May 8, 1947. MTIC, Portaria N.43 (May 8, 1947), published in *D.O.*, May 10, 1947, 6409. On the nationwide crackdown, see: Bethell, "Brazil," 62–64.

51. Relatório Externo, May 11, 1947, Pasta 1, Caixa 680, DOPS-RJ, APERJ; Relatório Interno da CSN, December 15, 1947, Pasta 1, Caixa 715, DOPS-RJ, APERJ.

52. "Relatório estatístico anual referente ao ano de 1947," Dossiê 15, Caixa 386, DPS, APERJ; cited in Duarte/Araújo, *História administrativa: DFSP—DPS.*, 16.

53. Relatório Anual de 1948, DPS, APERJ.
54. "Serviço de Polícia," *BSVR* 230 (November 27, 1947), 1992, and "Serviço de Polícia," *BSVR* 234 (December 3, 1947), 2018.
55. Parte de Serviço, April 20, 1948, Pasta 1, Caixa 715, DOPS-RJ, APERJ.
56. Relatório Interno, August 9, 1950, D155, folhas 7–9, Caixa 421, DPS, APERJ.
57. Relatório Interno da CSN, December 15, 1947, Pasta 1, Caixa 715, DOPS-RJ, APERJ.
58. Informações que presta o cidadão Elizeu Gonelli Filho, September 13, 1949, Pasta 3, Caixa 665, DOPS-RJ, APERJ.
59. Parte do Serviço, June 16, 1950, Pasta 2, Caixa 674, DOPS-RJ, APERJ.
60. Parte de Serviço 63, August 23, 1948, Pasta 1, Caixa 644, DOPS-RJ, APERJ.
61. Relatório Delegacia Especial de Polícia de Volta Redonda, February 11, 1948, Pasta 1, Caixa 715, DOPS-RJ, APERJ.
62. "Até do Carnaval se valem os Comunistas," *A Noite*, February 13, 1948, D155, folha 23, Caixa 421, DPS, APERJ.
63. "Violência policial em Volta Redonda," *Imprensa Popular*, November 14, 1950, D155, folha 15, Caixa 421, DPS, APERJ.
64. This was a rare case of cooperation between federal and state political police. Parte de Serviço, August 13, 1949, Pasta 2, Caixa 695, DOPS-RJ, APERJ.
65. Parte de Serviço, July 10, 1949, Pasta 2, Caixa 695, DOPS-RJ, APERJ; "Presos em Volta Redonda e trazidos incomunicáveis para o Setor Trabalhista," *A Cidade*, July 13, 1949, D155, folha 22, Caixa 421, DPS, APERJ; Informações que presta o cidadão Elizeu Gonelli Filho, September 13, 1949.
66. Relatório Interno, July 31, 1949, D155, folhas 10–11, Caixa 421, DPS, APERJ; Relatório–Volta Redonda, August 2, 1949, D155, folhas 5–7, Caixa 421, DPS, APERJ.
67. Internal Report, August 14, 1949, D47, folha 31, Caixa 445, DPS, APERJ.
68. Parte de Serviço, August 14, 1949, Pasta 2, Caixa 695, DOPS-RJ, APERJ.
69. "Incumbido de um plano de sabotagem em Volta Redonda," *O Globo*, August 22, 1949, D155, folhas 18–19, Caixa 421, DPS, APERJ.
70. Termo de Declaração—Domiciano Monteiro de Castro (eletricista), October 31, 1949, Pasta 1, Caixa 669, DOPS-RJ, APERJ; Termo de Declaração—Francisco Pinheiro da Silva (encarregado de construção), October 31, 1949, Pasta 1, Caixa 669, DOPS-RJ, APERJ.
71. Informações que presta—Antônio Pereira da Silva (encanador), August 18, 1949, Pasta 2, Caixa 695, DOPS-RJ, APERJ; Termo de Declaração—Antônio Pereira da Silva (encanador), October 31, 1949, Pasta 1, Caixa 669, DOPS-RJ, APERJ.

72. Termo de Declaração—José Nunes (mecânico), November 22, 1949, Pasta 1, Caixa 669, DOPS-RJ, APERJ.

73. Parte de Serviço, August 14, 1949, Pasta 2, Caixa 695, DOPS-RJ, APERJ; CSN to DOPS-RJ, August 16, 1949, Pasta 2, Caixa 674, DOPS-RJ, APERJ.

74. Serviço Secreto, April 21, 1950, Pasta 6, Caixa 643, DOPS-RJ, APERJ; Parte de Serviço, September 30, 1949, Pasta 1, Caixa 669, DOPS-RJ, APERJ.

75. The 1946 constitution had made strikes legal, but parliament never passed legislation to implement the provision. The labor courts applied earlier laws that outlawed strikes as *recursos anti-sociais* (anti-social means), but such rulings remained controversial. *BSVR* 075 (21/04/1949), 723; and *BSVR* 119 (23/06/1949), 1153.

76. Informação n. 1045/49—S.S.S., 13/10/1949, DOPS-RJ, Caixa 669, Pasta 1.

77. Relatório Reservado, 18/09/1950, DOPS-RJ, copy filed in CPDOC, EMS f-publ 47.04.02. Emphasis added.

78. On the Catholic roots of Brazilian anti-communism, see Rodrigo Patto Sá Motta, *Em guarda contra o "Perigo Vermelho:" o anticomunismo no Brasil (1917–64)* (São Paulo: Perspectiva, FAPESP, 2002), 18–29.

79. Marco Aurélio Santana, *Homens Partidos: comunistas e sindicatos no Brasil* (São Paulo: Boitempo, 2001), 80–82.

80. Recortes de Jornal, *Folha Carioca*, May 2, 1951; *Correio de Manha*, May 3, 1951; *Diário Oficial da União* n. 206, September 5, 1952; all in Dossiê "Fornecimento de atestados de ideologia," Administração 1-E, DOPS/DGIE, APERJ.

81. MTIC, Portaria N.53 (July 29, 1950), published in *D.O.*, August 1, 1950, 11249–11254.

82. Panfleto, September 4, 1951, Dossiê 1, folhas 181–182, Geral 21, DOPS/DGIE, APERJ.

83. Previsão Orçamentária STIMMMEBM, 20/12/1951, and Walter Millen, Interim President STIMMMEBM, to Delegado Regional de Trabalho, 30/06/1952, MTIC, Previsão Orçamentária—Sindicato, 1949/50, Caixa 7, ANdoB-B.

84. Interview, by the author, with Allan Cruz, STIMMMEBM president (1951–53), Volta Redonda, November 9, 1997.

85. Parte do Serviço n. 91, October 24, 1951, Pasta 4, Caixa 642, DOPS-RJ, APERJ.

86. Boletim Quinzenal, April 30, 1952, Estados 20B, folha 572, DOPS/DGIE, APERJ.

87. Internal Document, July 9, 1951, D155, folha 6, Caixa 421, DPS, APERJ.

88. Cap. Oswaldo de Assis Gomes, head of CSN security, to Major Cyro Alves Borges, Diretor Industrial, September 4, 1951, Dossiê 1, folha 185, Geral 21, DOPS/DGIE, APERJ.

89. Ibid., folhas 181–182.

90. Boletim Quinzenal, April 27, 1953, Estados 20C, folhas 730–733, DOPS/DGIE, APERJ.
91. Serviço Secreto, July 25, 1954, Pasta 2, Caixa 692, DOPS-RJ, APERJ.
92. Secção de Volta Redonda, July 27, 1954, Pasta 2, Caixa 692, DOPS-RJ, APERJ.
93. Regina da Luz Moreira, "Napoleão Alencastro Guimarães," in DHBB, 3:2702–2704.
94. Santana, *Homens Partidos*, 90–93.
95. Secção de Volta Redonda 282, October 6, 1955, Pasta 6, Caixa 645, DOPS-RJ, APERJ.
96. Secção de Barra Mansa, September 27, 1954, Prontuário P. 22.237—Aarão Steinbruch, DOPS-RJ, APERJ; "Edital para registro de chapas," March 23, 1955, MTIC, Processo Eleitoral, 1955, Caixa 24, ANdoB-B; Documento Interno: "Edital de publicidade de chapas," April 4, 1955, Pasta 2, Caixa 643, DOPS-RJ, APERJ.
97. Requerimento, March 17, 1955, Prontuário P. 17.782—Euclides Mendes de Souza, DOPS-RJ, APERJ.
98. This requirement had been established by the MTIC, Portaria 11, February 11, 1954.
99. José de Deus Alves to Delegado Regional de Trabalho, April 6, 1955, MTIC, Processo Eleitoral, 1955, Caixa 24, ANdoB-B.
100. Walter Millen da Silva, STIMMMEBM president, to Fenelon de Souza, Delegado Regional de Trabalho, n.d., MTIC, Processo Eleitoral, 1955, Caixa 24, ANdoB-B.
101. Walter Millen da Silva to Fenelon de Souza, April 27, 1955, MTIC, Processo Eleitoral, 1955, Caixa 24, ANdoB-B.
102. Ofício n. 292/55, Cap. Lúcio Marçal Ferreira, Delegado Chefe DOPS-RJ, to Fenelon de Souza, May 9, 1955. For the original *atestados*, see DOPS-RJ, Atestado—José Claudio Alves, March 17, 1955, and DOPS-RJ, Atestado—Nestor Lima, March 22, 1955; all in MTIC, Processo Eleitoral, 1955, Caixa 24, ANdoB-B.
103. Prontuário P. 17.767—Nestor Lima, DOPS-RJ, APERJ.
104. DRT to Ministro de Trabalho, May 24, 1955; DRT to DNT, June 10, 1955; DNT to MTIC, June 16, 1955; all in MTIC, Processo Eleitoral, 1955, Caixa 24, ANdoB-B.
105. Têrmo de Posse, June 22, 1955, MTIC, Processo Eleitoral, 1955, Caixa 24; Secção de Volta Redonda—Relatório, July 13, 1955, Pasta 5, Caixa 645, DOPS-RJ, APERJ.
106. STIMMMEBM to CSN directorate, August 23, 1955, Acordos Sindicais, CSN, Gerência de Assuntos Trabalhistas, Escritório Central.
107. José Pereira dos Santos to MTIC, August 17, 1955, MTIC, Processo Eleitoral, 1955, Caixa 24, ANdoB-B.
108. Parecer—Napoleão de Alencastro Guimarães, October 5, 1955, MTIC, Processo Eleitoral, 1955, Caixa 24, ANdoB-B; MTIC,

Portaria n.° 89 (October 10, 1955), published in *D.O.*, November 17, 1955, 21161/2.

109. Secção de Volta Redonda, October 23, 1955, Pasta 5, Caixa 645, DOPS-RJ, APERJ.

110. CSN to DPS, September 25, 1959, Dossiê 3, folha 15, Geral 75, DOPS/DGIE, APERJ.

111. Secção de Volta Redonda, October 23, 1955, Pasta 5, Caixa 645, DOPS-RJ, APERJ.

112. Acordo Sindical entre STIMMMEBM e CSN, October 21, 1955, Acordos Sindicais, CSN, Gerência de Assuntos Trabalhistas, Escritório Central.

113. Secção de Volta Redonda, October 23, 1955, Pasta 5, Caixa 645, DOPS-RJ, APERJ.

114. 1. BIB to Secretário de Segurança do Estado do Rio de Janeiro, Ofício n. 36 S/2—Secreto, Barra Mansa, September 15, 1966, Prontuário DOPS/DGIE 22.162—Othon Reis Fernandes, anexo n. 2, DOPS/DGIE, APERJ.

115. Interview, by the author, with Waldir Amaral Bedê, STIMMMEBM treasurer (1959–63), Volta Redonda, January 20, 1998.

116. Informações sobre ideologia política, March 30, 1957, Prontuário 40.497—Companhia Siderúrgica Nacional, DOPS-RJ, APERJ.

117. Parte de Serviço N. 150, Volta Redonda, May 1957, Pasta 3, Caixa 642, DOPS-RJ, APERJ.

118. Coronel Comandante do 1. BIB to Secretário de Segurança do Estado do Rio de Janeiro, Ofício n. 36 S/2—Secreto, Barra Mansa, September 15, 1966, Prontuário DOPS/DGIE 22.162—Othon Reis Fernandes e João Chiesse Filho, DOPS/DGIE, APERJ.

119. The record of the IPM/CSN lists all militants accused of subversion. It included all STIMMMEBM officers since 1955, even Nestor Lima, who had not played a prominent role in the union since losing the 1957 elections.

120. "Othon Reis Fernandes, Habeas Corpus N. 28.473," reprinted in Renato Lemos, ed., *Justiça fardada: o General Peri Bevilaqua no Superior Tribunal Militar (1965–1969)* (Rio de Janeiro: Bom Texto, 2004), 117–129.

121. For a more detailed discussion of this balance of power, see Oliver J. Dinius, "Work in Brazil's Steel City: A History of Industrial Relations in Volta Redonda, 1941–1968" (Ph.D diss., Harvard University, 2004), chapters 4, 5, and 7.

Chapter 8

Vargas on Film: From the Newsreel to the *chanchada*

Lisa Shaw

The screen image of Vargas and the state as depicted in both the official newsreels and the independently produced *chanchadas*, or popular musical comedies, that came to dominate Brazilian film production between 1930 and 1960 are examined in this chapter. The newsreels logically preached a pro-Vargas rhetoric of national integration, patriotism, and work ethic, as well as seeking to foster the cult of *o pai dos pobres*, the father of the poor, as the president came to be known. They were exhibited before both imported and domestically produced feature-length films, the latter most frequently examples of the irreverent, carnivalesque *chanchada* genre. The *chanchadas* hinged on ironic inversions of societal norms and hierarchies, and often blatantly made fun of the elite and its political representatives. Although both the newsreels and the *chanchadas* of the 1930–60 period have been studied independently,[1] this chapter adopts a fresh, revisionist approach to both by analyzing them within the context of a shared viewing experience. I argue that the juxtaposition of newsreels and these musical comedies would have undermined the self-congratulatory propaganda of the former, and underscored the countercultural messages and mocking tone of the latter.

Cinema and the State in the Vargas Years

Prior to 1930 film had already proved to be an important means of communication, second only to the press, and had been recognized as a key educational tool. Decree 21.240 of 1932 gave a flexible definition of "educational film," which embraced "not only films that have as their purpose the diffusion of scientific knowledge, but also those concerned in their musical or figurative composition with the development of artistic motifs, directed at revealing to the public the great aspects of nature or of culture."² Furthermore, the nascent Vargas regime recognized that "movies could be the conveyors of a nationalist ideology that identified a historical collectivity represented by the nation and guaranteed solidarity along ethnic, geographic, and cultural lines."³ In a speech given in 1934, Vargas, as honorary president of the Associação Cinematográfica de Produtores Brasileiros (ACPB; Association of Brazilian Film Producers) declared:

Among the most useful educational agents available to the modern state is the cinema. An element of culture directly inspiring reason and imagination, it sharpens the qualities of observation, increases scientific resources, and knowledge. . . . Thus cinema will become a book of luminous images through which our coastal and rural populations will learn to love Brazil, and it will raise confidence in the fortunes of our fatherland. For the many who do not read, it will be the perfect pedagogical tool, the easiest and most impressive. For the educated, for those responsible for the success of our administration, it will be an admirable [teaching method].⁴

The establishment of the *Estado Novo* signaled a turning point in the regime's attitude to the production of educational film: the incentives that had previously been suggested for involving private enterprise were forgotten, being replaced by an overwhelming emphasis on the Instituto Nacional de Cinema Educativo (INCE; National Institute for Educational Cinema), established on January 13, 1937, and headed by Edgard Roquette-Pinto.

The INCE was created in response to the fears of Gustavo Capanema, head of the Ministry of Education and Health between 1934 and 1945, that the unfettered growth of commercial film threatened to erode moral and educational standards. The institute's slogan was "Educational cinema in Brazil must be the school for those who never went to school,"⁵ and it produced or acquired hundreds of educational films for free distribution to schools and cultural institutions across Brazil. The regime also made it compulsory for movie theaters to show such short films before every screening of a commercial feature film.

The INCE films, some of which were of feature length, were exhibited in schools, cultural centers, sporting associations and workers' organizations, and provided regular work for actors and technical staff, as well as helping Brazilian cinema fulfill the quota system introduced by the Vargas regime, discussed in more detail later. As early as

1938, the acclaimed director Humberto Mauro, who produced and directed more than 200 documentaries for Roquette-Pinto's organization, took some of his productions to the Venice Film Festival, and in 1939 a number of the INCE's films were shown in the Brazilian Pavilion at the World's Fair in New York. The following themes were strikingly prevalent within the INCE's documentary production[6]: patriotic events and official celebrations or commemorations, such as the Dia da Bandeira (Flag Day) and the Dia da Pátria (Day of the Fatherland)[7]; the state's development projects and advances in manufacturing[8]; progress in the field of health care and medicine, often showing surgical operations or the development of vaccines, or advocating hygiene and safe sexual comportment[9]; literary works that celebrated national achievements[10]; key events of Brazil's history with which the Vargas regime wished to be associated, such as the imperial legacy and the Inconfidência Mineira independence movement of the late-eighteenth century[11]; Brazil's colonial heritage and historical preservation (known as *tombamento*)[12]; sporting events[13]; and folklore, particularly regional dances and songs, as recorded in Humberto Mauro's nostalgic, idyllic visions, including the recently rereleased *Brasilianas* series, seven short films made between 1945 and 1956.[14]

The year 1939 proved to be a key one for the *Estado Novo*'s relationship with Brazil's fledgling film industry. Keen to enhance the nation's image abroad, the regime introduced a law in September of that year to prohibit the export of films that gave an unfavorable view of Brazil or posed a threat to national security.[15] This legislation also set the screen quota for Brazilian films at a minimum of one full-length feature film and one short film per year in every cinema theater, casino, and sporting association in the country. In addition, the law introduced procedures for film censorship and the insertion of propaganda messages at the beginning or end of all film programs. Cinema was actively employed to enhance the image of the regime, and in 1939 the Hammann studios produced a film version of the theatrical revue *Joujoux e balangandans* (Knick-Knacks and Trinkets), staged at Rio de Janeiro's Municipal Theatre to raise funds for the charity work of the president's wife, Darcy Vargas. On December 1, Brazil's First Lady attended the premiere of the film version, which publicized the benevolent dimension of the state to a far wider audience.

The Departamento de Imprensa e Propaganda, established on December 27, 1939, actively promoted the production of films that valorized the natural beauty of Brazil, key historical events and the achievements of the regime. The DIP's cinema and theater division controlled prior censorship of all films, the organization of competitions to coopt filmmakers, and the production of the official newsreels, the Cine Jornal Brasileiro (CJB), enforcing the latter's screening before all feature films, in every cinema theater in Brazil. "[T]he DIP participated in every stage of film production, promoting, rewarding and punishing, censoring, registering, licensing and, finally, supervising the exhibition of the end product."[16] The Cine Jornal Brasileiro was produced between October 1938 and September 1946, first by the Departamento Nacional de Propaganda (National Department of Propaganda) and subsequently by the DIP. Production totaled 250 films between October 1938 and August 1941, and in 1944 of 1,600 cinema theaters in Brazil the official newsreels were exhibited in 608 of them, in 278 cities in 13 different states.[17] Average production sometimes exceeded two newsreels per week, and exhibitors were provided with a steady supply free of charge.[18] In the early 1940s, the DIP, which had previously used private companies, created a national film distribution agency to ensure the widespread exhibition of its productions, the Cooperativa Cinematográfica Brasileira (Brazilian Film Cooperative).[19]

With the introduction of decree-law 4,064 on January 29, 1942, the regime created the Conselho Nacional de Cinematografia (National Film Council), within the DIP, headed by the latter's director general, Lourival Fontes. With this law, the DIP had the authority to increase the screen quota for Brazilian films, but the regime effectively gave only token assistance to independent national filmmakers, even lowering the tariff on imported films. It placed much greater emphasis on cooption, state propaganda, and censorship. "Such a provision reflected the increasing power and ideological nature of the propaganda arm of Vargas's Estado Novo, incorporating instruments of mass communication such as radio and cinema into the corporative policies of the regime."[20] The makers of feature films were largely left to fend for themselves and thus most studios concentrated on the money-spinning, low-budget *chanchadas* or musical comedies that appealed to mass audiences.

After Vargas returned to the presidency in 1950, his democratically elected regime continued to draw on the support of newsreels, now called the Cine Jornal Informativo, to endorse its policies and mythology; indeed the dominant themes and implicit didactic messages are remarkably similar to those of the Cine Jornal Brasileiro, as examined in more details later. In 1951, Vargas invited the acclaimed filmmaker Alberto Cavalcanti to carry out a study of the state of Brazilian cinema, and in August of the following year the president submitted the initial proposal for the creation of the Instituto Nacional de Cinema

(INC; National Cinema Institute) that would promote national film production by running filmmaking courses, offering grants and awarding annual prizes for the three best shorts and feature-length films (in practice, the INC was established only in 1957). In 1952, Vargas also introduced the so-called eight-for-one law, which made it compulsory for all cinema theaters in Brazil to show at least one Brazilian film for every eight foreign ones. "With the price of a cinema ticket fixed at ten *cruzeiros* for years on end, in 1954 this figure corresponded to about US$ 0.25 and film importers were already threatening to cease all imports, since the box-office income obtained barely covered the cost of the copies and advertising."[21] In this favorable climate for national film production, the appeal of the *chanchada* endured throughout the 1950s. Carlos Manga's *Colégio de brotos* (College of Chicks, 1956), for example, attracted a quarter of a million viewers in the first week it was shown, a record that was not broken until 1975.[22] The *chanchada* played on the audience's feelings of alienation in the big city and encouraged them to identify with the characters and predicaments presented on screen. These Brazilian films were naturally favored by the semiliterate or illiterate masses over subtitled imports.

Vargas and the Newsreels

The CJB centered on a patriotic, militaristic discourse that, in turn, revolved around the iconic figure of Getúlio Vargas. The newsreels promoted a charismatic image of the president, characterizing him as omnipresent and omniscient, fully in line with the propaganda machine of his first regime that enhanced its leader's image as an accessible man of the people but equally conferred cult status upon him. These films intentionally created a "personality cult" around the figure of Getúlio Vargas himself, annually featuring his birthday celebrations. The president remained central to the official celebrations captured on film, even when he was not present in person. Official visits by Vargas, who is said to have logged 90,000 miles visiting every corner of Brazil during his first government,[23] and those made by his representatives to varied regions of Brazil are often evocatively titled. In volume 1, number 135 (1940), for example, *Na trilha dos pioneiros* [In the tracks of the pioneers] is the title of footage of the president in Rio about to set off for Goiás. Likewise, volume 1, number 133, 1940, is dedicated entirely to *A Marcha para Oeste* [The March to the West], the name given to a government program launched in 1940 during the inaugural celebrations for the new city of Goiânia, held up as a model of national integration. This newsreel item is composed of footage of Vargas's official visit to Goiânia, "beginning a trip through regions where Brazil still retains its primitive jungle." Such discourse evokes the memory of the *bandeirantes*—the pioneers of the colonial era who pushed Brazil's boundaries south and west in search of gold and Indians to enslave.[24] The newsreels cultivated the impression that Vargas could be in several places at once, and thus had a thorough knowledge and understanding of the entirety of his land and people that equipped him to take care of their needs best.

The mainstay of the newsreels from the Estado Novo years was footage of national celebrations, usually involving a display by the armed forces or commemorations of military feats. The Semana da Pátria military celebrations held on September 7 provided an annual focus for national pride.[25] The mise-en-scène was impressive, with a cast of 1000 people, highlighting the omnipotence of Vargas and all that he represented. Like any military parade, it was above all a show of force, in keeping with the view that "Vargas and his era were built around the metaphor of war."[26] Another dominant theme of the Estado Novo newsreels was modernity, and they frequently showcased industrial progress and public works schemes, such as the construction of dams in Brazil's arid northeast, and of hospitals, highways, and road tunnels. Aviation was a particularly favorite topic in the first half of the 1940s, with footage of the inaugurations of aerodromes, and the arrival in Rio of new aircraft for military use. Repeated features were the item *Asas para o Brasil* [Wings for Brazil], showing Vargas naming a new aircraft, and the official celebrations of the Semana da Asa.[27] Industrial development was seen in patriotic terms.

By 1944, the formal aspects of the newsreels reinforced the two central themes of patriotism/militarism and economic moderniza-tion. The opening titles were set against a split screen that contained five different images. The Brazilian flag was displayed in the center of the screen, and the remaining images that surrounded it were of vari-ous military scenes, such as soldiers marching and on horseback and a close-up of a warship. These then gave way to agricultural scenes, but with the workers using modern equipment and machinery. When the title "Cine Jornal Brasileiro" appeared on screen, a large plough in action formed the backdrop.[28]

A more detailed examination of one newsreel (CJB, volume 3, number 73, 1944) provides a clear indication of the medium's concern with celebrating industrial and agricultural progress, together with urban development. Like the other newsreels of the first Vargas regime, this example is silent but accompanied by a soundtrack of military marches and a male voice-over that describes the action on screen. The opening title, "Distributed by the Brazilian Film Cooperative" appear against a backdrop of a black and white Art Deco-Modernist design of muscular male workers, in hard hats, pulling on a rope with all their might. The anticipation of the audience is built up with a succession of written titles:

• The Press and Propaganda Department
• Presents
• A Special Edition
• Volume III, Number 73
• The President of the Republic in Belo Horizonte
• Important Works are Inaugurated by the Head of State, in the State Capital of Minas Gerais, Especially the 11TH National Exhibition of Animals and By-Products

At this point, the orchestration ceases and the narration begins: "Belo Horizonte, the beautiful capital of Minas Gerais, whose extraordinary progress constitutes a legitimate source of pride for all Brazilians, is witnessing a time of excitement and joy in the run-up to President Getúlio Vargas's visit." Simultaneously, the spectator is presented with images of the city, its modern buildings, bustling, traffic-lined streets, and the airport where Vargas's plane lands. To the extra-diegetic melody of a rousing military march, we see the crowds in the streets greeting the president, who opens the exhibition, raises the Brazilian flag and waves to those in attendance, from his stand. He looks on, applauding, as livestock are paraded before him. Later the president visits a state-of-the-art, mechanized dairy, where hygiene is emphasized by the crisp white uniforms and hats worn by the workers.

In the early 1950s, the CJI of Vargas's second government typically featured the president performing official duties at the Catete Palace, inaugurating public buildings, attending a display by the armed forces, and paying official visits to different parts of the nation. These newsreels also covered national commemorations, such as Independence Day, Dia de Tiradentes, Dia da Bandeira and Dia do Rádio, sporting occasions, and charitable events. Volume 3, number 29 (1952), is entirely dedicated, for example, to the official Independence Day celebrations on September 7. It opens with a split screen, divided into four sections, in each of which there is some kind of military scene, accompanied by the soundtrack of a military march. The audience is presented with Vargas watching a military parade from his platform on the Avenida Presidente Vargas. The staid spectators watch the file-past as military planes fly overhead. There follows an aerial shot of the ultraorderly and orchestrated procession, as the male narrator solemnly comments: "The precision of the march stands out even more when seen from the top of a large tower." Trucks, tanks, and artillery trundle past the assembled group of generals and admirals in the VIP stand sporting their medals and accompanied by their well-dressed wives. The camera focuses on the statue of the Duke of Caxias, patron of the armed forces, located in front of the Ministry of War. Vargas is then shown in his open-top carriage, waving and smiling at the crowds, as the narrator comments: "the people of Rio show once again their total trust in the man who leads the destinies of Brazil." This tour de force of pomp, ceremony, order, and authority could not differ more from the spontaneous, chaotic street celebrations of carnival that were the focus of short documentary films even before the arrival of sound film in Brazil in the late 1920s. Carnival was covered by the newsreels, but more often than not footage centered on the upscale costume balls of the elite, but both carnival music and the anarchic overturning of societal norms that characterized the annual celebration, found their fullest expression in the *chanchada* genre.

Vargas and the *chanchada*

Chanchada was the initially pejorative term used to refer to a genre of low-budget musical comedy films that emerged in the mid-1930s as vehicles for the promotion of carnival music and radio stars. In the 1940s and 1950s, these popular films dominated film production in Brazil, chiefly thanks to the Rio-based Atlântida studios, established in 1941. The *chanchada* espoused the counter-cultural ethos of *malandragem* or "living off your wits," embracing humble characters who succeeded in bypassing the social hierarchy, usually by a twist of fate, often played by the comic actors Oscarito or later Zé Trindade. Part of the appeal of the *chanchada* lay in the genre's irreverent humor that poked fun at the establishment, the pretentious social elite, and authority figures. Vargas and, later, President Juscelino Kubitschek were not spared such derision.[29] As early as 1936, *Alô. Alô. Carnaval* [Hello, Hello, Carnival], widely credited as being the first fully fledged *chanchada*, took *malandragem* as one of its themes. This film, produced by Rio's Cinédia studio, not only parodied elite culture in the form of a comic performance of the *Canção do aventureiro* [Song of the Adventurer] from Carlos Gomes's ultrapatriotic opera *O Guaraní* [The Guaraní Indian], but also featured two streetwise *malandro* hustlers, who set out to drink a casino dry at no cost to themselves, charm the wealthy female patrons, and cheat a gullible gambler out of his money. The *chanchadas* of the 1950s repeatedly made jokes about the state and its representatives.[30] The political regime and public administration are criticized via references to the mundane problems of everyday life, such as price rises, power cuts, unreliable public transport, petty bureaucracy, and an incompetent police force. A musical number from *Aviso aos navegantes* [Calling All Sailors, 1950], for example, sung by Emilinha Borba, repeats the refrain "Tomara que chova" (I hope it rains [so that there is water to wash with]). The president and his famous phrases and slogans are often made fun of; Watson Macedo's *chanchada O petróleo é nosso* [The Oil is Ours, 1954], for example, irreverently took its title from Vargas's nationalistic slogan employed to galvanize opposition to the *entreguistas* or "sell-outs," who supported the expansion of the operations of Standard Oil and Shell within Brazil. Poking fun at Vargas and his political legacy did not abate even after his death. In *O homem do sputnik* [Sputnik Man, 1959], all but one of the government officials are on an extended coffee break at the fictitious Departamento de Pesquisas Interplanetárias (DPI; Department of Interplanetary Research), clearly a tongue-in-cheek allusion to the Estado Novo's censorious DIP. Those in authority are often treated with suspicion by less educated characters, in a reflection of the mistrust commonly felt by migrant workers in the big city. In *Rico ri à toa* [The Rich Can Afford to Laugh, 1957], for example, Zé, the epitome of the humble man in the street, voices such fears: "Quanto mais elegante, mais vigarista" (The more well-dressed you are, the more likely you're a con man). His concerns prove to be legitimate when a bank clerk is exposed as a bank robber.

The São Paulo-based Vera Cruz studios, established in the late 1940s, became known for raising the production values of Brazilian cinema inspired by the Hollywood studio model, and produced the acclaimed drama *O Cangaceiro* [The Bandit, 1953], voted best film at the Cannes film festival. Although Vera Cruz set itself in direct opposition to the Atlântida studios in the rival city of Rio, famed for their low-brow *chanchadas*, the São Paulo studios recognized the commercial potential of harnessing popular comedy and music in a similar way. Thus, in 1952 Vera Cruz released the film *Sai da frente* [Get Out of My Way], starring the popular comedian and singer Amácio Mazzaropi in the role of the archetypal *jeca* or *caipira*, a country bumpkin who has migrated to the big city (migration from rural to urban areas was a common theme in the *chanchada*, striking a chord with vast swathes of the popular audiences, many of whom were displaced migrants from Brazil's arid northeast or the interior of the states of Rio de Janeiro and São Paulo). In this film Vargas is impersonated by a minor character, who adopts the president's rhetorical style, speech patterns, and accent when taking charge at the scene of a road accident. Standing on a box, he addresses the amassed crowd as "*trabalhadores*" ("workers"), and then emphatically declares: "O Brasil espera que cada um cumpra com o seu dever" ("Brazil expects everyone to fulfill his duty"—a well-known government slogan). Vargas is equally the butt of the joke in an earlier scene, in which Mazzaropi's character, Isidoro, asks his dog to perform a trick for Getúlio. Such light-hearted mockery extends to other aspects of the regime, not in the least to its legendary, unwieldy bureaucracy. In search of medical assistance, the half-witted Isidoro enters a civil service building (which bears the sign "Repartições Públicas" or "Public Office"), where he is fruitlessly sent back and forth by various officials in the shadow of a very prominent portrait of Vargas that hangs on the wall. In a comic swipe at officialdom and petty red tape, the audience is treated to a close-up of Isidoro's identity card, which bears a photograph of the back of his head. He is then told to join "a fila para entrar na fila para encher os questionários" ("the line to join the line to fill in the forms").

One of the more memorable consequences of Vargas's social legislation was the creation of a plethora of bureaucratic jobs and a civil service underpinned by nepotism and widespread corruption. It is thus no coincidence that the *barnabé* or idle civil servant, the butt of many a gag in the *teatro de revista*, Brazil's equivalent of vaudeville or music hall, should resurface in several *chanchadas* from the 1950s, such as *Barnabé, tu és meu* [Civil Servant, You're Mine, 1951] and *Esse milhão é meu* [That Million Is Mine, 1958]. In the latter, the poorly paid, work-shy government employee, who lives off his father-in-law, wins a prize of a million *cruzeiros* and a week's holiday for managing not to miss a day's work in one week. His equally indolent boss is a thinly veiled caricature of Getúlio Vargas, who informs an employee that he will be going on vacation for a month to the south of Brazil (Vargas, of course, came from the southern state of Rio Grande do Sul).

The *chanchada Nem Sansão Nem Dalila* [Neither Samson, Nor Delilah, 1954], very loosely inspired by the Cecil B. de Mille's Biblical epic *Samson and Delilah* (1949), features the most overt parody of Vargas and his regimes. In this comic reworking of the story of Samson, Oscarito finds himself taken back in time to 1153 BC, to Gaza, where the people are only required to work one day per year, on the so-called *Dia do Trabalho* (Day of Work). This is, of course, a humorous dig at Vargas's attempts to galvanize the Brazilian work force and dramatically increase economic development, and his introduction of various official commemorations, such as the *Dia do Trabalhador* (Workers' Day). Like Vargas, the Brazilian Samson (Oscarito wearing an obvious wig, which is the source of his legendary strength) uses radio broadcasts to disseminate his propaganda and introduces censorship.[31] It is no coincidence that written on the wall behind him are the words: "Votai em Sansão—um homem de ação" (Vote for Samson—a man of action) for one of President Vargas's popular nicknames was *o homem de ação* (the man of action). As João Luiz Vieira writes, this *chanchada* "uses the story of Samson and Delilah to satirize a certain Brazilian political context."[32] He continues:

> As Jean-Claude Bernardet has observed, *Nem Sansão Nem Dalila* is one of the best self-declared political films in Brazil, since it exposes with clarity the maneuvers of a populist *coup* and its counter-*coup*. Using some points of contact with the American original (the destruction of the temple, for example), Carlos Manga elaborates an allegorical parody where Sansão (Oscarito) is named governor of a fictional realm and is constantly watched by the military leader of the kingdom who aspires to total power. Sansão, naïve and unaware, does not perceive the military leader's intentions, which are counter to the measures taken by the hero in the interests of the people, such as lowering the price of wheat chaff and bread crumbs. The merchants complain, the court becomes unhappy, and there is an attempt to overthrow Samson.[33]

Cultural Dynamics: Newsreels versus *Chanchadas*

The head of the cinema and theatre division of the DIP, Henrique Pongetti, when called upon to film a luncheon for Vargas and high-ranking officials from the armed forces, was required to cut a sequence in which the president could be seen chewing on a toothpick. As Pongetti put it, "my job was to avoid a scene from a *chanchada* in a serious documentary."[34] But as much as the DIP tried to enhance the image of the president and his regime within the state-sponsored film production, this powerful and omnipresent government body could not prevent what must have been frequent unwitting juxtapositions of official propaganda and scurrilous comic attacks launched by the *chanchadas* on officialdom and its highest-ranking representatives. Cinema audiences would have subsequently delighted in the ironic mismatch of the regime's self-congratulatory propaganda and the counter-cultural messages of the *chanchada* that they had paid their money to see, particularly the genre's profane attitudes toward authority and its individual representatives. As examined earlier, the Cine Jornal Brasileiro promoted Vargas as a charismatic and powerful leader, a persona that would be remorselessly undermined by the antiestablishment discourse of these feature-length films.

The Sonofilmes studio's *chanchada Céu Azul* [Blue Sky, 1940], set in the wings of the *teatro de revista* and released in the run-up to carnival, included a scene that clearly joked about the ideologies of the New State. This scene centered on the parodic performance of the samba *Eu trabalhei* [I Worked], a big hit in the previous year's carnival performed by the well-known crooner Orlando Silva. This song's lyrics, which extolled the virtues of adopting a work ethic and rejecting the *malandro* lifestyle, in keeping with the demands of the DIP censors, were comically undermined in this tongue-in-cheek rendition.

The comic interplay between the *chanchadas* of the late 1930s and early 1940s and the official newsreels is illustrated by their respective treatment of the impact of the U.S. government's "Good Neighbor Policy" on Brazil. By 1941, the CJB featured a regular item entitled *Boa Vizinhança* [Good Neighborliness] that included items on political negotiations between Brazil and the United States, but more frequently news such as Walt Disney's visit to the DIP in 1941 (volume 2, numbers 59 and 60), and the reception hosted by Vargas at the Catete Palace for Disney and John Hay Whitney, head of the motion picture division of the Office of the Coordinator of Inter-American Affairs (CIAA) (volume 2, number 64).[35] An entire newsreel was dedicated to Orson Welles's visit to Brazil in 1942, on the CIAA's initiative, for example (volume 2, number 111, 1942). It began with footage of Welles and all his filming equipment arriving in Rio, to a soundtrack of military music. The film then went on to show him receiving a prize for best film of the year for *Citizen Kane* from the Associação dos Artistas Brasileiros (Association of Brazilian Artists), again to the strains of a military march. Within the *chanchada*, Welles was not afforded such respectful treatment; the Cinédia studio's *Berlim na Batucada* [Berlin to the Samba Beat, 1944] featured a rotund American tourist who had come to Rio in search of carnival, a clear comic spoof of the United States' "cultural ambassador" to Latin America.[36] This musical engaged satirically with the "Good Neighbor Policy" initiatives of Hollywood and the CIAA, more specifically Walt

Disney's creation, Zé Carioca, a *malandro* parrot that embodied Brazil and appeared in *Saludos Amigos* [RKO-Disney, 1943] and later in *The Three Caballeros* [RKO-Disney, 1945].

The *chanchada* equally encouraged similar "against the grain" interpretations of the newsreels after Vargas's return to power by democratic vote in 1950. In addition to mimicking Vargas and making fun of his policies and institutions, the genre incorporated locations identical to those used in the newsreels. In the CJI of the early 1950s, the iconic Copacabana Palace hotel, with all its glamorous associations with the rich and famous, was the scene of fashion shows attended by the elite in aid of good causes, as well as official dinners for Vargas and his ministers. Volume 2, number 43 (1950), contains an item on a photographic exhibition held at the luxurious Quitandinha hotel and casino in the state of Rio de Janeiro, attended by "*as mais ilustres*" (the most illustrious) according to the narration. Both the Quitandinha and, more frequently, the Copacabana Palace were used as settings in the *chanchadas* of the 1940s and 1950s. These sites of pleasure and luxury enable humble characters, who are employed there in lowly roles, such as cleaners, and members of the elite to come into contact with farcical consequences. In the paradigmatic Atlântida *chanchada Carnaval no fogo* [Carnival on Fire, 1949] the action unfolds in the Copacabana Palace, with all its associations with the rich and famous, where Oscarito's character is employed as a cleaner. The suspension of reality and social mores in the alien environment of the upscale hotel allows the marginalized to gain a taste of the elite lifestyle. Equally, however, the well-heeled patrons of such establishments are ridiculed for being vain, insincere, pretentious, and foolish, and the typically underprivileged audiences of the *chanchada* are encouraged to recognize the folly of social climbing. Sérgio Augusto comments that a recurrent motif in the *chanchada* was that of a member of the social elite opening his/her home to a gossip columnist to gain greater exposure.[37] In *Rico ri à toa* the nouveau-riche wife of Zé donates money to farcical charities to get her name in the newspapers, and in *O homem do sputnik* three "ladies who lunch," who visit the Copacabana Palace, boast of their so-called *Movimento da Pipoca* (Popcorn Movement) that aims to provide all Latin American children with free popcorn.

Carnival music dominated the soundtracks of the *chanchadas* until the end of the 1940s, with the films being launched in the run-up to the annual celebration as a vehicle for promoting what were likely to be the hit songs. The carnivalesque also permeated the genre in the form of the recurrent motif of inversion of established hierarchies, and the temporary suspension of society's unwritten rules about race, class, and gender for the duration of the film. The typical *chanchada* finale involved all the characters, even those previously at odds, coming together in a scene of jubilation and celebration, usually accompanied by a diegetic carnival samba or march sung by those on screen, and by all accounts, by the real-life audience. The contrast between the genre's veneration of carnival excess, freedom, and spontaneity and the newsreels' staid and somber reporting of the *Dia da Pátria* military celebrations could not be more marked, and provides another example of how the consecutive screening of both types of film could foster aberrant readings of official propaganda on the part of the audience. The cultural anthropologist Roberto DaMatta draws a distinct dichotomy between the pomp and ceremony of the elite's event of the year, in which the military must symbolically express their respect for authority and national emblems, and carnival, the quintessential festival of the people. He argues that the former emphasizes hierarchy, social distance, and bourgeois individuality, whereas the latter represents the intimacy and the collectivity of the poor masses, and symbolically flouts authority and overturns elite society's unwritten rules.[38]

Conclusions

The CJB of the first Vargas regime helped foster the personality cult of the president and forge a sense of patriotism by asserting the military force of the *pátria*, alongside the nation's links with its heroic past and its modernizing zeal. Yet, when screened before disrespectful, mocking popular musical comedies, this dominant discourse was unwittingly but inevitably subverted. Parallels can be drawn between such audience experiences during the Vargas dictatorship and those during the height of the military dictatorship in the 1970s. Film critic and scholar José Carlos Avellar describes audience reactions to the short government propaganda films that cinema theaters were obliged to show before the titillating comedies known as *pornochanchadas* in that decade.[39] These propaganda films invariably sought to put across an image of order, progress, national pride, and community spirit, and were in sharp contrast to the chaos, individualism, debauchery, and *malandragem* of the *pornochanchadas* that often followed them: "The sloppy narration of the *pornochanchada* belied the image of progress, edification, civilization, good manners, unity and common effort of the community as a whole that the authorities sought to create."[40] Audiences, in the true spirit of *malandragem*, would boo and heckle during these shorts, and would then settle down to watch images that quickly debunked the pompous and clearly erroneous notions that the government promoted regarding the state of development of the nation at that time.

After Vargas's return to the presidency by democratic vote in 1950, his government continued to produce official newsreels. Despite being rebranded as the CJI, these films bare a striking resemblance to their predecessors from the first Vargas regime, suggesting that surprisingly little has changed in terms of rhetoric with the move from autocratic to democratic regime. The *chanchadas* similarly maintained their own tacit conventions in the 1950s, continuing to view the state, its representatives and underlying ideologies through an irreverent, comic lens. The dynamic interplay between these independently produced feature films that targeted popular audiences, and the government's depiction of itself on screen thus also endured, maintaining a tradition initiated in the 1930s of what Marilena Chauí would define as popular resistance, characterized by a refusal to react to the state in the way the state expected.[41]

Notes

I am very grateful to the Arts and Humanities Research Board (AHRB) for a Research Leave Award that enabled me to carry out extensive archival research for this project from October to December 2003. I would also like to thank the staff of the Cinemateca Brasileira, São Paulo, the Arquivo Nacional, Rio de Janeiro, and the Fundação Getúlio Vargas, Rio de Janeiro, where I was able to view newsreels and/or related documentation.

1. On the newsreels see José Inácio de Melo Souza, "Ação e imaginário de uma ditadura: controle social e propaganda política durante o Estado Novo," *Anuário de inovações em comunicações e artes* (São Paulo: ECA/USP, 1992), 242–255; Anita Simis, "Movies and Moviemakers Under Vargas," *Latin American Perspectives* 29, issue 122, no. 1 (January 2002): 106–114; Daryle Williams, *Culture Wars in Brazil: The First Vargas Regime, 1930–1945* (Durham and London: Duke Univ. Press, 2001), 83–85. On the *chanchada* see, for example: Rosângela de Oliveira Dias, *O mundo como chanchada: cinema e imaginário das classes populares na década de 50* (Rio de Janeiro: Relume-Dumará, 1993); Sérgio Augusto, *Este mundo é um pandeiro: a chanchada de Getúlio a JK* (São Paulo: Companhia das Letras, 1993); Stephanie Dennison and Lisa Shaw, *Popular Cinema in Brazil* (Manchester: Manchester Univ. Press, 2004).
2. Quoted in Simis, "Movies and Moviemakers Under Vargas," 109.
3. Ibid., 107.

4. See Getúlio Vargas's "O cinema nacional: elemento de aproximação dos habitantes do país" in his *A nova política do Brasil*, vol. 3 (Rio de Janeiro: José Olympio, n.d.), 187–189, quoted in: ibid., 107–108.

5. Carlos Roberto de Souza, ed., Introduction to *Catálogo—Filmes produzidos pelo INCE* (Rio de Janeiro: Fundação do Cinema Brasileiro, 1990), iv. This and all other translations from Portuguese are my own.

6. Information taken from Souza, ed., *Catálogo—Filmes produzidos pelo INCE*.

7. Examples include Humberto Mauro's films *Dia da Bandeira I*, 1936, subtitled *Solenidades na capital da República, sob o patrocínio da Liga de Defesa Nacional; Dia da Pátria II*, 1937, subtitled *Aspectos dos festejos do dia 7 de setembro de 1936; 7 de setembro de 1936—Dia da Pátria*, a sound film lasting 132 minutes and showing troops on parade in Rio and military fanfares. Mauro's 1936 film *Visita do Presidente Franklin Roosevelt ao Brasil—27 de novembro 1936* featured the American President's arrival in Rio and excerpts from the speeches made to him.

8. See, for instance, *Abastecimento d'água no Rio de Janeiro* (1939), and films showing the manufacture of products as diverse as alcohol, cheese, perfume and screws.

9. Humberto Mauro's *Apendicite* (1937) showed an appendicitis operation performed by Professor Maurício Gudin. Other examples are *Combate à lepra no Brasil—Serviço Nacional de Lepra* (1943), also by Mauro, films on the production of vaccines for yellow fever, and of pharmaceuticals, and many others on surgical procedures, such as bladder and hernia operations. Hygiene and sexual behaviour were dealt with in films such as *Sífilis Vascular e Nervosa* (1942), a silent film of 127 minutes, directed by Eduardo MacClure, and *Sífilis Cutânea* (1943), a silent film lasting 105 minutes, by Mauro.

10. See *Um apólogo—Machado de Assis, 1839–1939*, directed by Humberto Mauro in 1939 to commemorate the one hundredth anniversary of the birth of the great nineteenth-century novelist Machado de Assis, and *Euclydes da Cunha, 1866–1909*, made in 1944 by Mauro, with Cândido Portinari as one of the scenographers, which recounted the life of the great Brazilian writer and focused on the War of Canudos that he wrote about in his most famous work, *Os sertões* (translated into English as "Rebellion in the Backlands"). This thematic strand of INCE's production extended to works by great Portuguese writers, such as the film version of the Adamastor section of the fifth canto of Luis de Camões's epic poem *Os Lusíadas* [The Lusiads], directed by Mauro in 1936.

11. *Os Inconfidentes* (1936), a sound film of 168 minutes in length, directed by Humberto Mauro, showed the arrival in Rio of the ashes of the conspirators on December 13, 1936. Mauro's *Bandeirantes* (1940) was described at the time as "the epic of the exploration and

conquest of the land, in search of gold and precious stones. The great expeditions and the most important pioneers, giving due prominence to the figure of Fernão Dias and the legend of the emeralds, recounted in the famous poem by Olavo Bilac." (quotation from *Catálogo de filmes e diafilmes*, Rio de Janeiro: MEC/INCE, n.d. [ca. 1965]).

12. Colonial-era churches were frequently filmed, such as in two silent films by unknown directors featuring the church of São Pedro and that of Nossa Senhora Bom Jesús, both in Rio, respectively. *Aspectos de Minas* (1943), directed by Humberto Mauro, depicted scenes of this state's baroque, "gold boom" architecture. Humberto Mauro's film *Museu Imperial de Petrópolis* (1942) was listed in the *Livro de Tombo* national heritage registry, as was *Relíquias do Império*, a silent film from 1942, lasting 200 minutes, by Genil Vasconcellos.

13. Documentaries often focused on football matches (*Copa Roca— Segundo Jogo—Brasil X Argentina—15 de Janeiro de 1939*, shot by Humberto Mauro) and motor racing (*Corrida de Automóveis*, held at Gávea in Rio in 1936, again by Mauro).

14. Júlio César Lobo lists the various themes set out for the INCE's films: " '*Brasilianas*', botanics, stories, dance, rural documentation, artistic education, fiction, physics, economic geography, history, industry, literature, mechanics, music and folklore, medicine, recreation of children, reports, technology, zoology and geography." Júlio César Lobo, "Nascimento, vida e morte de uma instituição pioneira em educação à distância no Brasil: o fenômeno INCE," *Revista da FAEEBA (Universidade do Estado da Bahia)* no. 3 (January– December, 1994): 25–37, quotation from 29. He also points out the discrepancies in terms of the number of films made on each theme; 61 films were produced for the medicine series, 37 on the subject of industry, but only two on economic geography and one on technology. Ibid., 31.

15. Silvana Goulart, *Sob a verdade oficial: ideologia, propaganda e censura no Estado Novo* (São Paulo: Marco Zero, 1990), 52.

16. Ibid.

17. Anita Simis, *Estado e cinema no Brasil* (Sao Paulo: Annablume, 1996), 64.

18. Carlos Roberto de Souza, "Cinema em tempos de Capanema," in *Constelação Capanema: intelectuais e políticas* ed. Helena Maria Bousquet Bomeny and Carlos Roberto de Souza (Rio de Janeiro: Ed. da FGV, 2001), 175.

19. Goulart, *Sob a verdade oficial*, 117.

20. Randal Johnson, *The Film Industry in Brazil: Culture and the State* (Pittsburgh: Univ. of Pittsburgh Press, 1987), 57.

21. Mário Audrá Jr., *Cinematográfica Maristela: memórias de um produtor* (São Paulo: Silver Hawk, 1997), 132–133.

22. Dias, *O mundo como chanchada*, 34. Also quoted by Augusto, *Este mundo é um pandeiro*, 138.

23. See the editors' introduction to the section. "The Vargas Era," in *The Brazil Reader: History, Culture, Politics*, ed. Robert M. Levine and John J. Crocitti (London: Latin America Bureau, 1999), 150.

24. Tellingly, the INCE produced a film in 1940 entitled *Bandeirantes*, which told the epic story of these pioneers. The INCE also favored films that portrayed the colonial splendor and natural treasures of Minas Gerais, such as *Lagoa Santa—Minas Gerais* (1940).

25. These official commemorations extend to such banalities as "Dia do Funcionalismo Público" [Civil Service Day]; in vol. 2, no. 81, under this sub-title we see Vargas signing two "important" decrees during a lunch held in his honor. In July 1938 the Departamento Administrativo do Serviço Público [Administrative Department of the Civil Service] was created with the aim of organising and rationalising the civil service.

26. Williams, *Culture Wars in Brazil*, 12.

27. For example, CJB, vol. 2, nos. 79 and 80, 1941.

28. It was no coincidence that the CJB opened with an image of the Brazilian flag, all regional standards having been burned in a public display of national unity in accordance with Article 2 of the New State's constitution.

29. The fact that the name of the villain in *Esse milhão é meu* is Juscelino would have raised a smile in cinema halls throughout Brazil in 1958. The fearsome wife of the diminutive adulterer in *Garotas e samba* [Girls and Samba, 1957] also just happens to be called Jocelina (virtually the female equivalent of the president's given name).

30. The *teatro de revista*, Brazil's version of music hall, established the tradition for irreverent attacks on the establishment, which took the form of comic impersonations of Mussolini and Hitler, and of Brazilian authority figures, such as President Getúlio Vargas, Luís Carlos Prestes, the Communist leader released from prison in 1945, and President Dutra (1946–51). In the revue *Música, maestro!* [Music, Maestro!, 1940], for example, Pedro Dias wore a mask of Vargas's face.

31. This film was released in April 1954, and Vargas committed suicide in August of that year.

32. João Luiz Vieira, "From *High Noon* to *Jaws*: Carnival and Parody in Brazilian Cinema," in *Brazilian Cinema*, ed. Randal Johnson and Robert Stam (New York: Columbia Univ. Press, 1995), 256–269. The quote is from 260.

33. Ibid., 262.

34. Quoted by Heloísa Paulo, *Estado Novo e propaganda em Portugal e no Brasil: o SPN/SNI e o DIP* (Coimbra: Minerva, 1994), 146.

35. Created in 1940 and headed by Nelson Rockefeller, the CIAA sponsored newsreels and documentaries for Latin American distribution and, along with the Hays Office, pressed studios to make films with Latin American themes. Rockefeller's official visit to Brazil in 1942

and his visit to the headquarters of the DIP were captured for posterity in newsreels vol. 2, nos. 149 and 150.

36. Orson Welles visited Brazil in 1942 to begin work on *It's All True*, the ill-fated film project in which Luiz de Barros was also involved. The Vargas regime clearly saw this as an opportunity to attract North American tourists to Brazil with dollars to spend. For the "Carnival" section of the film, Welles's team were strongly discouraged from filming in Rio's shantytowns by the Brazilian secret police, and elements of the conservative press in Rio, as well as RKO executives, objected to Welles's foregrounding of black and mixed-race Brazil in his recreation of carnival. Barros provided the decorations for a carnival ball that Welles filmed, and went on to make fun at him in *Berlim na batucada*.

37. Augusto, *Este mundo é um pandeiro*, 170.

38. Roberto DaMatta, *Carnavais, malandros e heróis: para uma sociologia do dilema brasileiro* (Rio de Janeiro: Jorge Zahar Ed., 1979), 41–49.

39. José Carlos Avellar, *Anos 70: Cinema* (Rio de Janeiro: Europa Empresa Gráfica Ed., 1979), 71–77 (section "Teoria da relatividade").

40. Ibid., 69.

41. Marilena Chauí, *Conformismo e resistência: cultura popular no Brasil* (São Paulo: Ed. Brasiliense, 1986), 66.

Chapter 9

"I Choose This Means to Be With You Always": Getúlio Vargas's *Carta Testamento*

Thomas D. Rogers

"To the wrath of my enemies I leave the legacy of my death." So began a note written in the hand of President Getúlio Vargas and found by one of his aides a week before Vargas took his own life on August 24, 1954, and permanently altered the twentieth-century history of Brazil. While the legacy he referred to has never been fully defined, one result of his death was a renovated cult of Vargas's personality and a political setback for his adversaries. Using another document as his tool, Vargas tried and arguably succeeded in giving direction to the legacy of his death. This longer and more famous letter was found near Vargas's body after he killed himself. Quickly acquiring a title, this *Carta Testamento* has been subject to persistent dispute, challenge, interpretation, and glorification. Opponents of *getulismo* obstinately dispute the letter's authenticity while each anniversary of the president's death finds political devotees offering homage to the text.[1]

This chapter analyzes the *Carta Testamento* on several levels: the contents of the document, the context and details of its authorship, and its abiding significance in Brazilian political culture. There are nearly as many opinions about the letter as there are people who mention it, with authors offering theories about whether Vargas intended to kill himself, who wrote the suicide letter and when, and what effects Vargas intended his letter to have. In two recent books, categorical statements about the *Carta* gloss a great deal of this controversy. One author states that "Vargas's suicide note was altered before publication" while another boldly asserts that there were two *Cartas*

Testamento.[2] A 2003 article brands Vargas's suicide a "grand political gesture" and observes that it "passed almost immediately from current event to popular myth." But while the *Carta Testamento* has been "studied, dissected, and appropriated," we are as far from a consensus about its meaning and significance as ever.[3] Indeed the suicide and the document associated with it remain as steeped in mystery (and mysticism) as ever. This chapter cuts through the profusion of accounts and opinions to offer the most likely scenario for the letter's authorship, its connection to other similar texts, Vargas's intentions for the document, and the uses to which the letter has been put since. The letter and Vargas's death clearly drew meaning from one another and this fact is crucial to understanding the document as an intervention. The *Carta Testamento* was the exclamation point following the suicide and the suicide sealed the letter with blood.

The "August Crisis":[4] The Context of Vargas's Death

The broad context of August 1954 is well known. Getúlio Vargas was several months away from entering the fifth and final year of his first term as the popularly elected president of Brazil. It was becoming increasingly clear, however, that his chances of finishing the term were dwindling. Spiraling inflation frustrated a public that had entertained high hopes for Vargas's administration.[5] A government inquiry had been launched the previous year into unseemly connections between the pro-Vargas newspaper *Última Hora* and the Bank of Brazil.[6] In February, Vargas had bowed to the strength of his detractors and removed the recently appointed João Goulart from his position as minister of labor. In May, impeachment proceedings were initiated against him, hinging on his alleged support for a coalition with Chile and Argentina against U.S. hegemony in the region.[7] In the same month, a member of the civil police in Rio de Janeiro beat a crime reporter to death, tarring the image of the local government and by association Vargas.[8] But the worst blow to the president's legitimacy came with the assassination attempt against the anti-Vargas muckraker Carlos Lacerda on August 5.

The bungled assault wounded Lacerda and killed his bodyguard Rubens Vaz, a major in the Air Force. Already split in their stance toward Vargas, the armed forces went into further turmoil when news of the murder spread. An Inquérito Policial Militar (IPM) was begun, accompanied by a massive investigative operation. Within days, the alleged gunman had been found and detained and the military traced the origin of the attempted hit all the way to the presidential guard. Eventually, the head of the guard, a long-time associate of Vargas named Gregório Fortunato, was implicated in the murder and people even closer to the president came under suspicion. On receiving the information about his personal guard, Vargas uttered the famous phrase "I have the impression of being on a sea of mud."[9] On August 22, a group of Air Force officers wrote and delivered to Vargas an ultimatum demanding his resignation.[10] Vargas gave a defiant refusal to General Mascarenhas de Morais who transmitted the reply back to the protesting officers.[11]

The president held a ministerial meeting in the early morning of August 24 to assess the situation. With the armed forces apparently uniting against him and popular opinion slipping rapidly toward the opposition, Vargas sought the counsel of his ministers and advisors (the details of this conference have been exhaustively examined and some are reviewed later). The outcome of the meeting was an agreement that Vargas should request a leave of absence from the presidency. When the meeting ended after 4:00 a.m., Vargas retired upstairs to his rooms. He was followed by Finance Minister Oswaldo Aranha, who helped him vet the text of a message announcing the leave of absence.[12] According to Zenha Machado, this short note was read over the radio at 4:45 that morning.[13] This makes sense, considering that there are a number of accounts of public reactions to the news of Vargas's departure from the presidency in the very early morning on 24.[14] Vargas's message stated simply that he would transfer his mandate to his legal substitute, Vice President Café Filho, providing order was maintained.[15]

At 6:00 a.m., representatives of the IPM invited Vargas's brother Benjamin to their headquarters at Galeão Airport to testify for the inquiry. He refused, claiming that he could not leave his brother in such trying times. An hour later, Justice Minister Tancredo Neves and Benjamin learned that General Zenóbio da Costa, the minister of war, had informed the military leadership that Vargas would be stepping down. Benjamin spoke with his brother about the general's reaction—they believed that Vargas must resign. Getúlio asked, "so I am deposed?" and his brother responded: "I don't know, but I know that it is the end." Asking to be left alone so that he might rest, Vargas changed into pajamas and went to his bedroom. Shortly after 8:00 a.m., he shot himself in the heart with a .32 caliber revolver of his ownership. Family and friends immediately rushed into the room and noticed an envelope sitting on his bedside table. It contained a signed copy of the *Carta Testamento*.[16]

The suicide letter found its way to a large audience immediately after Vargas's death. Aranha, whom Benjamin had called at home to say only that Vargas had died, heard on the car radio en route to Catete Palace (the presidential residence) that it had been suicide. Aranha read the letter out loud to everyone in Catete shortly before it was read over the telephone to radio stations, which broadcast the text at 9:00 a.m. and repeatedly throughout the day.[17] The August 24 edition of the *getulista* newspaper *Última Hora* carried the *Carta's* text also, and the next day the *New York Times* published a translation.[18] According to innumerable eyewitness accounts, the public reaction to the suicide was swift and remarkable. A crowd surrounding the presidential palace that had been crying angrily for the president's ouster immediately began shouting *vivas* to the now departed leader. People moving through the downtown area trumpeting the news of Vargas's impending renunciation changed their tune completely as word of his death spread.[19] Angry crowds now began circulating through the capital, attacking anti-Vargas newspapers and advertisements for anti-*getulista* politicians.[20] The contents of the suicide note was at least partly responsible for the popular reaction, since the text circulated at virtually the same time that news of the death broke. In addition, *Última Hora's* version of the events, including its prominent treatment of the *Carta*, became the most widely seen newspaper account because the crowds demonstrating in front of the other newspapers' facilities prevented their editions from being circulated widely.

Última Hora's Samuel Wainer remembered in his memoirs that the radio announced the news "incessantly." "The only [newspaper] to circulate," Wainer reported, "was *Última Hora*, which sold almost 800,000 copies."[21] In other words, most people learned of, and probably remembered, the suicide through the lens of the most devoted *getulista* paper. Responding to worries that the popular unrest was being fed by "dramatic readings of the Carta Testamento" over the air, Rádio Nacional stopped broadcasting the text. The labor ministry's station, Rádio Mauá, also stopped transmitting it at mid-day, under orders from Under-Secretary of Labor João Oliveira Santos.[22] Other stations persisted, reading the letter over a background of solemn music.[23] Carlos Lacerda recognized the effect on the public and exhorted distracted members of the brand-new administration to shut the broadcasts down. "What you are doing is crazy," he told them, "you are throwing the people against the . . . government and soon we shall have riots in the streets."[24]

"I Choose This Means to Be with You Always": The Text of the *Carta Testamento*[25]

The document that contributed to firing so much passion has been called by Darcy Ribeiro the "essential document of contemporary Brazilian history."[26] Sociologist Octavio Ianni claimed that the *Carta Testamento* marked the "apex of the historical period of populist democracy."[27] Despite these grand claims, few scholars have devoted sustained attention to the actual text of the letter. It is to this that I now turn.

For the most part, the *Carta Testamento* directs itself to a group interpellated as "the people," implicitly Vargas supporters and distinct from those endowed with political or economic power. In the *Carta*, Vargas details the pressures that mounted against him, his efforts to fight for liberty and the well-being of his followers, and the choice to die for them. In a certain very clear sense, it is a narrative, telling a story with a protagonist and a series of morals. The letter does not take place in a vacuum or establish its own temporality, which might be expected of a document that talks of ultimate sacrifice and an epic battle against hate. Its very first words link the text to history, to a very personal past, as Vargas wrote, "once more, the forces against the people are newly coordinated and raised against me." He then sketched out the broad trajectory of his political career, claiming to have brought to an end "decades of domination and plunder by international economic and financial groups" when he made himself "chief of an unconquerable revolution." This one line constitutes one half of his account of the entire period between 1930 and 1945. After making the revolution, he wrote, "I began the work of liberation and I instituted a regime of social liberty." The narrative of the period ends unceremoniously with the statement, "I had to resign."

He then devoted a paragraph and a half to recounting the political efforts he put forth and the challenges he faced during the 1950–54 term, which began when he "returned to govern on the arms of the people." He described his attempts to defend the price of coffee, to establish the nationally owned energy and electricity companies, and to raise the minimum wage. These are policy-oriented issues, with almost quotidian details included, such as the fact that passage of the law of excess profits was delayed in congress. The tone of these lines does not match the rest of the document, since the concrete and mundane details clash with the elevated tone and elegiac passages that open the text, as well as those that follow.[28]

After the account of politics past, Vargas shifted into apostrophe. To that point he had maintained an oratorical tone, as if he were making a general speech, referring to the beneficiaries of his travails simply as "the people." But then he changed the mode of address, writing, "I cannot give you more than my blood," and thereby making the apostrophe explicit. This structure defines the rhythm of most of the rest of the letter. "When they humiliate you, you will feel my soul suffering at your side. When hunger knocks at your door, you will feel within you the energy to fight for yourselves and for your children. When you are scorned, my memory will give you the strength to react."

The second half of the letter, from the beginning of the apostrophe and continuing through Vargas's final flourish—leaving life to enter history—is written in such a way that he *must* have known that he was going to die. Telling the people that he chose "this means to be with you always," and offering his life "in the holocaust" are not positions consistent with plans for a peaceful retirement to his ranch in São Borja. But they could be consistent with a president planning to defend his mandate through force against what he knew would be superior numbers. An imagined final spectacle of bullets whizzing through the Catete garden might also explain the "holocaust" in which Getúlio planned to offer his life. He referred to the scandal-ridden environment in the capital as an "inferno" several days before his death, but that does not reach the level of a "holocaust."[29] It is worth asking what Vargas meant by the "means" through which he would forever be with his people. Was he talking simply about death or about the more immediate (in the sense of an authorial present) letter?

The two halves of the letter are clearly linked, but the bond is fragile.[30] In closing his message, Vargas returned to the language of the very beginning. The "hatred, infamy, and calumny" of which he was the object did not "defeat [his] spirit." But everything else, led by tone, is different. The "people" has become a unified subject, where in the first half he drew a distinction between "the people" and "the humble," claiming to have always defended "the people and principally the humble." Such distinctions become cumbrous when one seeks to create a tone of sweeping drama and "exalted mysticism."[31]

In analyzing the *Carta Testamento*, many people have, with good reason, pointed to Vargas's letter of renunciation when he was forced from office in 1945 at the end of the Estado Novo. Indeed, the first line of the *Testamento*, claiming that "forces against the people" are *once more* raised against him, no doubt references the experience of 1945. While some instructive similarities can be found between the two letters, a comparison reveals that the two texts are notable for their divergences. In the 1945 letter, he explicitly stated that he would "abstain from analyzing the grave events that brought me to renounce."

"In all the decisive moments of my public life," he wrote, "I sought to stay above the personal passions and battles, thinking only of the good of the *Pátria*." His "serene elevation" above the dirty details of politics corresponds to his pretensions to grace and to the role of savior in his final letter.[32] However, though he might claim to be "serenely" taking the first step into history in the famous final line of the *Carta Testamento*, the rest of the letter descends into the details of his political efforts and the obstacles constructed by his opponents.

Vargas tried hard to maintain some sense of grace in the midst of his strong language and denunciations, even if by simply attributing it to himself. In his 1945 resignation, he hoped "that serenity will return to people's spirits and that everyone will acknowledge the tremendous responsibilities of the moment." And his final line of the *Testamento* is: "Serenely I take the first step on the road to eternity and I leave life to enter history."[33] As James Dunkerley has observed of this line, "there can be little doubt that Vargas meant not the general history of the past but the particular history of the great."[34] Vargas had made such a sweeping appeal to the verdict of history before. Upon giving up his mandate in 1945 he claimed that "History and time will speak for me," at which moment he probably thought that his projects and policies (including the Estado Novo) would eventually be more appreciated.[35]

One of the final lines of the *Carta Testamento* reveals a great deal about Vargas's intentions. "To those who think they have defeated me, I respond with my victory." This claim reflects a remarkable self-consciousness about the probable effect of his death, and the efficacy of the final message accompanying his death. Many people refer to his final "gesture" as "turning the tables" on the right-wing opposition— the perfidious generals, the União Democrática Nacional, and Carlos Lacerda. He knew that dying, and leaving a (melo)dramatic message behind, was the best means of snatching victory from the jaws of defeat.

In the Chamber of Deputies the day after Vargas's death, a deputy from Rio Grande do Sul, representing the Partido Trabalhista Brasileiro, claimed a parallel between Vargas's end and Christ's, and pointed out that Vargas identified himself with Christ. "There is an extraordinary similarity between the heroic death of President Getúlio Vargas and the evangelic death of the Nazarene, on the cross," the deputy declared, citing the *Carta Testamento* as his evidence. He instructed his colleagues: "Christ said, upon seeing that screaming and reactionary multitude, that though they might spit in his face and blaspheme his tragedy, 'Father, forgive them for they know not what they do.' 'To hate, I respond with pardon.'" The letter itself, the deputy said, has "all the characteristics of an evangelical document."[36] Vargas would probably have been pleased by the observation. He cultivated the sense that he had been chosen to lead and ultimately sacrifice himself for "the people" by claiming that all he did was "follow the destiny that is imposed on me." And he sprinkled Christ imagery throughout the course of the letter. He made the ultimate sacrifice—giving all that he could before, the only way to give more was to give his blood. He twice mentioned "my sacrifice," and he claimed to have "renounced" himself and to be giving his life for the people.

The self-abnegation, however, went only so far. His claim that "my name will be your battle flag" points to his sense of his own importance and of the history he was entering. Obviously no other name would be so closely associated with the political legacy Vargas envisioned than his own name. And in the final analysis, what more individual act is there than suicide? In what way can a person more completely turn attention and the making of meaning inward than by killing himself?

Writing a Manifesto to the Nation: The Authorship of the *Carta Testamento*

There are four copies of the *Carta Testamento*. Besides the copy found on Vargas's dressing table after his suicide, Alzira found in her father's safe a signed copy with errors and corrections and an unsigned copy, as well as penciled notes in Getúlio's hand.[37] Finally, Goulart had a copy, which Vargas gave him before the final ministerial meeting, saying, "take this, Jango. Keep this letter to read at home and take it tomorrow to Rio Grande. I have been heavily targeted. Prepare yourself, because now you're the target."[38]

Several factors contribute to confusion about the authorship and the authenticity of the *Carta*. Since Vargas's death, a number of witnesses, friends, and scholars have published accounts that mention different or overlapping texts (confusion about multiple texts actually began on the day of the suicide, as we see shortly). And many sources have revealed the participation of someone besides Vargas in the *Carta*'s crafting.

A week before the president's death, Vargas's daughter Alzira Vargas do Amaral Peixoto was approached by one of the president's aides.[39] Major Fitipaldi showed Alzira a note that he had found among the papers on Vargas's desk. The note began with the line at the beginning of this chapter—"to the wrath of my enemies I leave the legacy of my death"—and continued, "I carry with me the sorrow of not having been able to do for this good and generous Brazilian people and principally for the most needy, all the good that I desired."[40] Though these two sentences constituted the entire note found by Fitipaldi, a longer letter beginning with these lines turned up later.[41] Consistent with Vargas's well-known habit of writing small notes or *bilhetes* to himself, the shorter message was probably an outline for the longer one.[42]

The various texts, and their similarities, continue to cause confusion. The longer "legado da morte" (legacy of death) text has been taken by some to be the original message, Vargas wrote when contemplating his impending death. That text has also been seen as the "true" suicide letter, probably because it contains the two lines of the short "legado" note that Major Fitipaldi had found and apparently memorized since he transmitted them to the press in the immediate aftermath of the suicide. Fitipaldi's recitation might also explain why some scholars think that those two lines constitute the entirety of the "legado da morte" text.[43] The tone is bitter and the content explicitly anticipates death. "If a simple resignation of the post to which I was elevated by the votes of the people let me live forgotten and calm in the Fatherland, I would happily resign," he wrote. But instead, "old and tired, I preferred to settle accounts with the Lord, not for crimes that I did not commit, but for the powerful interests I opposed." "Let the blood of an innocent," he continued, "placate the wrath of the Pharisees."[44]

Most scholars agree that Vargas received help in the drafting of the *Carta Testamento*. He seemed to be planning a message for some period leading up to his death. In a conversation with his speechwriter Lourival Fontes, he directed the latter to think "of a type of manifesto to the Nation, that will be strong, but that will also be generous." This same conversation has also been cited as evidence for Vargas's lack of intention to kill himself, since it came in the context of planning a trip to Amapá for August 27. "This trip is good," Vargas is supposed to have said, "I will rest my spirit and get out of this inferno."[45] But the likeliest collaborator in composing the *Carta* was Vargas's close confidant and another speechwriter (as well as a friend of Fontes), José Soares Maciel Filho. A devout Catholic and a newspaperman, Maciel Filho became close to Vargas at the beginning of the president's term in 1950 and wrote most of his speeches from that date onward.[46]

Though we can safely acknowledge Maciel Filho's participation in the drafting of the *Carta*, assessing the *degree* of his involvement is difficult. Alzira and Luthero Vargas said that Maciel Filho simply inserted some details and typed the note, the latter a point frequently mentioned since Vargas could not type.[47] Robert Levine argues that words of the *Carta Testamento* "were dramatic, but they were not Vargas's usual language."[48] Maciel Filho's daughter, Izabel Maciel Veloso Borges, has her own observation with regard to the language of the *Carta*. She contends that one word choice in the letter proves that her father was the author. She says, "my father spoke, wrote, and thought in two languages, Italian and Portuguese. There was one word there, 'obstaculando,' that doesn't exist in Portuguese. The word is 'obstando' [obstructing]. 'Obstaculando,' or 'ostacolare,' is Italian."[49] Robert Levine further relates that Maciel Filho revealed to him in a 1965 interview that he had changed the letter's wording while typing from Vargas's notes.[50]

Maciel Filho is known to have written the speech Vargas gave at the inauguration of the Mannesmann steel mill in Belo Horizonte, which contained some similarities to the *Carta Testamento*.[51] Some even assume that Maciel Filho used this address as a template for the suicide letter, while others suggest that he worked from the "legado da morte" note.[52] According to one source, Maciel Filho said in a meeting with Oswaldo Aranha that Getúlio had come up with the idea for the letter as well as its final phrases but had given his speechwriter the responsibility of composing the final text.[53] And Izabel Maciel, for her part, claims that her father authored almost the entire text. Francisco Antonio Doria prints the text of a document found among Maciel Filho's papers and written in his hand that is extremely close to the first half of the *Carta Testamento*. Izabel further claims, in a strange detail, that her brother typed more copies of the *Carta* and her father distributed these to newspapers.[54] This, if true, would indicate a far greater degree of premeditation on Vargas's part, and it would underscore the staged drama of the episode.[55]

Analyzing the text of the discovered letter, Doria argues that Maciel Filho penned a letter of renunciation, not suicide. He points to references in the letter to the abdication and deposition of Pedro I and II, and argues that Maciel Filho as a strict Catholic would not have been party to a suicide. Also, he says that witnesses attest to the final sentence of Maciel Filho's draft being, "I leave *public* life to enter History," as opposed to "I leave life."[56] But if, as Doria suggests earlier, Maciel Filho worked from the "legado da morte" text, then he surely must have been aware that Vargas was facing certain death, if not necessarily suicide.

Ana Maria de Abreu Laurenza joins many scholars who have been misled by confusion surrounding the *Carta Testamento* when she declares that "there are two *Cartas Testamento*. The one published in *Última Hora*, written, actually, by the journalist José Soares Maciel . . . with the celebrated ending 'I leave life to enter History'; and the President's actual letter, found beside the body."[57] According to a reasonable interpretation of the preponderance of evidence, Abreu Laurenza's claim is wrong. But considering the range of extant accounts, opinions, and rumors, not to mention the fact that there *were* several different texts relevant to Vargas's death, there seems ample reason for the mistake. In her construction of the situation, Abreu Laurenza appears to be conflating several misunderstandings that swirl around the *Carta*, in this case involving the "legado da morte" note and Maciel Filho's role in producing the *Carta*.

The most careful conclusions seem to be that Vargas wrote at least one *bilhete* that took the rough form of a letter to be found after his death, dealing with ideas current in his consciousness including some that made it into a public speech. Probably based partially on that note and with the help of Maciel Filho, Vargas expanded the letter and elaborated some of the central themes. This process took at least two drafts, which would explain the annotated and corrected copy found in his safe. Maciel Filho or an aide typed at least three copies of the final edition and Vargas signed two of them, giving one to João Goulart and eventually placing the other on his bedside table.

The Suicide and the Letter: Interpreting Vargas's Final Gesture

Of persistent importance to the analysis of August 1954 is the relationship between the *Carta Testamento* and Vargas's suicide. Many authors have speculated about Vargas's mental state in the hours immediately before his death, operating under the assumption that such an inquiry could yield some insight into the letter. We must dispense with the idea that the final moments of Vargas's life have anything to do with the contents of his suicide note. By dawn of August 24, the letter was long finished, with several copies typed and signed by the president.[58] However, I will appropriate the larger question about the relationship between the death and the text as a frame for analysis. I propose that the best means of thinking about the two is as complementary parts of a larger gesture.

It is telling that many authors refer to Vargas's suicide as a gesture. The word speaks to the political salience of the act and to its deeply dramatic character. "Under profound pressure and without a solid support base," Lucília de Almeida Neves Delgado writes, Vargas "opted for the political gesture of suicide."[59] Tancredo Neves refers to the suicide as a "gesture of bravura" and Cleanto de Paiva Leite observes, "whatever the interpretation of the personal gesture, of the personal, intimate reasons that pushed Getúlio to commit suicide, this gesture, as a historical fact, as a political fact, certainly represents a defeat for his adversaries."[60] So while the act was political and dramatic, it was also a deeply personal choice. Importantly, though, this might be for Vargas a false distinction. That the personal was also the political in Vargas's world is clear from the *Carta*, which was marked by an intense fixation on his individual relationship to the people. The bold gesture encompassing the suicide and his message was consciously crafted to defeat his opponents.

In the days leading up to the suicide, Vargas is said to have made a number of statements that appeared to foreshadow his death, at least in retrospect. As the crisis heated up following the attack on Carlos Lacerda and the murder of Major Vaz, Vargas indicated that he would like his son Manuel to cut short the European honeymoon that he had recently begun. Upon hearing from his daughter on August 12 that Manuel was headed home, Vargas said, "good, the time has come for my burial."[61] That same day, he delivered the Belo speech, in which he referred to the insults and calumny directed against him, and he claimed that his opponents would fail to "defeat [his] spirit." He promised to maintain his "serenity" and to "pardon the injustices." He also, though, vowed to remain in government and warned his opponents that he knew how to resist against attacks on the public order.[62]

Nearly a week later, Major Fitipaldi showed the "legado da morte" note to Alzira Vargas and she confronted her father the next day, August 18. He told her "it's not what you think" and, taking the note back, claimed he had no intention of killing himself.[63] But he added, "though I am certain that they want to hurt me and humiliate me, I will not resign. I will only leave here dead."[64] Vargas seemed attracted to the drama of this bold claim, as it resurfaced various times. On 21, Vice President Café Filho met with Vargas and proposed that they both resign simultaneously, a solution to the crisis he felt the armed forces would tolerate. "By no means will I resign," Vargas responded, and then exclaimed, "I will only leave here dead."[65] The repetition of the quote could be a fabrication of the memories of those reconstructing the events of Vargas's last few days, since the phrase would later come to acquire such resonance. But just as likely it could be the result of Vargas's warming to the idea. He is said to have uttered the same line at a ministerial meeting on the morning of 22 and then to have repeated it the next day to Mascarenhas de Morais while responding to the ultimatum the latter brought from the group of 30 Air Force officers demanding that the president step down.[66] Vargas was so taken with the quotation, in fact, that on 22 he sent his son to the *Última Hora* office with the request that Samuel Wainer print the line in the next day's paper. Wainer was happy to oblige and he too played up the line's drama when, upon hearing of the suicide on 24, he reprinted the headline containing it over a picture of Getúlio with his hands covered in oil (which in the black and white photograph clearly evoked blood).[67]

The separate names that have been given the president's farewell message bring up questions of the divisions between the personal and the political and the suicide and the letter. It is known most popularly as the *"Carta Testamento,"* or testament letter. More than the political, this evokes the personal angle of the message and Vargas's preoccupation with the importance of his legacy, since "testament" implies last wishes for the future more than explanations of the past.[68] But it has also been called his *"testamento político"* (political testament), an interpretation of the message the PTB would certainly advocate.[69] So we are left with the question, how do we read the *Carta*? What is it? What was its role? Getúlio himself dropped a hint in his short conversation with Benjamin the night before the suicide, when he told his brother that a document he was reading (presumably the *Carta*) was a "political document," that he would give to Benjamin were the latter a politician.[70] Other remarks in the days leading up to his death would support this view; for instance, his comment to speechwriter Lourival Fontes of the need to make a manifesto to the nation, one that is "strong, but generous." Also, in his response to Mascarenhas de Morais, who brought the ultimatum from the Air Force officers, Getúlio said, "if by chance they want to depose me, I will present a manifesto to the Nation and I will die fighting, with a weapon in my fist, against those who intend to strip me of Power."[71]

To separate the letter from the suicide would be like separating the personal from the political in Vargas's world; both efforts would be doomed to fail. His politics, as has been observed by many analysts at the time and since, were an extension of his identity. This comes through clearly in his emphasis on his opponents' efforts to humiliate him, a theme that appeared in the "legado da morte" note, in his conversation with Alzira, and in his conversation with Mascarenhas de Morais, in which he claimed that he had never shown himself to be cowardly. In the *Carta* he wrote, "they do not accuse me, they insult me; they do not fight me, they slander me and refuse to give me the right of defense." The tactics of the forces raised against him were dishonorable and he was being dragged into the "sea of mud" instead of being able to stay "above the personal passions and battles," as he had written in 1945.[72] Killing himself and leaving the type of document that he did, then, were actions on the same plane. Indeed, they depended on each other for their shared power.

On the day that Manuel Vargas visited him at *Última Hora* to talk about the dramatic headline, Samuel Wainer says that the president's son indicated that the phrase was to be the "password for the resistance that would be unleashed on 24." Upon telling Manuel that he thought that "such a strong phrase could detonate violent reactions," Wainer was told that the "objective was precisely this: to force the confrontation."[73] By the time of the ministerial meeting in the wee hours of 24, Oswaldo Aranha and Tancredo Neves had already agreed to resist with force and protect the president if necessary.[74] And, interviewed about the episode 30 years later, Neves was convinced, first, that the mounting opposition to Vargas could have been controlled with some ease and, second, that in the week leading up to the suicide the president intended to resist. "All of our conversation a little before the last ministerial meeting was about resistance," Neves said, and "when one reads the letter today, one sees that just as it serves to justify the suicide it also justifies resistance or a gesture of bravura."[75]

While Neves clearly thought that Vargas intended to fight to the end, at least until the ministerial meeting, the president may have changed his mind as he listened to his ministers. Most accounts of the meeting make a point of mentioning Vargas's demeanor, and most agree on his detachedness. In his biography, Dulles describes Vargas as appearing "thoroughly at peace and exceptionally friendly" as the meeting started and then being "in a daze" while his ministers shared their opinions.[76] After the discussion about his fate had worn down, Vargas said: "since you gentlemen did not decide, I will decide. To the military ministers I indicate that order be maintained and the Constitution respected. In these conditions, I am disposed to solicit a leave of absence, provided that the responsibilities are decided. But if an insurrection breaks out, I warn that they will find in Catete only my dead body."[77]

Seeking to explain the suicide, Neves suggested that Vargas saw it as a means of salvaging the difficult situation. "When Vargas made the decision to commit suicide, his gesture was no longer an act of desperation or dissension, or of impotence in the face of the events, and became a political act of great wisdom."[78] Robert Levine agrees, making no bones about the calculation of Vargas's act: "Suicide was the form of resistance he chose, a calculated political act."[79] But the key to the suicide's power, Neves thought, was the *Carta Testamento*; the letter lent persistent power and symbolism to the act. Neves quoted some of the important lines to his interviewers in 1984, commenting admiringly that "he has phrases in the letter that translate perfectly his idea." And, as one of the interviewers put it, the letter helped Vargas "turn the tables" on his opponents.[80]

A Historic Document Left to Posterity: The *Carta Testamento's* Ongoing Career

"Goodbye my beloved Brazil/Where I was born/The moment has come/For me to die/By my own hand." Verses like this from *cordel* literature, along with innumerable other forms of popular adulation, welled up throughout the country immediately following Vargas's death. The *Carta Testamento* proved particularly compelling for composers of *cordel* and musicians, and frequently the letter was simply reprinted in pamphlet form.[81] The popular reaction in the streets of Rio following the president's death overwhelmed city officials. The crowds accompanying Vargas's body to Santos Dumont airport, from where it was flown to Rio Grande do Sul, dwarfed any political demonstration the city had seen, with people expressing their grief loudly and publicly.[82]

Politicians from the PTB quickly seized on the *Carta Testamento*, recognizing in it a means for making political gains. The day after Vargas's suicide the federal Chamber of Deputies held a session devoted to the dead president. Vice President of the party Aziz Maron, like Vargas a *gaúcho*, read into the record a statement in which he pledged that he and his colleagues would "stay at the barricades, defending the unforgettable memory of the greatest of Brazilians, sacrificed in the holocaust for order and public tranquility." "The blood of Getúlio Vargas," he continued, "was the communion that united us forever."[83] The *petebistas* adopted Vargas's language as their own, drawing liberally from the *Carta* in their eulogies to the dead leader. Religious imagery was and remains quite common in the party's statements about their departed founder's letter; one PTB scholar states that the *Carta* became the "Biblical document" of the PTB.[84]

In fact, the PTB explicitly embraced the *Carta Testamento* as a foundational document. Already during the session of 25, Maron intoned this solemn vow: "We swear, with our hands on the lifeless body of our great Chief—whose spirit will guide us till death—to make his ideal our ideal, to make his final declarations our platform, in order, within the law, to defend our Fatherland and the advances of the workers."[85] Another deputy chimed in to praise the exalted memory of the departed leader for his wisdom in penning "the historic document that he leaves to posterity," a carefully composed text with every comma in place such that his "thought should be faithfully expressed."[86] On the same day, the national executive committee of the party released an official statement declaring complete support for the "principles contained in the last letter of President Getúlio Vargas, which are: (a) combat against the abuses of economic power; (b) defense of the regime of social liberty; (c) struggle for the economic liberation of the Brazilian people."[87]

Ângela de Castro Gomes argues that the PTB made strong gains, in electoral terms and in basic party strength, in 1955 and 1960.[88] Almeida Neves Delgado agrees that the PTB was "reinvigorated" after Vargas's death and pushed its agenda with new life, "rooted in the prestige of the ex-President and inspired by the nationalist principles of his *Carta Testamento*."[89] Vargas's death also helped pull the Brazilian Communist Party closer to the PTB. The Communists met for their fourth congress in November, "still under [the suicide's] impact."[90] Though Luís Carlos Prestes claimed that Vargas's suicide was not "an event that had great repercussions," most people agree that it shifted the Communists' strategy significantly.[91] Moisés Vinhas observed that the Communists had called for Vargas's head not long before his death and were then required to "spin 180 degrees overnight to accompany the masses."[92]

A year after the suicide, Manuel Vargas spoke about the *Carta Testamento*. Asked if it should be used as a political tool, he responded that his father had left it as a political testament to the people of Brazil, and they should use it as they saw fit. Its importance, he thought, was clear. "The problem for *getulistas*," he said, "is not to try to figure out what the President would do were he alive, but to decide what we should do after his disappearance. It isn't a matter of imitating him but of being faithful to his political testament, left in written form in his *Carta*."[93]

Though the suicide strengthened the PTB in the short term, the loss of Vargas's leadership and the ensuing competition over claims to his legacy weakened the party system as a whole, in the argument of Castro Gomes. "The suicide was a point of flux in the party system," she writes, and served to "retard its consolidation."[94] His famous exhortation "my name will be your battle flag" acquired a truth that could not have been foreseen by Vargas, as different politicians squabbled over the right to invoke his memory and his political projects.[95]

"Contrary to what one would expect," Claudio Lacerda observed, "political exploitation of the image of Vargas . . . grew with time."[96] Asked whether Vargas's suicide ended the *getulista* era or extended it, Tancredo Neves mused that the president's death did not extend his era but rather projected his image through the political life of the country. "Consciously or unconsciously," he said, "all governments follow Getúlio's politics. Even the 'revolutionary' [military regime] governments, whatever they did that was positive was *Getulista*-inspired."[97]

One justly famous political maneuver undoubtedly owed its inspiration to the dead president. After spending less than a year in office following his election in 1960, Jânio Quadros resigned the presidency on August 25, 1961. When Quadros resigned, "there was no reaction such as had followed Vargas' suicide," John Dulles observes. "Tearfully departing by steamer, Quadros quoted a statement attributed to Vargas in 1945: 'Though they send me away, I shall nevertheless return.' "[98] It is generally agreed that Quadros intended his odd and mishandled gesture as a ploy to gain fuller presidential powers. He clearly sought to profit from the symbolism of the anniversary of Vargas's death but executed his political maneuver in a manner that did not do justice to the dead president's legacy of political savvy.

In the tension-filled atmosphere of João Goulart's presidency, when the presumptive heir to Vargas's legacy was trying to push through congress a set of "basic reforms," evidence of the ex-president and his *Carta Testamento* was not hard to find. Goulart presided over a large rally in Rio on March 13, 1964, only a couple of weeks before he would be deposed in a military coup, and he railed against those who had pushed Vargas "to the supreme sacrifice." A large picture of Vargas was accompanied by the words, "this people whose slave I was will no longer be slave to anyone."[99]

There was a small burst of interest in Vargas's suicide and the letter he left in 1964. Not only did this mark the ten-year anniversary of the event, but the coup that brought a group of generals to power in April spurred reflection on the country's recent political history. John Saunders wrote an article for the May 1964 issue of the *Hispanic American Historical Review* documenting Vargas's fall from power, devoting his final two pages to the notes left by the dead president.[100] Four months later, the same journal published a short piece by John W. F. Dulles, which assessed questions about the *Carta Testamento* and other documents related to the suicide.[101] Scholars have continued to see a relevant connection between the 1964 military coup and Vargas's death, with many arguing that the suicide forestalled by a decade what was an inevitable seizure of power from the right.[102]

Tancredo Neves's opinions about Vargas's suicide, quoted above, came from a book called *Tancredo Speaks about Getúlio*, which transcribed a long interview carried out by scholars from the Centro de Pesquisa e Documentação de História Contemporânea do Brasil at the Fundação Getúlio Vargas. Published in 1986, the book was at least partially designed to bolster public confidence in the first civilian president following the military regime that had begun in 1964. It is revealing, then, that the interview revolved around Vargas, the memory of whom was still powerful enough to lend some credibility and allure to a politician who had worked with him 30 years before.

More recently, the fiftieth anniversary of Vargas's suicide provoked a predictable flurry of publishing about the event and its legacy. The popular historical magazines *Nossa História*, *Desvendando a História*, and *História Viva* each carried multiple treatments of Vargas's death and the *Carta Testamento*.[103] Ronaldo Conde Aguiar published his explanation for Vargas's suicide, Carlos Heitor Cony's 1960s articles on the subject found their way back into print, and Juremir Machado da Silva wrote a novel about the dead president.[104] In *Caros Amigos*, Gilberto Vasconcellos argues that Vargas intended his death and final message as an emphatic denunciation of imperialism and the encroachment of North American capitalists.[105] While Aguiar suggests that Vargas's was an "egoistic," rather than "altruistic," suicide, in Durkheimian terms; an act marking his isolation rather than his heroic defense of the "humble."[106] Half a century later, Vargas's suicide and the discovery of the *Carta Testamento* remain a powerful and multivalent episode. And they carry persistent political power. The funeral cortege of lifelong politician and self-proclaimed heir to Vargas's political legacy Leonel Brizola stopped in front of Catete Palace, where the crowds of mourners heard a reading of the *Carta Testamento*.[107]

Vargas's suicide carries such incredible weight in large part because of the unrelenting drama surrounding it. Vargas's "gesture" resonated backward and forward in time, giving new meaning or relevance to events in the past and lending gravity and symbolism to later acts. Vargas's penchant for political spectacle was revealed by many more acts than his suicide—his move to power in 1930, the consolidation of his regime with the 1937 coup, his renunciation in 1945—and these previous experiences only took on a more intense aura following his suicide.

Why did he make his final gesture? We could take him at his word, when he said to Alzira shortly before his death, "I've had enough and I am tired; I am too old to take the iniquities and injustices with which they try to hurt me."[108] It is the second part of this quotation that seems most revealing. He said the day before his death, "The main thing I need to do is defend my honor . . . I cannot leave here with dishonor." Vargas could not bear to see his power threatened, to suffer the indignity of prosecution by the military, of "being linked to theft and murder."[109]

Vargas began thinking about a means to rise above his problems weeks before he killed himself. He scribbled down ideas and justifications for his actions. He considered resigning his position. And he began to write a letter of farewell to the people. But had he delivered the *Carta Testamento* in the form of a "manifesto" or address to the nation, it would have been comparatively powerless, ringing hollow to a frustrated public. In suicide, his gesture became complete. Besides the shock value of death, Vargas's suicide gained tangible political power through his letter. And by sealing with death his self-portrait as a noble but battered leader, Vargas regained his ebbing public popularity and reshaped his legacy, entering history a legend instead of an old, weary politician.

A Note on Versions of the *Carta Testamento*

For the purposes of this chapter, I have worked from the *Carta Testamento* text printed in the appendix of Hélio Silva's *1954: um tiro no coração*.[110] The differences between this text and the other versions I consulted are minimal, though small discrepancies are of course magnified in such a short document. The text that appears on the Brazilian Senate website has many apparently typographical errors while another web version has some infelicitous spacing.[111] The Human Rights Network version has one error, though a large one; it is missing an entire sentence.[112] The only apparent errors in the Silva version appear near the end of the second paragraph, in a sentence where "Petrobrás" and "mal começa" should be separated by a semicolon, not a comma, and a verb should be "se avoluma," not "se voluma."

For translated versions, I consulted Robert Levine's translation, in an appendix to *Father of the Poor?* and *The New York Times* translation reprinted in Burns.[113] It is difficult to know if Levine and the *Times* translator were working from the same source. Levine says he translated the letter from a clipping in the Brazilian National Archives and the *Times* probably got the text from a Brazilian newspaper as well. It seems reasonable to assume that there was minimal divergence between versions that appeared in major newspapers at the time, and from which reprints and translations have presumably been made. Perhaps some punctuation and spacing were altered (there seem to be no two versions that share these elements exactly) but no larger changes. Of the two translations, Levine's is clearly better. The *Times* version is a much more literal translation, which occasionally leads to awkwardness and even an error. They translate "Contra a justiça da revisão do salário mínimo se desencadearam os ódios" as "Hatreds were unchanged against the justice of a revision of minimum salaries." They probably meant "unchained," the literal translation. Levine uses "unleashed," which I think is better. Levine's, though, also has apparent typographical errors. He twice repeats lines or parts of lines. In one case it appears that he had given himself two options and meant to take one out when he had decided which was better.

Silva's and Levine's versions follow, with the appropriate corrections made.

Mais uma vez, as forças e os interesses contra o povo coordenaram-se novamente e se desencadeiam sobre mim.

Não me acusam, insultam; não me combatem, caluniam e não me dão o direito de defesa. Precisam sufocar a minha voz e impedir a minha ação, para que eu não continue a defender, como sempre defendi, o povo e principalmente os humildes. Sigo o destino que me é imposto. Depois de decênios de domínio e espoliação dos grupos econômicos e financeiros internacionais, fiz-me chefe de uma revolução e venci. Iniciei o trabalho de libertação e instaurei o regime de liberdade social. Tive de renunciar. Voltei ao governo nos braços do povo. A campanha subterrânea dos grupos internacionais aliou-se a dos grupos nacionais revoltados contra o regime de garantia do trabalho. A lei de lucros extraordinários foi detida no Congresso. Contra a justiça da revisão do salário mínimo se desencadearam os ódios. Quis criar a liberdade nacional na potencialização das nossas riquezas através da Petrobrás; mal começa esta a funcionar, a onda de agitação se avoluma. A Eletrobrás foi obstaculada até o desespero. Não querem que o trabalhador seja livre. Não querem que o povo seja independente.

Assumi o Governo dentro da espiral inflacionária que destruía os valores de trabalho. Os lucros das empresas estrangeiras alcançavam até 500% ao ano. Nas declarações de valores do que importávamos existiam fraudes constatadas de mais de 100 milhões de dólares por ano. Veio a crise do café, valorizou-se o nosso principal produto. Tentamos defender seu preço e a resposta foi uma violenta pressão sobre a nossa economia a ponto de sermos obrigados a ceder.

Tenho lutado mês a mês, dia a dia, hora a hora, resistindo a uma pressão constante, incessante, tudo suportando em silêncio, tudo esquecendo, renunciando a mim mesmo, para defender o povo que agora se queda desamparado. Nada mais vos posso dar a não ser o meu sangue. Se as aves de rapina querem o sangue de alguém, querem continuar sugando o povo brasileiro, eu ofereço em holocausto a minha vida. Escolho este meio de estar sempre convosco. Quando vos humilharem, sentireis minha alma sofrendo ao vosso lado. Quando a fome bater à vossa porta, sentireis em vosso peito a energia para a luta por vós e vossos filhos. Quando vos vilipendiarem, sentireis no meu pensamento a força para a reação. Meu sacrifício vos manterá unidos e meu nome será a vossa bandeira de luta. Cada gota de meu sangue será uma chama imortal na vossa consciência e manterá a vibração sagrada para a resistência. Ao ódio respondo com o perdão. E aos que pensam que me derrotaram respondo com a minha vitória. Era escravo do povo e hoje me liberto para a vida eterna. Mas esse povo de quem fui escravo não mais será escravo de ninguém. Meu sacrifício ficará para sempre em sua alma e meu sangue terá o preço do seu resgate.

Lutei contra a espoliação do Brasil. Lutei contra a espoliação do povo. Tenho lutado de peito aberto. O ódio, as infâmias, a calúnia não abateram meu ânimo. Eu vos dei a minha vida. Agora ofereço a minha morte. Nada receio. Serenamente dou o primeiro passo no caminho da eternidade e saio da vida para entrar na História.

—Getúlio Vargas

Once more the forces and interests against the people are newly coordinated and raised against me. They do not accuse me, they insult me; they do not fight me, they slander me and refuse to give me the right of defense. They seek to drown my voice and halt my actions so that I no longer continue to defend, as I always have defended, the people and principally the humble. I follow the destiny that is imposed on me. After decades of domination and plunder by international economic and financial groups, I made myself chief of an unconquerable revolution. I began the work of liberation and I instituted a regime of social liberty. I was forced to resign. I returned to govern on the arms of the people.

A subterranean campaign of international groups joined with national interests revolting against the regime of workers' guarantees. The excess-profits law was held up in Congress. Hatreds were unleashed against the justice of a revision of minimum wages.

I wished to create national liberty by developing our riches through Petrobrás, which had scarcely begun to operate when the wave of agitation clouded its beginnings. Electrobrás was obstructed to the point of despair. They do not want workers to be free. They do not want the people to be independent.

I assumed my government during an inflationary spiral that was destroying the rewards of work. Profits by foreign companies reached as much as 500 percent annually. In declarations of goods that we import, frauds of more than 100 million dollars per year were proved.

I saw the coffee crisis increase the value of our principal product. We tried to maintain that price but the reply was such violent pressure on our economy that we were forced to surrender. I have fought month after month, day after day, hour after hour, resisting constant, incessant pressures, unceasingly bearing it all in silence, forgetting everything and giving myself in order to defend the people that now fall abandoned. I cannot give you more than my blood. If the birds of prey wish the blood of anybody, they wish to continue to suck the blood of the Brazilian people. I offer my life in the holocaust. I choose this means to be with you always. When they humiliate you, you will feel my soul suffering at your side. When hunger knocks at your door, you will feel within you the energy to fight for yourselves and for your children. When you are scorned, my memory will give you the strength to react. My sacrifice will keep you united and my name will be your battle standard. Each drop of my blood will be an immortal call to your conscience and will uphold the sacred will to resist.

To hatred, I reply with forgiveness. And to those who think that they have defeated me, I reply with my victory. I was a slave of the people and today I am freeing myself for eternal life. But this people whose slave I was will no longer be slave to anyone. My sacrifice will remain forever in your souls and my blood will be the price of your ransom. I fought against the looting of Brazil. I fought against the looting of the people. I have fought bare-chested. The hatred, infamy, and calumny did not defeat my spirit. I have given you my life. Now I offer you my death. Nothing remains. Serenely I take my first step on the road to eternity and I leave life to enter history.

—Getúlio Vargas

Notes

1. Sérgio Lamarão, "Carta Testamento," *DHHB* online, CPDOC, http://www.cpdoc.fgv.br/dhbb/verbetes_htm/5759_1.asp, accessed October 12, 2003; PDT, "PDT critica na carta testamento os falsos trabalhistas que usam a memória de Vargas" (2002), http://www.pdt.org.br/personalidades/getulio_historia_8.asp, accessed March 8, 2004.

2. With regard to the first statement, see Shawn C. Smallman, *Fear and Memory in the Brazilian Army and Society, 1889–1954* (Chapel Hill: Univ. of North Carolina Press, 2002), 239. Smallman cites Robert M. Levine, *Father of the Poor? Vargas and His Era* (Cambridge: Cambridge Univ. Press, 1998). Ana Maria de Abreu Laurenza, *Lacerda X Wainer: o corvo e o bessarabiano* (São Paulo: Ed. SENAC, 1998), 129. Laurenza probably based her claim of two Cartas Testamento on José Murilo de Carvalho's essay "As duas mortes de Getúlio Vargas," originally published in *Jornal do Brasil*, August 24, 1994, and reprinted in *Pontos e*

bordados: escritos de história e política (Belo Horizonte: Ed. UFMG, 1999). As we will see later, though, Laurenza mixes up her facts with regard to the discoveries of the different texts.

3. Bryan McCann, "Carlos Lacerda: The Rise and Fall of a Middle-Class Populist in 1950s Brazil," *Hispanic American Historical Review* 83, no. 4 (2003): 661–696. The quotation is from 661.

4. The phrase is from, among other sources, the title of Claudio Lacerda's book, *Uma crise de Agosto: o atentado da Rua Toneleros* (Rio de Janeiro: Ed. Nova Fronteira, 1994). It is interesting that Lacerda chose "*an* August crisis," as opposed to "August crisis," or even "*the* August crisis," which other authors have used. See, for instance, Paulo Brandi, *Vargas: da vida para a história* (Rio de Janeiro: Jorge Zahar Ed., 1983), 285. The choice of title is consistent with Lacerda's intention of demystifying Vargas's death. Also representative of this effort is the fact that the crisis to which he refers is the attempt on Carlos Lacerda's life, not the president's death. Also, later prominent political crises (including one mentioned later in this chapter) took place in August. And finally, one might point out the fearsome reputation of the month of August in Brazilian popular culture. Larry Rohter, "The Devil Take August. In Brazil, It's Just Too Scary," *The New York Times*, August 5, 2004.

5. Brandi, *Vargas: da vida para a história*, 265–270.

6. Laurenza, *Lacerda X Wainer*, 59, 61–62; John W. F. Dulles, *Vargas of Brazil: A Political Biography* (Austin: Univ. of Texas Press, 1967), 318.

7. John W. F. Dulles, *Carlos Lacerda, Brazilian Crusader*, vol. 1, *The Years 1914–1960* (Austin: Univ. of Texas Press, 1991), 144, 146.

8. Ibid., 147–148.

9. F. Zenha Machado, *Os últimos dias do govêrno de Vargas* (Rio de Janeiro: Ed. Lux, 1955), 193.

10. Dulles, *Vargas of Brazil*, 324.

11. Julio de Sá Bierrenbach, *1954–1964: uma década política* (Rio de Janeiro: Domínio Público, 1996), 17–18.

12. Dulles, *Vargas of Brazil*, 330.

13. Machado, *Os últimos dias do govêrno de Vargas*, 115.

14. Araken Távora, *O dia em que Vargas morreu* (Rio de Janeiro: Ed. do Repórter, 1966), 77; Laurenza, *Lacerda X Wainer*, 130.

15. Machado, *Os últimos dias do govêrno de Vargas*, 114.

16. Levine, *Father of the Poor? Vargas and His Era*, 332–333.

17. Bierrenbach, *1954–1964: Uma década política*, 21; Dulles, *Vargas of Brazil*, 333–334.

18. Laurenza, *Lacerda X Wainer*, 129; Bradford Burns, *A Documentary History of Brazil* (New York: Knopf, 1966).

19. Laurenza, *Lacerda X Wainer*, 130. Lamarão, "Carta Testamento." The transformation in the emotions of the crowd outside Catete Palace makes for good drama, though the presence of the crowd itself is questioned by Bierrenbach, who said that on arriving at the beginning of

the ministerial meeting and leaving later there was no crowd. See Bierrenbach, *1954–1964: uma década política*, 20.

But Oswaldo Aranha told John Dulles in a 1963 interview that a large and very hostile crowd surrounded the palace immediately after the ministerial meeting. See Dulles, *Vargas of Brazil*, 331.

20. Samuel Wainer, *Minha razão de viver: memórias de um repórter* (Rio de Janeiro: Ed. Record, 1987), 205; Lamarão, "Carta Testamento."

21. Wainer, *Minha razão de viver*, 203, 205.

22. John D. French, *Drowning in Laws: Labor Law and Brazilian Political Culture* (Chapel Hill: Univ. of North Carolina Press, 2004), 92.

23. McCann, "Carlos Lacerda, 691.

24. Dulles, *Brazilian Crusader*, 168.

25. For the full text of the *Carta Testamento*, in Portuguese and English, see the Note at the end of this chapter.

26. Darcy Ribeiro, "Getúlio Vargas," PDT, 1994, http://www.pdt. org.br/diversos/gvperf.htm, accessed March 8, 2004.

27. Octavio Ianni, *O colapso do populismo no Brasil* (Rio de Janeiro: Ed. Civilização Brasileira, 1968), 68.

28. While this apparent dissonance could be explained by the degree to which Vargas was absorbed by these details of governance, later arguments will elaborate my position on Vargas's mixing of the personal and the political to such a degree that he saw these different issues as closely related.

29. Machado, *Os últimos dias do govêrno de Vargas*, 94. It should be pointed out that "*holocausto*," always translated into English versions of the *Carta Testamento* as "holocaust," means "self-abnegation" or "self-renunciation," and refers to the sacrificial practice of the ancient Hebrews in which the victim was completely burned. The layers of meaning surrounding the word are perhaps less dense in English. Antônio Houaiss and Mauro de Salles Villar, *Dicionário Houaiss da Língua Portuguesa* (Rio de Janeiro: Objetiva, 2001), 1544.

30. Others have noted the two-part structure. Marquilandes Borges de Sousa, "50 Anos sem Getúlio Vargas: o suicídio que marcou a história do Brasil," *Desvendando a História* 1, no. 1 (2004): 32–41, see 40. Carvalho suggests a three-part structure, simply including an introduction. See his "As duas mortes de Getúlio Vargas," 411.

31. Luthero Vargas, *Getúlio Vargas: a revolução inacabada* (Rio de Janeiro: Bloch Ed., 1988), 143.

32. The 1945 letter is reprinted in Gileno dé Carli, *Anatomia da renúncia* (Rio de Janeiro: Ed. O Cruzeiro, 1962), 20.

33. By writing down his claim of serenity, Vargas made it real. In a letter to the nation two days after the suicide, General Zenóbio da Costa praised the "serene and heroic figure of the intrepid president Vargas." Adelina Alves Novaes e Cruz and CPDOC, eds., *Impasse na democracia brasileira, 1951/1955: coletânea de documentos* (Rio de Janeiro: Ed. da FGV, 1983), 311.

34. James Dunkerley, *Political Suicide in Latin America and Other Essays* (London: Verso, 1992), 30.
35. From the 1945 renunciation letter, reprinted in dé Carli, *Anatomia da renúncia*, 20. This line recalls Fidel Castro's famous speech when he was being tried for his failed attack on the Moncada barracks, in which he claimed "history will absolve me."
36. José Queiroz Junior, *Memórias sôbre Getúlio* (Rio de Janeiro: Ed. COPAC, 1957), 191–192.
37. Cícero Antônio F. de Almeida lists five letters, including the pencilled notes as a copy. "A carta de muitos autores," *Nossa História* 1, no. 10 (August 2004): 22–25, see 23.
38. Machado, *Os últimos dias do govêrno de Vargas*, 100; Vargas, *Getúlio Vargas: a revolução inacabada*, 338.
39. Alzira's husband Ernani was the governor of Guanabara.
40. John W. F. Dulles, "Farewell Messages of Getúlio Vargas," *The Hispanic American Historical Review* 44, no. 4 (November 1964): 551–553, the quote is from 551.
41. The letter is printed in its entirety as an appendix to Hélio Silva, *1954: um tiro no coração* (Rio de Janeiro: Civilização Brasileira, 1978), 375. Silva, in turn, took it from a July 16, 1978, interview with Alzira Vargas do Amaral Peixoto, published in *O Estado de São Paulo*.
42. For Vargas's *bilhetes*, see Lourival Fontes and Glauco Carneiro, *A face final de Vargas: os bilhetes de Getúlio* (Rio de Janeiro: Ed. O Cruzeiro, 1966).
43. Silva, *1954: um tiro no coração*, 338. This issue is dealt with in an appendix to Silva, titled "The two versions of the text" and signed "A. C."
44. Silva, *1954: um tiro no coração*, 375.
45. Machado, *Os últimos dias do govêrno de Vargas*, 94. Fontes recounted this in an interview with *O Cruzeiro*, on September 11, 1954.
46. Levine, *Father of the Poor? Vargas and His Era*, 80.
47. Lamarão, "Carta Testamento"; Vargas, *Getúlio Vargas: a revolução inacabada*, 336.
48. Levine, *Father of the Poor? Vargas and His Era*, 90.
49. Francisco Antonio Doria, *No tempo de Vargas: memórias, reflexões, e documentos* (Rio de Janeiro: Ed. Revan, 1994), 153.
50. Levine, *Father of the Poor? Vargas and His Era*, 90. Some might say that the statement of the individual in question should put an end to speculation. However, Maciel Filho could have had a variety of motives for downplaying his involvement, including the desire to protect Vargas's legacy or his own moral qualms about the issue (mentioned later).
51. Dé Carli, *Anatomia da renúncia*, 22–23.
52. Gustavo Borges, *Getúlio e o mar de lama: A verdade sobre 1954* (Rio de Janeiro: Lacerda Ed., 2001), 184; Silva, *1954: Um tiro no coração*, 373; Carvalho, "As duas mortes de Getúlio Vargas," 409–410.
53. Lamarão, "Carta Testamento."

54. Doria, *No tempo de Vargas*, 153–154, 168. Doria writes that he is a relative of Maciel Filho's.

55. Joel Wolfe actually describes the *Carta* as a "rambling suicide note that Vargas *left to be read on the radio that morning*" (emphasis added). This is perhaps the strongest statement of opinion about the degree to which Vargas engineered the drama of his death. Joel Wolfe, "Guest Editor's Introduction: Getúlio Vargas and His Enduring Legacy for Brazil," *Luso-Brazilian Review* 31, no. 2 (1994): 1–3, quote from 1.

56. Doria, *No tempo de Vargas*, 168.

57. Laurenza, *Lacerda X Wainer*, 129.

58. Regarding treatments of Vargas's final hours, Machado actually recreates the president's thoughts during that morning. These creative renderings must be seen as simply dramatic additions to the narrative of the President's final days. Their inclusion, though, contributes to the confusion about which parts of Machado's book are supported by evidence and eyewitness accounts. His footnotes are sparse enough to raise this question repeatedly and the inclusion of the personal thoughts of a man who shortly afterward killed himself undermines the book's credibility. Machado, *Os últimos dias do govêrno de Vargas*, 82, 85, 133–147.

59. Lucilia de Almeida Neves Delgado, *PTB: do getulismo ao reformismo, 1945–1964* (São Paulo: Marco Zero, 1989), 175.

60. Valentina da Rocha Lima, ed., *Getúlio: uma história oral* (Rio de Janeiro: Ed. Record, 1986), 262, 265. Other examples, from other interviewees, are on 263 and 268. See also Wainer, *Minha razão de viver*, 207, Távora, *O dia em que Vargas morreu*, 87.

61. Machado, *Os últimos dias do govêrno de Vargas*, 45.

62. Dé Carli, *Anatomia da renúncia*, 22–23.

63. Silva, *1954: Um tiro no coração*, 282–283. These pages recount Alzira's version of this, or Silva's prosopopeia of Alzira.

64. Machado, *Os últimos dias do govêrno de Vargas*, 56–57. This conversation was recounted by Alzira in an interview she gave *Última Hora* on August 30, 1954.

65. Queiroz Junior, *Memórias sôbre Getúlio*, 165.

66. Wainer, *Minha razão de viver*, 173, 203; Dé Carli, *Anatomia da renúncia*, 25.

67. Wainer, *Minha razão de viver*, 203. For the edition of August 24, Wainer reprinted the "historic front page," adding the words, "he kept the promise," in reference to Vargas's vow to stay to the death. The image carried a significant charge for a number of reasons, since besides the visual invocation of blood Vargas had explicitly mentioned Petrobrás in the *Carta Testamento*. The combination of the photograph with the *Carta* retains its potency. In an August 2004 article on the suicide, Gilberto Felisberto Vasconcellos writes, "Oil is blood and the blood spilled by the *Carta Testamento* carried the nationalist

message that all oil and all electricity belong to the State." "Um suicídio épico-didático, reflexo das contradições entre o povo brasileiro e o imperialismo norte-americano," *Caros Amigos*, no. 21 (August 2004): 6–7, quote on 6.

68. Cícero Almeida also draws attention to the word *testamento*, deriving as he points out from the Latin *testamentu*. "A carta de muitos autores," 22.

69. Queiroz Junior, *Memórias sôbre Getúlio*, 180.

70. Carvalho argues that the letter was, "above all, political." See his "As duas mortes de Getúlio Vargas," 411.

71. Dé Carli, *Anatomia da renúncia*, 25.

72. Ibid., 20.

73. Wainer, *Minha razão de viver*, 203.

74. Valentina da Rocha Lima and Plínio de Abreu Ramos, *Tancredo fala de Getúlio* (São Paulo: L&PM Ed., 1986), 36.

75. Ibid., 39. João Neves da Fontoura, writing to Vargas's former secretary a month after the suicide, suggests that Vargas wanted to fight but lost hope at the ministerial meeting. *Impasse na democracia brasileira, 1951/1955: coletânea de documentos*, 313. Lourival Fontes, Vargas's secretary at the time, also argues for this interpretation. See Fontes and Carneiro, *A face final de Vargas*, 151. Finally, this is the argument of Ronaldo Conde Aguiar in his recent book *Vitória na derrota: a morte de Getúlio Vargas* (Rio de Janeiro: Casa da Palavra, 2004), 180.

76. Dulles, *Vargas of Brazil*, 327, 329.

77. Machado, *Os últimos dias do govêrno de Vargas*, 108–109. Machado actually provides *four* different versions of this short statement, with slight differences between them. This version cleaves closest to the first of the three that are consigned to a footnote on page 109.

78. Lima and Ramos, *Tancredo fala de Getúlio*, 38.

79. Levine, *Father of the Poor? Vargas and His Era*, 89.

80. Lima and Ramos, *Tancredo fala de Getúlio*, 38.

81. Origenes Lessa, *Getúlio Vargas na literatura de cordel* (Rio de Janeiro: Ed. Documentário, 1973), 122. Cordel literature is a popular creative form generally consisting of verses printed and bound into a rudimentary pamphlet-sized booklet and sold in markets at cheap prices. The name—"string literature"—derives from the usual manner of presentation, with rows of the booklet hanging on a string for viewing.

82. Jorge Ferreira has analyzed this episode in, among other places, "O Carnaval da tristeza: os motins urbanos do 24 de Agosto," in *Vargas e a crise dos anos 50*, ed. Ángela Maria de Castro Gomes (Rio de Janeiro: Relumé-Dumará, 1994), 61–96.

83. Queiroz Junior, *Memórias sôbre Getúlio*, 189.

84. Maria Celina d'Araújo, *Sindicatos, carisma, e poder: o PTB de 1945–1965* (Rio de Janeiro: Ed. da FGV, 1996), 116.

85. Queiroz Junior, *Memórias sôbre Getúlio*, 189.

86. Ibid., 190–191.
87. Lamarão, "Carta Testamento."
88. Ângela de Castro Gomes, "Trabalhismo e democracia: o PTB sem Vargas," *Luso-Brazilian Review* 31, no. 2 (1994): 115–136, see 118. This issue of the *Luso-Brazilian Review* was devoted to assessing Vargas's legacy on the fortieth anniversary of his death.
89. Delgado, *PTB: do getulismo ao reformismo, 1945–1964*, 159.
90. Ibid., 176.
91. Ibid., 165; Dênis de Moraes and Fransisco Viana, *Prestes: lutas e autocríticas*, prefácio de Raymundo Faoro (Petrópolis: Ed. Vozes, 1982), 125.
92. Quoted in Delgado, *PTB: do getulismo ao reformismo, 1945–1964*, 174.
93. Queiroz Junior, *Memórias sôbre Getúlio*, 112–113.
94. Gomes, "Trabalhismo e democracia: o PTB sem Vargas," 115.
95. The battle simmers even still. In 2002, at the ceremony held in front of the *Carta Testamento* at Vargas's graveside, members of the PDT denounced the PTB "who use the name of the ex-president and his banner to support the government of Fernando Henrique Cardoso, which has the publicly-declared objective of ending the Vargas era." PDT, "PDT critica na carta testamento os falsos trabalhistas que usam a memória de Vargas."
96. Lacerda, *Uma crise de Agosto*, 306.
97. Lima and Ramos, *Tancredo fala de Getúlio*, 55.
98. Dulles, *Vargas of Brazil*, 338.
99. Ibid.
100. John V. D. Saunders, "A Revolution of Agreement among Friends: The End of the Vargas Era," *The Hispanic American Historical Review* 44, no. 2 (May, 1964): 197–213.
101. Dulles, "Farewell Messages of Getúlio Vargas."
102. See José Augusto Ribeiro, Interview with Elio Gaspari, PDT. http://www.pdt.org.br/livros/era_vargas_5.htm, accessed March 8, 2004; Wainer, *Minha razão de viver*, 207; Ivete Vargas interview in Lima, ed., *Getúlio: uma história oral*, 265.
103. See *Desvendando a História* 1, no. 1 (2004) (cover headline "50 anos sem Getúlio Vargas"—Fifty Years Without Getúlio Vargas); *Nossa História* 1, no 10 (2004) (cover headline "Os 50 anos do suicídio que abalou o país"—Fifty Years Since the Suicide which Made the Country Tremble"); and *História Viva*, no. 10 (2004) (cover headline "O legado de Vargas"—The Legacy of Vargas).
104. Aguiar, *Vitória na derrota*; Carlos Heitor Cony, *Quem matou Vargas, 1954: uma tragédia brasileira* (São Paulo: Ed. Planeta, 2004); Juremir Machado da Silva, *Getúlio* (Rio de Janeiro: Ed. Record, 2004).
105. Vasconcellos, "Um suicídio épico-didático," 6–7.
106. Aguiar, *Vitória na derrota*, 179–182.
107. Almeida, "A carta de muitos autores," 25.

108. Dulles, *Vargas of Brazil*, 325.
109. Queiroz Junior, *Memórias sôbre Getúlio*, 187. For a similar conclusion, see Barbosa Lima and Eugênio Gondin in Lima, ed., *Getúlio: uma história oral*, 264.
110. Silva, *1954: um tiro no coração*, 347–348.
111. http://www.senado.gov.br/web/historia/carta_testamento.htm, accessed October 12, 2003; http://www.losvargas.org/personaj/pers0020.html, accessed October 12, 2003.
112. http://www.dhnet.org.br/desejos/sonhos/getulio.htm, accessed October 12, 2003. The sentence is: "Quando vos humilharem, sentireis minha alma sofrendo ao vosso lado."
113. Levine, *Father of the Poor? Vargas and His Era*, 150–152; Burns, *A Documentary History of Brazil*.

Chapter 10

Myth and Memory: Getúlio Vargas's Long Shadow over Brazilian History

Jerry Dávila

O raiar de um novo dia
Desafia meu pensar
Voltando à época de ouro
Vejo a luz de um tesouro
A Portela despontar (lálalaiá)

Aclamado pelo povo, o Estado Novo
Getúlio Vargas anunciou
A despeito da censura
Não existe mal sem cura
Viva o trabalhador ô ô ô

Nossa indústria cresceu (e lá vou eu ...)
Jorrou petróleo a valer ...
No carnaval de Orfeu
Cassinos e MPB

O Rei da Noite, o teatro, a fantasia
No rádio as rainhas, a baiana de além-mar
Tantas vedetes, cadilacs, brilhantina
Em outro palco o movimento popular
E no Palácio das Águias
Ecoou um grito a mais
Vai à luta meu Brasil
Pela soberana paz
Quem foi amado e odiado na memória
Saiu da vida para entrar na história

Meu Brasil-menino
Foi pintado em aquarela
Fez do meu destino
O destino da Portela

The shining rays of a new day
Challenges my thoughts
Returning them to the golden age
I see the light of a treasure
Unveiled by Portela (lálalaiá)
Acclaimed by the people, the Estado Novo
Getúlio Vargas announced
Despite the censorship
There is no ailment that can't be cured
Long live the worker ô ô ô
Our industry grew (and with it go I . . .)
We got the oil . . .
Orfeu's carnival
Casinos and Popular Brazilian Music
The King of the Night, the theater, the costume
On the radio the queens, the baiana from overseas
So many stars, cadillacs and glitter
On another state the popular movement
And in the Palace of the Eagles
Echoes one more shout
Go to war my Brazil
For the sovereign peace
He who was loved and hated in memory
Exited life to enter history

My Brazil child
Was painted in watercolors
It made my destiny
The destiny of Portela

"Trabalhadores do Brasil—A época de Getúlio Vargas"
[Workers of Brazil—the Getúlio Vargas Era]
—Zezé do Pandeiro, Amilton Damião, Ailton Damião,
and Edyne and Edinho Leal, Portela 2000

The Rio de Janeiro Carnival of 2000 commemorated the fifth centenary of the discovery of Brazil by the Portuguese. The city's leading samba schools, which organize the parades that march through the 80,000-seat Sambadrome and are televised worldwide, chose to showcase different facets of Brazilian history. One of the largest and most successful samba schools, Portela, chose "Workers of Brazil—the Getúlio Vargas Era" as their theme. The lyrics of Portela's samba, put to music by hundreds of drummers and sung and danced by thousands of dancers as they made their way through the filled Sambadrome in the early hours of the morning of March 6, reflect the curious hold of Getúlio Vargas over Brazil's historical memory in the half century since he famously took his "first step into history." The Getúlio Vargas celebrated by Portela on that hot summer night was depicted as a curiously complex figure. He was acclaimed as a defender of the popular classes and the father of the country's developmental model. Most significantly, he serves as the bridge between the elegant world of the mid-century Brazilian elite and the difficult realities experienced by the overwhelming majority of Brazilians, both then and now. Portela did not praise Vargas uncritically. It gave a nod to the repression that characterized his first presidency, and acknowledged that he is "both loved and hated in memory."

Portela's characterization of Vargas reflects the enduring significance of his historical memory as a site for reflecting upon facets of Brazil's past as well as a space for considering contemporary issues in Brazilian society. Members of the popular classes (as the leaders of samba schools typically are), political leaders (most notably during the military regime), museum curators, and historians (both Brazilian and foreign), have often set upon Vargas, the Vargas era, and the Revolution of 1930 in order to interpret Brazilian society. Most notably, interpretations that have used Vargas and his era as an analytical site surround issues of authoritarianism and democracy, national development and industrialization, populism and a bridge between popular classes and the elite, and finally to grasp at a supposed golden age of cinema, radio, and samba.

This chapter looks at both the construction of Vargas's image as chief of the nation during those years in which he governed, as well as the enduring public memory of the man. A sustained thread of symbolic meaning extends from official constructions of the leader's image during the Estado Novo, through the posthumous reflections— both popular and scholarly—of Vargas: from the moment he assumed the presidency in the Revolution of 1930 to the present, Getúlio Vargas has singly and unwaveringly represented his historical moment in Brazil. Vargas presided over the transformative Vargas era.

Even Vargas's contemporaries saw him as a symbol. For supporters, he was a populist who championed the popular classes—workers, and the poor, and who was a defender of Brazilian culture and *brasilidade*.

This was the image he left in his suicide note. Opponents saw him as a symbol of populist demagoguery, a man who interrupted and perhaps even derailed the course of Brazilian history in order to placate the masses and perpetuate his power. Both of these symbolic roles endured in the later imaginings about Vargas. The leadership of Brazil's military dictatorship (1964–85) saw Vargas as the latter, and justified their authoritarian monopoly on power in part upon the suggestion that they were righting a Brazil set amiss by Vargas. The trajectory of Vargas as a symbol of social inclusion has been more complicated but much more engaging, as Portela's characterization illustrates. Few among Vargas's champions are uncritical of his leadership, stressing his ideological elasticity and the repressiveness of his first regime (especially his decision to deport Jewish Communist Olga Prestes to Nazi Germany, where she faced death in a concentration camp), even as they note his connection to the popular classes and his image as "father of the poor."

This has been the vision advanced by most historians of Vargas and the "Vargas era." In the attempt to identify meaningful patterns in the twentieth century Brazilian experience, historians have naturally had to tangle with the image of Vargas and with his time. More often than not, these historians have reproduced the myths of Vargas because of the ways in which the symbol of Vargas has remained present in Brazilian history. For example, scholars who studied the Vargas era during the 1960s faced obstacles put in place by a military dictatorship that was mistrustful of their efforts. Meanwhile, university students who opposed the military regime used analyses of the Vargas era as a means of visualizing the possibilities for social revolution in their own time. Ultimately, the historical analysis of Vargas and his time has helped keep the symbolic role of Vargas alive by continuing to connect the man and the age to the concerns of the present. The Vargas era was a divider of waters between an agricultural and largely rural Brazil run by a small semiaristocracy and an urban and industrial Brazil that has oscillated between periods of populism and authoritarianism. Since for historians studying Brazil—and for contemporaries living in it—these two worlds remain present and linked, Vargas still stands at a kind of symbolic center of the Brazilian national experience.

The Vargas Era

The Vargas era came amidst the increasing visibility of two basic and lasting questions: who should by rights rule Brazil and what course should these rulers set for the nation? These questions touched all regions, they were debated by rich and poor, they addressed (or failed to address) the challenges of gender, racial and social inequity, and they involved an assessment of everything that was old and everything that was new about Brazil. Brazil was a country that was changing rapidly: it was becoming more urban and more industrial. A growing population shaped by patterns of immigration and internal migration, as well as Western cultural influences, demanded political and economic rights. Both political and economic landscapes changed. Vargas's historical significance lies primarily in the fact that he presided over the changes and the continuities of Brazil's twentieth-century transformation.

Getúlio Vargas's administrations from 1930 to 1945, and again from 1951 to 1954, reflected in different ways the challenges of governing the changing Brazil. Corporatism, the political formula that Vargas put into practice after 1930, was a system of government intended to indirectly represent the interests of both new and established social groups. A ministry of labor would recognize progovernment unions and promised, with ambiguous results, to act on behalf of workers. Government-sponsored institutes as well as federations of merchants and industrialists would represent the dominant economic sectors. Individuals were to have their identity provided by their affiliation to a social group—the "student classes," the "defensive classes," the "liberal classes," the "conservative classes"—and social rights would flow from these affiliations. In turn, Vargas and his swelling bureaucracies would balance and advance the interests of Brazil's different corporate groups, much the way a brain coordinates the organs of a body.

While from 1930 through the end of World War II this system functioned under an authoritarian regime, Vargas predicated his return to power through the 1950 elections on a different political formula: populism. He claimed to represent the interests of workers and the "humble," an appeal that was enough to win him the presidency, but which pitted him increasingly against the old "defensive" and "conservative classes" that had supported his earlier regime. In this regard, Vargas typified other populists of twentieth-century Latin America. Yet the pragmatism with which Vargas experimented with different forms of political power over his many years in office is illustrative of the difficulties of governing a country as vast, as diverse and as rapidly changing as was Brazil. Indeed, only a small minority of the political leaders to succeed Vargas could boast the legitimacy of being elected or the success of serving out their term. In most cases it would be the military that would install or remove the president, as they had done with Vargas in 1930 and 1945, respectively.

Thirty-four years after the Revolution of 1930 and a few months after the military's 1964 coup, a lawyer lectured the Army's Superior War College on the topic of Vargas's influence over Brazilian history. The lawyer declared:

> I like to compare Vargas with a Napoleon from the countryside . . . spreading the *caudillismo* of the remote southern frontier until it covered the vast continent-like expanse of Brazil . . . and bringing to those placid lands, once conquered by Portugal, an Indian-Hispanic unrest which was unknown to Brazil until 1930 . . . all of this accompanied by the tumult of horses from the pampas and of men of song and drawling accents. Like Bonaparte, who dreamed of unifying Europe by reviving the empire of Charlemagne, Vargas grasped the reigns of the Federation which the Republic had held so loosely. Arrogant regionalisms, semi-confederate states with their own small local armies, their Senates patterned after legislatures in the United States, and their feudal baronies dominated by "colonels" . . . all of these tumbled before the unifying magnetism of Vargas. . . .[1]

By 1964, the military thought little of Vargas, choosing to remember him not for the tight partnership he shared with the armed forces between 1930 and 1945, but for his populism of 1951 through 1954, years in which he governed on the promise of expanded economic and political rights for workers. The structure of this discourse was fascinating: by describing Vargas as a *caudillo* who brought "Indo-Hispanic unrest" to Brazil, the lawyer suggested that Vargas was somehow alien to Brazil's history and culture—and that his political era was an aberration. This argument must have played well with the military, which conveniently blamed Vargas for the political instability of Brazil since 1930 and defined its national security state as the savior of the nation. There was great irony in this perception: the military had played a decisive role in the Revolution of 1930, the installation of the 1937 Estado Novo, the toppling of Vargas in 1945, the plotted coup that drove Vargas to suicide in 1954, as well as other crises in the years that followed and culminated in the 1964 coup that placed the armed forces in power until 1985.

The lawyer's address pointed to one of the main political tendencies of the Vargas regime: political centralization. Indeed, this process culminated on November 27, 1937, when each of Brazil's state flags was burned at a pyre mounted at the base of a pole bearing the Brazilian flag—symbolizing the yielding of regional identities to *brasilidade*, and regional authorities to central power. But alongside the regional integration of Brazil, Vargas presided over ambitious programs of social integration that ranged from an expanded right to vote (largely moot given Vargas's reticence about elections) to a labor code that recognized certain labor unions, and established pensions, a minimum wage and other benefits. Indeed, these initiatives would give rise to Vargas's identity as a champion of the workers despite the limited scope of these reforms and the high cost of union dependence on an often diffident government. Significantly, these benefits only applied to urban workers; Vargas steadfastly avoided rural reforms of any sort, seeking not to disturb entrenched political and economic structures.

Vargas's centralizing political authority and his social policies marked an expanding role for the national state that was echoed in economic policy. While the Republican government had been active in promoting the coffee economy, the Vargas regime embarked on a more extensive and deliberate politics of economic development. Vargas organized industrial and trade groups, stimulated domestic industrialization, pushed for the nationalization of key sectors of the economy, and used political competition between the United States and Germany before the war to deftly negotiate the construction by U.S. engineers of a massive and economically consequential national steel production complex. Brazil's emergence as an industrial powerhouse owes much to the economic conditions created by the Great Depression and to the emergence of the state as a major industrial patron and engineer of industrial policy.

Vargas's political activism stretched beyond political centralization, the implementation of developmentalist economic policies, and the articulation of a system of labor relations. For instance, though Vargas did not particularly promote his own image, he did create a federal Departamento de Imprensa e Propaganda that sought to manage the emerging media of cinema and radio. The DIP wielded broad powers of censorship over the press and produced its own film shorts and radio programs. A prominent centralizing initiative was the "Hour of Brazil," a mandatory hour of government-produced news broadcast daily on every licensed radio station in the country, an institution that continues to survive. Similarly, both the DIP and the ministry of education also created by Vargas promoted the concept of *brasilidade* that celebrated cultural traditions, led to the recognition and state promotion of carnival and samba, and introduced an aesthetic fixation on modernism in public art and architecture.

The demographic and economic dynamism of the mid-century were matched by the political activism of the Vargas regime. More than any other, the Vargas regime emerged as a mediator bridging regional and social groups by extending the federal government into the sinews of the nation's economic, political, social, and cultural life. Both this age and the active role of the government within it are periodized as "The Vargas Era." Scholars unflinchingly embrace the notion of a Vargas era as a conceptual framework to understand what they deem to be a key moment in Brazil's recent history. Debates surrounding this concept have only chiseled at its edges. Does the Vargas era refer only to the uninterrupted reign of 1930–45, or does it extend to the second administration of 1951–54? Does the Vargas era represent a true break with the past? Did not much change? Or, as scholars have increasingly argued, did the Vargas era give expression to political, economic, and social tendencies already afoot in the years after World War I? Even the most revisionist challenges to the mainstream periodization of Brazilian history have reinforced acceptance of a Vargas era by simply questioning its extent.

This unchallenged reliance on the concept of a Vargas era is all the more surprising given the rarity of equivalent frameworks linking political leaders in other countries to their historical moment. No candidate appears from among the cohort of strong leaders with whom Vargas shared the interwar years. The United States remembers a New Deal and a Great Depression, but not a Roosevelt era. Hitler's Germany was Nazi Germany, and Mussolini's Italy was Fascist. Peronism has become such a diffuse and lingering concept that it is hard to envision a Perón era for Argentina. Perhaps the closest analogue comes, interestingly, out of Salazarist Portugal from which Vargas took many of his cues.

Part of the explanation for a Vargas era is easy: Vargas was so politically and ideologically elastic that there is no single defining idea or political initiative by which to characterize these years. Other easy explanations quickly fall apart. Vargas cultivated his public image as the "Chief of the Nation," and this image was celebrated in public facilities, in civic events, in official publications and controlled press. Yet the cult of personality was much more understated than that of other contemporary leaders whose names do not define their times. Nor is the memory of Vargas uncritical: in most cases he is remembered through both successes and excesses.

The memory of Vargas has come to mean many things in the past half century, yet perhaps the most prevalent image associated with Vargas, ever since it was cultivated by the regime's handlers in the 1930s, has been that Vargas bridged the social gap between the rich and the poor in Brazil. It is perhaps because of this image more than for any other reason that the memory of Vargas is indispensable and the man has come symbolize his time, since there are few other events, symbols, individuals, or values capable of credibly bridging what are some of the greatest social inequalities in the world. Vargas supporters called him the "Father of the Poor." His detractors suggested he was merely the "Mother of the Rich."[2] Vargas's historical legacy is that he was uniquely both.

Chief of the Nation

The promise to bridge the social gap was one of the hopes ignited by the Revolution of 1930. In its aftermath, tangible—if limited—steps were taken in this direction, including the creation of a Ministry of Labor, Industry and Commerce that, for the first time, systematically regulated labor relations, and the creation of a Ministry of Education and Public Health, which endeavored in earnest to expand public educational opportunities (though with more success in the cities than in the countryside). Both of these new ministries were part of a broader campaign to expand the role of government in preserving social welfare, and in expanding the terms of political, social, and cultural integration. Other areas of federal policy also reflected the drive to increase social inclusion. These include the extension of political autonomy to the government of the Federal District of Rio de Janeiro (which opened an exciting period of populist political experimentation), the enfranchisement of women, the introduction of meritocratic government hiring practices, and the creation of limited social security benefits.

While these innovations were examples of a broader cycle of political change made possible by the Revolution of 1930, they alone offer an incomplete vision of the revolution and its aftermath. What *was* the Revolution of 1930? Was it *even* a revolution? Did it mark the victory of the industrial bourgeoisie over the coffee barons and other traditional elites? Did it usher in a revolution in governing, from the liberal Republic to a strong, interventionist, and centralizing regime? Did it ignite the industrialization of Brazil? The integration of the working class? Was this even something new? These are the lines of scholarly analysis that have directed historians for the most part away from Getúlio Vargas as an individual or as a leader, and drawn them instead to the interpretation of the Revolution of 1930 and the ensuing political regime.[3] While historians will always debate the significance of the Revolution of 1930, one outcome is clear: the political events that brought Vargas to power unleashed a revolution of expectations that touched both traditional and emerging elites, as well as radicals on both the Left and the Right, the emerging urban working and middle classes (and a small segment of the rural poor), nationalists, progressives, artists, and intellectuals. The expectations these groups held for a postrevolutionary Brazil, whether met or frustrated, were symbolically borne by Vargas.

The *Revolution of 1930* by Boris Fausto is one of the principal Brazilian texts that engages the causes and outcomes of Vargas's rise to power.[4] In determining whether the Revolution of 1930 represented the triumph of new groups such as the industrial bourgeoisie and working class over a traditional planter oligarchy, Fausto finds broad evidence for the political participation and reformist attitudes of the emerging groups. Yet he does not believe the industrial bourgeoisie or the middle class displayed a clear opposition political program. Instead, Fausto suggests that an emerging class and political consciousness among these groups did not translate into political action toppling the prevailing order. The Revolution of 1930 was not a class conflict simply because different social classes were involved.

Instead, Fausto suggests that 1930 marked a watershed in which both international and domestic economic changes weakened the coffee barons' influence. This group could no longer monopolize power. Yet the revolution did not mean the defeat of the oligarchy, nor the triumph of emerging sectors. Instead, Fausto proposes that a "compromise state" emerged from 1930. Without a clear social, political, or economic victor, the state was forced to mediate between competing groups and popular pressures. This was not a social tie, but a delicate balancing act that took Brazil through decades of short-lived populist and authoritarian governments.[5] While a long-term structural transition from an agrarian to an industrial society was *related* to the Revolution of 1930, it did not cause the revolution, nor did the revolution resolve it. Instead, it was a symptom of a widening gap between regions, between social classes, and between rural and urban groups.

Historian Edgar de Decca has challenged this concept of a "compromise state," arguing instead that, by 1930, the São Paulo industrial and economic elite had already established a new model of state-society relations and a new political philosophy, both of which were gradually absorbed by the federal government after 1930.[6] Barbara Weinstein echoes this analysis in her examination of São Paulo industrialists' adaptation of the principles of scientific rationalism from a system of industrial management into a social philosophy that placed the state in the role of mediator between workers and industry and laid the foundations for a limited system of social welfare.[7] Certainly, this vision of the state as cultural mediator and social manager is echoed in a number of areas of public policy, among them the realm of public education. While the principles of education reform were visible as early as the 1910s, only after 1930 did the political opportunity and institutional momentum make it possible for the most substantial of these reforms to take root.[8]

Enter Vargas, the individual who spent the most time (19 years) at the center of the political balancing act set in motion by the Revolution of 1930. The heterodox mix of populist and authoritarian tactics that he used to juggle competing groups framed the dimensions of national power for at least half a century. From João Goulart and Juscelino Kubitschek to the long list of generals who shared power after 1964, every individual or group exercising national leadership has emulated or reacted to facets of Vargas's political style. This reach has been so great that, when President Fernando Henrique Cardoso took office in 1994, he defined his administration by proclaiming the end of the Vargas era.[9] Despite this bold declaration, important parallels link the Brazil of Vargas and of Cardoso. The social gap, measured either in wealth or in citizenship, remains the country's most pressing issue. Even more striking, perhaps, is the parallel in the two leaders' political styles. In the midst of Cardoso's politically costly campaign for a constitutional amendment allowing him to succeed himself, historian Thomas Skidmore suggested to readers of Brazil's leading daily newspaper, the *Folha de São Paulo*, that Cardoso followed in Vargas's—and 1960s military dictator Castelo Branco's—undemocratic footsteps by presenting himself as Brazil's indispensable man.[10]

Vargas's pragmatic political style, lack of a clear or consistent ideology, and gift for bringing together diverse groups and interests, all facilitated his consolidation of power in the fragile political moment. These personal characteristics also emerged as the dominant elements of his official public image, beginning with the title he assumed: chief of the nation. Vargas's appeal to the working class, his use of popular media, and his reliance on paternalism—seen especially in his invitation to ordinary Brazilians that they write him about their problems— presaged the political persona he created for himself during the Estado Novo. He cultivated an image of being above politics. Instead, he cast himself as paternal, impartial, transcending political differences.

In 1942, foreign observer Karl Lowenstein captured the extent— and the limits—of the official image of Vargas. The political scientist noted that, as an individual, Vargas shunned the limelight: "He disdains the customary manifestations of dictatorial condescension such as baby-kissing and dog-petting. Vargas has little in common with his bombastic glorification-hungry colleagues in Europe."[11] But beyond the private man lay a well-choreographed campaign to promote his image nationally. Lowenstein adds:

> Most conspicuous in the drive for making the people emotionally responsive to the regime is the pictoralization of Vargas himself. His portrait, prominently displayed in shops, offices, hotels, railroad stations, and all places generally accessible to the public—though rarely in private homes—shows the president in a rather complimentary pose as the chief of state, in formal dress and with a sash, expressing stern if benevolent paternalism and thus personifying both the forceful leader and the good father of his people. In reality he is rather small of stature and with his glasses and a very well-sculptured forehead he looks more like a lawyer—which he is—than like the man on horseback whom he is supposed to impersonate. But he is portrayed as a civilian and not as a military man.[12]

Lowenstein did not see Vargas as a leader hungry for personal glorification. Instead, his regime's propaganda used him as a symbol of the government, building a paternalist emotional connection between the public and the chief of the nation.

Textbook Vargas

Between 1930 and 1945, Getúlio Vargas's image as chief of the nation was ubiquitous in Brazil. It was described by foreign observers, reproduced in the censored press, and promoted by federal authorities and state governments run by federal interventors (governors appointed directly by Vargas who wielded exceptional local power). High school history books are a particularly thorough source for various perspectives on Vargas's regime. Three books used in the then contemporary Brazilian history course students took in their fifth year of high school (*Epítome de história do Brasil* and two *Histórias do Brasil*) and one World Civilization book for first year high school students (*História da civilização*), all published between 1932 and 1947 and discussed later in this chapter, illustrate the extent to which the image of Getúlio Vargas was linked to the conditions and aspirations surrounding the Revolution of 1930.

These depictions of Vargas are all the more striking because of the elite nature of Brazilian secondary education. Very few students would ever read these books. In 1946, Mário Augusto Teixeira de

Freitas, the director of the Brazilian census bureau, concluded that of the centennial generation born in 1922 and raised largely during the Vargas era, only 17 percent had completed the third grade and fewer than 4 percent had concluded high school.[13] Indeed, in 1940, only 45 percent of Brazilians between the ages of 15 and 19 even knew how to read. Fewer than one-third of individuals who identified themselves as black or racially mixed, and fewer than a third of the population in the north and northeast of Brazil were literate.[14] According to one textbook author of the period, in 1942 Brazil's few high school students studied in a combined total of 750 public and private schools.[15]

High school history books were a luxury. Each cost in 1940 around a tenth of the monthly minimum wage.[16] The cost of school texts—and history books were among the most expensive—was so high that they drew the attention of the head of state security for the capital, Filinto Müller, who in 1938 assigned a team of agents to interview book vendors and determine the causes and possible solutions to their high cost. In their report, the agents agreed that the books "continue to be luxury items affordable only to the wealthiest among us."[17]

These textbooks were intended to reach only a few: secondary education trained elites, and a select number of aspiring elites. High schools were overwhelmingly private and mostly Catholic. In each of the state capitals, one or two public high schools might maintain a classical curriculum that would teach history, along with science and literature. The rest—that were very few in number—were vocational schools. Freitas classified high school graduates as subleaders who would assume roles of social responsibility.[18] The ways in which Vargas and the regime were introduced into the high school curriculum held a special significance: this was not an image created for mass consumption, like a portrait in a railway station. Instead, the image of Vargas presented in the texts was a primer to those individuals who would as adults be part of the *classes conservadoras*, the conservative classes.

While the image of Vargas and the Revolution of 1930 that appeared in history textbooks was consistent with the regime's propaganda, the textbooks were not produced under government supervision, nor was content dictated or censored. The textbook industry during the Vargas era was the principality of leading publishers, and no government mechanism regulated the political or ideological content of the books. Beginning in 1938, the ministry of education created a Comissão Nacional de Livros Didáticos (CNLD; National Commission on Didactic Books) aimed at regulating the quality of Brazilian texts. The preeminent textbook writer, Catholic nationalist

Jonathas Serrano, headed the CNLD's study of history texts. Between its creation and the end of the Vargas regime in 1945, the commission scrutinized each of the history texts then in publication. The CNLD's records show an absence of explicitly political concerns. Instead, Serrano and its other members focused on the abundant historical inaccuracies, faults in grammar, and the number of texts whose new editions had failed—sometimes for decades—to update their information. The most political endeavor undertaken by the CNLD rested in its recommendation that regionally produced histories of Brazil include not only local, but also national, historical figures.[19]

The visions of the world, of Brazil, and of Vargas presented in the history textbooks written by Jonathas Serrano represented the mainstream textbook perspective. Jonathas Serrano was the senior high school history teacher and textbook writer in Brazil during the Vargas era. He was the ranking chaired professor of history at the federal Colégio Pedro II. Until Vargas created the Ministry of Education and Public Health, Pedro II served as the national model school; other secondary schools had to follow the Pedro II curriculum if their students were to gain admission to the public law, engineering, and medical schools. Because of its historic role, the Colégio's chaired professors typically produced the texts their fields demanded. Yet even after the Colégio's curriculum-setting role passed to the ministry, Serrano's prominence and influence continued through his prolific textbook writing and his role on the ministry of education's CNLD.

Of Jonathan Serrano's books, the fifth edition of the *História da civilização* [History of Civilization], published in 1939, and the third edition of *Epítome de história do Brasil* [Epitome of Brazilian History], published in 1941, offer particularly rich images of Getúlio Vargas's and Brazil's place in the world. The *História da civilização* culminated with the rise of European fascism and the American New Deal, both seen by the author as the zenith of human progress. It reproduced excerpts of a 1933 speech on world peace by Franklin Roosevelt, and chronicled the rise of Mussolini. Serrano declared: "In a decade fascism has built Italy into a respectable power, with a first-rate army, navy and airforce, and extraordinary enthusiasm for developing all of the resources of the country, as well as admiration for the man who has realized such a spectacular transformation." The book ends with a quotation by Mussolini: "The Fatherland is not an illusion: it is the greatest, the most human, the purest of realities."[20]

This conservative and nationalist tone carried over to the *Epítome de história do Brasil*. This book, largely founded upon a Catholic and Portuguese historical experience, described the Revolution of 1930 as "the greatest and most important [movement] of our nation's history." As told to high school students, the Vargas administration was a combination of nationalist will and political genius: "President Getúlio Vargas knew how to increase constantly his personal prestige both within and outside Brazil, understanding how to unite energy and serenity, prudence and fearlessness, choosing dedicated and capable auxiliaries, revealing himself to be an administrator of exceptional moral character."[21] He praised Vargas for advances in social policy and national organization, strengthening the military, and for being committed to visiting each region of the country, "so as to understand Brazil as a whole." Yet with Vargas's hand at the helm, "Brazil as a whole" shifted course between the 1939 publication of the *História da civilização* and the 1941 publication of *Epítome de história do Brasil.* The regime that had flirted with fascism and been courted by Nazi Germany to form wartime alliances found a more solicitous suitor in the United States, which offered considerable economic aid in exchange for military and political cooperation during World War II.

Reflecting the change in political currents, the book's conclusion dealt with Pan-Americanism. A speech by Vargas stressed the common objectives of the American nations and traced the idea of an American system back to José Bonifácio, the drafter of Brazil's first constitution. Students were taught that Pan-Americanism was a Brazilian tradition. This theme in the closing chapter of the book published in 1942 represented a sudden break from the praise of Mussolini that appeared in the 1939 edition of *História da civilização.* As the political currents of the Vargas era changed, the major textbooks followed suit.[22] Still, whether Brazil was a nation that respected the gains of fascist powers, or turned against fascism and embraced the American system, Vargas stood at its center.

Another history textbook for the fifth grade published during the Vargas era, *História do Brasil* [History of Brazil] by Basílio de Magalhães, spoke less specifically about Vargas, but echoes the vision of the era presented by Serrano.[23] Magalhães taught at another of Brazil's most prestigious schools, the Rio de Janeiro Institute of Education, and based his text on his lectures for the history class. Organized by the nation's leading progressive educators, the institute served as a national model for teacher training and a center for pedagogical innovation. Originally from São Paulo, Magalhães referred to his native state as the national leader and stressed the significance of its "Constitutionalist Revolution" of 1932, in which São Paulo revolted against the Vargas regime, as a turning point in Brazilian history. The text never referred to Vargas as chief of the nation, and used the honorific "Sr," rather than "Dr.," to refer to Vargas, though, in contemporary usage, holders of a degree in law—as Vargas did— typically assumed the title.

Though Magalhães was in some respects a political outsider, his text nonetheless hailed the proclamation of the Estado Novo in 1937 as opportune and adroit, and described Vargas as the "supreme realizer of the political ideals of the Revolution of 1930."[24] Magalhães concluded the text with a chapter, "Contemporary Brazil," that detailed national issues and Vargas's government policies. It was divided into six sections. "Economic-Financial Aspects" discussed Brazil's export production and noted that Brazil had already acquired from the United States the matériel for developing a national steel industry. The "Politico-Social" section of the text described the ways the Estado Novo consolidated a

> corporative regime representing families, the working class, liberal professionals, workers and bosses—all is syndicalized and in solidarity, forming strong social cells, for defense and for the collective upward march. Social welfare was also organized. This way, in a mixed process of communion of interests and social cooperation, each is moved by imponderable forces for the same pragmatic ideal, the chalking new plans, carrying stones, harvesting wood, forging girders, building scaffolds for the grandeur, the solidification of the unperishable edifice of the fatherland.[25]

In a footnote to this declaration, Magalhães elaborated that the Estado Novo had also decreed the minimum wage, regulated work hours as well as women's and child labor, set up protection against sickness and injury, organized vocational education, and established aid for proletarian families. Though Magalhães did not directly link each of these realizations to the image of Vargas, the vision of the era remained consistent. The Vargas regime realized the objectives of the revolution, chiefly in integrating the nation's social groups and classes.

The seventeenth edition of Joaquim Silva's *História do Brasil* [History of Brazil] was released in 1947, two years after Vargas was forced to resign from power, by São Paulo's leading publisher, the Companhia Editora Nacional. Though this text was no longer beholden to Estado Novo paradigms and was a product of a region that prided itself on political and intellectual autonomy, Silva's text nonetheless echoed Serrano's and Magalhães's themes. Silva declared: "The Revolution of October of 1930, by its extent and its consequences, was among the greatest of our history . . . healing the great ills that the existing regime lamented."[26] Vargas regained the honorific titles "Dr." and "Chief of the Nation." Silva described the first accomplishments of the regime as the realignment of priorities in education and labor (citing the creation of the two ministries), and the introduction of a new electoral code establishing the secret ballot, class representation, and women's suffrage. Each of these issues symbolized a closing of the social gap.

Like Magalhães, Silva devoted a chapter to the accomplishments of the regime. He declared that "the measures in favor of the proletariat did not cease . . . these measures have made our social legislation among the most advanced in the world. Other laws . . . protect the family, maternity and infancy."[27] Similar words were used to describe advances in public and vocational education. Indeed, despite the Depression and the outbreak of World War II, "our general national progress is evident."[28] But what of Getúlio Vargas, deposed in 1945? Silva states only that the people chose a return to democracy—rather than a rejection of his leadership—and closes the chapter with a biographical sketch of the leader and his tenure in power.

The image of Vargas and of the Revolution of 1930 was consistent throughout these texts, which represented both Estado Novo and post–Estado Novo visions, as well as perspectives from Rio de Janeiro and São Paulo. The Revolution of 1930 was a watershed, marked by the arrival of a more vigorous government and the introduction of overdue social policies. Vargas's personal abilities made him the natural choice to lead Brazil, and to navigate the shoals of left- and right-wing agitation. In this interpretation, the Estado Novo was the supreme expression of Vargas's able and necessary leadership.

Singing Vargas's Praise

Within the city of Rio de Janeiro, and to a lesser extent in other city school systems, the curricular representation of Vargas was complemented by a cocurricular nationalist music program led by the composer Heitor Villa Lobos. It was in this space, rather than the classroom, that the representation of the regime resembled a cult of personality. The practice of choral song, which records show was carried out extensively, illustrates what children actually did in school, as compared to textbooks, which only reveal what elite children might have been taught. Beginning in the early 1930s, Villa Lobos organized schoolchildren into mass musical manifestations aimed at generating collective discipline and a love of the fatherland. His assemblies of tens of thousands of students commemorating the national civic calendar had more than a whiff of European fascism, and became the element of Vargas era Brazil that most resembled the images of Nazism captured on film by Leni Riefenstahl. Indeed, the similarity was no coincidence, since Villa Lobos's and other educators saw the cohesive power of the chorus as a way of getting students to actively participate in the formation of a national identity.

Beginning in the city of Rio's public school system, and in 1938 moving to the federal ministry of education, Villa Lobos' Serviço de Educação Musical e Artística (SEMA; Musical and Artistic Education Service) implemented a curriculum of orpheonic choral music in order to "awaken the racial energies."[29] Elementary and secondary students learned hymns that followed a progression from primitive African and Indigenous folk music for younger children, to more complex odes to the Vargas regime, the military, and Brazil. As Villa Lobos explained, "this is easily understood by the analogy that exists between the naïve, primordial, and spontaneous mentality of the masses and the infant mentality, equally naïve and primitive."[30] Villa Lobos sought to create a disciplined and nationalistic Brazilian culture that would serve as the basis of a strong, corporate race unified under the leadership of the chief of the nation. The nationalist choral song, with its enormous cohesive power, creates a powerful collective organism and integrates the individual within the social patrimony of the Fatherland.[31]

Throughout the 1930s and 1940s, Villa Lobos organized frequent student assemblies in Rio de Janeiro stadiums. These gatherings of 10,000–40,000 students from around the city—a major logistical operation—celebrated the Day of the Race (September 4), Independence Day (September 7), Proclamation of the Republic (November 10), and Proclamation of the Estado Novo (November 7). Children sang such hymns as *Hymn to the Sun of Brazil, Brazil United*, and *Salute to Getúlio Vargas*. The *Salute to Getúlio Vargas*, composed by Villa Lobos in 1938, read: "Viva Brazil Viva! / Long Live Getúlio Vargas! / Brazil Places its Faith / Its hope and Its Certainty / Of the Future on the Chief of the Nation!"[32]

Villa Lobos hymns fit into three general categories: patriotic and nationalist anthems (often referring to Vargas or the military), primitive folkloric hymns, and songs about labor and workers. The last category included such pieces as *Come on, Comrades* ("Come on, comrades, let's all go to work / Because where one works, joy must reign"); and the *Song of the Worker* ("The worker is the motor force / Which, smiling, builds the potential / And the Nation cannot be happy / Without work and the light of science / Power, grandeur on Earth / Have their origins in the labor laws").[33]

Villa Lobos tied the concept of a unified Brazilian race to the disciplined leadership of Vargas and to the promise of love and respect of work. The tens of thousands of students would sing in a single voice, tying Vargas as chief of the nation to the project of building a unified nation and integrating the working class.

Remembering Vargas

Long after Villa Lobos's nationalist hymns had been forgotten, and half a century after the Vargas era, voices rose up again to hail the chief of the nation and tout his connection with the workers. The Portela samba school's homage to Vargas during the 2000 Carnival, "Workers of Brazil—the Vargas Era", placed a dismal tenth in the official ranking of performances. Enough to keep it in the "Special Group" that parades before the world in the Sambadrome, but distant from any of the prizes. Neither an allegory about labor nor about Vargas, Portela's project linked the idea of a Vargas era again to the integration of the working class into national life. Though acknowledging that Vargas was both loved and hated, the Portela samba nonetheless characterized Vargas as the bridge between the rich and the poor. Looking back on that golden age, the samba reminisced: "So many stars and cadillacs and glitter / On another stage the popular movements / And in the Palace of the Eagles / Echoes one more shout / Go to war my Brazil / For the sovereign peace / He who was loved and hated in memory / Exited life to enter history." Portela acclaimed Vargas for his courage, and for his place in Brazilian history, steering the nation between the rich and the poor.

The lingering image of Getúlio Vargas has been subject to the oscillations of Brazil's political history and eventually subject to the currents of historiography. Brazilianists Thomas Skidmore and Robert Levine, for example, who began studying the Vargas era in the aftermath of the 1964 military coup, saw the nation's turbulent present as intimately tied to its *varguista* past. Levine recalls that the image (and lingering popularity) of Vargas was deemed inconvenient by the early military regime, whose leaders made it difficult for both foreign and Brazilian scholars to work with sources on the Vargas era.[34] Despite these obstacles, Skidmore considered the 1964 coup impossible to explain without looking back to the Revolution of 1930. Echoing Fausto, Skidmore explains 1964: "one can regard this political conflict as part of the deeper institutional crisis resulting from the failure to create political institutions and processes that could channel and direct the rapid social and economic changes which have transformed Brazil since 1930."[35]

For Edgar De Decca, the way the Revolution of 1930 was remembered by Brazilian historians of the 1960s and 1970s was influenced by these historians' opposition to the military regime (1964–85), and by sympathy for the Cuban Revolution held by intellectuals pushed to the fringes by military repression. De Decca suggests that with the end of the Vargas regime, which had sustained official the image of the Revolution of 1930 as a historical turning point, the revolution faded from popular memory. Yet for intellectuals opposed to the military regime, both the themes of militarism and of revolution brought discussion of 1930 back to the forefront. These intellectuals debated the role of the military as both a source of repression, as in Brazil, Argentina and Chile, or as an instrument of the Left, as in Bolivia and Peru. Consequently, these scholars chose to focus on the volatility of the Brazilian military leading up to 1930, looking especially at the role of insurgent junior officers, the so-called *tenentes* or lieutenants. These officers led both left- and right-wing uprisings and prepared the armed forces for an active role in both politics and administration during the Vargas era.[36]

More significantly, the idea of the Revolution of 1930 as a turning point resurged as opponents to the military regime flirted with revolutionary tactics to oppose the dictatorship. When students occupied parts of the University of São Paulo in 1968, they held seminars on the theme of revolutions in Brazil, within which the theme of the Revolution of 1930 was a highlight. Students and historians did not seek a return to the Vargas era, nor did they romanticize the Revolution of 1930. Instead, they seized upon the symbolism of the Revolution for two reasons. First, 1930 showed the real possibility of revolution in Brazil. Second, it could be interpreted as evidence of Marxist class struggle—that 1930 was a *bourgeois* revolution that in turn created conditions that would make possible a subsequent and perhaps imminent *proletarian*, or social, revolution. De Decca suggests that this renewed interest in the Revolution of 1930 and in the Vargas era failed to challenge the basic paradigms and myths that the Vargas regime itself had produced. Instead, scholars revitalized the old official vision of the revolution and Vargas as part of a 1960s and 1970s project of intellectual and political opposition, rather than applying a new critical eye to Vargas regime propaganda. By contrast, De Decca's rereading of a "loser's history" of the Vargas era suggests that the turning points the revolution symbolized had already taken place by 1930.[37]

Since the end of military rule, Vargas's memory has taken a different turn. Rather than serving as a symbolic threat to the regime, the image of Vargas instead has come to serve as a reminder of the failure of Brazilian institutions (including those created by Vargas) to address the nation's social inequalities. Portela embraced the populist image of Vargas—the image that his suicide letter reinforced—as a leader who echoed the will of the popular classes. This is one element of a larger image: Vargas as the bridge over Brazil's social gap as a leader who stood between the rich and the poor. One of the sites in which this vision is most conspicuous is Rio de Janeiro's Museum of the Republic. The former presidential palace in which Vargas committed suicide is a museum of the Brazilian presidency, but it has emerged as a shrine to Getúlio Vargas. Its centerpiece is the bedroom in which he killed himself, ornamented by his bloodstained nightshirt, his chrome revolver, and the bullet that ended his life.

The Personal, the Past and the Present

In January 2001, I led a group of American college students to Rio de Janeiro to study Brazilian history. One walking tour took the students to the Museum of the Republic to witness firsthand the ostensible shrine to Vargas. It is not a crowded museum, and most of the public that enters it skirts the entrance to the old presidential palace and walks past the driveway to the public park on the grounds of the museum, or goes to the small theaters located in the former carriage house to watch an art film or a play. Yet the museum that few enter is a powerful and unusual space, a place in which the past and the present meet and interact.

The students' trip to the Museum of the Republic shocked them. Upon entering the museum, they passed through an exhibit entitled *I, Getúlio*, which has attained a near permanent status. This exhibit has evolved from a series of rooms containing photographs and artifacts linked to Vargas (his golf clubs, a grand piano shaped in the outlines of Brazil, cigars), into an interactive display intended to develop a bond between Vargas and his public. On the day of the visit, the security guard—a *getulista* who spoke passionately about Vargas's ability to bridge the gap between rich and poor—carefully seated each student on a bench before an apparatus that contained Vargas's death mask, set behind polarized glass. At a certain angle, the light on half the face of the student and on the other half Vargas's mask created an illusion on the plate of glass in which the student's face blended into

Vargas's: looking at her reflection, the student saw Vargas, his eyes animated by hers and his contours blending with her own. This was an unsettling experience for the students from the United States. It placed them within an uneasy proximity with a past they had considered remote—something I had myself experienced through an unexpected encounter with another copy of Vargas's death mask, when I conducted dissertation research in 1995.[38] Interacting with Vargas's death mask was a different type of relationship with the past than the students were accustomed to. The museum exhibit gave them an instrumental experience intended to draw a bond between Vargas and his present-day public that provided a way of looking at contemporary Brazilian social issues. The experience with the mask was followed by a series of rooms whose displays explored the dimensions of the social gap. The most striking of the exhibits was a room with a collection of busts of Brazilian presidents lined at one end, facing a display containing a pair of Nike Air Jordan basketball shoes and a machine gun. The message implied by this arrangement was that Brazil's republican leaders had failed to speak to the realities of the poor, and now sat in mute witness of the world they had begotten. This exhibit was followed by other rooms illustrating dimensions of Brazilian social inequality in the twentieth century.

The *I, Getúlio* exhibit at the Museum of the Republic helped these students to make sense of the tremendous disparities of lifestyle and opportunity that they experienced during their first stay in Brazil. Like many museum exhibits in Brazil today, *I, Getúlio's* style of presentation was avant-garde and eclectic, at first difficult to decipher. But after a moment of thought, its meaning was clear even to the outsider. Grounded in the Brazilian approach to the past as a tool for understanding the present, the exhibit induced its public to confront the social gap from a different perspective—Vargas's. This new way of confronting a familiar problem was grounded in an old image of the leader: the didactic role of Vargas at the Museum of the Republic exhibit differed little from the didactic characterization of Vargas in 1940s textbooks.

Both Brazilian and U.S. historians accept and use the concept of a Vargas era with little debate. For some scholars, these years represent a turning point, and for others it is a period that consolidates continuities in Brazilian history. Regardless of these interpretations, Vargas and the Vargas era symbolized the aspirations that diverse Brazilians held for the Revolution of 1930 and its aftermath. The enduring legacy of the Vargas era is paradoxical and contradictory (Father of the Rich? Mother of the Poor? Time of change? Period of continuity?).

It is also incomplete and unique. The unmet potential of the Vargas era rested in creating a strong nation and overcoming the country's huge social gap. This vision accompanies the detritus of corporatist institutions that have endured since the Vargas era whose depth President Cardoso's administrative reforms have hardly begun to plumb. Historians and others remain drawn to the Vargas era because the period's model of limited and nonparticipatory inclusion of marginalized groups still remains the maximum expression of social egalitarianism in Brazil. The nationalism and *brasilidade*, or "Brazilianness," of the Vargas era included the popular classes as minority partners. Despite its limits, this paradigm is one of the most visible linkages between the popular classes and the formal sector. So long as the distance between these groups is not addressed in a more earnest manner, the historical memory of the Vargas era will endure.

The visitor to the Museum of the Republic finishes the tour in the bedroom in which Vargas committed suicide. The room is dark, shrouded by diaphenous black curtains. Inside, it is sparsely furnished. There are only two wall hangings: a painting of Vargas seated alongside Franklin Roosevelt during the war, and a portrait of Jesus. On a sole dresser sat a clock and the figure of a black saint. Was this how Vargas kept his room? Here, a life lived yields to a shrine to its memory. As visitors to the bedroom are serenaded by a solemn voice reciting, over and again, the text of the suicide note, they contemplate the two exhibits encased in glass at the center of the room. One is the bullet. The other is Vargas's nightshirt, with the blood-stained bullet-hole just above the GV monogram on the breast pocket. Like the image of the death mask downstairs, this exhibit is unsettling because of its intimacy—the physical proximity to Vargas's stigmata. It makes his presence in the life of Brazil seem so immediate.

Notes

An early version of this chapter was presented at the New Approaches to Brazilian Studies Symposium at Tel Aviv University, Israel, June 4, 2001.

1. Thomas Leonardos in John W. F. Dulles, *Vargas of Brazil: A Political Biography* (Austin: Univ. of Texas Press, 1967), 10.
2. Joel Wolfe, "Father of the Poor' or 'Mother of the Rich'?: Getúlio Vargas, Industrial Workers, and Construction of Class, Gender and Populism in São Paulo, 1930–1954," *Radical History Review* 58 (1994): 80–111.
3. Only one English-language biography of Vargas exists, Dulles's *Getúlio Vargas: A Political Biography*.

4. Boris Fausto, *A Revolução de 1930: historiografia e história*, 16th rev. ed. (São Paulo: Companhia das Letras, 1997[1970]).

5. Fausto adopts Francisco Weffort's definition of a compromise state: "A state in crisis that organizes and reforms itself in search of responses to the new situation created by the agrarian economic crisis, by the local (and global) crisis of liberal institutions, by the efforts toward autonomous industrialization of a traditionally dependent society, by the social dependence of the middle sectors, and by growing popular pressure." See ibid., 29. See also Francisco Weffort, *Classes populares e política* (São Paulo: Ed. da Universidade de São Paulo, 1968).

6. Edgar de Decca, *O silêncio dos vencidos* (São Paulo: Ed. Brasiliense, 1981).

7. Barbara Weinstein, *For Social Peace in Brazil: Industrialists and the Remaking of the Working Class in São Paulo, Brazil, 1920–1964* (Chapel Hill: Univ. of North Carolina Press, 1996), 50–66.

8. On the expanded role of the state in Brazilian education, and more broadly, on the role of educational policy in shaping race relations, see Jerry Dávila, "*Diploma of Whiteness:*" *Race and Social Policy in Brazil, 1917–1945* (Durham: Duke Univ. Press, 2003).

9. Robert Levine, *Father of the Poor? Vargas and his Era* (Cambridge: Cambridge Univ. Press, 1998), 12.

10. Emir Sader, "O transformista FHC," *Folha de São Paulo*, April 9, 1997, 3; Carlos Edouardo Lins da Silva, "FHC adia 'hora da dor,' diz Skidmore," *Folha de São Paulo*, February 28, 1997, 6.

11. Karl Lowenstein, *Brazil Under Vargas* (New York: Macmillan, 1942), 287.

12. Ibid., 286.

13. Mário Augusto Teixeira de Freitas, *A escolaridade primária e a política educacional*, chapter 5, "Revelações dos números no terreno social (1946)," Freitas Collection, AP 48, Box 55, Folder 15, Arquivo Nacional [do Brasil], Rio de Janeiro (hereafter ANdoB–RJ).

14. Instituto Brasileiro de Geografia e Estatística, *Contribuições para o estudo da demografia do Brasil* (Rio de Janeiro: IBGE, 1961), 399–407.

15. Joaquim Silva, *História do Brasil para o quarto ano ginasial, de acordo com o último programa oficial*, 17th ed. (São Paulo: Companhia Ed. Nacional, 1947), 197.

16. "Condições do livro didático no Brasil," by José Augusto de Lima, Conselho Nacional do Livro Didático do Ministério de Educação e Saúde, November 29, 1940, AGC, GC 38.01.06g, folha 790, FGV/CPDOC; MES/INEP, *Oportunidades de educação na capital do país (Informações sobre as escolas e cursos para uso de pais, professores e estudantes)* (Rio de Janeiro: Imprensa Nacional, 1941), 60. Estimate of the relationship between the cost of schoolbooks and the monthly minimum wage is calculated based on the industrial minimum wage in São Paulo in 1940, cited in Joel Wolfe, *Working Women, Working*

Men: São Paulo and the Rise of Brazil's Industrial Working Class,
1900–1955 (Durham: Duke Univ. Press, 1993), 104.

17. "A indústria do livro, considerações gerais," November 21, 1938,
Arquivo Filinto Müller, FM/Relatórios chp. SIPS, pasta 1,
FGV/CPDOC.

18. Freitas, "*A escolaridade primária,* AP 48, Box 55, Folder 15,
ANdoB–RJ.

19. Records of the Comissão Nacional do Livro Didático can be found in
the AGV, FGV/CPDOC, and in the Jonathas Serrano Private
Collection at the ANdoB–RJ (AP 55, Jonathas Serrano, Folder
CNLD).

20. Jonathas Serrano, *História da civilização (em cinco volumes, para o curso*
secundário), 5th ed. (Rio de Janeiro: F. Briguet & Cia., 1939), 209.
The Campos Reform of 1931 ended the separation of the disciplines of
Universal History and History of Brazil, by creating a single discipline
referred to as either Universal History or History of Civilization. This
discipline was to give preference to Brazilian history in the context of a
world history. The main text used for this discipline was Serrano's,
which was divided into five volumes, one for each year of secondary
education. The first volume, referred to here, was a general orientation
that did not discuss Brazil. It made recourse to biographies of historical
figures, followed by brief discussions of the historical contexts or events
within which they participated. The intention was to incite student's
interest in history. In later years, the books were divided into time periods that were explored in greater thematic depth, and with Brazilian
history holding a privileged position. A decade later, the Gustavo
Capanema Reform (1942) again divided Brazilian and world history,
giving preference to Brazilian history.

21. Jonathas Serrano, *Epítome de História do Brasil,* 3rd ed. (Rio de
Janeiro: F. Briguet & Cia., 1941), 235–236.

22. Ibid., 242.

23. Basílio de Magalhães, *História do Brasil,* vol. 2 (Rio de Janeiro:
Livraria Francisco Alves, 1942).

24. Ibid., 203, 208.

25. Ibid., 211.

26. Silva, *História do Brasil para o quarto ano ginasial,* 183.

27. Ibid., 197.

28. Ibid., 203.

29. Heitor Villa Lobos, *A música nacionalista no governo Getúlio Vargas*
(Rio de Janeiro: DIP, 1940), 25.

30. Ibid., 33.

31. See chapter "Educação musical," in Heitor Villa Lobos, *A presença de*
Villa-Lobos, vol. 13 (Rio de Janeiro: Museu Villa-Lobos, 1991), 8.

32. Heitor Villa Lobos, *Canto orfeonico: marchas, canções e cantos marci-*
ais para educação consciente de "Unidade de Movimento" (Rio de
Janeiro: E.S. Mangione, 1940).

33. Ibid.
34. Levine, *Father of the Poor? Vargas and his Era*, ix.
35. Thomas Skidmore, *Politics in Brazil: An Experiment in Democracy, 1930–1964* (New York: Oxford Univ. Press, 1967), xv.
36. De Decca, *O silêncio dos vencidos*, 22–24.
37. Ibid, 22, 26.
38. This experience is related in an article by this author which explores the role of the scholar's clinical distance in the process of studying history. See Jerry Dávila, "Under the Long Shadow of Getúlio Vargas: A Research Chronicle," *Estudios Interdisciplinarios de América Latina y El Caribe* 12, no. 1 (2001): 25–38.

Glossary of Selected Terms

belle époque: literally, beautiful epoch; more freely, splendid era. The term, used in the French original, stands for France's Third Republic before World War I, a time when peace reigned between the country and its neighbors and the sciences, arts, and culture prospered, with a significant impact on other nations. While the establishment in Brazil, including the academies of letters and fine arts, largely imitated nineteenth-century French fashion and aesthetic style, a new generation of artists studied the European avant-gardes and, from the end of World War I, advocated an abandonment of the *belle époque*, a creative digestion of European modernity, and the search for Brazil's historical roots, reevaluating the country's Amerindian and Afro-Brazilian legacies. The 1922 Week of Modern Art in São Paulo showcased their work.

bairrista spirit: from *bairrismo*, localism; intense feeling of local/regional patriotism, in São Paulo sometimes approximating chauvinism.

baiano: a native of, or appertaining to, the state of Bahia.

bandeirante: participant in a *bandeira* (literally, flag; i.e., *bandeirantes* followed the flag of their leader). *Bandeiras* were colonial-era armed expeditions from São Paulo that set out to explore the hinterland, find precious metals, recapture runaway slaves, and enslave new Indians. *Bandeirantes* pushed forward the frontier (some would say: "made Brazil"), and in this sense of "pioneers" *paulista* elites consider themselves their heirs.

brasilidade: Brazilianness. The Modernists' search for Brazil's national identity was the expression of an increasing cultural and intellectual nationalism in the 1920s that soon became politicized. Vargas's regime, keen to rebuild state and nation, worked feverishly on shaping national culture but the contents of Brazilianness remained highly contested.

à la brizolismo: in a Brizola-like (populist) style, referring to populist leader Leonel Brizola (1922–2004).

borgista: a supporter of Rio Grande do Sul's long-time "president" Antônio Augusto Borges de Medeiros (1863–1957).

Brigada Militar: Military Brigade; since 1892 the name of the state armed forces of Rio Grande do Sul. With the installation of Vargas's Estado Novo, the Brigada Militar was subordinated to the federal armed forces; it gradually assumed police functions.

café-com-leite: coffee with milk, a popular drink in Brazil; used to describe the informal agreement between the two most populous and hegemonic states of the Old Republic, coffee-producing São Paulo and dairy producer Minas Gerais, to alternate the presidency between them. When the last president of the Old Republic, *paulista* Washington Luís Pereira de Sousa, violated this agreement and nominated another native of his own state, Júlio Prestes, he was interested in guaranteeing the continuation of his economic stabilization program. However, he caused indignation in Minas Gerais; *mineiros* would approach Rio Grande do Sul and, together with other dissident oligarchies, overthrow the government and end the rule of the Partido Republicano Paulista.

carioca: a native of, or appertaining to, the city of Rio de Janeiro (the equivalent for the state of Rio de Janeiro is *fluminense*)

charqueador: owner of a *charqueada*, a (rural) property in Rio Grande do Sul that produces *charque*: salted and dried beef (*charquear* means: to salt and dry meat).

castilhismo: the political philosophy, institutional edifice, and policies of Rio Grande do Sul's republican "patriarch" and first "president," Julio de Castilhos (1860–1903), who used Auguste Comte's positivism to foster conservative modernization and legitimate his "enlightened" rule. The developmental and educational dictatorship, installed by Castilhos and adjusted by his successors to suit changing economic and political conditions, remained an important normative influence on *gaúchos* when they took power in 1930.

castilhista: a supporter of Julio de Castilhos or an adherent of *castilhismo*.

caudillismo: Spanish term that describes the rise to power and rule of *caudillos*, regional and national strongmen who exercised personal power. In Spanish America, independence resulted from a war of liberation that produced a highly militarized society. Military leaders— some from the property-owning elite, others from a more humble background—were admired for their heroism. After independence they often remained in command of military divisions or could mobilize a paramilitary force from the dependents living on the landed estates they had inherited or received as a reward for their services in the war. By exploiting their status as war heroes, further fostering their popularity among followers through political clientelism, and using violence against enemies, these strongmen, rather than far-away central governments of little-understood enlightened intellectuals, became the recognized civilian leaders. Widespread resistance against the central authorities' unpopular reform programs could produce new *caudillos*, as with Juan Manuel de Rosas in Argentina. In periods of political instability, especially at times of popular discontent or uprisings, only *caudillos* were able to restore law and order and prevent the undermining of the existing social pyramid. It was in such times that regional *caudillos* rose to national power. The chronic *caudillismo* during the three decades that followed Spanish America's political emancipation reflected the fact that real power rested in the provinces. Even after nations had been forged and the state and its bureaucracy strengthened, republican governments had difficulties in holding rival regional *caudillos* and military factions at bay. Moreover, bossism and patronage also characterized and fractionalized urban interest groups. In Brazil, the terms *caudilhismo* and *caudilho* are rarely used; while the more empirical *coronelismo* comes close, it has a different historical origin and meaning, and it is applied primarily to local politics. References to the *caudillismo* of the *gaúchos*, emphasizing the southern state's similarity to the River Plate states and exceptionalism within Brazil, fail to recognize both the nature of provincial conflicts in Rio Grande do Sul and the peculiarities of the state's *coronelismo burocrático*.

chanchada: popular musical comedy. From the 1940s to early 1960s, *chanchadas*, mostly produced by Atlântida studios in Rio de Janeiro, attracted large audiences. They originally incorporated carnival music, chiefly samba, into the soundtrack, but by the 1950s the carnivalesque element increasingly took the form of inversions of social norms, irreverent critiques of authority, and parodies of Hollywood movies.

classes conservadores: the (property-owning, wealthy, and educated) elites and traditional middle class.

clientelismo (político) or (political) clientelism: a personal relationship between the *patrão* (patron) and his *clientela* (clientele) that is based on an exchange of favors: the patron offers jobs, little services, and protection in exchange for labor, support, and loyalty.

Consolidação das Leis do Trabalho: The Consolidation of Labor Laws, or CLT, was approved on May 1, 1943. This labor code synthesized (most of) the legislation that had been promulgated since Vargas's 1930 Revolution and eliminated the inconsistencies and contradictions inherent to it. However, it was also innovative and included many new labor laws. With the CLT, workers' rights were, at least nominally, recognized. Moreover, this code also displayed, as John D. French has shown, signs of a relaxation of the repressive corporatist industrial relations system that the Estado Novo had established in 1937. Therefore it allowed for an engineered mobilization of workers. Numerous amendments and reforms would follow after Vargas's death but in its very core the CLT has survived until now.

coronelismo: The term is usually defined as either *mandonismo* (from *mandar*: to order; the habit and misuse of ordering, or just bossism) or a Brazilian variant of political clientelism that had its peak during the decentralized Old Republic (1889–1930) and became especially visible at election time. When landowners created a National Guard in 1831, essentially in order to counterbalance an army that had been founded after independence and often sided with revolutionary movements, they conferred the rank of a *coronel* (colonel) to themselves; commissions went almost exclusively to members of the (land- and slaveholding) elite. After the formal abolition of the Guard in 1918, they kept their honorific titles. By then large landowners faced increasing economic decline and their private power had long waned, a major difference from the heyday of *caudillismo*. However, these local bosses continued to command a considerable workforce, living under miserable conditions and held in personal dependence but representing a large percentage of the vote. At the same time, state governments gained more power but were still not strong enough to infrastructurally penetrate rural areas. From there the possibility for compromise arose: in order to retain social prestige and control over local politics, the *coronel* would have to subject himself to the ruling republican party. In exchange for loyalty and the collective vote of his dependents, state authorities would allow him to fill public posts with his relatives and favorites and provide funds for public works and communal services that neither the *coronel* nor the *município*, with its lack of financial autonomy, could raise on their own. At a time when the traditional rule of local bosses was eroding, there could be no worse situation for a *coronel* than having the state government against him. The latter could shift its loyalties but needed the support of at least a substantial majority of the *coronéis* if it wanted to maintain the stability of the oligarchic system as a whole. Scholars have controversially discussed whether *coronelismo* continued to exist after 1930 and whether it extended to urban areas. Recent research by James P. Woodard has questioned the usefulness of the entire concept of *coronelismo*, pointing out that it is too simplistic to describe the wide variety of relations between local clans and state government. This concept would ignore the real bargaining power of rural bosses, particularly in dynamic regions, and underestimate both the *economic* dependence of families in decaying areas on public employment and opposition within *coronelismo*.

coronelismo burocrático: bureaucratic *coronelismo*; a concept developed by Sérgio da Costa Franco, Joseph Love, and others to describe a form of *coronelismo* in Rio Grande do Sul that differed from other states (under liberal-constitutionalist governments). At Brazil's southern frontier, with its highly militarized society and authoritarian polity, it was not primarily the economic position and social prestige of an *estancieiro-coronel* that implied control over local politics; rather such power resulted from his role in the machine politics of the ruling Partido Republicano Rio-Grandense. The government party required obedience from its local satraps and intervened in the (nominally autonomous) *municípios* when its hegemony was challenged. The *coronel* became a "bureaucratic *coronel*." It should be added that in the state's zones of foreign colonization large-scale landed property was absent and the hegemonic party had to look for other stewards. As with *coronelismo* more generally, this concept has been contested.

desenvolvimentismo: derived from *desenvolvimento*: development; an ideology and policy that aimed at closing the gap with the developed nations and focused on generating economic growth on the basis of rapid industrialization and investment in the infrastructure. In Brazil, the term is primarily linked to the government of Juscelino Kubitschek (1956–61) but in many ways this administration could build upon the think tanks, social services, technocratic advisory councils, financial institutions, planning agencies, and nationalized key industries it had inherited from Vargas. In the late 1950s and early 1960s, economists and social scientists at the Instituto Superior de Estudos Brasileiros (Superior Institute of Brazilian Studies) who were influenced by the ideas of *cepalismo* (derived from the Spanish name of the United Nation's Economic Commission for Latin America) explored the causes for the country's underdevelopment. CEPAL advocated state-led development on the basis of import-substituting industrialization (by then an economic doctrine, rather than an emergency strategy) and domestic structural reforms. Kubitschek's government remained within the limits of modernization. It represented a bridge between Vargas's *nacional-desenvolvimentismo*, characterized by an economic nationalism that was no longer applicable if the country, lacking sufficient internal funding and know how, wanted to shift to the domestic production of consumer durables, and the military's more liberal economic strategy. Despite a strong nationalist rhetoric, Kubitschek already practiced "associated-dependent development." He produced significant economic growth and change (though not quite matching his slogan of "fifty years of progress in five") and invited foreign investment and technology. However, inflation increased and he neglected those "basic reforms," especially an agrarian reform, which only João Goulart would promise. Thereby Goulart left the *castilhista* consensus of a conservative modernization and prompted the military to intervene and restore it.

estadonovista: adjective referring to the Estado Novo, Getúlio Vargas's 1937–45 dictatorship.

estancieiro: owner of an *estância*, a large ranch.

exaltado: a person displaying an extreme enthusiasm and excitement (for a cause).

favela: a Brazilian shanty town, usually at the periphery of big cities. *Favelas* originated not only from the migration of former black slaves (and, before abolition, runaway slaves) and other marginalized groups from rural areas but also from the displacement of poor residents from downtown as a consequence of urban "improvements." The population of these shanty towns is rarely integrated into the reproduction process and survives in the informal sector of the economy.

fazenda: farm or estate; a *fazenda de café* is a coffee plantation.

feira livre: free market.

Força Pública: state armed force. With the installation of Vargas's Estado Novo, the Forças Públicas were subordinated to the federal armed forces; they gradually assumed police functions.

gaúcho: term of unclear etymological origins. The *gaúcho* (Spanish *gaucho*) is a herdsman or cowboy in the larger River Plate area, in

Rio Grande do Sul especially in the grasslands of the Campanha along the borders to Uruguay and Argentina. The term has become a synonym for a native of, or something appertaining to, Rio Grande do Sul (also *sul-riograndense*), though its sociological meaning never matched the state's socioeconomic structure during the twentieth century.

getuliana: academic or artistic works dealing with Getúlio Vargas and his era.

getulismo: derived from Getúlio Vargas. In Brazil, it is common practice to use first names when referring to a (popular/populist) public figure. *Getulismo* stands for (the official interpretation of or supporters' praise for) the political ideas and policies represented by Vargas, especially his *trabalhismo* and *desenvolvimentismo* (see also *varguismo*).

Independência: Independence. In contrast to Spanish America, Brazil's independence was not the result of a nation-wide war of liberation but of a more reformist, some would say: restorative, process. Brazil not only preserved the monarchical form of government; the empire also continued to be governed by the Bragança dynasty. However, the declaration of political emancipation "from above" in 1822 should not be separated from the aborted 1817 revolution in Pernambuco, then the country's economic center. Journalist Evarista da Veiga's "Let us have no excesses. We want a constitution, not a revolution" summed up the slaveholding elites' social conservatism, and this position is echoed by *mineiro* Antônio Carlos Ribeiro de Andrada's warning on the eve of Vargas's takeover of power: "let's make the revolution, before the people does it."

integralista: member of the Ação Integralista Brasileira.

intendente: intendent, the executive of a *município*, later prefeito (prefect).

Intentona Comunista: literally, the Communists' insane intention or plan (to overthrow the Vargas regime), expressing the official, deprecatory reading of three barrack revolts under Communist leadership in November 1935 (23. 11. in Natal, Rio Grande do Norte; 24. 11. in Recife, Pernambuco; and 25. 11. in the Federal District of Rio de Janeiro); a more appropriate, neutral translation would be Communist Conspiracy or Communist Complot. All three revolts, involving primarily enlisted men, were instigated under the banner of the popular front Aliança Nacional Libertadora that had been founded in March 1935. On July 5 that year—the anniversary of the 1922 and 1924 *tenentismo* revolts—its honorary president and Communist activist,

Luís Carlos Prestes, a former *tenente* who had been trained in Moscow and was in charge of a team of Comintern agents, called for the armed overthrow of Getúlio Vargas's government though, in orthodox Marxist terminology, no "revolutionary situation" existed. While Moscow hoped, rightly as it turned out, that in Chile the popular front could gain power through elections, an armed revolt seemed to be the only way to seize control of Brazil, and Brazilian delegates to the Comintern's seventh world congress declared it was do-able. Such a strategy, considered to be pure adventurism by some Communist dissidents, suited the leftist *tenentes* in the movement who were confident that these revolts would be the igniting spark for a popular revolution throughout Brazil. However, forced into illegality on July 11, the popular front lost its initial mass backing and converted ever more into the Trojan Horse of the Communists. The revolts were quelled by November 27. Vargas applied the National Security Law, in place since April 4 of that year, and declared a state of siege that allowed him to persecute the democratic opposition (not only Communists and popular front activists). On November 27 every year the army would commemorate the successful suppression of the *Intentona Comunista*, and in 1964 it would depict the coup as the ratification of its 1935 promise not to tolerate communism.

interventoria: the office/administration of an *interventor* (literally: intervener), a state's chief executive during the Provisional Government and the Estado Novo. The *interventor* was not an elected official but appointed by Vargas and vested with extraordinary authority. Still, a 1931 code (*Código dos Interventores*) established the rules for *interventor* government, and during the Estado Novo the appointee's decree-laws were subject to approval by an administrative department (*departamento administrativo*) that replaced the state's legislative assembly. This department also approved and watched over the execution of the budget and was to guarantee efficient public administration. The *interventorias* tamed, rather than broke, the power of regional and local oligarchies. While appointments could be contentious in the years of the Provisional Government (that of a left-leaning *tenente* and non-*paulista* in São Paulo triggered the events culminating in the 1932 "Constitutionalist Revolution"), after 1937 the relations between Vargas's satraps and local elites remained rather close. Some *interventores* originated in the state's dominant sociopolitical groups or used public funds and nominations for the administrative departments to build themselves a political basis in the region. They would still benefit from it after Vargas's overthrow in 1945.

malandro: literally (and in criminal proceedings), a vagabond, rough, or scoundrel; best translated as "scoundrel," tongue-in-cheek for a person (usually of low social standing) for whom diligent and honest work and respect for societal norms have little meaning but who takes enormous pleasure from gaining little advantages through illicit acts, such as cheating authorities, bending rules, outfoxing officials, and stealing little things from his social superiors (an act of *malandragem*). The *malandro* acts alone, with great ingenuity, and so subtly that those affected almost do not notice. He does not set out to gain wealth or prestige; instead, he tries to survive in an unjust and unequal society and enjoy the small sensual pleasures of life. The *malandro* has become a popular icon.

mineiro: a native of, or appertaining to, the state of Minas Gerais.

município: municipality; a county-like administrative unit.

Pátria: Fatherland or Motherland; used when declaring patriotic allegiance to one's native country.

paulista: a native of, or appertaining to, the state of São Paulo and its antecessor, the *capitania* (captaincy) of São Vicente. The latter had its administrative center first in São Vicente and later in São Paulo dos Campos de Piratininga.

paulistano: a native of, or appertaining to, the city of São Paulo.

pecebistas: members of the PCB, the Partido Comunista Brasileiro.

pelego: literally a sheepskin that is placed between a saddle and the horse; deprecatory name for the spineless leader of an official trade union in Brazil's corporatist system who stood between the ministry of labor, which paid him, and the workers, to whom he was not accountable. This union bureaucracy benefited from representing the interests of employers and government, rather than rank-and-file members.

perrepista: a member of the PRP, the Partido Republicano Paulista.

petebista: a member of the PTB, the Partido Trabalhista Brasileiro.

pornochanchada: a genre in Brazilian cinema that gained prominence during the 1970s and in fact had little in common with the *chanchadas* that had dominated the film industry during the 1940s and 1950s. These films were not pornographic, but relied on double entendres, risqué humor, female nudity, and titillation. Under the conditions of severe censorship, sharp-tongued social criticism was no longer possible.

primeiro mundo: literally (and as a praise): First World. Despite the end of the cold war, breakdown of "real socialism," and therefore superfluity of "neutral" and "non-alignment" policies for developing nations, the term has strangely survived. It should be replaced by developed nations or industrial countries.

provisório: literally, provisionals; forces that could be mobilized by Rio Grande do Sul's government to reinforce the state's Brigada Militar.

Queima das Bandeiras: "Burning of the Flags," referring to the ceremony on Rio de Janeiro's Russell Square on November 27, 1937, when, on Vargas's orders, all state flags went up in flames—a symbolic act of ending state autonomy.

queremista: supporter of the 1945 *queremismo* campaign for the nomination of Getúlio Vargas as presidential candidate. *Queremismo* is derived from "queremos Vargas": "we want Vargas." The campaign began in March 1945 when the end of the Estado Novo was imminent and the opposition against Vargas and his policy of *nacional-desenvolvimentismo* and *trabalhismo* began to organize. Interestingly, it started in São Paulo from where it extended to the federal capital and other states. The *queremistas* called for the convocation of a constituent assembly and ensuing presidential elections, hoping that this would guarantee Vargas's sustenance in power. The campaign was supported by the legalized Partido Comunista Brasileiro. Vargas's overthrow by the military dashed the *queremistas'* hope but the two parties the dictator had founded in the last months of the Estado Novo secured his election as a senator in his native Rio Grande do Sul (PSD) and São Paulo (PTB) and as federal deputy in six states (PTB).

Reação Republicana: literally, Republican Reaction; a conflict between primary and secondary regional oligarchies in 1922, revealing the fragility of the Old Republic's clientelistic system of interstate compromise. The seeds of this conflict can be traced back to the presidency of Marshall Hermes da Fonseca (1910–14) who owed his office to the rivalry between São Paulo and Minas Gerais and the suggestion of a non-civilian (*gaúcho*) candidate by Rio Grande do Sul (notwithstanding the strong opposition of the urban middle class against a militarization of politics). For the first time, the *gaúchos* claimed control over national politics; their powerful man in the federal senate, Pinheiro Machado, a *castilhista* to the core, had become kingmaker, and he did his best to act as gray eminence in Fonseca's administration. However, he failed to shift the political center to the south. Hermes who let himself be maneuvered by military and civilian plotters intervened in several secondary states to depose the old oligarchies and Machado was not always able to protect those who were devoted to him. In 1914, São Paulo and Minas Gerais united their forces to prevent Machado's candidature (he was assassinated one year later) and reclaim the presidency for themselves. During the war years, *mineiro* Venceslau Brás governed Brazil. When his successor, *paulista* Rodrigues Alves, died briefly after his election in 1918, renewed destabilization could only be avoided by choosing a neutral candidate, Brazil's representative at the Versailles Peace Conference, Epitácio Pessoa, until 1964 the only president from a northeastern state. It was then when *paulistas* and *mineiros* reached the *café-com-leite* agreement; in 1922, a *mineiro* was to become president. However, they had not counted with the *gaúchos* who (unsuccessfully) opposed the candidature of Minas Gerais's Artur Bernardes and gained the support of Bahia and Pernambuco that had failed to secure the vice presidency for themselves. Their "republican reaction" was part of a wider political crisis, and it was essentially the threat of this intraoligarchic conflict extending to nonoligarchic sectors and becoming a social revolution that allowed for the recooptation of the dissident factions.

republiqueta: diminutive of *república* (republic), that is, a small or miniature republic.

ruralismo: a policy that, in the words of Fernando de Azevedo, wanted to tackle the problems of rural life in order to civilize the country; especially used for the strategy of ruralizing education. During the interwar period, education reformers emphasized the need to extend public schooling to rural areas, adjust the contents and forms of education to the rural environment, and supply these schools with specially trained teachers. For the Vargas government, this was also an eminent political question. If the rural population could be fixed to the land, it would not migrate to the cities and thereby contribute to a further aggravation of the "social question." The state of Rio de Janeiro, placed under the command of Vargas's son-in-law, Ernani do Amaral Peixoto, in many ways pioneered *ruralismo*. During the Estado Novo, Peixoto focused on the construction of *escolas típicamente rurais* (typical rural schools) that were to become "irradiating centers of civilization and progress." Eugenicist objectives fused with liberal principles of the Escola Nova (New School) reform pedagogics. After his election as governor during Vargas's 1951–54 administration, Peixoto continued to place emphasis on rural education, for instance by developing a pilot project for teacher training, the rural normal course in Cantagalo. However, these initiatives failed to produce the desired results. Teachers could not be retained in rural areas, leaving a large percentage of the school-age population without access to education. Few children completed a primary school course.

sindicato: trade union. During the state-corporatist Estado Novo, unions were organized by trade, on a territorial basis, usually the *município*, and along vertical lines. As a consequence, workers of different trades were represented by different *município*-based official *sindicatos* that were forbidden to establish relations between themselves and to operate within the factories. Five or more *sindicatos* of the same trade within one state were allowed to unite in a *federação* (federation), and more than three federations of the same trade or of different professional categories in a national *confederação* (confederation). There was one confederation for each of the eight economic sectors that the regime had defined. However, federations of different trades and confederations of different sectors were not allowed to unite or directly cooperate. The ministry of labor watched over this system: it legalized and closed unions, coordinated their activities and arbitrated in disputes, collected the *imposto sindical* (union tax), compulsory even for unorganized workers, and determined for what purposes it was to be spent.

situacionista: somebody who represents the "situation" or status quo, that is, a member or supporter of the party or political group in power.

técnico: literally, technician; a specialist in the expanding government technocracy. The term *tecno-burocrata* (techno-bureaucrat) emphasizes the technocratic aspect of governance even more but has a more pejorative connotation, stressing bureaucracy, rather than efficiency.

tenente: lieutenant; in the context of *tenentismo* a junior officer (lieutenant to captain) or army cadet more generally.

tenentismo: The term refers to a radical reform movement of junior officers that organized during the political crisis of 1922 and disintegrated after the 1934 reconstitutionalization (though some of its activists would continue to play a prominent role in national politics). The 1922 and 1924 *tenente* revolts and the ensuing Prestes Column (1924–27) revealed that these junior officers were united in their rejection of inefficient oligarchic politics, including the neglect of the armed forces, but vague and divided with regard to the polity that was to replace the *café-com-leite* cartel. These divisions increased after

1927 and worried senior officers, like Pedro Aurélio de Góes Monteiro, who wished to strengthen the role of the army as a corporation. With Vargas's 1930 Revolution, the *tenentes* gained political influence and Góes Monteiro succeeded in uniting their dominant national-revolutionary wing and so-called civilian *tenentes*, like Oswaldo Aranha and Pedro Ernesto, in the *Clube 3 de Outubro* (Club October 3). It advocated centralism, state corporatism, economic nationalism, and social reforms and was to stop, or at least delay, reconstitutionalization. However, neither the Club nor the *tenentes-interventores'* electoral alliance, the União Cívica Nacional, could prevent the return of state particularists and the gradual decay of *tenentismo* as a political movement. As Góes Monteiro had wished, the Estado Novo strengthened the *corporate* power of the army. In 1964, it would take power as an institution.

trabalhismo: term that links the late Vargas era's labor doctrine and the regime's social policies, implemented through a corporatist trade union system. After 1942, Labor Minister Alexandre Marcondes Filho installed this structure, while simultaneously the Estado Novo's propaganda office, the Departamento de Imprensa e Propaganda, constructed the image of Vargas being the protector of the working class and, more generally, the father of the poor. The dictatorship disguised itself as an "economic" or "social democracy" that subordinated individual rights to the public good represented by the state, identical with the nation, and its leader. In contrast, liberals would define freedom in a formalistic, rather than authentic, way. During Brazil's post-war *democradura*, a formally democratic regime with remnants of a state-corporatist polity, unions remained subordinated to the ministry of labor. While scholars have shown the limited impact of Vargas's social policies, the dictator-turned-populist was successful in securing himself the support of labor and thereby preserving his own legacy. For many, especially the members and adherents of the Partido Trabalhista Brasileiro and its self-declared heir, the Partido Democrático Trabalhista, *getulismo* was/is almost identical to *trabalhismo*.

udenista: member of the UDN, the União Democrática Nacional.

varguismo: referring to Getúlio Vargas but much more distanced (and critical) than *getulismo* and therefore better suited to capture the contradictions in Vargas's legacy. The term *getulismo* is linked to the "invention" of *trabalhismo* and an increasingly populist style of leadership (even personality cult); it could not be sensibly applied to the early, at times cruel, authoritarian-corporatist Estado Novo. Arguably, one could say that in the years before Vargas's death, *getulismo* politics collided with the remnants of a *varguista* polity and prevented the government from implementing new public policies. This would support Thomas E. Skidmore's argument according to which the military, when they intervened in 1964, used the techniques of Vargas's Estado Novo against those of his second administration.

Jens R. Hentschke*

* I would like to thank Gunter Axt, Frank McCann, James Woodard, and Lisa Shaw for some suggestions.

Index

INDEX

305